HARVARD ECONOMIC STUDIES

Volume I: The English Patents of Monopoly, by William H. Price. 8vo, $1.50, *net.*

Volume II: The Lodging-House Problem in Boston, by Albert B. Wolfe. 8vo, $1.50, *net.*

Volume III: The Stannaries: A Study of the English Tin Miner, by George R. Lewis. 8vo, $1.50, *net.*

Volume IV: Railroad Reorganization, by Stuart Daggett. 8vo, $2.00, *net.*

Volume V: Wool-Growing and the Tariff, by Chester W. Wright. 8vo, $2.00, *net.*

Volume VI: Public Ownership of Telephones on the Continent of Europe, by Arthur N. Holcombe. 8vo, $2.00, *net.*

Volume VII: The History of the British Post Office, by J. C. Hemmeon. 8vo, $2.00, *net.*

Volume VIII: The Cotton Manufacturing Industry of the United States, by M. T. Copeland. 8vo, $2.00, *net.*

Volume IX: The History of the Grain Trade in France, by Abbott Payson Usher. 8vo, $2.00, *net.*

Volume X: Corporate Promotions and Reorganizations, by A. S. Dewing. *In Press.*

HARVARD UNIVERSITY PRESS
CAMBRIDGE, MASS., U.S.A.

HARVARD ECONOMIC STUDIES

PUBLISHED UNDER THE DIRECTION OF THE DEPARTMENT OF ECONOMICS

VOL. IX

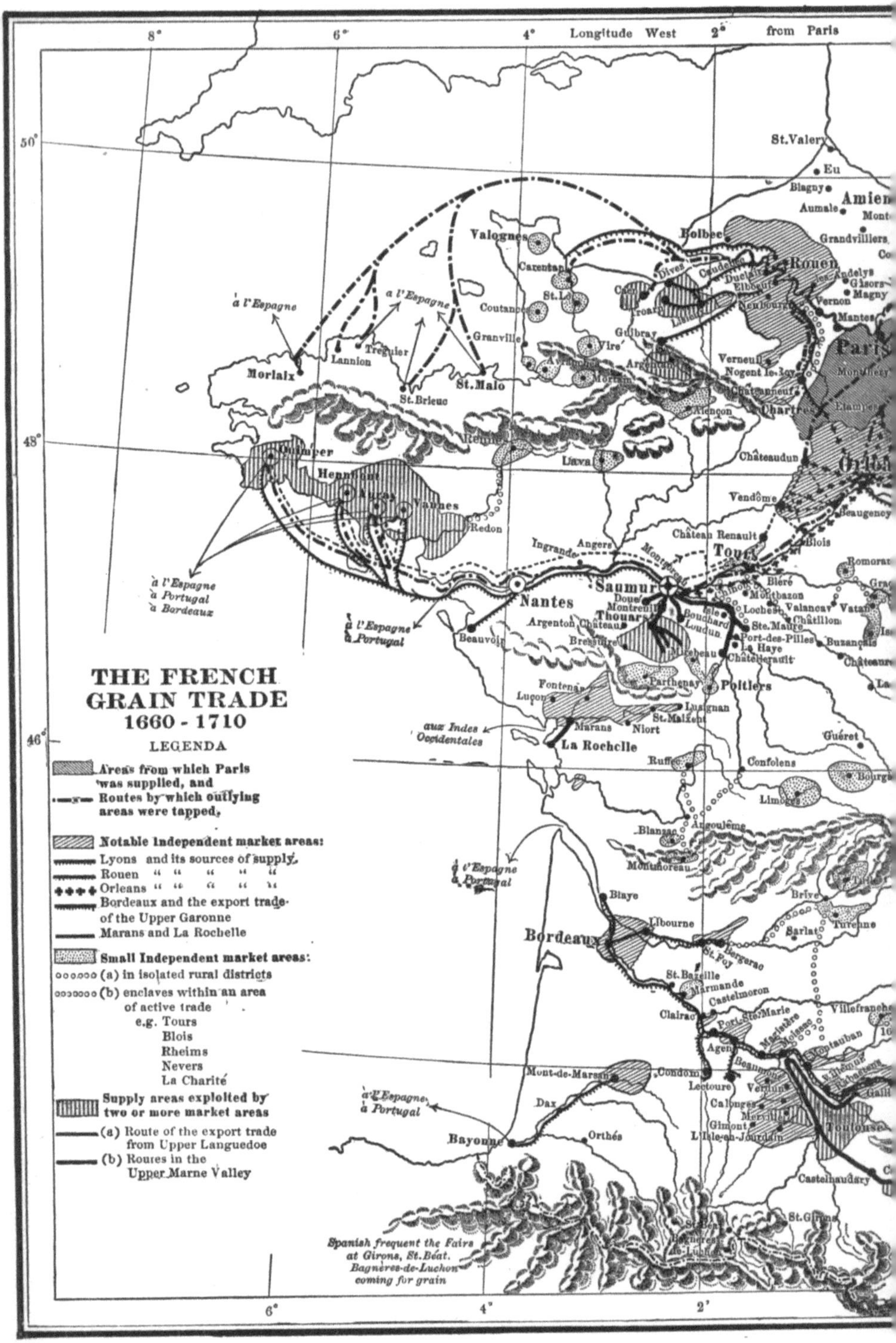

THE FRENCH GRAIN TRADE 1660 - 1710
LEGENDA
Areas from which Paris was supplied, and
Routes by which outlying areas were tapped.
Notable independent market areas:
Lyons and its sources of supply.
Rouen " " " " "
Orleans " " " " "
Bordeaux and the export trade of the Upper Garonne
Marans and La Rochelle
Small Independent market areas:
(a) in isolated rural districts
(b) enclaves within an area of active trade
e.g. Tours
Blois
Rheims
Nevers
La Charité
Supply areas exploited by two or more market areas
(a) Route of the export trade from Upper Languedoc
(b) Routes in the Upper Marne Valley
Longitude West
from Paris
8°
6°
4°
2°
50°
48°
46°
St.Valery
Eu
Blagny
Aumale
Grandvilliers
Valognes
Carentan
St.Lo
Coutances
Granville
Vire
Bolbec
Dives
Rouen
Elbeuf
Neubourg
Vernon
Magny
Mantes
Paris
Verneuil
Nogent le Roy
Chateauneuf
Chartres
Alençon
Châteaudun
Vendôme
Beaugency
Blois
Château Renault
Tours
Orleans
à l'Espagne
Morlaix
Lannion
Tréguier
St.Brieuc
St.Malo
Quimper
Hennebont
Auray
Vannes
Redon
Rennes
Laval
Angers
Ingrande
Montsoreau
Saumur
Nantes
Doue
Montreuil
Thouars
Argenton Chateau
Bressuire
Loudun
Mirebeau
Chatellerault
Port-des-Piles
La Haye
Ste.Maure
Loches
Montbazon
Valancay
Chatillon
Buzançais
Beauvoir
à l'Espagne
à Portugal
à Bordeaux
Fontenay
Luçon
Parthenay
Poitiers
Lusignan
St.Maixent
Niort
Marans
La Rochelle
aux Indes Occidentales
Ruffec
Confolens
Guéret
Limoges
Angoulême
Blanzac
Montmoreau
Blaye
Libourne
Bordeaux
Bergerac
St.Foy
Brive
Sarlat
Turenne
St.Bazeille
Marmande
Castelmoron
Clairac
Port-Ste.Marie
Agen
Moissac
Montauban
Villefranche
Mont-de-Marsan
Condom
Lectoure
Beaumont
Verdun
Calonges
Gimont
L'Isle-en-Jourdain
Toulouse
Castelnaudary
Dax
Bayonne
Orthés
St.Girons
St.Béat
Spanish frequent the Fairs at Girons, St.Béat, Bagnères-de-Luchon coming for grain

Longitude East 2° from Paris 4° 6° 8°
50°
48°
46°
44°
2°
4°
6°
Trade to Thulain
Avesnes
Philippeville
Chimay
Charleroi
Cambrai
Hirson
Capelle
Rocroi
Vervins
Charleville
Rosoy
Laon
Soissons
Rethel
Pontavert
Rheims
Crepy
Epernay
Chalons-sur-Marne
Meaux
Bar-le-Duc
Nancy
Strasbourg
Schlestadt
Vitry
St. Dizier
Provins
Arcis sur Aube
Troyes
Bar-sur-Aube
Sens
Bar-sur-Seine
Montargis
Langres
Montbard
Huningue
Fontaine Française
Gray
Dijon
Auxonne
Pontailler
Besançon
St. Jean de Losne
Salins
Nevers
Moulins
Riom
Bourgoin
Montélimar
Sisteron
1700
Manosque
Pertuis
Aix
Marseilles
Toulon
Tarascon
Arles
Martigues
Frontignan
Cette
Agde
Narbonne
Rodez
Millau
à Marseille
à Arles
à l'Italie
à Toulon
Venant
du Cap Negre
et Bastion de France
PETERS, ENGRS., BOSTON

THE HISTORY OF THE GRAIN TRADE IN FRANCE

1400–1710

BY

ABBOTT PAYSON USHER, Ph.D.

INSTRUCTOR IN ECONOMICS IN CORNELL UNIVERSITY

CAMBRIDGE
HARVARD UNIVERSITY PRESS
1913

PATRI DILECTO
FILIUS GRATUS

PREFACE

The history of the grain trade acquired great prominence in France in the eighteenth century. The Physiocrats made it one of the issues in their struggle for commercial freedom, and the scandal attached to the King's name in connection with the Pacte de Famine still furnishes the political historian with an interesting episode in pre-Revolutionary history. The earlier history of the grain trade does not appeal to the same interests. There is none of the intensely dramatic tone of the great episodes of the eighteenth century. It is a chapter in the history of social evolution, interesting perhaps, but complicated and difficult because it involves an understanding of conditions so strangely different from those of our own day. Changes in the mode of marketing seem to be relatively unimportant and it is only with an effort that we bring ourselves to realize how closely these changes are associated with the development of economic solidarity.

The increasing complexity of the division of labor creates a necessity for more accurate determinations of value. Everyone is concerned either as a producer or as a consumer. Today there is a high degree of refinement in the valuation of the great staples, and the achievement of this success is one of the triumphs of modern institutions. Grain, cotton, wool, oil, iron and steel, beef, and some other products are valued today with reference to the demand of the world. It is perhaps the greatest novelty in our modern economic organization. The history of the grain trade is significant because it presents most clearly some of the first steps in the evolution of these new modes of marketing. France is peculiarly important, not because the general development is different in Germany and in England, but because the history of France exhibits more clearly some of the stages in the process. The story is more easily read. The crises leave a deeper impress on the records. The great dearths of the seventeenth century revealed the defects of the local market systems. The need of wholesale markets becomes unmistakably clear. Then, too, conditions in Burgundy exhibit the strength of the old system and make it possible to understand the extreme slowness of the evolution.

The study of the limitations of the market area is essential to an understanding of the history of commerce, though other topics usually attract more attention. The importance of foreign trade and the greater volume of records available tend to distort our views. The general character of trade between tropical and temperate zones, too, creates an appearance of world marketing that is somewhat deceptive. The history of the great stream of trade that flowed through Europe from the Mediterranean countries does not belie the conclusions reached by a study of domestic trade. The analysis of price-making, the characteristic problem of domestic trade, merely emphasizes the need of a more careful study of the cosmopolitan trade of the middle ages. This stream of commerce, which we would today designate as foreign, presents as its characteristic problem the liquidation of trade balances. Development in the organization of domestic trade is measured in terms of market organization; the changes in the mechanism of the general trade of Europe can best be appreciated in terms of the growth of financial machinery for the handling of commercial credit. The principal topics in that story are the development of credit instruments, the history of banking, and the development of money markets. The history of European commerce in this sense is still unwritten. The subject is gradually taking form, material is being collected and rendered available, but the narrative is still incomplete. As yet we know only the vague outlines of the history of the bill of exchange. Ehrenberg has laid the foundations for an understanding of the money markets of the transition period, but much remains to be done. The histories of banking are becoming more genetic; there is less of antiquarianism and a deeper sense of consistent growth. But the history of financial organization is truly European in its scope. It is a story that begins on the shores of the Mediterranean, that contains many intricate chapters on the trade and commerce of Central Europe, and that is finally concluded only in the Low Countries and in England. The breadth of the field constitutes a serious obstacle to adequate research. It is not enough to work over the archives of any single country or of any single period, in the end the historian will be obliged to follow the thread of the narrative wherever it leads him.

The history of the grain trade furnishes only a chapter in this larger history of commerce and trade, but this episode is sufficiently independent to be treated separately.

This study has been the outcome of work with Prof. E. F. Gay, and in a two-fold sense. The interest in these problems of economic growth was first kindled by his lectures, and this particular investigation, begun at his suggestion, could not have been carried to a conclusion without the assistance he has so willingly given at every stage of the work. His suggestions have repeatedly opened up new aspects of the problem and made the study more comprehensive than would otherwise have been possible, and his criticisms have been invaluable both in judgment of material and in preparation of the text.

It gives me great pleasure also to have this opportunity of thanking the officials of the various libraries and archives for their courtesy and kindness. The staff at the Archives Nationales at Paris, M. Rochez, Archivist at Lyons, and the Archivists at Dijon helped me through many difficulties and saved me errors and much loss of time. In other libraries, too, the character of the manuscripts was carefully explained to me and the relation of the deposit to my work made clear.

A. P. U.

GRAFTON, MASSACHUSETTS,
September, 1912.

TABLE OF CONTENTS

PART I

CHAPTER I

CHAPTER II

CHAPTER V

PART II

CHAPTER I

CHAPTER II

CHAPTER III

CHAPTER IV

THE HISTORY OF THE GRAIN TRADE IN FRANCE

PART I

THE HISTORY OF THE GRAIN TRADE IN FRANCE

CHAPTER I

Markets and Market Organization

I

The transition from the local market of the middle ages to the wholesale markets of the nineteenth century presents a difficult problem in the study of value. The theorist is content to state the principle. It is sufficient for his purposes to recognize that prices are approximations, attempts to ascertain values that are never completely successful. The historian must study the relation of price to value somewhat more closely, if he would gain insight into the fundamental factors in the development of new forms of marketing. Changes in the form of markets imply that the community needed more accurate determinations of value. The simple forms of market were adequate as long as economic interests were confined to a small area. The expansion of trade made the problem more complicated. New factors in valuation were introduced, to which the local market could not give effect. The historian is concerned with the degree of approximation between prices and values. A system of marketing that secures a close approximation is efficient and good. A system that results in prices which bear no close relation to values is inefficient and in need of reorganization.

A market is an assemblage of buyers and sellers, but any assemblage of buyers and sellers does not constitute a good market. A market, in the ordinary sense of the term, is associated with a territorial area. It is an assemblage of buyers and sellers from a given area. What then is an efficient market?

Clearly, a market which gives effect in its prices to all the factors that should influence the value of the commodity within that area. Those who wish to buy should be able to ascertain the full extent of the demand for their goods. All the buyers and all the sellers from the area concerned should be present on the market, and no buyers or sellers from any other area should be there. The area from which the supply is drawn must correspond to the area from which the demand comes. A local supply can be efficiently valued only with reference to local needs. Demand that can be satisfied only by drawing upon the supplies of the known world can be handled only on markets which take cognizance of the supply available in the known world.

The medieval market was in form self-sufficient and isolated; in reality, it was part of a complex system. Market regulations assumed that the town was isolated, and municipal authorities persistently placed the interest of the town before the well-being of the community as a whole. Despite the recognized importance of trade with neighboring towns, such trade had no definite status nor any well defined organization. It was illegal in France to store grain except for one's own use, but granaries were formed in town and country which were important sources of supply for the large towns and for the export trade. This grain never appeared on the local market, and consequently did not enter into the trading system that was recognized by law. The granary trade existed by sufferance. The municipal authorities and their friends were usually engaged in the trade, so that they were reasonably secure from interference, but their action was illegal. When the inter-market trade was small in volume, it was usually in the hands of *blatiers*. They were persons with little capital who carried small quantities of grain from one market to another. They were tolerated because it was not supposed that they would be a factor of any consequence in the local market. This was true as long as they were not numerous, but in many places they became the predominant factor on the market. The old form remained, but the essence was gone. The *blatier*, however, had no right to attend the market. He could be excluded at any time by the local authorities.

The central problem in the history of the grain trade is the organization of this inter-market trade. A solution involved two changes; the creation of a legal basis for the wholesale trade, the recognition of the predominance of general over local interests. Reorganization was the result of the efforts of Paris and Lyons to secure an adequate and assured supply of grain. In a community dominated by petty municipal selfishness, they alone represented the higher ideal of interdependence and solidarity. In their advocacy of the general interest there was much that was selfish. A public spirited policy was forced upon them by their necessities, but the achievements of their officials laid the foundations of our modern organization of distribution. The small towns were reactionary, seeking to perpetuate in law an isolation that had ceased to exist. The large towns endeavored to break down the old system and create new administrative traditions that should be in accord with the needs of the time.

The element of selfishness in the policy of the large towns was important historically. They were interested in supplying their own wants. They were not concerned with the necessities of the producing regions, and many of the reactionary measures of the small towns were an attempt at self-preservation. In time of dearth, the large towns might secure supplies at the expense of the small towns and villages of the producing regions. The distress was likely to be felt most intensely in the small markets. Each local market affected by metropolitan demand was influenced not by any particular part, but by its full intensity. This was an inevitable consequence of the independence of the markets, and it was the perennial source of complaints. The market was designed to make prices with reference to local conditions; the division of the supply between the town and the metropolis was not one of its normal functions. The organization of this inter-market trade was, in fact, the most pressing necessity. The local market could not discharge such a function, and until the wholesale markets were established both province and metropolis suffered. There was no means of giving effect to the general interest.

Consider the situation in a local market with a surplus. Present in the market are the townsmen buying for their immediate needs, wealthy bourgeois who would like to secure grain for hoards, merchants from the metropolitan town. Under these circumstances, it is clear that the only limit [1] to the price in such a market is the price that can be obtained in the metropolitan town. As long as the metropolitan merchant can be relatively certain of getting a higher price at home, so long will he bid against the bourgeois, unless he is restrained by positive administrative regulation. Consequently, the equilibrium of demand and supply upon such a market cannot be described as a local supply, balanced against a local demand: it is a supply that is somewhat in excess of local needs pitted against the full intensity of the joint demand of the locality and of the metropolis. Such a concentration of demand is dangerous as it tends to carry away from the local market more than the actual excess of supply over consumptive wants.

An illustration will make this relation between local and metropolitan demand somewhat less abstract. To represent the local market let us take the little village of Attichy in Soissonnais. There was a market here every Saturday, "to which come the inhabitants of the villages for two or three leagues in the vicinity. They buy the grain, bread, and meat which they will need for the following week." [2] It is, thus, just such a market as we have had in mind throughout the previous discussion. The constant export of grain to Paris from this section introduces the other factor that is under discussion, — the metropolitan demand. In ordinary seasons there was little trouble; but a severe dearth generally revealed all the dangers of this connection with the metropolis. In May, 1709, the purchases for Paris were so heavy that no grain whatever appeared on the market at Attichy. "There was a great tumult in the three preceding markets, and in today's market," writes Marillac, May 12, "the officers of my jurisdiction appeased the first

[1] I omit, for the present, the effects of special hours at the opening of the market reserved for bourgeois buyers.

[2] G[7]. 1650. Attichy, 12 Mai 1709. Marillac.

troubles by compelling the steward of my estates to expose some of my grain on the market, though I really have none to sell. . . . I then wrote to d'Ormesson to have him cancel my contracts with a merchant of Soissons named Pannier, who had purchased all the grain that I had for several years received as rent. He had also stored in my granaries grain purchased by him of several farmers of this vicinity. In all there are about 160 muids (8,520 bushels) and I urged d'Ormesson to have this merchant bring some of his grain to the market." [1] This depletion of the local supply by the intensity of the metropolitan demand was general for the rural parts of Soissonnais. The Bishop writes on May 4: "I see it is no longer possible to prevent the shipments which Sr. Pannier is making from this vicinity, but it must not be carried too far. . . . The situation is most serious in the rural districts where Pannier has made his purchases. All the markets of this section, Ferre-en-Tarlenois, Braine, Vailly, Coucy, and the rest are without grain, and it is because there is none in the region. Paris has taken so much and in such a short space of time. There is a gentleman living near Braine, — M. le Comte d'Aumale — who has more than 100 muids (5,200 bushels) in his granaries. This would be a great resource for all this countryside, both for food and for seed. . . . Within the last four days, all that grain was taken up by the agents of this Pannier, and yesterday there was no grain on the market at Braine. There was a very considerable riot, and, if these little markets of the country continue to lack supplies, the disorder will increase." [2]

In these particular cases, the supplies of the local market had been carried off by purchases from the peasant cultivators [3] outside the market, or by purchases of hoards that might have supplied the region even if all the year's crop had been taken up by merchants.

[1] G[7]. 1650. Attichy, 12 Mai 1709. Marillac.

[2] G[7]. 1650. Soissons, 4 Mai 1709. Évêque de Soissons. See also the letter of 25 April 1709. Évêque de Soissons.

[3] The French word is "laboureur," for which peasant cultivator is perhaps a more exact rendering than laborer.

But this exhaustion of the locality is not the most significant feature of these disorders. The prices paid for the grain are the most definite indication of the intensity of demand, and there is fortunately enough evidence to indicate the tendency of the merchants of Paris to set the price at any figure necessary to secure the grain. Thus, at Provins, in 1693–94, one Colmet purchased 100 muids, paying 100 livres per muid when "the highest price current at Provins was 25–30 écus" (75–90 livres).[1] At Bray, the peasants said that it was well known that the wife of Colmet offered 2 sous per sack above the current price for any grain that they would bring in from the country.[2] Some time after their first dealings with Colmet, the latter told them that he would "take any grain they could buy of peasant proprietors and farmers, paying whatever the peasants asked."[3] Illustrations can be multiplied, but these few references are enough to bring out the point at issue. When metropolitan demand began to influence a local market, there was nothing to protect the local market from its full intensity. The only limit to prices in the locality was the highest price that could be had at the metropolis. Ignorance on the part of the peasants of these conditions, their inability to realize how high prices could rise in the large towns enabled the merchants to secure the local grain at prices which were high perhaps in the opinion of the peasants and townspeople, but still much lower than the prices prevailing in the great markets at such times of crisis.

Under the pressure of dearth, the local market was thus entirely disorganized. The region might be drained, and saved only by official intervention, or it might merely suffer from high prices. In any event, all its troubles were due to the metropolis, and to the inadequacy of local market machinery for the determination of the actual extent of the surplus of the locality. But dearths were by no means a frequent phenomenon, and to understand the local market it must be studied not only in time of dearth but in time of plenty. The ordinary function-

[1] Bib. Nat., Fr. 21643. 320. Déposition de Pierre Brisard.

[2] Bib. Nat., Fr. 21643. 320 et suiv. Déposition de Fiacre Pionnier, Vigneron, demeurant à Servan.

[3] Same deposition.

ing of this mechanism is quite as significant as its disorders. In normal circumstances the surplus available for export might be determined in two ways, without in the least disturbing the efficiency of the market. The metropolitan demand might be supplied with grain taken from the granaries of landlords and bourgeois, which had never appeared on the local market; or the surplus of each market day might be purchased by small merchants who made it their business to buy on the less important markets, to sell on the larger markets where the metropolitan merchants appeared. We know of the existence of both of these forms of wholesale supply, but their effect on the local market is necessarily pure conjecture. The reasoning involved, however, is simple. The formation of hoards in regions where there was an excessive supply was the only means of preventing such an overstocking of the market that prices would fall abnormally low. Any marked tendency to form hoards is indeed the surest indication of a considerable surplus. Where such stores were seen to be essential, the large land-owners were obviously the best fitted to forego immediate realization on the crop. The withdrawal from the market of the grain received as rents was thus an advantage to the peasant, as it protected him against excessively low prices. Unless there was an obvious likelihood of dearth, there would be little temptation to form granaries by purchases on the market. If prices were lower than usual, such hoards might be formed. In such a contingency there would probably be purchases on the market until prices reached the customary level. If there was a slight scarcity, the granaries would not be likely to afford immediate relief, as the possibility of a dearth would hold out such prospects of gain that the doors of the granaries would remain closed. The hoard could be formed in ordinary years without greatly affecting the market, and such hoards could be purchased by metropolitan merchants without disturbing the local trade. The possibility of dealing in large quantities was eminently satisfactory to both landlords and merchants, and the granaries played a prominent part in the history of the wholesale trade. These granaries did not represent a very exact determination of the surplus of the region, but when there was no pressure minute precision was not essential, and the rough and ready separation of the hoards and market supply was quite adequate.

This is undoubtedly the most important and most wide-spread mode of satisfying general and local interests. But the relation of metropolitan to local markets takes another form. Where a market was situated in a fertile region, it was quite possible, and in many cases probable, that the supply offered would be in excess of the simple consumptive demand. Several things might happen: the surplus might be carried home again by the peasants; prices might be reduced to such a point that some of the townspeople would be induced to buy two or three weeks' supply instead of one; or the surplus might be sold to merchants. The unwillingness to carry the grain home was frequently supplemented by a regulation prohibiting such practices, or at the most permitting the storage of the grain in some public place till the following market day. A great reduction of price was contrary to the practice of the time.[1] The prohibition against removing unsold grain from the market led regularly to a market surplus in many sections. The possibility of disposing of this grain on other markets created a class of small itinerant merchants known as *blatiers*. They were occupied in buying the surplus on the small markets, carrying the grain to the larger towns in the vicinity that could not be adequately supplied by the peasants. The inter-market trade of this type was very considerable in the total amount, though the dealings of any particular *blatier* were conducted on a very small scale. Grain that once entered the trade in this way might pass through several markets, each larger than the last, until finally it reached a market frequented by metropolitan merchants. The striking fact here is the relatively accurate determination of the excess of local supply above local needs. The *blatiers* were not allowed to buy on many markets until after a fixed hour and in that event the surplus would be determined in the most convincing manner possible. These regulations, however, were

[1] This I infer from ordinances about speculative dealing, comments on the practices of merchants, and the characteristic speculation on hoarded grain.

by no means universal, and were not very stringently enforced, so that the *blatier* was generally able to enter the market as freely as anyone. Even then the relation of the *blatier* trade to the market is not essentially altered. The exports are still a real surplus. The *blatier* was not possessed of a large capital: he must needs realize what little profits he could in a small way, without exposing himself to large risks. He could not undertake any great strokes: recklessly running up the prices in one market on the chance of selling higher elsewhere. He could not purchase in large enough quantities to affect the market notably. Every aspect of his position confined his dealings to conservative purchases at the current market price. His presence merely assured the maintenance of the customary price, and obviated the inconvenience of a surplus. Even if he was not actually forced to wait until the bourgeois and peasants had made their purchases, he represented merely a contingent demand, standing ready to take any excess at current rates.

In ordinary years, both the hoards and the *blatier* trade promoted stability and tended to maintain the local price that would be made if there were no excess supply and no metropolitan demand. The influence of the metropolitan trade ruled in times of dearth; the influence of local stability and conservatism was predominant in years of plenty. In the lean years, the trade was disorganized by the intensity of metropolitan demand, and prices were so largely dependent upon ignorance and fear that they represented no true equilibrium of demand and supply. In the fat years, local prices governed. The trade on the market, the inter-market trade, and the dealings of landlords and merchants, everything was dominated by *real* local prices. The local surplus was taken off the market by the formation of hoards or by the *blatiers* buying the market surplus, so that the conduct of the market and the prices were made practically what they would have been if the market were completely isolated. The defects of the medieval market organization, though serious, were, thus, for the most part, latent defects. Prices did not represent a very exact equilibrium of demand and supply; the surplus in the producing regions was very crudely determined;

the larger towns could never be very certain where they would be able to get supplies. But ordinarily no degree of accuracy was necessary in any of these particulars. Any greater elaboration of market machinery would generally have been a superfluity. Today, these matters have acquired an importance that renders such machinery a primary necessity, and to us the medieval system is difficult to understand because of its ability to dispense with any great degree of nicety of adjustment. It is difficult for us to become accustomed to a system that is so exclusively adapted to normal local conditions that the least departure from the ordinary disrupts and disorganizes the whole. Yet this is the most fundamental feature of medieval institutions. The State drags out a troubled existence even in ordinary times, but it requires very little to dissolve a feudal kingdom into the anarchy of Stephen's reign in England, or the disorders of Louis XI's reign in France. The Church maintains itself for centuries, but national sentiments in the College of Cardinals can create the Great Schism. Heresy was dreaded with a fear that to us seems unreasoning, simply because the unusual was so powerfully associated in medieval thought with social disintegration. Disruption under pressure of extraordinary circumstances was so common, that it was assumed as an axiom. The economic organization was no exception to the rule, and we must not forget either the tendency to disorganization under stress or the fairly adequate functioning in the general routine of daily life.

It would not be just to suppose that the bourgeois of the medieval town had any special fancy for this element of discontinuity in the economic or social life. It was no "*parti pris*" that made them prefer institutions that worked most of the time to institutions that would work all of the time; they did not see how institutions could be given the desired elasticity.

II

A local market in the narrowest sense of the term would be an isolated market in which producers and consumers were brought together without the intervention of middlemen. In most of our thinking about the middle ages we assume that such local markets were really characteristic of the period, but there is reason to doubt the validity of the conception. Even the smallest of the organized markets were not entirely isolated, and the existence of some middlemen is at least possible. We must remember, too, that many towns and villages did not possess organized markets, and that intense isolation would probably be evidenced by the absence of definite mercantile organization. The significance of a market can be essentially local even if it is not completely isolated, and it can be a very simple mechanism even if some middlemen are present. These qualifications of the abstract conception of the local market center about the *blatier*. He was a middleman, sometimes engaged in trade between two markets, sometimes bringing grain from the farms to the town market. The characterization of the *blatier*, however, is difficult. Most of the available information is contemporary with trade conditions which must have exerted a great influence upon even the most backward regions. The comparative method is not entirely trustworthy, and, even if it were, the proper sequence of the various functions of the *blatier* would necessarily be somewhat conjectural. Probably the *blatier* was characteristically engaged in inter-market trade.

If the evidence from the Seine basin is excluded, as representing influences of metropolitan "country buying" which were too new to be typical, the only detailed descriptions of the *blatier* are the letters from Orléannais and Bourbonnais in 1693 and 1709. These are contemporary with the letters from the Seine Basin, but conditions were not so far advanced, and there was less likelihood of reflex influences from "country buying."

De Séraucourt, writing from Bourges in December, 1694, describes the operations of the *blatier*. The grain supplies from the vicinity of Bourges are small, he says, and do not appear on the market, because the poorer farmers cannot spare any and the richer farmers are holding in expectation of higher prices. "The markets of this town (Bourges) have been supplied only with such grain as comes from Bourbonnais, and from Vatan and Graçay, which are in Orléannais. This trade is carried on by the poorest peasants of those provinces, and of this province. With 40 ll. or 50 ll. capital, borrowed from their masters, and four or five little horses, they make a trip every week and bring 20–22 bushels of grain on which they gain 5–6 sols per bushel above expenses. This is sufficient to support their families. . . . It is easy to see that the bad roads are very disadvantageous, as these petty merchants called *petons* [1] do not come so often. They load their horses less heavily and sell more dearly in order to gain the usual profit." [2] The suggestion of Vatan and Graçay makes it difficult to avoid interpreting the passage as a description of an inter-market trade. But the letter is really too ambiguous to warrant any conclusion. Letters from Romorantin in 1709 say much about market purchases, but nothing sufficiently definite to connect these purchases with *blatier* trade. May 11, Pronard writes to Bouville (Intendant at Orleans): "The Intendant at Bourges actually prevents the peasants *and other individuals* of your Generality from buying grain in the markets of his department, either for food or to sow. The town officials here are obliged to have the markets supplied by individuals, even when it trenches on the provision made for their own households." [3] Later, Pronard repeats much of this criticism of prohibitions. New towns are mentioned, notably Vierzon, Graçay, and Valençay. "For more than two months," he says, "this town has not been able to get ten muids of grain from Graçay or Valençay, on account of the obstacles opposed by Foullé." [4] This would confirm the supposition that the *blatier* trade previously referred to originated on the markets and not on the farms.

This interpretation, however, is very seriously affected by a letter of Creil from La Charité, in October, 1693. This is a report on the edict of September, 1693, in regard to the declarations of grain, and the bringing of grain to the nearest market. This interfered with the ordinary course of trade on the provincial boundaries, as the local authorities interpreted the edict

[1] Almost the only reference to a term other than *blatier*.
[2] G^7. 1634. Bourges, 16 Dec. 1694. De Séraucourt.
[3] G^7. 1646. Romorantin, 11 Mai 1709. Pronard à Bouville (enclosed).
[4] G^7. 1646. Romorantin, 1 Juin 1709. Pronard.

to mean the nearest place within their own jurisdiction. On these grounds "several judges refused to furnish any grain to inhabitants of Romorantin, and refused to permit sales to '*blatiers*' who *come to buy grain in the farms* (*dans les lieux*) *to carry it to the wool workers and weavers*."[1] This is a fairly clear statement of buying in the farms, as the phrase "*dans les lieux*" is nearly always used in such a sense. But there certainly is not enough evidence to permit of any definite statement. Probably it would be unwise to endeavor to draw a very sharp issue on the question. It is quite possible that there should have been some buying in farms, even if the characteristic mode of purchase was on the markets. This is on the whole the safest view. The *blatier* did buy, at times, of the peasants for a rather distant market, but before 1660 he ordinarily secured his supplies on some local market, and this aspect of his trade was most prominent.

An additional difficulty is created by the occasional character of the *blatier*. During the late spring and summer he frequently seems to have been a day laborer. When the harvesting was finished and his summer employment was at an end, he earned small sums by turning *blatier* during the most active period of trade. He is in a sense a *laboureur*. Can we be sure that the *blatier* is not frequently confused with farmers bringing their own crops to market? A letter from Bar-sur-Seine illustrates the difficulty. If "*particuliers*" is taken to mean farmers and proprietors, the letter describes a purely local market supplied entirely by the peasants of the countryside and having no relations with other grain markets. "This region," write the magistrates collectively, "is a part of Burgundy. It is devoted to wine culture, and produces scarcely enough grain to maintain its inhabitants a month. Accordingly, it could not subsist without the aid of several parishes of the wheat country, among others Magnan, Fralignes, Chefaine, Villensade, Court-

[1] G^7. 1632. La Charité, 19 Oct. 1693.

See also a letter of Bouville, 17 July 1694. Boislisle, *op. cit.*, I, 371, 1350. But all these references are after 1660. The real question is the character of the *blatier* before 1660. Was his buying in the farms an imitation of merchants buying wholesale in the farms?

enot, Beuré, Briel, Montreuil, and others, in the province of Champagne. But these places are only one or two leagues distant from Bar. The inhabitants of those parishes bring hither grain for the maintenance of this town."[1] The distinction between a purely local market and a market with the minimum inter-market trade must not be pressed too far. The distinction is doubly difficult if the question is considered from the general point of view. Bar-sur-Seine, while probably presenting an instance of a purely local grain market, might have been the seat of a brisk trade in wine. But with all these qualifications, we can regard the *blatier* as the outward sign of the transition from the purely local market to a market engaged in trade with other markets.

In the regions where the inter-market trade is long established the position of the *blatier* is much clearer. With possible exceptions, the *blatier* is the intermediary in this trade based upon the local market. Once the *blatier* becomes a permanent feature, too, the chief difference between the markets lies in the degree of elaboration of the net work of inter-market relations.

One of the simplest cases of the inter-market trade appears on the border of Provence and Dauphiné. Gap, one of the principal towns of lower Dauphiné, received much of its food supply from the market of Sisteron, which was supplied by peasants. The interruption of trade at Sisteron " causes famine at Gap and in the environs, as Sisteron is the granary of this section." "This interference with trade has another result. The merchants, who usually form granaries there with the intention of shipping grain to Dauphiné, no longer send out any grain. They buy no more on the market at Sisteron and that affects Sisteron. The parishes in the vicinity which have grain to sell no longer carry their grain thither, as the merchants have ceased buying."[2]

This trade is somewhat distinct from the ordinary type of simple trade, as the merchants are evidently fairly well-do-to.

[1] G[7]. 1641. Bar-sur-Seine, 24 Nov. 1708. Magistrats de Bar-sur-Seine.

[2] G[7]. 1634. Gap, (3) Juin 1694. L'Évêque de Gap à Lebret, Intendant en Provence.

The Bishop of Gap says in his letter that the merchants at Sisteron professed themselves ready to maintain granaries in the town sufficient to supply all its needs till the harvest, if the municipal officials would leave their trade free. Merchants capable of making such an offer are obviously possessed of considerable capital.

In central Provence there was a similar trading connection between the markets of Manosque and Pertuis, and between Aix and Marseilles. The details are not very full, and it is impossible to say whether the inter-market trade was in the hands of *blatiers* or merchants of greater wealth.[1] The possibility of a change in the direction of this trade indicates significantly the fluidity of medieval supply. In 1709, Marseilles and Aix complain because the supply that should come down from Manosque and Pertuis is all moving north to Sisteron and thence to Gap.[2] The difficulties experienced at Aix and Marseilles disclose the weakness of this market system. The larger towns could never be sure of controlling their supply area. Even if the tributary market had its usual excess, very little was required to deflect it to another town where prices were higher and gains more considerable.

Other cases of a trade between a single local market and the market of a larger town appear in lower Guienne between Mont-de-Marsan and Bayonne; in Poitou between Mirebeau and Poitiers. The volume of trade between Mont-de-Marsan and Bayonne was considerable; as much as 100 wagon-loads were sold each market day. Some of this grain was exported; most of it, however, was consumed by Bayonne.[3] Apparently the trade was controlled by merchants of means. The trade between Poitiers and Mirebeau is merely mentioned incidentally; it was probably in the hands of *blatiers*.

The curious feature of this trading relation between two markets is the presence of well-to-do merchants instead of

[1] G[7]. 1648. Aix, 18 Mars 1709. Lebret.
G[7]. 1648. Aix, 17 Avril 1709. Lebret.

[2] Letters cited above.

[3] G[7]. 137. Bordeaux, 2 Fev. 1697. Bezons au C. G.
G[7]. 138. Bordeaux, 26 Mai 1699. Bezons au C. G.
G[7]. 1640. Agen, 18 Avril 1709. de la Bourdonnaye au C. G.

blatiers. This was doubtless the result of the volume of trade. Where there was only one tributary market, it was likely to be located in a town scarcely inferior in size to the town supplied. The concentration of trade was considerable and business could be done on a scale that was attractive to merchants of wealth. All these factors were present both at Sisteron and Mont-de-Marsan.

When there is one market supplied by several smaller markets, the trade is so small on each local market that it falls to the *blatiers.* Fontainebleau illustrates this type, deriving its supplies from the markets of Melun, Malesherbes, Nemours, and Montereau.[1] This suggests a complication that frequently occurs. One local market sends supplies in two or even three directions, just as most of these towns sent grain both to Paris and to Fontainebleau. But the clearest and simplest case of this type of trade is Tours and its subsidiary markets. The officers of the Présidial at Tours describe the market arrangements. "Tours has the misfortune of possessing no granaries within its walls or even within six leagues. The bourgeois form no granaries for their own use, and never were accustomed to make such provision for the future. There are no wealthy merchants engaged in wholesale grain trade. We have only small retail merchants called *blatiers,* who twice a week bring to our market the grain that they buy in the neighboring markets. This is a kind of regrating that renders the market at Tours absolutely dependent upon the other markets, both in regard to price, and in regard to the supply of grain. . . . The neighboring towns, such as Langeais, Chinon, Loches, Corméry, Sainte-Maure, Richelieu, Montbazon, Château-Regnault, close all the roads from which we might procure subsistence from Berry and Poitou, and these towns themselves draw no more grain from the outside."[2] The ordinary supply markets are not distinctly mentioned, but probably the towns named are usually supply markets. The officials, at this juncture, desire to reach the country districts from which the local markets are supplied,

[1] G[7]. 1647. Fontainebleau, 23 Mai 1709. Dorchemer.
[2] G[7]. 1651. Tours, Avril, 1709. Les Officiers du Présidial.

since they represent the action of these towns as very hostile to Tours.

The trade supplying Rouen combines the inter-market *blatier* trade with inter-market trade in the hands of wholesale merchants. There were two groups of markets, four fairly near the town which were frequented by the wholesale merchants, and beyond these, smaller markets in the country which supplied the wholesalers' markets. The inner markets were Elboeuf, Caudebec, Duclair, and Les Andelys. In addition to these supplies, much grain was brought directly to the Halle at Rouen by peasants and land-owners.[1] The four markets were supplied by *blatiers,* and the grain was brought thence to the market at Rouen by ninety-nine titular grain merchants, licensed by the municipality. "They are under contract to furnish the Halle with such quantities of grain as may be needed for the sustenance of the inhabitants of the town. They shall procure this grain in the four neighboring markets, Elboeuf, Caudebec, Duclair, and Andelys, where they shall have preference over all other merchants."[2] The market of Elboeuf was supplied largely by *blatiers* coming from Neubourg and that vicinity.[3] Caudebec was supplied from an even wider range. Much came thither from Caen and the markets on the right bank of the Orne, Argences, and Troarn. The grain was carried along by *blatiers* from market to market;[4] grain was also brought to Caudebec from Bolbec near the mouth of the Seine, but the people there made trouble at home. "The inhabitants of Bolbec are numerous and ill disposed, for it is an industrial section, where there are many workmen who have nothing to lose. They are beginning (25 April 1709) to wish to prevent the *blatiers* from coming to this market to buy. . . . This *blatier* trade, however, is quite necessary, as it furnishes the market at Caudebec."[5]

[1] G[7]. 496. Rouen, 3 Juillet 1700; Boislisle, *op. cit.*, III, 216, 559; G[7]. 1632. Rouen, 17 Avril 1693; G[7]. 496. 5 Dec. 1698.

[2] Boislisle, *op. cit.*, III, 216, 559, letter of 14 Sept. 1709.

[3] G[7]. 496. Rouen, 5 Dec. 1698.

[4] G[7]. 1635. Rouen, 1 Juillet 1694. Montholon. Boislisle, *op. cit.*, III, 129, 375. Caen. G[7]. 1642. Caen, 23 Dec. 1709, Mémoire.

[5] G[7]. 1650. Rouen, 25 Avril 1709.

G[7]. 1650. Lillebonne, 17 Juin 1709.

The market of Duclair drew its supplies from markets of the pays de Caux, which are not clearly indicated in the correspondence; Andelys was furnished from Gisors, Magny, and Vernon.[1] The market system around Rouen was the most complicated development of trade based entirely upon local markets. It represents the highest achievement of what we may call the pure medieval system.

III

Wholesale trade developed in the large towns, particularly Paris and Lyons, and in regions which regularly exported grain to foreign ports: notably, parts of Touraine, Brittany, the upper basin of the Garonne, and a district on the borders of Poitou and Saintonge. In all these districts, the local markets were affected by the existence of this trade with distant points. The relation of the trade to the markets of the locality varied. In some regions, the wholesale trade was concentrated in towns which were supplied by a system of markets reaching back into the country districts. The trade at Saumur and Montsoreau is one of the best instances of this form of organization. Elsewhere, the wholesale trade was usually based on granaries, and was relatively independent of the markets although it frequently exerted an unfortunate influence upon them. In the upper basin of the Garonne and on the coasts of Brittany trade was of this type. In the course of the seventeenth century the market systems were gradually disorganized by canvass of the farms and the formation of granaries by direct purchase. This occurred in Touraine and in many parts of the Seine Basin. It was illegal, because it was an infringement of the prohibitions against the purchase of grain in the farms or on the way to market; its prevalence led to the reiteration of the old ordinances, and determined efforts were made to suppress these practices. Buying grain outside the market was not in itself a new phenomenon, but it was a great break with the past when merchants

[1] G[7]. 1650. Rouen, 25 Mars 1709; Rouen, 28 Avril 1709, and other letters in the same carton. Pavilly and Bourgachard are noted near Duclair, but their relation is not quite clear.

and their agents began to scour the whole countryside, paying practically any price asked and buying all the grain in sight. It was a new fact because different persons were the active purchasers, and because the object of their purchases was different. This practice may be described as "country buying," and, although the words might be applied to the infrequent extra-market dealings that always existed, the phrase will be applied in succeeding chapters only to that late development which was the result of greater activity on the part of the wholesale merchants.

"Country buying" was not the primary or ordinary means of securing grain for the large towns, but an extraordinary device to secure supplies when the granaries of the towns ceased to promise all that could be sold in the metropolis. Then, the merchant must buy on the market in competition with the townspeople, or he must go among the farms. With this alternative before him, it required little perspicacity to see the wisdom of scouring the country and dealing separately with each individual. The merchant might, indeed, be forced to pay the full market price, but he need never pay more, and in all probability he could secure the grain for less. This work was at first undertaken by the chief agents of the metropolitan merchants. Later, they pressed *blatiers* into service, and many bourgeois, seeing the possibility of gain, profited by the example. Finally, the *blatiers* who had dealt almost exclusively on the markets, began to buy systematically on the farms as well.

The effect of this practice upon the local market was fatal. The other developments of wholesale metropolitan trade had left the local machinery intact. This form of buying tended to destroy the local market. There was no pretence at local price-making; the predominance of metropolitan influence was complete; it was the first manifestation of the idea that prices could most adequately be made with reference to metropolitan interests.

But "country buying" is significant for much besides a mere destruction of old customs, and of old forms of market organization; it also indicates a new attitude toward the supply. The local market had been passive. No attempt was made to get the supply out into sight. The peasants were left to themselves, and when they chose to bring grain to market, it would be included in the equilibrium of supply and demand. If no grain came to market, there was no remedy except interference by the administrative officials. No machinery, formal or informal, existed by which the grain was brought in contact with the market, until each individual felt moved to act. The initiative was with the seller, not with the buyer, — largely no doubt because the buyer was not a professional merchant. Even the wholesale trade was relatively passive in so far as it was limited to granaries. The merchants had to rest content with what they could find in such granaries as the owners saw fit to open, and granaries were habitually concealed. " Country buying " was the first indication of an active mercantile attempt to hunt out the whole supply. It was above all an effort to discover how much grain was hidden away in farms, châteaux, and tithe-barns, how much secluded in little villages, guarded by ultra-conservative farmers or grasping proprietors waiting anxiously to secure the highest possible price. This endeavor to widen the scope of the " visible " supply is quite as significant as the destruction of the local price-making machinery.

The wholesale trade assumed three forms: the system of local markets; the granary trade of the older type, in which the granaries were owned by residents of the producing region; the granary trade of the newer type, in which the granaries were formed by merchants coming from the consuming or shipping center. Until the latter half of the seventeenth century the older type of granary trade was doubtless the most important. Where the trade was considerable, it was based on such granaries. The systems of markets contributed relatively small quantities of grain to the metropolis or export point. In regions where the surplus was large, granaries were sure to be formed. The territorial distribution of these different types of wholesale trade was thus definitely related to the agricultural character of the region, and to the extent of its surplus.

In the vicinity of Paris there were many tributary market systems of varying degrees of complexity. The simplest of these centered about the market of Montdidier. A petition of the inhabitants asserts "that all the grain sold on the markets of the town and in the villages of the élection, amounting to 2000 sacs per week, comes from the vicinity of Peronne, Artois, and Cambresis."[1] Much grain came to Paris from Montdidier, brought overland by *blatiers,* doubtless to some of the markets near Paris, though we have no details. Another line of trade of the same type begins in Soissonnais. *Blatiers* bought grain in the markets of Crépy-en-Valois and the vicinity, bringing it down to Dammartin and Gonesse, markets within a few leagues of Paris, much frequented by bakers.[2] The trade from the Beauce on the south side of the city and from Brie on the east came up to Paris through just such a system of local markets.[3] The *blatiers* were everywhere the active intermediaries in this inter-market trade. Where this trade was wholly in the hands of *blatiers,* it was small in volume and passed through a great number of markets.

In the Loire Valley the grain trade presents a degree of complexity unequalled in any part of France. The demand acting upon the local markets is the metropolitan demand of Paris, the demand arising in connection with the export trade from Nantes, the demand of cities in the Loire Valley, notably Nantes and Orleans, and at times Blois, Tours, and others seeking supplies here. The intensity of demand concentrated on the supply area is extraordinary in every respect. The complexity of inter-market relations is no less unusual. The merchants from Paris, Orleans, or Nantes seldom went beyond Saumur and Montsoreau where the grain supply of the valleys of the Vienne and Creuse was concentrated. This is the primary division of the trade: the major wholesale trade at Saumur and Montsoreau; the minor wholesale and the *blatier* trade engaged in collecting the grain in the back country and in conveying it to the Loire. Even this simple statement shows that the system is more

[1] G[7]. 1634. Montdidier, Fev. 1694. Placet des Habitants, envoyé par Chauvelin, 1 Mars 1694.

[2] G[7]. 513. Soissons, 16 Mai 1700. Sanson.

[3] See *infra* in connection with "country buying."

elaborate than any yet considered. There is an additional group of wholesale merchants: the minor wholesale merchants who help the *blatiers* bring the grain to the Loire. But this is not the most serious complication. Trade in this region was developing very actively in the latter seventeenth century. The minor wholesale merchants were probably a relatively recent phenomenon. Besides this development of an additional group of wholesalers, the trade here was much influenced by the practice of "country buying." In the Seine Valley the new mode of purchase was extremely significant. There its effects were less far-reaching, but it did much to complicate the inter-market trade. The forms of trade previously considered were in existence before 1650 and maintained their integrity well into the seventeenth century. They had become fixed, either from lack of capacity of further growth or from lack. of necessity for expansion.

In the Loire Valley, the activity of trade required more efficient organization, and the letters from Touraine in 1693, 1698, and 1709 afford interesting insight into the possibility of a development of trade based upon *blatier*-supplied wholesale markets. The main line of trade is described very comprehensively by the Subdélégué at Thouars. "There are several grain merchants who live in the parishes on the border between Anjou and Poitou. They usually have a very extensive trade in grain, buying much in our markets in this town and much in the country. They ship it at once to Montreuil and Saumur, where there are boats that are loaded for Paris or Nantes. . . . The grain comes to our markets from Saint-Jouin, Assais, and Airvault, where the merchants buy. The Bureaux, merchants of Doué, and other merchants from Montreuil-Bellay buy the grain here and carry it to Montreuil-Bellay where boats are waiting to carry it to Saumur."[1] Grain also came to Saumur from Doué and Loudun.[2] With the omission of the "country buying" referred to, this description would probably represent the conditions in this region before the changes that appear in 1693. The grain

[1] G⁷. 451. Thouars, 28 Dec. 1698. M. le Subdélégué à d'Ableiges.

[2] G⁷. 1651. Saumur, 2 Fev. 1709. Boisayrault.

passed through three or four markets successively before it started on its journey up or down the Loire. Trade was partly in the hands of *blatiers*, partly in the control of merchants.

The changes consist primarily in the development of " country buying " both in farms and in country granaries, and in the simplification of machinery between the farm and the market at Saumur. The merchants send out agents to buy directly for them. The trade falls into the control of the merchants; and these are of two types, the local dealers who propose to sell at Saumur or Montsoreau and the richer merchants from Nantes and Paris. The efforts of these merchants develop new sources of supply which concentrate at Montsoreau.

This exploitation of the valleys of the Vienne and Creuse is first mentioned in 1699. " Miroménil was informed in the month of July that merchants and commission agents from Saumur, Chinon, and Isle-Bouchard were buying standing grain in the environs of Châtelleraud, Le-Port-du-Pille, and Sainte-Maure, along the Creuze and the Vienne. They pay five sous more per bushel than the market price of old grain, and take up all the grain among the peasants and *metayers*." [1]

The buying in the farms had appeared around Thouars in 1693 and continued with even greater disorders in 1698–99 and 1709. " The Bureau and one Trois Cheminée of Doué . . . go day and night through the country districts, with valets and other men, buying grain. They form extensive granaries and raise prices on the markets; so that the poor cannot get a bushel of grain in any way whatsoever. A few days ago at Argenton-Château near Bressuire, the common people rose against them saying that the grain was sent to foreign countries." [2] In 1698, d'Ableiges writes: " There are persons in the markets who force prices up by leaps and bounds. They take all the grain so that the bourgeois and inhabitants cannot get any. This has happened at Thouars, which is only seven leagues from Saumur, . . .

[1] G[7]. 524. Feuille en main de Secrétaire. Abrégé d'une lettre perdue. Boislisle, *op. cit.*, II, 4, 13, 10 Oct. 1699.

[2] G[7]. 1632. Thouars, 9 Dec. 1693. La Veuve Marie.

and at Montaigu."[1] The same abuses appear "near La Haye, Sainte-Maure, and in all Touraine." "The merchants buy of the peasants."[2]

In 1708–09 the formation of country granaries appears more clearly. Before the dearth became generally known, the merchants of Saumur were eagerly seeking permits to export grain. Granaries had been formed in the châteaux. Turgot said that he knew personally of more than ten châteaux filled with grain for export. He proposed to prohibit export and thus force the merchants to sell on the markets.[3] The Lieutenant du Roi at Saumur tells the same story. "The merchants are buying all the grain in the province, forming stores in all the châteaux and abbeys, and finally shipping to Nantes. . . . As the merchants take up practically all the grain in the back country, little or none comes to the market here. Prices are excessively high, and the people are restive as they see the grain going abroad."

The trade, which was originally carried through a series of markets, gradually left the markets and was carried on entirely apart from the market system of the locality. The trading was conducted without any formalities and without organization. At Saumur, the merchants bid against each other in some of the granaries whose owners were not engaged in trade with Nantes or Paris,[4] but many of the merchants were shipping to Nantes or Paris from country granaries of their own. Much of the grain stored in châteaux and abbeys by the merchants never came in contact with any market. The intensity of demand had been too great for the market system, and trade around Saumur had become completely disorganized.

The export trade from lower Poitou which passed through Marans is not unlike this Saumur trade in some respects. There were wholesale merchants buying directly in the country, per-

[1] G7. 451. Poitiers, 8 Dec. 1698. d'Ableiges.

[2] G7. 524. Tours, 8 Juillet 1699. Miroménil. G7. 524. Saumur, 5 Août 1699. Dandenac.

[3] G7. 1651. Tours, 17 Nov. 1708. Turgot. See also G7. 1651. Tours, 6 Fev. 1709. Turgot.

[4] G7. 524. Tours, 15 Juillet 1699. Miroménil.

sonally or through agents. Granaries were formed in the country in anticipation of this demand. The grain that was the basis of the wholesale trade left the country without touching the wholesale market. The principal difference is the apparent relation of the trade to the market at Marans. The market was supplied by peasants and *blatiers* and was a considerable feature in the trade of the vicinity. But all the trade of Marans did not pass through the market. The larger merchants, who collected in Poitou by agents, sold at Marans in the granaries. There were thus two phases of the Marans trade: one, the normal trade of the ordinary local market; the other, a highly systematized wholesale trade which had no more connection with the market at Marans than the trade at Saumur with the local country markets or the town markets.

This curious duality of the Marans trade is not easily perceived, and the descriptions do not bring it out clearly. The practice is most distinctly indicated in a memorial drawn up by Roujault, the Intendant at Poitiers. He puts the case in dialectical form. "The issue between the inhabitants of Aunis and Poitou is not to determine whether or no the peasants of Poitou may carry grain to the market at Marans, as they do to markets in Poitou. The real question is: does the edict permit the merchants of Marans to buy their grain at wholesale in the granaries of Poitou? Does it permit them to sell at wholesale to other merchants at Marans? Does it permit them to ship ten, twenty, thirty tons of grain at a time to the markets at Marans, under the pretext of selling there at retail? Can this go on, without our being able to force them to carry a grain of corn to the markets of Poitou? [1]

"Then, too, there are peasants of Poitou who have granaries at Marans, although they live far from that town. They are all registered as grain merchants, and, under pretext of carrying grain to the market at Marans, which they never enter, they ship all the grain from their farms to their granaries at Marans." [2]

[1] The French of the original is extremely involved; the translation is free, but reproduces faithfully the ideas of the text.

[2] G^7. 1647. Mémoire pour le Commerce des Bleds entre le Poitou et l'Aunis, fait par Roujault à Poitiers, 6 Dec. 1709.

This is couched in rather rhetorical form but it is evidently meant to be a concise description of the trade. "It must be admitted," he says, "that this wholesale trade between Poitou and Marans has been established since time immemorial (est estably de tout temps)." Then he describes the trade in more detail. "Rochelle is supplied in two ways; by the markets of the parishes of Aunis and Saintonge which send grain to the market at Rochelle; by the bakers who buy at wholesale at Marans. The wholesale trade of Poitou is thus merely concentrated at Marans for further sale. . . . The trade is also important for the maritime undertakings and the provision of merchant-men setting out from La Rochelle." [1]

Many of the assertions of Roujault are confirmed by a memoir of d'Ableiges drawn up in 1699. This inquiry was primarily concerned with the mode of purchasing in Poitou and the granaries at Marans. The tone of the letter suggests the separation between the wholesale trade and the market trade. "I have secretly made a very exact investigation of the grain trade from Poitou. I have the honor to submit a memoir by which you will perceive that Marans is the principal *dépôt.* Some grain, however, passes through the Isle de Ré and Rochelle. The memoir contains all the details and you can trust it. . . ." The memoir then continues: "The principal merchants at Marans are Large, Grignon, and Aurard who say they have commissions to buy grain. They have agents and merchants in Poitou who buy for them. Sr. Clereau, formerly Greffier at the Cour des Aides, has a lease of the abbey of Neuil. He has his steward buy for him and carries on a great trade. He has the grain delivered at Marans, La Rochelle, and Isle de Ré. Martineau de Brilhouet and his son-in-law buy extensively. It is supposed that they are agents for Sr. Jouet, Receiver of the Taille at Fontenay. One La Fontaine, agent of this Martineau, says that Martineau has three granaries at Luçon. According to his mother-in-law he has also three granaries at Marans. Boutet de Nailliers also buys incessantly and ships

[1] See in this respect the letters of Colbert de Terron. Bib. Nat., Mél. Colb., 101, 85. *Ibid.*, 86, 222.

to Marans. He is agent for the said Jouet, Receiver of the Taille at Fontenay. . . ."[1] The memoir continues in this fashion giving a detailed account of all the merchants. It is quite clear that the buying in Poitou is very extensive. Merchants, agents, granaries in the country and at Marans, we have here all the machinery for an invisible wholesale trade that we found at Saumur. But while this trade in lower Poitou is essentially a wholesale trade entirely independent of markets, the appearance of connection with the local market at Marans must not be forgotten.

A more ordinary type of wholesale trade is based on granaries formed in river towns by residents, who sell to merchants from the large towns. This form suggests a rather passive trade at every stage, presenting a sharp contrast to the feverish energy that appears in the Saumur district and at Marans. The persons forming granaries make no energetic canvass of the country to secure grain. They wait passively for the arrival of the merchants from the larger town. The latter rest content with the supplies in the granaries. This form is prevalent in the Saône and Marne Valleys in the sixteenth and seventeenth centuries, in the Upper Loire in the latter seventeenth century and possibly earlier, and in the Upper Garonne.

Conditions in the valleys of the Marne and Saône will be considered in detail later, and as the general aspects of this type of trade appear sufficiently well in the Garonne Valley and on the Upper Loire, it will be most expedient to confine our attention to these cases.

The trade of the Garonne was devoted only in part to supplying Bordeaux. Grain was frequently sent abroad, although Bordeaux was also an importing region. The organization of the wholesale trade was designed to cover both means of disposing of the surplus of the Upper Garonne. The characteristic feature in the producing regions is the formation of granaries in the principal towns, especially, but not necessarily, river

[1] G⁷. 457. Poitiers, 22 Jan. 1699. d'Ableiges. For additional details see G⁷. 1645. Mémoire sur le Commerce des Bleds en Poitou et Aunis, envoyée par les Maire et Échevins de la Rochelle, 2–5 Nov. 1709.

towns. "The élection of Rivièreverdieu of which Grenade is the capital," writes Foucault in 1681, "is the most fertile section of the Généralité of Montauban. In almost all the towns of this élection I find that the principal inhabitants have large stores."[1] De Ris reports, in 1683, that there are rumors "of many granaries, made by individuals, who hope to double their money in a very short time."[2] In 1701, de la Bourdonnaye says, "the inhabitants around Agen and above are already (10 Sept.) beginning to form granaries, in the hope that war or inclement weather will prevent Bordeaux from procuring grain from abroad, so that they can sell at their own prices." In 1709, the granary trade was recognized and regulated by local ordinances. All wholesale merchants were required to give statements of the quantities of grain they bought, with the name and residence of the sellers.[3] The principal depots of this granary trade were Montauban, L'Isle-en-Jourdain, Grenade, Verdun, Beaumont, Gimont, Gaillac, Magistère, Agen, and Port-Sainte-Marie.[4]

In bringing the grain from the granaries to Bordeaux two sets of merchants found occupation; merchants resident in the producing regions and merchants resident at Bordeaux. The former

[1] G[7]. 390. Grenade, 6 Mai 1681. Foucault.

[2] G[7]. 132. Bordeaux, 30 Avril 1683. de Ris.

[3] G[7]. 1646. Montauban, 17 Août 1709.

[4] The most detailed indications of the sources of supply are found in a group of notices of grain arrivals at the port of Bordeaux. G[7]. 132. 23 Dec. 1682–2 Jan. 1683. 10 Mars 1683–5 Juin 1683. The names mentioned are Magistère, Montaigne, Agen, Mast, Boué, Verdun, Villemur, Saint-Surin-de-Mortaigne, Moissac, Laspeyres, Gaillac, Saint-Christolly, Castelmoron, Couserans, Conac, Calonges, Clayrac, Montauban, Saula. The relative importance is indicated in part by frequency of appearance but more accurately by a report of the amount of grain in store in the Généralité of Montauban in September, 1684.

Estat des Bleds qui sont dans les magazins des élections de Montauban.

Montauban	21,600 sacks	Le Burgaud	750 sacks
Anconville	2,050 "	Grenade	13,650 "
Le-Mat-en-Verdun	2,250 "	Beaumont	7,350 "
Merville	1,300 "	Saint-Sardos	1,200 "
L'Isle-en-Jourdain	25,300 "	Colonger	900 "
Verdun	7,000 "	Gimont	9,300 "
Bouret	1,450 "	Total,	96,600 sacks.

G[7]. 390. Montauban, 28 Sept. 1684. Bois du Baillet (enclosed in letter).

were called *marchands forains* and sold their grain through agents called *courtiers*. These *courtiers* or brokers were not supposed to engage in trade on their own account, but complaints indicate that abuses were numerous. "These agents frequently have grain of their own to sell, so that they take pains not to execute the orders of foreign merchants immediately, for fear of causing prices to fall, or of selling less of their own grain. Nor is this their only interest in delaying the sale of grain addressed to them. After grain has been exposed three days, they are allowed to unload the boats and to store the grain in warehouses which they own. The agents store the grain and charge the foreign merchants rent for the use of the granary." [1]

But this is not the only source of abuses in the wholesale trade. "There was no regulated market. All the grain came down the river, and, when a boat came in, it was straightway sold. The only persons who bought were bakers, as the well-to-do bourgeois provided for their own needs and the poor were not able to buy except at retail." [2] In short, there was no market and the bakers were the principal buyers on the port. These conditions invited underhanded practices, and Courson felt assured that the bakers acted in concert to maintain prices by controlling the trade. Some were engaged in the grain trade. "They would have grain sent down to Bordeaux, and when it arrived they would feign to buy it at a price much higher than they paid." It was impossible to remedy this abuse at once, as there was no grain in Bordeaux except what was in the hands of the bakers, who took care not to have much in their granaries. . . . "I thought it most expedient to engage several merchants to buy grain on their own account so I inquired after merchants while touring the department to levy the taille, and I had them promise to send grain down to Bordeaux giving them names of agents whom they could trust. In the end I secured in this way 20–25,000 bushels, including what was in individual granaries in the town. Then it was no longer possible

[1] G[7]. 139. Avril, 1702. Mémoire des Jurats de Bordeaux concernant le placet presenté au Roy pour le Courtage des Grains.

[2] G[7]. 1641. Bordeaux, 8 Fev. 1710. Lamoignon de Courson.

to doubt the combination of the bakers. Only the grain in the boats of men we did not know was bought. Nothing was offered for the grain which my merchants placed on sale, though it was quite as good, and they were willing to sell it cheaper. . . . This induced me to speak to the bakers, and to let them know that I understood their game. I told them I would make trouble for them if the price of grain at Bordeaux did not fall to the level of prices in the Généralité. It was hard for them to make up their minds, but when they saw that I was prepared to execute my threats, 2,500 bushels of grain suddenly appeared on the ports from some unknown source. It was sold at a considerable reduction." [1]

It is not of great consequence to know whether all Courson's suspicions were justified, for the significance of the incident does not depend on the truth of Courson's allegations. The important fact to note is the complete invisibility of the wholesale trade. The bakers may or may not have had a controlling influence, but this much is certain, — the trade was entirely independent of any formal market both in the producing regions and in the town. Under such circumstances wholesale prices were practically guess work: there was not enough competitive dealing to make a satisfactory price.

Such little wholesale trade as existed on the Upper Loire was based primarily upon granaries. In 1693, d'Ableiges writes: "It is true that merchants in the vicinity of Aigueperse and Cusset formed granaries last year. This year too they are again at work." [2] Other letters report "that Sanson and Levassor (merchants from the lower river) have purchased, directly or through agents, all the grain in the large farms and in the granaries in the vicinity of Aigueperse." [3] Evidently there was some active work on the part of the metropolitan wholesalers, but the more usual local trade was also in evidence. "Several persons of quality in the province, Dallègre de St. Herent, Du Terrail, d'Estain Ribeyre, have boats ready to ship down

[1] Letter cited previously.

[2] G^7. 1630. Clermont, 15 Sept. 1693. d'Ableiges au C. G.

[3] G^7. 1630. Aigueperse, 3 (?) Nov. 1693. Grimaudet à d'Ableiges.

stream. Besides these, the "Receveurs Généraux," the lessees of the coal mines in Nivernais, and other individuals are engaged in the same business."[1]

This trade in the Upper Loire was part of the supply of Orleans and Paris. In Brittany there was a considerable wholesale trade for foreign export. Some of this grain went to Bordeaux, occasionally grain was shipped to Paris by way of the Loire through Nantes, or by sea through Rouen. Most of the Breton grain was sent to Spain or Portugal. The trade was not a general provincial trade in the sense of being comprehended in one trading system, but conditions were essentially the same throughout the province. On the south coast, the trade fell into two general classes: it was in part concentrated at Nantes and shipped thence up the Loire, or to Spain and Portgual; in part the grain was shipped directly from the coast ports, Vannes, Quimper, Auray, and Hennebont. On the north coast, there were two or three rather distinct trading systems, notably centered around Saint-Brieuc and Saint-Malo. A small coasting trade was carried on by many of the small ports: little places that now scarcely afford anchorage for light pleasure craft were then considered favorable for trade.

Apart from these geographical aspects of the trade there is a more significant difference between conditions in Brittany and conditions in the producing regions which were tributary to some domestic consuming center. In the Garonne Valley, on the Upper Loire, on the Marne, the merchants who bought in the granaries came from the metropolis. There was a sharp differentiation between resident and foreign merchants. In Brittany there was no distinction of this type. The merchants who handled the export trade resided, in a general way, in the district from which they drew their supplies. But these Breton merchants amassed large resources and gradually developed extensive systems of correspondents and agents.

[1] G[7]. 1630. Clermont, 4 Nov. 1693. d'Ableiges à Pussort. See also G[7]. 1632. Ord. du Lieu. Gén. d'Aigueperse, 23 Nov. 1693. G[7]. 1635. Letter of 24 Fev. 1694. Boutz, Marchand d'Orléans. G[7]. 1630. 3(?) Nov. 1693. Grimaudet à d'Ableiges, enclosed in a letter of d'Ableiges to Pussort.

The wholesale trade here was primarily based on the rents of the province. "All the rents are paid in grain, very rarely in money. Consequently little grain is to be found in the country as elsewhere. Almost all of it is carried to the granaries of persons in easy circumstances and landed proprietors. The rest is used for seed, and for the maintenance of towns and communities. All the (wholesale) purchases are made in these granaries, which are closed whenever the proprietors please. Most of them, indeed, sell only when grain is high."[1] As another writer says almost twenty years earlier: "Brittany waits to sell her grain not only until there is a light harvest in the province and the adjoining provinces, but until there is a general dearth throughout Europe. All the granaries are near the coast, shipments are easily made, and the profits are large. It is worthy of note that the wealthiest men in the province are engaged in the trade, and these companies buy large quantities of grain when prices are low."[2] In ordinary seasons, therefore, the separation of wholesale and retail trade was based on these rents in kind. A definite portion of the crop was, of course, applied to these payments and in a rough way the division doubtless represented the proportion actually available for export.

As the Duc de Chaulnes suggests, the merchants engaged in this trade were men of means. Royal projects bring us in touch with one St. Vast Foliot, who describes himself as a "native of Saint-Lô, engaged in this wholesale trade for the last twenty years." Replying to the proposals made by the administrative authorities, he says: "As our means are not large, we cannot undertake to secure more than two or three hundred tons of grain. Grain is high at present and we would be obliged to form associations with our friends. . . . I have correspondents at Quimperlé, Hennebont, Auray, and Vannes, which are cantons where the harvest promises to be fine. I could give orders to correspondents to buy what grain they can."[3] Similar indica-

[1] Boislisle, *op. cit.*, III, 96, 298. 6 Fev. 1709. Ferrand.
[2] *Ibid.*, I, 166–167, 638. 6 Dec. 1688. Duc de Chaulnes, Gouv. de Bretagne.
[3] G7. 1641. Quimper, 12 Juillet 1709. St. Vast Foliot, Marchand à Quimper.

tions of the scale of operations, and of the associations, are furnished in a letter from Desgrassières, a royal official in Brittany. "Falconneau, who is employed to buy in the Bishoprics of Vannes and Quimper, has received word from Hennebont that M. Coetmadeu has delivered to one Le Sage and his associates 150 tons of wheat and 150 tons of rye. These merchants are forming large granaries. Billy and Mercier, merchants of Vannes, have 120 tons of grain in their granaries. It is reported that one Rallet, buying in the Bishoprics of Saint-Brieuc and Tréguier, has already taken up 6–7,000 bushels (103 tons)." [1]

In general there was probably little interference with the markets, but in 1693 and 1709 troubles appeared here as elsewhere. The merchants persisted in scouring the country and in buying in the markets to the exclusion of the peasants. The purchases of Rallet just mentioned were made with such indifference to local needs that there were riots, notably at Paimpol. The market there was completely drained of supplies, and to quiet the people the sénéchal forced him to place some of his grain on sale. At Quimper, in 1709, the wholesale merchants bought grain "at the gates of the town and on the highways without higgling at all over prices. They gave the peasants what they asked." [2]

In the Oise Valley, we find wholesale trade that is based in part on granaries of *rentiers*, and in part on granaries formed by bourgeois who buy on the market. The wholesale merchants also buy directly on the market. The evidence is so contradictory that it is difficult to be at all certain of details. It was apparently most usual for the wholesale merchants to buy on the market or in the granaries of bourgeois who had bought on the market. The Lieutenant Civil, who was examined in 1660, comments particularly on the quantity of grain brought to the market to supply the wholesale trade. It was then early in November, so that the new grain was coming rapidly to market,

[1] G^7. 1641. 18–19 Juillet 1709. Desgrassières et Barclay, copie, avec apostilles par Nointel.

[2] G^7. 1641. Quimper, 30 Sept. 1709. Le Proc. du Roy à Quimper. See also G^7. 1630. Mémoire sur les Bleds. Bretagne, 1693.

and the arrivals were probably greater than usual as the trade had attracted particular attention. He thought that "there was an unusual quantity of wheat and oats in the town, for much had been coming in from Saint-Quentin, Santerre, Bapaume, Arras, Brussels. The *blatiers* arrived daily from Monday to Saturday when the market was held, so that the market-place was completely filled. For some time, eighty, ninety, or one hundred muids (Parisian measure) had come daily to the market and had been sold. It was bought by merchants trading with Paris and by the bourgeois of Noyon. Most of the residents were accustomed to form granaries which they sold ultimately to merchants of Paris."[1] This movement of grain to the market of Noyon is also indicated by the complaint that some merchants had been buying at the sources of the supply so that grain which should have come to Noyon failed to appear. This complaint is made by Valentin Meniole, Charles le Brun, Toussaint, and La Maire, merchants resident at Noyon trading with Paris. "Every week boats come up from Beaumont, Creil, Pont-Sainte-Maxence, and Compiègne, which take loads not only of grain bought at Noyon, but also of grain purchased at Nesle and Peronne. All this grain should come to the market at Noyon. Furthermore, certain merchants of Gonesse and Saint-Denis go even as far as Peronne, where they buy grain which they carry on horses to Pont-l'Évêque near Noyon, where they load it on boats." But they had been doing the same thing themselves. "Within the last three months they had bought grain at Ham where there is much to be had both on the markets and in granaries. But when they wished to carry the grain to Noyon, the pack trains were robbed."[2] The merchants at Chaulny were also buying directly in the towns of Picardy whence the *blatiers* came. They frequented Saint-Quentin.[3] The land-owners also played a considerable part in the trade, although they are not so much in evidence.[4]

[1] Bib. Nat., Fr. 21641. 240. Noyon, 4 Nov. 1660. Procès Verbal.
[2] *Ibid.* 245v. Noyon, 4 Nov. 1660. Procès Verbal.
[3] *Ibid.* 247. Chaulny, 4 Nov. 1660. Procès Verbal.
[4] *Ibid.* 245v–6. Noyon, 4 Nov. 1660. Procès Verbal.

The buying on the market, and the independent buying in the country continues after 1660. Le Vayer in 1682 speaks of the great quantity of grain coming to the markets at Noyon from Cambresis, Vermandois, Artois, and Santerre. He also speaks of grain brought by the merchants of Noyon to Pont-l'Évêque and shipped thence to Paris.[1] On the whole this seems to have been the characteristic form of the wholesale trade at Noyon: — a combination of buying on a *blatier*-supplied market with buying in granaries formed by well-to-do bourgeois and land-owners. The different modes of purchase are not always equally important. Some years the merchants from Paris are active, buying extensively in the towns of Picardy. Then, when the harvests have been plentiful, the *blatier* supply on the market becomes so considerable that the wholesale trade is largely supplied from this source. The general appearance of the trade at Noyon was thus likely to change somewhat, although the essential features remained unaltered.

This description has possibly failed to suggest the great variety in the forms of market organization, for the common principles that can be traced and above all the universal inadequacy efface the impression of diversity that is most apparent when the analysis is not carried so far. The market systems fall into three general classes: those based entirely on town markets; wholesale trade based on *blatier*-supplied markets; wholesale trade based on granaries in the producing regions. The inter-market relations based on the town markets present by far the greatest variety of individual forms. They vary both in the different degree of the dependence and in the number of markets brought together in one system. Every possible combination can be found. One consuming market trading with one supply market, or a great town market like that of Rouen with an elaborate system of small local markets passing the grain along from remote sections of the back country. In the second general group, the variety of form is not so great. There

[1] G[7]. 510. Mémoire de Le Vayer sur L'Élection de Noyon, 23 Mai 1682. See also G[7]. 512. Soissons, 11 Juin 1697. de la Houssaye. The granaries formed by residents of Noyon.

is the large town market supplied by smaller markets. Noyon was supplied in this way from Flanders. The wholesale merchants appear on the market and buy for the metropolitan town. Differences in this group are largely confined to the relations between the town market and tributary markets. The conduct of the merchants and their relations to the metropolitan and local markets are very much the same in all places. In the last general group of trading systems, the differences are very slight and seldom significant or essential.

All the forms of the inter-market relation were inadequate. The machinery for price-making and distribution did not assure a competitive price. The system that is based throughout on the local markets over-emphasizes local interests. It inverts the relation between central and local market. The demand of the central market is sure to control in the end, but this system of market organization persistently endeavors to ignore the presence, or at any rate, the importance of the demand of the central market. It represents an effort to transact wholesale business on the basis of local prices. The combination of wholesale trade with *blatier*-supplied markets introduces no factor that overcomes the deficiencies of the simple town market system. The preponderance of the local market is still assured. The only new feature is the emancipation from the market of the later stages of the trade. This affords opportunities for deals and combinations among the merchants, it decreases competition, and renders the supply more invisible than if the trade were more closely connected with the markets. The wholesale trade that is entirely independent of the markets is the most dangerous of all. It is in a sense the most advanced form of trade organization, but in respect to price-making it is certainly the least efficient. There is no organized market in the granary towns. There is no strictly regulated market on the ports of the metropolis. In most places the merchants were required to fix a price on each boat-load when it was first placed on sale,[1]

[1] KK. 1014. Ms. "Le Commerce d'Eau à Paris." G[7]. 132. Reports of grain arrivals at Bordeaux, 1683, with the prices set for each boat-load. H. 1837. Reg. du Bureau, 404. 31 Juillet 1677. Statuts et Règlements des Jurez Mesureurs, Art. 24.

and that price could not be increased. As the boats were frequently large, the grain might not be sold within a fortnight of its arrival. Prices would naturally change, but the old grain must be sold at the first price or at a reduction. There was little competition in the ports in any event, and the natural tendency was much restrained by the limitations imposed in imitation of the town market regulations. In addition to the defects in price-making, the supply coming from this wholesale granary trade was almost completely invisible. The extent of such supplies could never be estimated in advance. In short, every form of market that appears before 1680 is inadequate and inefficient: all types involving wholesale trade are more inefficient than the simpler types based on the old town markets.

The process of evolution is in an inverse direction. Extension of any one of these three forms of organization merely made matters worse, emphasizing all the latent defects of the primitive system. All three forms had been developed as far as possible, and any further effort to widen their scope or secure additional supplies would result in a complete destruction of the market system. The dearths of 1693, 1698, 1708–09 created this need for additional supplies; greater efficiency in marketing became necessary, and reorganization of the trade was inevitable.

Reform of the market system could only be based on some type of market different from any that had existed and unlike any of the varieties that were the outcome of the three general forms that had developed more or less logically on the basis of the local markets, wholesale merchants, and granaries. The new variety of market that was so sorely needed appeared at Bray. It was first noticed in 1693 by Delamare, but its full significance was not perceived till 1709. The investigation of 1693, however, showed conclusively that the new type of market had developed at Bray shortly after 1680. No exact dates can be determined since the new departure was at first merely an informal commercial usage.

The appearance of this new variant at such a crucial time was by no means pure accident, neither was it a natural development out of any of the three general forms of market organization.

It combined features of the *blatier*-supplied market with the independence of local markets that characterized the granary trade. The traits that had been fundamental in the old *blatier*-supplied market do not appear at all in the new form. What had been incidental in the old local market is alone adopted. Similarly in the selection of features from the wholesale granary trade, the independence of the local market system is preserved, but the complete absence of organization is not retained. The market at Bray was, indeed, a natural product of all the circumstances of the time, but it is more than a mere progressive modification of any one of the three general types of market. The curiously felicitous blending of old elements in a new combination was made possible by the breaking-down of many of the sharper distinctions that had previously differentiated the primary types. All the lines became blurred so that new combinations were not only probable but almost inevitable.

The character of this period has already been suggested in the description of the various types. In the Saumur system we have already noted the efficiency of the active canvass for the old *blatier*-supplied market. In Brittany, the wholesale merchants tended to encroach on the local markets and the supplies held by peasants for local needs. The *blatier* trade was developing new affiliations with the country and with the wholesale merchants. The wholesale trade was coming into closer contact with the markets. The *blatiers* acquired a new freedom and independence; the wholesale merchants became more visible, and were less inclined to keep their trading secret. All these changes were the result of the practice of "country buying."

The form of the market at Bray prior to 1660 is largely a matter of conjecture.[1] The wholesale trade at Provins, Nogent, Pont-Sainte-Maxence, and Méry was primarily based upon granary supplies. The Parisian merchants bought in local granaries formed by rent-owners, and, to a very limited extent, by persons purchasing on the markets. Probably conditions at Bray were not very different. Possibly it was not then as

[1] Full details will be given in the following chapter.

important as it became later. The trade of this region was very much affected in 1660 by the "country buying," and the transformation of the market system under the influence of this new ferment is the most significant incident in the history of the grain trade in this period.

Buying in granaries was advantageous to the merchants, but only part of the supply of the region was accessible in that form. Consequently, the pressure of a dearth would impel the merchants to seek additional supplies either in the farms or on the markets. It is a natural development of the increased needs of the consuming center. Profits rose so high that the merchant was not content to limit his trade to the granary supply. The dearth of 1662 in the Seine Basin was the first occasion when these conditions became sufficiently intense to render them significant. Already there had been indications that such troubles were possible, but they became serious only in that year. The energy of the merchants is most notable in the sections near Paris especially at Montereau, where they invaded the markets in addition to buying in the farms. One Nepveu, agent of the Widow Rousseau, "was in the granaries at Montereau and in the environs, buying all the grain there, so that no grain came to market on the following market day."[1] According to another account, this same Nepveu "visited the peasants within six leagues of Montereau, raising the price and buying of everyone."[2] "Lavallé, a servant of the Widow Rousseau, has also been in this section running around among the farms where he has bought all the grain held by the peasants." Louise Martin heard that several merchants of Paris were scouring the country in the vicinity of Provins, especially Rebigois, and one Le Brie, agent of the Widow Rousseau.[3] Three years later, a Parisian merchant declared in court that all the grain he shipped from Bray was bought in the farms and villages of the vicinity. None was bought on the market at Bray. "This," he says, "is the

[1] Bib. Nat., Fr. 21641. 261. Procès Verbal. 31 Juillet 1660. Marie Coudray.

[2] *Ibid.* 216. Louise Pigre.

[3] Same Procès Verbal.

practice of most of the Parisian merchants at Bray."[1] Apparently the commercial customs of the region had been considerably modified.

The natural result of this energetic canvass of the country districts was to call attention to the intensity of the demand for grain. The apathetic peasantry would be roused to a realization of the possibilities of trade. They saw that the Parisian merchants would take all the grain they carried to Bray, and would pay good prices. It was no longer merely the quiet local trade of a small town, doubly dull because of the large excess of local supplies over local needs. The feverish restlessness of the metropolis, the stimulus of feeling that the demand was limitless, the assurance of high prices to be had for the asking: all this combined to give a different tone to the trade of the region. The stimulus of the suggestions of 1660 worked powerfully, and produced a marked flow of trade to Bray.

No contrast could be more striking than that presented by Bray in 1663 and the same town forty years later. In 1663, as we have seen, trade was dead, confined to granaries and to the shipment of additional supplies purchased in the country. After the change, the town was the scene of an active and steady trade. "The peasants and *blatiers* have begun to bring grain to town daily. They expose it at the Halle so that it is a sort of continuous market. . . . The fertility of the country around Bray and the facilities for shipment to Paris attract such a volume of trade that the spacious Halle of the town could not contain the whole supply, if it were all brought in the same day. The peasants and *blatiers* come from Champagne, Burgundy, and other distant places. This extension of the market is not authorized by any ordinance. It is a mere custom, but the municipal officials and the principal inhabitants say that their experience proves that the practice is advantageous. The *blatiers* from a distance could not arrange to arrive each time on Friday, the regular market day, and if they were obliged to stay in town until the market day, it would increase their expenses and cause them to sell at higher prices. In Brie the roads are

[1] H. 1817. Reg. du Bureau, v^{e}iiii. 13 Juillet 1663.

so rough and difficult that in winter the country folk could not be sure of arriving on the day prescribed. Liberty to sell at any time attracts them and produces abundance. Notwithstanding this freedom, the Halle is always well supplied on Friday, and the ordinary market day sees a greater quantity on hand than the other days of the week. This liberty to sell grain every week-day gives the Parisian merchants greater facilities. They can ship daily to Paris." [1]

This is a real wholesale market. The supply flows into the town in anticipation of a metropolitan demand, and the anticipation is so keen that practically all the available supply comes to market without any special canvassing. The purpose of the market is frankly avowed, and no pretence is made of controlling the trade from the point of view of local interests. The local market has been completely engulfed in a wholesale market. The new practice was not very firmly fixed. There was no legal basis for the system, and the habits were not firmly settled. But the idea of a wholesale market had taken visible form. The conception was so new that Delamare did not sympathize with such a complete departure from the ordinary market regulations. The practical efficiency of the idea, however, commended it, and it was allowed to survive.

It was long before the full significance of this new market was impressed upon the administrative officials. Even more time was required before the new form supplemented completely the older modes of handling the wholesale trade. But this was destined to be the solution of all the difficulties. The wholesale organization was defective in two respects: lack of real wholesale price; invisibility of supply. Both of these defects would be remedied by the application of the new principle. The assembling of the wholesale merchants and the concentration of the available supply obviated the most distressing feature of the old system in the producing regions. Metropolitan demand was no longer pressing upon a supply that was assembled primarily with reference to local conditions. This concentration

[1] Delamare, *op. cit.*, II, 981. The order of the paragraphs has been altered to give the description more continuity.

of trade had made the supply visible. The purchases of grain merchants could no longer be secret. The market in the producing region was public, and if each producing region had a public wholesale market of this type, the available metropolitan supply would be definitely known long before it appeared at Paris. Then it would no longer be possible to play upon the apprehensions of the Parisians by forming subsidiary granaries or by delaying grain in transit. The supply would be visible. The price would represent a serious attempt to meet the conditions of the wholesale trade.

CHAPTER II

The History of the Parisian Markets

The changes that took place in the market systems of Paris were important and considerable, but the development is not obvious since the outward appearance of the grain trade was only slightly affected. When the trade appears in the records of the late thirteenth century, it is already highly organized and acquainted with distant sources of supply. Some grain came to Paris overland, much came by water.[1] There were wholesale merchants, some residents of Paris, some from the provinces; there were retail dealers, called *blatiers*, and the usual peasants and tithe owners. The market system of Paris in 1300 was quite as highly developed as the system of Bordeaux in 1700. But the trade of Paris in 1300 was not quite what a general description might lead us to expect: there were merchants indeed, but doing a very small business; supplies from a wide area, but they were very occasional and they did not represent any attempt to exploit the region systematically. The native merchants leave no trace in the records, but the *bourgeois forains* were required to enter into partnership with some native merchant, whenever they wished to trade at Paris, and this formality gave them a place on the registers of the municipality. Michel Dean, who had brought fourteen muids of grain to the city in 1293, without forming any association with a native of Paris, was fined.[2] Other merchants complied with the regulations and are duly recorded. " Maci de Gigors brought ten muids of grain from Noyon, the Thursday after Saint Honoré. It was put in a granary. Geoffroi of Dammartin brought four muids,

[1] *Livre des Métiers* d'Étienne Boileau, p. 21. " Si Mesureur mesure aucun grain quelqu' il soit, *soit en granier, soit en nef* il aura de chascun muid IV deniers."

[2] Le Roux de Lincy, *Histoire de l'Hôtel de Ville. Sentences du Parloir des Bourgeois*, p. 120.

which was put in a granary. Symon Dandin brought four muids."[1] The merchants are thus much less important than they became later, if these figures are at all representative of the ordinary amounts of their purchases. In the seventeenth century, the larger merchants handled several hundred muids, and frequently had several boats (20–30 muids each) on the ports at one time.

The *Livre des Métiers* of Étienne Boileau mentions the merchants, but without revealing any essential feature. The resident and non-resident merchants are clearly distinguished. The principal interest of the *Livre des Métiers*, however, is the establishment of the dues to be paid by the various dealers in grain. The wholesale merchants seem to enjoy the privilege of exemption from the obligation to employ the official measurers. This was the most marked difference between the obligations of the merchants and the *blatiers*. "Buyers and purchasers are not required to pay the two deniers per mine, if they do not have the grain measured. They are not required to have the grain measured unless they are *blatiers*."[2] The *blatier* was not allowed to sell more than one setier without having it measured by the sworn measurer.

This *blatier* was evidently quite a different person from the small inter-market trader known by that name later. The *Livre des Métiers* is explicit. "*Whoever wishes to be a blatier, that is, a buyer and seller of grain at Paris*, may engage freely in that occupation on paying the *tonlieu* and the other dues that are levied on grain. Whoever is a *blatier* at Paris may have as many journeymen and apprentices as he desires. He may have a measure, sealed with the royal seal, and may measure up to a setier."[3] The distinction between the *blatiers* and the *talemalers* is not very clear; both were retail dealers, but the *blatiers*

[1] Le Roux de Lincy, *Histoire de l'Hôtel de Ville. Sentences du Parloir des Bourgeois*, p. 176.

[2] *Livre des Métiers* d'Étienne Boileau, p. 312. But compare p. 21. "Nus marchans de grain, c'est asavoir vendeur ou achateur de grain quelqu'il soit, dedanz la Ville de Paris ne puet ne ne doit mesurer chose qu'il vende, plus haut d'un sextier a une fois." This must refer to the *blatier*.

[3] *Livre des Métiers* d'Étienne Boileau, p. 20.

seem to have dealt in grain only, while the *talemalers* might deal in other commodities.

The inter-market *blatier* does not appear in any of these early sources. He is probably confused with the peasants, possibly with the *blatiers* mentioned by Étienne Boileau. It is hardly conceivable that there were no middlemen of the type of the *blatier* of the seventeenth century.

This supposition is strengthened by the indication of a widely extended trade that appears in the *Sentences du Parloir des Bourgeois* in 1304. It was a year of dearth, and commissioners were sent out to discover how much grain was available in the producing regions. Two groups of agents were sent out: some, with royal commissions to the Baillis of Sens, Tours, Orleans, Gizors, Troyes, Senlis, Vermandois, Vitry, Chaumont-en-Bassigny, and Amiens; others, with commissions from the Provost of Paris, to the towns in the vicinity of Paris, Gonesse, Saint-Cloud, Châteaufort, Claye, Montgay, Dammartin, Poissy, and Marly.[1] Two years later, Robert Ausgans and Matthew of Gisors were sent out to the environs to stimulate shipments of grain to Paris. Instead of discharging their commission they bought grain and shipped to Rouen.[2] Then, too, we must remember the shipments from Noyon to Paris that are noted in another passage of the *Sentences*. The exact significance of these obscure references cannot be determined, but it is clear that we must not conceive this early Parisian trade to be highly concentrated in a small region close to the city. The land trade with the immediate environs certainly existed and doubtless constituted the principal part of the supply. If we may draw inferences from the commissions of 1304, the plains to the north and west of Paris were at that time a more important source of

[1] Leroux de Lincy, *op. cit.*, *Livre des Sentences du Parloir des Bourgeois*, 161, anno 1304, Mardi avant Pasques.

It is impossible to decide which Marly is intended. There is a Marly la Ville not far from Dammartin. The other and more famous Marly is between Versailles and Saint-Germain-en-Laye. Poissy is on the Seine northwest of Saint-Germain. Châteaufort is south of Versailles on the upper border of the Beauce.

[2] Delamare, *op. cit.*, II, 339. *Les Olim*, III, 193–194. 1306, Mercredy avant St. André.

supply than the Beauce and Brie, which became the principal sources of the overland trade in the seventeenth century. The markets of Gonesse, Dammartin, and Claye drew from the north and sent the grain on to Paris. On the west side of the city, Poissy and Châteaufort served as tributary markets. The location of Châteaufort, on the northern edge of the Beauce, suggests that trade was soon likely to push farther into that fertile region. But none of the later markets of the Beauce or of Brie are mentioned. Besides this land trade, there was a river trade that reached well up the Oise, the Seine, and the Marne. Probably this river trade was very irregular, carried on by merchants to whom a shipment of grain was incidental to other commercial ventures which occupied most of their attention. The general trading relations between Paris and the towns of the Upper Seine Basin were intimate. The fairs of Champagne carried many traders to Provins, Bray, and Troyes. The textiles of Châlons and Rheims attracted merchants from Paris. Shipments of grain were an occasional source of profit. This early acquaintance with the possible sources of supply, however, is a noteworthy feature of the Parisian trade.

The fourteenth century leaves almost no record of the grain trade. The lacuna is in part due to lack of material, but there is good reason to suppose that little notable change occurred. The marked institutional advance of the later thirteenth century was a crisis, which was followed in the grain trade, as in other matters, by a period of relative stagnation.

I

Delimitation of the Supply Area

The late thirteenth and the fourteenth centuries are notable for the evident acquaintance with a wide supply area; the fifteenth century affords the first definite indication of a serious effort to utilize more completely the great resources that lay so close to the city. The Parisian merchants extended their operations in the Upper Beauce, and most especially in the Seine Valley between Mantes and Rouen. Some of this grain was brought to Paris overland but the larger part came by water. The development of the Upper Basin, curiously enough, was primarily the work of merchants of Rouen, while the Parisians developed what would seem to be properly a source of supply for Rouen. Here we find a confusion of commercial relations that is thoroughly typical of medieval trade. But such crudity of organization could not continue permanently. Paris and Rouen had distinct market systems, and it was practically necessary to bring about some close connection between the market systems and the territorial areas from which the markets were to be supplied. Each market would work most efficiently if it had the assurance that its supplies would not be taken by merchants from other towns. In the latter part of our period the acceptance of this policy is evident. Each market town had a fairly well defined sphere of influence, and any encroachment upon the supplies of this area was keenly resented. The development of this aspect of the Parisian and Rouenese markets is the principal episode in the history of the fifteenth and sixteenth centuries.

When all the possible sources of supply are considered, it is singular that the extension of the Parisian trade should first proceed westward to Rouen. Probably there was then an exportable surplus in Normandy that was not needed by Rouen herself until later. Doubtless the intimacy of general trading relations tended to draw the grain trade in that direction. Whatever the reason, the first considerable movement does take that direction; the trade pushes down the river from Poissy to Mantes, from Mantes to Andelys, from Andelys to Elboeuf, and even to Rouen itself. The merchants also work into the back country.

These movements are somewhat obscure and the paucity of information renders great caution necessary in drawing inferences; it is above all essential to avoid minute conclusions in regard to dates. There is a lacuna of more than thirty years (1411–47) in the registers of Rouen from which much of the evidence is drawn, and the records of the *Compagnies Françaises* for the succeeding generation show that many aspects of the trade are very inadequately indicated by the municipal registers. The dates of the available evidence are probably of no significance; the movements indicated are general for at least the first half of the fifteenth century. At the beginning of the century Rouen was deriving her supplies from the Vexin and the "*pays de Neubourg*," which were the most important sources of supply in the seventeenth century.[1] The markets of Andelys, Gisors, Elboeuf, and Neubourg are not definitely mentioned, but the relation of the markets to each other was probably approximately the same as it was later.

The appearance of Parisian merchants in the immediate vicinity of Rouen naturally caused some apprehension, but in this period it spent itself in deliberation and discussion. In 1457, we find the Échevins considering "the great export of grain that is taking place daily, from Andelys, from the farms of the Vexin, from Elboeuf, from the vicinity of Neubourg, from Rouen itself, and from other parts of the duchy. This grain is carried up the Seine to 'France'[2] or down to the sea."[3] Some Parisian merchants were frequently engaged in such ventures. In 1430, a group of merchants had been operating more or less independently beyond Rouen, in the parts of Normandy that were not at that time very closely bound to the Rouenese market. "The Cotentin, Bessin, Pays de Caux, and other places" furnished a very considerable field for operations.[4] The ports from which the grain was shipped are not indicated, and it is quite possible that the frequent shipments from Rouen and Elboeuf were purchased in this back country to the west of Rouen. The registers of the *Compagnies Françaises* give nothing beyond categorical statements of quantity, place, and price.[5] The proposition to execute prohibitions at

[1] *Arch. Som. de Rouen, Reg. Consulaires*, p. 28. 8 Jan. 1406–07.

[2] "France" is applied to the district along the Marne from its confluence with the Seine to the border of Champagne.

[3] *Arch. Som. de Rouen, Reg. Consulaires*, p. 60. 27 Dec. 1457. They conclude that prohibitions would be expedient.

[4] Delamare, *op. cit.*, II, 345.

[5] Bib. Nat., Col. Moreau, 1062, ff. 28v, 21 Fev. 1455; 45, 24 Mars 1457; 47, 29 Mai 1458; 47, 5 Juillet 1458; 47v, 9 Juillet 1458; 47v, 11 Juillet 1458; 48,

Bouillé, Caumont, La Poterie, Quilleboeuf, and Pont-Audemer would confirm the inference that exports by Parisian merchants, at this time, were from the plains west of Rouen.[1] But the merchants might at any time invade the regions on the east which generally supplied Rouen, and complaints in 1460 would indicate that extensive purchases were made there. "Ever since August there have been heavy shipments from the Vexin, and from the environs of Neubourg. Wheat and other kinds of grain have been purchased and sent up the Seine." The merchants were said to have "purchased much in the farms and in the villages,"[2] and if the rumours were true there would be added reason for supposing that the purchases in the back country were shipped from Rouen and Elboeuf.

But the movement was not all in one direction. Almost contemporaneously with the trade from Normandy to Paris there was an equally extensive trade from the Oise Valley to Rouen. Less frequently there were shipments from the Seine or Marne Valleys to Rouen. There are few instances in which the movements take place in both directions in the same year, but some cases of this do appear even in the scanty material available. The year 1459 was most notable for the shipment of grain from the vicinity of Rouen to Paris, but Jean de Bilain, a merchant of Rouen, enters into *Compagnie Française*, 23 June 1459, in order to ship thirty muids of grain to Rouen from some place in the commercial jurisdiction of Paris.[3] In the following year there is a similar instance of cross-trade.[4] Throughout the fall of 1460 there were shipments from Rouen, Elboeuf, and Neubourg to Paris. In the spring, the trade turned; merchants of Caen, Elboeuf, and Rouen bought in the Oise Valley, shipping

17 Août 1458; 49, 2 Sept. 1458; 63, 21 Juin 1459; 66v, 24 Nov. 1459; 72, 7 Fev. 1459; 72, 5 Dec. 1459; 78v, 18 Juin 1460; 98v, 21 Dec. 1461; all these cases, Rouen or Elboeuf to Paris. f. 29, 1 Mars 1455, Saint-Clère to Paris.

[1] *Arch. Som. de Rouen, Reg. Consulaires*, p. 60. 15 Jan. 1457–58.

[2] *Ibid.*, p. 61. 16 Dec. 1460. The reference to "country buying" at this date shows the impossibility of making any rigid classifications. Even if the practice were relatively common, it does not have the significance that it acquires later.

[3] Bib. Nat., Col. Moreau, 1062. f. 63, 23 Juin 1459.

[4] *Ibid.* f. 78, 5 Juin 1460.

to Rouen and Elboeuf. Possibly supplies in the vicinity of Rouen were exhausted and all the wholesale merchants were obliged to transfer their activity to a new source of supply. Additional color is lent to this explanation by the shipments from the Oise Valley to Paris in the spring of 1462. In short, everything points to the conclusion that Paris and Rouen drew supplies from Normandy up to the last of December, 1461, or even through January and February, and then perforce turned to Noyon and Compiègne till the following harvest.[1] There is doubtless some truth in such an interpretation but the Rouenese trade from the Oise Valley is so considerable that it is probably an export trade. The quantities mentioned in the registers are: "60 muids, 260 muids, 155 muids, 136 muids, mesure de Compiègne"; "68 muids, 87 muids, 31 muids, 18 muids, mesure de Rouen; 205 muids, mesure de Crépy. 100 muids, mesure de Paris." The measures differ considerably, those of Compiègne and Crépy are only a fourth or a fifth of the Parisian or Rouenese measure. But even with all allowance for this factor, the trade is much more considerable than the trade from Rouen, which generally consisted of consignments of less than ten muids. Furthermore, the registers of *Compagnies Françaises* give us only a part of the whole commercial movement, as the trade by resident Parisian merchants does not appear. For this reason it is not safe to conclude that the turn of the trade took place in February and March, 1462 as the records of trade of non-resident merchants seem to indicate. Even if the exact character of the episode could be established, the successive exploitation of Normandy and Santerre is not the significant feature. It gives an impression that can easily be misinterpreted in the light of modern commercial practice. It looks too much like the well-directed buying that characterizes the modern metropolitan market. In reality the whole incident is strikingly medieval. Paris and Rouen are distinct markets, each supplied by different groups of merchants. Their operations are relatively short-sighted. The Parisian merchants

[1] Bib. Nat., Col. Moreau, 1062. ff. 102, 103, 104, 105, 106, 107, 15 Mars 1461–2 Août 1462.

buy in the vicinity of Rouen where they come into competition indirectly with the merchants of Rouen. As much of the trading is done in granaries and farms, this competition amounts to little. But the supply available for export is not as considerable as the supply in the Oise Valley; the latter is somewhat more difficult to reach and consequently is not touched except in last resort. The merchants of Rouen perceived the activity of the Parisians, and bought in distant places for the supply of the town or for export; but there was no determined effort to drive the Parisians out of the neighborhood in order to preserve the supply for the town and its export trade. Two entirely distinct trades cross each other, leading to much unnecessary transportation and to a confusion of trading relations that is hardly comprehensible. There are indications in 1458 and 1460 that the Échevins of Rouen were beginning to feel strongly on the question. They resented the intrusion of the Parisians and endeavored to prevent export from the duchy. The activity of the merchants, however, shows that the idea was not carried out. Great latitude in all these matters apparently prevailed throughout the fifteenth century.[1]

In the early sixteenth century the effort to secure a sharp limitation of areas becomes insistent and finally triumphs. The Parisians cease to buy in Normandy except with permission; the Rouenese no longer buy in the Oise Valley unless they have been granted special licenses.

An important factor in the new development of policy and organization was the necessity for a wider area to supply Rouen. In the fourteenth century, the Vexin and Pays de Neubourg had sufficed. In 1520, the agents of the town work up into the Beauce to Nogent-le-Roy and Chartres.[2] The efforts of the municipality to secure grain are in themselves significant. This edge of the Beauce gradually came to be considered a regular source of additional supply.[3] In 1528, the Échevins speak of the

[1] This is inference. There is a serious lacuna in the Registers of Rouen from 1472–90.

[2] *Deux Chroniques de Rouen*, pp. 124–125. 1521–22.

[3] *Arch. Som. de Rouen, Reg. Consulaires*, pp. 124–125. 18 Avril 1522.

Beauce as the region which has "always been our principal resource in time of necessity."[1]

The pressure was in part due to the growth of the city, but it was primarily caused by the closing of the Valley of the Oise to Rouen. There is a striking contrast between the brisk trade on the Oise in 1462, and the humble petition of the Échevins in 1528, craving permision to buy grain along the Oise. "We believe that you are informed of the great distress which we have suffered twice in the last seven years from dearth of grain, and inasmuch as we apprehend similar trouble in this current year we have commissioned Gilles des Froisses, a merchant of this town, to go to Santerre, where we have been advised of the existence of considerable quantities of grain. He was instructed to buy one or two hundred muids. He has made his purchases and engaged to place the grain on sale at Rouen. . . . Dear brothers and friends, you know that we have always freely permitted the passage of all the goods that you have found necessary, raising no obstacles. So we beg you to assist us in this affair of ours, and to permit that the grain be transported incontinent to Rouen."[2] Such complete acknowledgment of the power of Paris is an interesting commentary on the change that had taken place since 1462. The Oise had been closed to the merchants of Rouen, except under special permission. For foreign export and for maintenance Rouen was ordinarily dependent on Norman grain. As in this case, the permission was generally granted but under strict limitations and subject to much formality. "Gilles des Froyses," declare the Échevins of Paris, "is given leave to export 100 muids of grain to Rouen, upon furnishing security not to export in excess of that quantity. On condition also that he will within six weeks certify that the grain has been sold and distributed at the markets of Rouen."[3] Besides this consignment secured directly by the intervention of the Échevins of Rouen, merchants of Paris made some shipments to Rouen on their own initiative. But they were required

[1] *Reg. du Bureau*, II, 16. 20 Mars 1528.
[2] *Ibid.*, II, 16. 20 Mars 1528.
[3] *Ibid.*, II, 16–17. 24 Mars 1528.

by the Provost of Paris to obtain special permits from him. Even this degree of intercourse seemed dangerous to the Provost of Merchants, who represented the authority of the municipality, and partly to protect the supplies of the city, partly to assert his power over the royal official, a very vigorous protest was entered against the assumption of this jurisdiction by the Provost. The case was laid before the Council and decision rendered in favor of the Provost of the Merchants.[1] The policy of Paris was thus clearly asserted. The Seine Basin outside of Normandy was subject to the jurisdiction of the Provost of Merchants of Paris. No towns in other parts of France could make purchases in this region without first securing permission.[2] Permits would be issued under certain conditions, but such exports were closely watched. Thus, in April, 1536, permission to export was cancelled on account of "the great shipments of grain by the river Seine to Rouen, and because the merchants of Normandy make great exports from divers places, which they have amassed at Rouen and other places in Normandy, so that grain is cheaper at Rouen than at Paris."[3] The movement of grain from the Parisian sphere of influence was thus forcibly stopped in the first half of the century.

The trade from Rouen to Paris leaves little trace. There seems to be little effort at Rouen to stop such movements of grain, but despite this apparent indifference there is nothing to suggest the continuance of the extensive operations of Parisian merchants in Normandy. What the Normands gave up unwillingly and under pressure, the Parisians abandoned voluntarily. The development of the Upper Seine, of the Marne, of the Oise, of parts of the Beauce, all probably took place in this century, though the evidence is not very definite. The full possibilities of the Upper Seine Basin seem to have been realized for the first time. The perception of the value and richness of these sources of supply rendered the city jealous of

[1] *Reg. du Bureau*, II, 28. 26 Juin 1528.

[2] At times, Lyons seeks grain in the Beauce.

[3] *Reg. du Bureau*, II, 218. 27 Avril 1536. See also *ibid.*, II, 225. 30 Juin 1536.

any encroachment from outside, and the great resources of the area made the city quite independent. The renunciation of the exploitation of Normandy cost little, when greater abundance was to be had nearer Paris in the upper waters of the Seine, even more advantageously situated for water transport.

The abandonment of trade with Rouen was not absolute. The dearth of 1563, more severe in the Seine Basin than in Normandy, sent Parisian merchants down stream to make purchases for the town.[1] In 1596, also, purchases were made at Rouen in behalf of the Échevins of Paris.[2]

The extension of Parisian influence, which took the form of excluding the competition of other towns from the Upper Seine Basin, assumes in the seventeenth century an entirely different character. After a moderate degree of consolidation of trade within the sixteenth century area, the capital town begins to reach out still farther. There is a real attack upon the supply areas of other towns. The old Norman trade is revived; Parisian merchants again invade the vicinity of Rouen, as in the fifteenth century, but in a very different manner. Aspects of modern metropolitanism appear. Then, too, the trading system of the Loire Valley is invaded. A supply area in Touraine that had been developed by Nantes for export trade is entered by Parisian merchants who carry off a continually increasing portion of the supply. From Saumur, the ubiquitous merchants pass on to Nantes; from Nantes, they are led on to the other source of her export trade — Brittany. The larger history of the export trade in the seventeenth century is thus concerned with a remarkable extension of Parisian influence. The Rouenese market area is invaded; the Loire Valley is tapped; the Breton granaries pour their supplies into the boats of Parisian merchants. It is all a great movement towards a centralization of the northern grain trade in Paris, a revelation of the growing tendency of Paris to dominate the commercial life of northern France.

The new phase of the relation between Rouen and Paris appears as early as 1626. The municipality of Rouen issued

[1] *Reg. du Bureau*, V, 221. 10 Mai 1563.

[2] *Ibid.*, XI, 221. 21–22 Fev. 1596.

prohibitions against exports from its jurisdiction by Parisian merchants.[1] In 1629 and 1630, the Parlement of Normandy undertook the defence of the Rouenese area against the encroachments of Paris. The apprehensions of the authorities were amply justified by the facts. In 1643 the Parisians had organized the trade in Normandy. We find one Pierre Pinon of Paris, in partnership with Jean Renault of Elboeuf, engaged in trade from Rouen to Paris. Pierre Pinon describes the condition of their trade to the officials at Paris: "They have a boat on the Port de l'École charged with 100 muids of grain, none of which has yet been sold. Besides this they have 300 muids of grain in their possession, in the Beauce, at Pont-de-l'Arche, Elboeuf, and at Rouen: — all destined for Paris. But it must pass Pont-de-l'Arche, Andelys, and Vernon, which are all within the jurisdiction of the Parlement of Rouen. The Parlement, however, has prohibited the export of grain from the province. These *arrêts* must be annulled by the Council, and the officers of Pont-de-l'Arche, Andelys, and Vernon must be summoned to give account of their conduct. A distinction is drawn between the upper and lower Beauce. All the grain of the Upper Beauce is sent to Paris from Étampes where no difficulties are placed in the way of the merchants. But the grain of the Lower Beauce is brought ordinarily to Nogent-le-Roy, where the merchants of Paris and of Normandy go to buy. Purchases for Rouen in the Lower Beauce should be stopped in retaliation against the prohibitions made by the Parlement of Rouen against exports from the province. The prohibitions in Normandy ought not to apply to grain purchased by merchants of Paris within the jurisdiction of Paris and passed through the jurisdiction of the Parlement of Rouen merely for the convenience in shipping. The 300 muids, which the said Pinon and Regnault have declared, can reach Paris only by way of Pont-de-l'Arche, Andely, and Vernon."[2] Pierre de Vaux,

[1] H. 1802. Reg. du Bureau, viii^{xx}ii. 25 Avril 1626.

[2] H. 1806. Reg. du Bureau, iii^{c}xl. Enquête par les Prévost des Marchands et Échevins, 28 Mars 1643. There is a copy of this at the Bib. Nat., Fr. 16741. f. 9. The name of the merchant is there given "Pierre Simon."

another merchant, declares that he has a boat-load of 25 muids of grain at Elboeuf, about 80 muids arrested at Oudan below Pont-de-l'Arche, and about 200 muids at Chartres, Nogent-le-Roy, Elboeuf, and Rouen.[1] The encroachment is thus obscured in some degree by the legal dispute over jurisdiction. There is a tacit admission of the legal independence of each area, but the Parisian merchants propose nevertheless to restrict the sphere of influence of Rouen. The right to carry grain through the Rouenese area would have opened endless opportunities for the shipment of grain purchased within the jurisdiction of the Parlement of Rouen.

In 1649, the municipality of Paris was again seeking to annul the prohibitions in Normandy,[2] and without great success. But despite the opposition of the Parlement of Rouen, the trade to Paris continued from this period to 1693, when the aggressiveness of the Parisian merchants became more marked. The apparent lacuna in the evidence is bridged by the history of Jean Roger, in 1694 one of the wealthiest grain merchants of Paris. His father was a merchant of Rouen engaged incidentally, if not principally, in the grain trade with Paris. Jean began his career as a clerk under his father. In 1650, Jean moved to Paris and acted as Parisian agent for the house until 1656, when he set up in business for himself. His father continued his business, and a few years later, when his son lost heavily on certain ventures, the elder Roger took him into partnership again on some consignments from Normandy. Between 1662 and 1693, Jean changed the basis of his operations to Soissons.[3] Jean Regnault and the widow of Pierre Simon, of whom we first hear in 1643, are engaged in the Rouenese grain trade as late as 1661, though the partnership has apparently been dissolved.[4] The Parisian encroachment thus persists without intermission.

[1] H. 1806. Reg. du Bureau, iii^e^xl. Enquête par les Prévost des Marchands et Échevins, 28 Mars 1843. There is a copy of this at the Bib. Nat., Fr. 16741. f. 9. The name of the merchant is there given "Pierre Simon."

[2] H. 1809. Reg. du Bureau, iii^e^xlv. 13 Oct. 1649.

[3] Bib. Nat., Fr. 21642. 368. Factum pour Jean Roger. Paris, Juillet–Août, 1693.

[4] H. 1816. Reg. du Bureau, cli. 10 Juin 1661.
Ibid., cxxviii. 7 Mai 1661.

Towards the close of the century the movement becomes more aggressive. It is no longer an attempt to carry grain from the edges of the Rouen market area, but a deliberate invasion of the whole region from which Rouen drew supplies. Beuvron writes from La Mailleraye, 3 January 1694: "A great quantity of oats has been shipped to Paris from Caudebec, and from the country round about within a radius of seven or eight leagues. Oats have become dear and very scarce, so that many have been impelled to form partnerships to engage in trade. . . . They are constantly shipping and buying. They take up all that is to be had of the peasants, forming granaries at Caudebec and other places, so that very little is available for the markets. In a short time there will be absolute dearth in this section." [1] Three months later Montholon writes: "Elboeuf, which ordinarily furnished the market at Rouen with 60–80 muids of grain per week, brings now only 14 or 15 muids. The day before yesterday only 4 muids came from Elboeuf. *The blatiers carry everything off to Magny and thence to Paris. They buy even on the market to Rouen.*" [2] In July, the Parisian merchants were still active. "The market of Elboeuf furnishes nothing, all its supplies go to Paris. Caudebec has been supplied from Caen and has sent considerable quantities to Rouen." [3] The local authorities made some futile attempts to oppose this encroachment of Parisian merchants, but neither the Parlement nor the Échevins of Rouen dared take the drastic measures that would have been effective. In 1698 and 1699 the same problem confronted Rouen.[4] "There is always a swarm of *blatiers* in the markets of Elboeuf, Du Clère, Caudebec, and Andelys, buying up the grain that should come to Rouen, so that little comes to town. The grain of Neubourg and of that whole section is carried off without even passing through the market at Elboeuf." [5] Then, in the following year we find

[1] G7. 1635. La Mailleraye, 3 Jan. 1694. Beuvron.

[2] G7. 1635. Rouen, 6 Mars 1694. Montholon.

[3] G7. 1635. Rouen, 1 Juillet 1694.

[4] G7. 495. 1697, Placet envoyé par Jean Patty et Jean Mulheau.

[5] G7. 496. Rouen, 5 Dec. 1698. Also letters of 16 and 22 Nov. 1698; 15 and 19 Dec. 1698.

similar reports. "Several millers, peasant proprietors, and farmers of the élections of Mantes, Chaumont, and Pontoise, especially in those parts of the élections which are in the jurisdiction of the Parlement of Normandy, buy grain on the local markets, convert it into flour, and ship to Paris."[1] "At Magny, Gisors, Vernon, and other places the merchants who declared their intention of selling at Paris, Saint-Germain-en-Laye, Mantes, and other places bring back no certificates of sale. They assert that the local officials refuse to issue the certificates."[2]

During the great dearth of 1709 every aspect of this invasion of the supply area of Rouen appears in clearer outline. In a letter of April 10, 1709, the Intendant says: "I fear that the *blatiers* who are shipping to Paris will cause a rise in prices. They have already invaded the market of Du Clère, three leagues northwest of Rouen, buying at any price that is asked without stopping to haggle."[3] Two days later he writes: "they have reached Louviers and Neubourg on the south side of Rouen. I am afraid they will go next to Bourgachard, and in that way drain all the local markets. It would bring Rouen to the verge of famine."[4] A fortnight later his fears were realized. "The *blatiers* have surrounded us. They have invaded the markets of Routot, Bourgachard, and Caudebec, where they are buying at any price that is asked."[5]

The careful delimitation of supply areas so gradually worked out in the course of the sixteenth century was thus completely broken down. The metropolitan importance of Paris was asserted. The idea that a supply should be reserved for a particular city was abandoned. The grain trade acquired a ubiquitous character that is distinctly modern: the supply of Paris, like that of the modern metropolitan market, was recruited freely wherever a merchant from Paris could find grain.

[1] G[7]. 430. 26 Août 1699.

[2] G[7]. 496. Rouen, 1 Dec. 1699.

[3] G[7]. 1650. Rouen, 10 Avril 1709.

[4] G[7]. 1650. Rouen, 12 Avril 1709. Courson au C. G.

[5] G[7]. 1650. Rouen, 28 Avril 1709. See also letters of 29 Avril, 15 Juin, 7 Juin, 14 Sept. 1709, all in the same carton.

But while the Parisian market was metropolitan in its far-reaching canvass for supplies, it was itself distinctly medieval in regard to distribution of supply. It was a consumptive rather than a distributive market. Supplies were poured in from every quarter of northern France; nothing was sent out.

The same general features were disclosed in the extension of Parisian trade in the Loire Valley. In this way, Paris acquired control of the only important source of supply in northern France not previously tributary to the growing capital. The date of this movement is obscure. Indications of Parisian trade in the Loire Valley do not appear in the Parisian sources before 1650, but it is quite possible that local material would carry the date back to a more remote period. The approximate coincidence with the encroachment upon the Rouenese area, however, might suggest that the Loire Valley trade with Paris really began in the middle of the seventeenth century.

Previous to this connection with Paris, the trade of the Loire Valley was dominated by Nantes and by Lyons. The supplies available in Touraine, coming to Saumur from the back country, were purchased by merchants from Nantes who were engaged in foreign export trades in addition to the local trade of the town. Nantes was engaged in a considerable trade with Spain and Portugal in which grain played a subsidiary but significant part. The possibility of foreign export attracted to Nantes a quantity of grain far in excess of the needs of the town, and this is doubtless the primary factor in the sixteenth century trade of the Lower Loire.[1] On the upper reaches of the river the surplus was small and trade was irregular. The principal sources of supply were in the vicinity of Clermont-Ferrand and Aigueperse. In the sixteenth century Lyons drew supplies from the region through Roanne.[2] The appearance of Parisian merchants on the Loire led to a complete reorganization of trade throughout the valley. The grain from the upper river was

[1] See *Arch. Communales de Nantes*, ff. 176, 180, 186, 187, 188, 189. It was impossible for me to see this material, but the printed inventory indicates its general character, and the conclusions stated above.

[2] Archives Municipales de Lyon. See ch. iii for details.

deflected from Lyons and came down to Orleans, passing thence to Paris. From Saumur a large portion of the available supply came up stream to Orleans and Paris. The trade of the river converged on Orleans, and proceeded to Paris, either by way of the Canal de Briare or overland.

The Loire Valley trade, however, was tending to assume this form quite independently of Parisian influence. At an early date Lyons ceased to purchase grain in Auvergne, and, as the grain of the Beauce went primarily to Paris, Orleans found it necessary to seek supplies both in Auvergne and in Touraine. In years of dearth, too, Blois and Tours frequently needed supplies beyond what could be secured in the immediate vicinity. The similarity of the development of the trade of Orleans and of Paris renders the history of the Loire Valley curiously complicated. There are three distinct lines of trade: to Paris, to Orleans, and to Nantes. The first two draw both from the upper and lower river, the latter derives its supplies wholly from Touraine. The distance of the sources of supply from the consuming towns makes the encroachment upon these areas less distinct than in the case of Rouen where the Parisian merchants bought in the immediate vicinity of the city. There is less feeling of exclusive right to the supply here in the Loire. The local officials have the same feeling towards all wholesale merchants; the merchants feel a certain community of interest. Orleans and Nantes, whose interests are most seriously threatened, have no jurisdiction over the producing regions, though the position of Orleans enables her to exert some control over the grain passing to Paris. The appearance is somewhat different; the movements are essentially the same. Both in Normandy and on the Loire the larger towns suffered from the competition with Paris for supplies previously left to them without external interference.

In 1662, Parisian merchants were buying in Auvergne.[1] Their operations were based on purchases in the granaries, but the resources of the region were not considerable and no

[1] Bib. Nat., Mél. Colb., 107 bis. Riom, 3 Jan. 1662. De la Barre. *Ibid.*, 107 bis. 632. Riom, 24 Jan. 1662. De la Barre à Colbert.

great quantity could be obtained. De la Barre says in his letter of January 3, that 1200–1500 setiers might be obtained for Paris, and this probably represents about the proportion that could be secured by Parisian merchants. March 11, he reported that 5000–6000 setiers had gone down the river to Orleans, Blois, and Tours.[1] May 30, he writes: "I have just returned from the ports of the Allier where more than eighty boats, loaded with 13–14,000 setiers of wheat are waiting for the river to rise. It is extremely low just at present, but the weather has been very wet lately and the river will soon become navigable."[2] But the boats did not get off at once, and by the time the river had risen the grain fleet had increased remarkably. June 19, he writes: "I have left the ports of the Allier only after having sent off a fleet of two hundred boats, charged with more than 20,000 setiers of grain. . . . I have no doubt that the fleet will relieve the misery throughout the Loire Valley."[3] The ambiguities here are typical. The Parisian merchants are mentioned. De la Barre is himself possibly buying on royal account for Paris; but there is no means of distinguishing the activities of Parisian merchants from those of merchants of Orleans or of Auvergne and Bourbonnais. All are mentioned, but the fleet of two hundred boats goes down the river "en masse."

In 1693 the Parisian merchants do not appear. "Several individuals proposed to ship oats to Paris," but d'Ableiges, the Intendant, refused to grant the necessary permits.[4] In the fall of 1698, several Parisian merchants, who generally made their purchases in Champagne, were forced to seek supplies elsewhere. They went to Auvergne, Nivernais, and Normandy.[5] In January there were considerable arrivals of grain from the Upper Loire, presumably the result of the purchases made in November. On the third of January, eight boats

[1] Bib. Nat., Mél. Colb., 107, 275. Mémoire sur Auvergne, 11 Mars 1662.

[2] *Ibid.*, 108, 833. Clermont, 30 Mai 1662.

[3] *Ibid.*, 109, 352. Clermont, 19 Juin 1662. See also *ibid.*, 109 bis. 696. Orléans, 7 Juillet 1662. Brachet, Maire à Orléans.

[4] G[7]. 1630. Clermont, 4 Nov. 1693. d'Ableiges à Pussort.

[5] G[7]. 428. (Paris), 7 Nov. 1698. Dubois.

arrived at the Port de Grève from Bourbonnais. Ten days later, d'Argenson writes that "the Port de Grève is well supplied. There are at least thirty boats with grain from Auvergne and Brittany, in all about five hundred muids." [1]

On the Lower Loire the operations of the Parisian merchants are quite as completely lost in the general trade. The officials make no attempt to distinguish. It is likely that the Parisians went down to Saumur as early as they went up to Auvergne, but in 1662 they could have found little incentive to seek grain in Touraine as the dearth was more extreme there than in most parts of the Seine Basin. In 1693, 1698, and 1709,[2] the merchants of Paris are referred to, but it is impossible to form any idea of the extent of their dealings except through the measures taken by the officials at Orleans to prevent complete exhaustion of the supplies of their town. This is indeed the curious feature of the Loire Valley trade — its elusiveness in the producing regions, its volume when it passes Orleans.

The position of Orleans was peculiar; situated on one side of the Beauce, the most fertile plain of all France, placed in a commanding location on the Loire with the possibility of receiving grain from either Auvergne or Touraine, it was nevertheless in constant dread of dearth. The grain, which seemed to be at hand on every side, had a tendency to move towards Paris. Orleans was in the center of a brisk trade, but it moved around the city, without affecting the market. Bouville's letter of November 14, 1699, gives the most complete description of the situation of the town. "The individuals who have previously carried on a great business have ceased entirely. All the grain they could get hold of has been shipped to Paris, so that Orleans is without resource. Every week the town consumes 12–1400 muids of grain (mesure d'Orléans). There are only two markets, in each of which there is generally about four hundred muids, so that even when the markets are well supplied quite as much

[1] G7. 430. Paris, 4–14 Jan. 1698. d'Argenson.

[2] G7. 1635. Estat des bleds qui sont entré dans le Canal de Briare. Sept., 1693–Juillet, 1694. G7. 524. Divers Estats des bleds sorties par les Bureaux de Touraine pour Orléans et Paris, 1698, etc.

must come by river. The water trade, however, has ceased, as only the poor bourgeois are still engaged in the grain trade. Consequently, there is every reason to fear a dearth. Paris will carry off all the grain in the Beauce, and, if the ice forms soon, the river will be so low that no aid can be expected from that source."[1] Creil, the predecessor of Bouville, had been similarly struck by the tendency of the grain of the Beauce to go to Paris. He thought "it would be expedient to prevent the peasants from carrying to Étampes, Dourdan, and Montlhéry grain which they could sell for almost as much here at Orleans."[2] In years when there was any trouble, Orleans was always on the point of suffering from dearth in the midst of abundance.

The volume of trade passing Orleans on its way to Paris is best indicated by the figures giving the monthly shipments through the Canal d'Orléans for Paris, between September, 1693 and July, 1694. This does not include the overland trade, or the trade passing through the Canal de Briare, which were both considerable:

	Wheat muids	Oats muids	Rice lbs.
1693 November	453½	280	....
December	1,452	583	....
1694 January	103	139½	....
February	60	400	....
March	1,242	308	300,000
April	4,162½	2,315½	420,240
May	1,099	175½	91,913
June	3,462	960	....
July	1,311	920[3]	....

In 1699 the volume of trade must have been greater. Bouville writes, January 15: "within the last three months more than eight thousand muids has entered the Canal d'Orléans alone. There is much on the river and there is no accurate measure of the great quantity that has been shipped overland."[4]

[1] Boislisle, *op. cit.*, II, 11, 42. 14 Nov. 1699. Bouville.

[2] *Ibid.*, I, 304, 1146. 8 Dec. 1692.

[3] G⁷. 1635. Estat des Bleds qui sont entré dans le Canal d'Orléans pour estre porté à Paris. Sept., 1693–Juillet, 1694.

[4] G⁷. 419. Orléans, 15 Jan. 1699. Bouville. There are some figures from

Orleans had good cause for serious apprehension many times, but the much-dreaded dearth never arrived. The appearance was deceptive. The Intendant understood this situation and never lost confidence in the liberal policy of permitting this trade to continue without restriction. Orleans was never assisted by grain destined originally for Paris, but the independent efforts of the merchants were generally successful in supplying the city. In December, 1698, prices were rising despite the abundance of grain on the markets. Shipments were made to Paris from all sides. Speculation had developed to such an extent that the same lot of grain would pass through five or six hands without leaving the granary, rising in price from 250 ff. to 360 ff.[1] Despite all this, Bouville could write, two days later: "I know that prices cannot fall in the provinces, especially in this province, until prices have gone down in Paris, which must be supplied by the provinces. I can assure you that I leave no stone unturned to secure safety for the transportation of grain. I am convinced, also, that the merchants of Paris and the bakers should be allowed to buy in the markets."[2] Why should he adopt such a policy? Because Orleans could secure supplies in the lower river. The Parisian trade floating by the town was not to be reckoned upon. It could not be touched, because that would call in question the privileges needed to bring grain up the river past Blois and Tours. It was easier to stimulate the independent trade of Orleans than to stop the Parisian grain boats. Bouville states this as his policy. "At the beginning of 1694, I found the city much less adequately supplied than it is today, but it did not suffer. I even permitted shipments to Paris, *because a number of wealthy merchants, grocers, and others, on the strength of my promises, were willing to make large purchases in Brittany*."[3] Orleans was in reality seriously menaced by the extraordinary development

Touraine for December, 1698. They purport to distinguish between the shipments for Paris and the shipments for Orleans, but they must be based on false declarations by the merchants. G[7]. 524. 22 Dec. 1698–7 Jan. 1699.

[1] Boislisle, *op. cit.*, I, 508, 1800. 4 Dec. 1698. Bouville.

[2] *Ibid.*, I, 508, 1800. 6 Dec. 1698.

[3] *Ibid.*, II, 11, 42. 14 Nov. 1699.

of Parisian trade, but no consequences were felt, as the burden could be shifted to the producing regions, Auvergne, Touraine, or Brittany. The principal effect upon Orleans of the extension of Parisian influence in the Loire was an increased emphasis on the river trade. Orleans could count less on the Beauce, and became more dependent upon Auvergne, Touraine, and Brittany. The spectacle of Parisian exports was tantalizing but not serious. The sources of supply were somewhat different and the market of Orleans was left relatively intact.

Below Orleans, the influence of the intrusion of Parisian demand was more serious, both in the region supplying the wholesale trade at Saumur and Montsoreau, and in the independent river towns. These places, like Orleans, saw the Parisian trade passing by, but they had neither the energy to procure supplies independently nor the patience to permit the shipments for Paris and Orleans to pass unmolested. In November, 1693, the boats coming to Orleans were stopped at Blois. The merchants were obliged to sell at prices fixed by the officials although this was less than the grain cost in Brittany. This continued despite ordinances, and despite the passports carried by the merchants.[1] In April, 1694, the disturbances were quite as frequent.[2] Boats were stopped at Saumur, Amboise, and Tours.[3] The merchants feared that scarcely one-tenth of the quantity shipped would arrive at Orleans. They were even inclined to countermand their orders. The Échevins of Lorris, a little town on the Canal d'Orléans, described the popular feeling in most detail: "The people of our town and of the neighboring parishes," they say, "are without bread and without grain. They are on the point of mutiny, and there is little security for the boats passing on the Canal. Threats of pillage are rife, and we have been obliged to go twice to the Canal to maintain order. Three boats were stopped at Coudrey, and we were obliged to withdraw. We have just come from the

[1] G[7]. 1632. Orléans, 12 Nov. 1693. de Creil. G[7]. 1632. Vendôme, 19 Nov. 1693. Bertin.

[2] G[7]. 1635. Orléans, 30 Avril 1694. Bouville.

[3] G[7]. 1635. Tours, 18 Mai 1694. Huot.

Canal, where we had the boats released on account of their passports, issued by Pontchartrain, on behalf of the Hospital at Paris. All the merchants who pass on the Canal have similar passports, so that we do not know what to do. We are even resolved to leave town, in order to escape the violence that may appear. The people wish us to procure bread for them from the boats passing on the Canal, but we do not dare to do so, although the people are literally starving." [1]

The larger towns could secure material relief only by making special efforts to stimulate trade. The amounts secured from passing merchants were generally too small to afford more than temporary respite. Angers, in 1709, formed a public fund for the purchase of grain.[2] Other towns frequently did likewise. At Tours the Intendants often made purchases on the royal account.[3] At times very considerable royal purchases were made, and distributed at less than cost. Such supplies generally came from a distance, as the vicinity was either exhausted or the people so much incensed at the conduct of the merchants that no grain could be taken from the towns in the producing regions.

At La-Ferté-Bernard, the Maire says: "I have found it impossible to furnish the markets, as there is no grain in the parishes of my jurisdiction." The other sources of trouble were more frequent. Tours was often menaced by the closing of Poitou and Berry. May 1, 1709, an inhabitant of Tours writes: "the city cannot subsist fifteen days unless Berry, Brittany, and Poitou permit exports. The merchants and millers who take the risk of going to buy there are robbed. Famine will be upon us before the end of the month." [4] A description of a market at Châtillon tells the same story in more detail: "The person that I sent to the market at Châtillon yesterday reported that there was great disorder. The inhabitants would not permit any grain to leave the town for Touraine;

[1] G^7. 1635. Lorris, 26–28 Avril 1694. Échevins de Lorris.
[2] G^7. 1651. Angers, 27 Mars 1709. Autichamp, Lieu. du Roi.
[3] G^7. 1651. Tours, 30 Avril 1709. Turgot.
[4] G^7. 1647. 1 Mai 1709. Anon.

not even barley. More than two hundred persons were obliged to return home without any grain. Barley is needed for seed, and the markets of Tours, Cormery, Loches, and Eseville are all inadequately furnished." [1]

The effect of the Parisian trade upon the markets of the producing regions has already been considered.[2] The chain of *blatier*-supplied markets was disorganized. Buying in the farms and in granaries spread throughout the region. The agents of the large wholesale merchants, the resident merchants, and even the *blatiers* scoured the countryside over a considerable area. The grain in the Valley of the Vienne was collected at Montsoreau without coming in contact with any markets. On the Thouet, the markets of Montreuil-Bellay and Thouars were seriously affected, but not completely disorganized. The bulk of the trade, however, was quite independent of the market system. To attribute all these disorders to the appearance of the Parisian merchants is perhaps unjustifiable, but there is much to warrant such a severe judgment. These abuses appear only where the demand becomes very intense, and it is hardly probable that the trade of the Loire Valley itself would have been sufficient to develop the requisite pressure to lead to such practices. The Parisian merchants increased the demand in the producing regions, indirectly as well as directly; it was not only what they bought that influenced prices and modes of buying, but also what the depletion of the supplies of Orleans made it necessary for Orleans to buy. The addition of Parisian demand in times of dearth was practically certain to create an intensity of demand that far exceeded the supplies available. Such pressure was sure to develop the new practices that would disorganize the local markets.

The invasion of Normandy and of the Loire Valley by Parisian trade was a step towards the formation of a metropolitan area; but it was only the prelude to the great change that finally completed the fabric of the new organization. The overthrow of the system of relatively limited supply areas was the purely

[1] G[7]. 1651. Loches, 8 Mai 1709. Puiguibaut.

[2] See ch. i.

destructive aspect of the new tendencies. In the Loire Valley this destructive element does not appear as clearly as in the invasion of Normandy. On the Loire, the independent supply areas were transformed rather than destroyed. The depletion of the supply affected the rural districts and the small towns, rather than the large towns of the region. But here, as in Normandy, the breaking-down of old customs, the formation of new commercial habits, the intrusion of a ubiquitous metropolitan demand created new problems. Questions were raised which led to the development of new forms of commercial organization. The fundamental importance of problems of marketing was emphasized. Beneath all these difficulties lay the question of the relation between the local market and the wholesale trade, or between the wholesale trade and the metropolis. The local markets needed protection against the intensity of metropolitan demand; the metropolitan market needed some means of rendering its supplies more completely visible.

II

The Upper Seine Basin and Problems of Marketing

The evolution of market machinery in the Seine Basin is one of the most important and most interesting aspects of the commercial history of Paris. In no other section of France are the difficulties inherent in the old market system and the transition to the freer modern system more clearly revealed. The basic factor in the Parisian area is the presence of a large and easily available food supply. By no means the only foundation for the predominance of a commercial center, it is none the less the most important consideration in the development of a great inland capital like Paris.

The influence of abundance upon the development of trading organization will be more apparent after the subsequent study of the grain trade in the Rhone basin. There, the constant dread of dearth, the prohibitions in the producing regions, the elaborate negotiations in regard to the trade, everything militated against a free development of commercial machinery.

In the Seine Basin, the abundance of the supply reduced supervision to a minimum and rendered the crudity of the market organization less serious. The merchants were not forced to make so many concessions to the medieval system, and in time of dearth the supplies were sufficiently great to make trade possible. The distribution of the supply was no easy matter, but it was seldom necessary to prohibit trade entirely. This was of the utmost importance, for it was in such times of stress that significant changes most frequently occurred. In the less fertile regions, where trade was completely disorganized in time of crisis and discontinued for an interval, the trade was resumed without any considerable alteration. In the Seine Basin, where trade continued despite dearths, innovations of far-reaching consequences were at times made under the pressure of the crisis. The dearths of 1693–94, 1698–99, 1708–09 are for this reason more interesting in the Seine Basin than in Burgundy. Conditions there became so serious that trade was suspended during the crisis of the dearths. In the Seine Basin, the trade was maintained upon an organized basis though with difficulty. The tendency to break down under stress was the primary defect of the medieval market system. No solution could be found unless there was enough grain in the region to make continuous trade a possibility. The dearth must not be so severe that the dreaded famine could become an actuality. The market could develop only in a region where the difficulties were due not to lack of grain but to inefficient markets; where it was not a question of getting grain, but of distributing a supply that was barely adequate.

The character and the extent of the available supply is most evident in the latter part of the seventeenth century, when it was more completely utilized than previously. The supply falls into two classes: the overland grain from the Beauce, Brie, and France; the water-borne grain from the Valleys of the Oise, Marne, and Seine. The most valuable figures appear in a few reports of the year 1700. Quantities are given in the Parisian muid, which is equivalent to 51.4 bushels English. Some of the headings are ambiguous, but I have used the classi-

1700	Châlons & Vitry	France & Brie	Unspecified Seine and Marne	Oise	Total by Water	Halle
	muids	muids	muids	muids	muids	muids
22 Sept.–2 Oct.	413	360	368	20	1,161	181
2–20 Oct.	1,416	92	...	85	1,593	232
22–27 Nov.	350	80	400	30	860	135
4, 18–22 Dec.	250	250	800	64	1,364[1]	222

fications of the reports. "France and Brie" means, primarily, the region shipping from Bray, Nogent-sur-Seine, and Mary. The significant feature is the proportion between the water-borne grain and the grain coming overland to the Halle. The figures for the Halle should be increased somewhat as only wheat is reported regularly in the letters. Other kinds of grain amounted to half as much again. Then, too, flour came in considerable quantity, but the flour frequently represented water-borne grain. In all probability, the overland grain constituted in 1700 about one-fourth or one-third of the supply. The proportion between the various branches of the water trade is probably indicated justly, but as the reports are not comprehensive the total quantities received do not appear. There are comprehensive reports of shipments from the ports of the Oise for nine months of 1700 and for January, 1702. These are based on the declarations of the merchants and seem to be accurate in every respect. The Parisian figures for 1700 happen to include only the less considerable arrivals so that the Oise figures are low. From March, 1709, to December, 1710, we have very careful reports of arrivals at Paris. The water-borne trade is at times

Exports from the Generality of Soissons to Paris.[2]

		muids			muids
1700	April	801	1700	September	102
	May	139		October	210
	June	345		November	181
	July	212		December	206
	August	23	1702	January	397

[1] G⁷. 431. Reports of different dates, 22 Sept.–22 Dec. 1700.

[2] G⁷. 513. Letters of 16 Mai, 7 Juin, 6 Juillet, 6 Août, 8 Sept., 8 Oct., 7 Nov., 5 Dec. 1700. 5 Jan. 1701 to 11 Fev. 1702.

Grain Arrivals on the Ports and on the Halle, at Paris[1]

In Muids, Mesure de Paris

	Vitry & Châlons	Bray & Provins	France & Brie	Noyon & Soissons	Total by Water	Halle
1709 March	105	290	340	190	1,175	1,160
April	...	140	400	120	1,060	605
May	78	295	875	26	2,074	853
June	239	340	460	115	1,688	1,186
July	137	230	760	...	1,487	1,220
August	70	128	195	...	838	1,253
September	76	68	261	...	755	882
October	216	120	158	...	1,064	1,536
November	20	65	565	50	1,000	961
December	24	108	161	30	323	1,025
1710 January	227	142	280	4	673	1,293
February	80	145	281	84	590	825
March	70	178	285	44	697	1,018
April	20	...	270	40	1,230	854
May	35	231	...	25	791	993
June	254	283	643	30	1,210	1,098
July	185	257	390	...	832	1,056
August	120	100	457	...	677	1,198
September	80	40	472	...	847	1,493
October	135	70	688	...	893	1,441
November	60	140	475	48	1,263	1,080
December	345	25	470	2	1,002	1,211

described only as so many boats, but the load of the boats was sufficiently uniform to admit of satisfactory estimates of the quantity. The abnormal condition of the trade makes it necessary to refrain from any precise deductions, but the statistics are suggestive. The arrivals on the Halle are extraordinarily large, on the whole equal to the total arrivals by water. This is partly due to overland trade from Orleans, and to arrivals from a wider area in the Beauce than usual. Much of the trade from Normandy was doubtless overland. In part, too, the dearth in the Upper Seine Basin reduced the shipments from those sections. This interpretation of the effect of the dearth is supported by the comparison of the average semi-weekly

[1] G^7. 1654 and 1655. Semi-weekly reports of d'Argenson.

arrivals in 1709. For the thirteen weeks reported in 1700, the highest figure is 87 muids; the average is 45–50 muids. In 1709–10, the highest figures are 500 muids, 260 and 228 muids. These unusual arrivals are ascribed in the reports to the shipments overland from Orleans. The lowest figures are 45 and 53 muids. Scattering reports from 1708, which are not included in the table, confirm the impression that the normal semi-weekly market seldom saw more than 60–70 muids on the Halle.[1] The dearth of 1709 reduced the water-borne supply and the deficiency was made up in part by a more intense exploitation of the Beauce, France, and Brie. The continuity of the trade with the Seine and Marne Valleys is really the most significant fact in these reports. Despite the severity of the dearth, despite the heavy drain caused by the campaign of 1709 in the Low Countries, trade with Paris continued with no serious interruption.

The abundance of grain in the distant river valleys which made such continuous trade possible, even in time of dearth, freed the merchants from any serious interference from the officials in those regions. The abundance of grain in the immediate vicinity of Paris freed the merchants from harassing regulation by the Parisian authorities. The *blatier* trade to the Halle was very steady, and, as it brought nearly one-fourth of the total supply, the irregularities of the river trade were not of moment. At Lyons, where there was no such volume of land trade, the municipality was obliged to play an important part in the grain trade, largely to secure some guarantee against the irregularity of water-borne supply. Ice on the river, low water, intentional delays in shipment combined to render the river trade singularly erratic. In April, 1710, nine hundred muids arrived at the Port de Grève during the first two weeks. From the sixteenth to the twenty-sixth of April, only ninety muids came in. From April thirtieth to May twentieth only one hundred and fifty-five muids arrived; on May twenty-first, two hundred and fifty muids arrived.[2] But this uncertainty

[1] G⁷. 1654. 7 Avril, 5 Mai, 2 Juin, 4 Juillet, 5 Sept., 3 Nov., 1 Dec. 1708, 2 Jan., 6 Fev. 1709. Reports of d'Argenson.

[2] G⁷. 1655. Letters of d'Argenson. Dates indicated.

was not serious. The Halle sufficed to tide the city over the intervals between arrivals of grain on the Ports. The wholesale merchants of Paris were thus subjected to the minimum amount of regulation and the trade was allowed to develop naturally.

The absence of energetic administrative supervision involves the history of the Parisian trade in considerable obscurity. Official regulation and interference are responsible for nearly all our information about the trade, so that the relative freedom of the trade appreciably diminishes the bulk of our evidence. This difficulty of obtaining information is further enhanced by the destruction of the Municipal Archives of Paris during the Commune. The Registers of the city which had been transferred to the Archives Nationales are now the only considerable extant record of the activities of the municipality. These circumstances make it impossible to treat the sixteenth century with much certainty, but the main features of the period can be reconstructed by reading the scanty material available in the light of seventeenth century evidence.

The abundance of supply made very simple modes of trading practical. The early systems of marketing continued with little apparent change in all the producing regions until the seventeenth century. Consequently, the investigations that were made when the active development began disclosed not only the new conditions and the innovations, but also the old trading system that was soon to be supplanted. The differences in the market systems of the three valleys of the Upper Seine Basin were not great, and no distinction can safely be drawn before 1660. Trade in granaries and wholesale buying upon the market are found on the Marne, Seine, and Oise. There are differences in the emphasis placed upon these modes of buying, but it is practically certain that both forms existed throughout the sixteenth century. In 1649, the concentration of the trade in the towns appears clearly in an examination of grain merchants at Paris. Charles Ferre says there are six thousand muids of grain at Soissons; and other merchants also testify to the existence of hoards in Soissons.[1] Louis Presle

[1] H. 1809. Reg. du Bureau, ii^c iiii ^xx vi. 20 Août 1649.

declares that there are twelve thousand muids at Châlons, and four thousand muids at Vitry.[1] But the details of this granary trade do not come fully to light till 1660. Inquests in October and November of that year brought out the real character of the trade. "Louis Lallement and Pierre Coq depose that there are great quantities of grain at Vitry and Châlons in the houses of divers individuals."[2] "Charles Appert, grain porter at Châlons, said he acts as grain factor at Châlons; that is to say he buys for the merchants of Paris in accordance with the orders given by Farez of Châlons, Lallement, and others who are agents of Parisian merchants. In the month of July, the present witness, together with Hemary and Lambert, bought two thousand setiers of grain in different houses. The witness believes that there are 200,000 muids of grain in different houses where it has been stored for five or six years."[3] "Pierre Châlons, merchant of Châlons, says that he acts as agent for merchants of Paris, and that he buys ordinarily in the granaries."[4] In 1660, the granaries of Châlons were supplied in part by the *blatier* trade from Lorraine and from the region south of the Marne,[5] but the general form of the trade was not changed, as this grain was purchased by resident merchants and bourgeois who hoarded it until it suited their interest to sell to the Parisian merchants who came to their granaries. The simpler form of the trade appeared at La-Ferté-Gaucher and Coulommiers. The commissioners felt that many persons in these towns falsified their testimony, but the witnesses summoned declared on oath that the grain they handled came from their estates. At the house of Jean Montguillon, at La-Ferté-Gaucher, the commissioners "found 9–10 muids of wheat which Montguillon declared to be the product of the payments made by his tenants. He affirmed that he had no more than 20–25 muids of grain which he had collected in the course of seven or eight years. He has sold much to merchants who have come

[1] H. 1809. Reg. du Bureau, ii^{c}iii ^{xx}vi. 20 Août 1649.

[2] Bib. Nat., Fr. 21641. 357. 4 Nov. 1660. Procès Verbaux à Châlons. Depositions de Louis Lallement et Pierre le Coq.

[3] *Ibid.* 4 Nov. 1660. Procès Verbal à Châlons.

[4] *Ibid.*

[5] *Ibid.* Magdelaine Goudouin.

to buy, and he is ready to sell whenever merchants offer to buy."[1] This passive attitude of the landlord is one of the most interesting features of the granary trade. There is no effort to find a market. The landlord waits patiently year after year till the merchants come to buy. At Coulommiers the commissioners found 105 muids of wheat and 20 muids of rye in granaries. "There was much more in the town," they say, "but we are not able to make a more comprehensive report because the municipal officials and the officials of the élection are all engaged in this trade. They have stores in their granaries and in their country houses." "Most of the witnesses deposed that Lambert and his associates had more than 400 muids of grain at Coulommiers and in the environs."[2] D'Alençon, the Lieutenant General, who was accused of participating in this trade, declared that "he carried on no trade, that he hoarded only the grain coming from his estates, and that he sold daily to such as presented themselves. He had about twenty-six muids. He showed us also another granary of wheat, belonging to Sr. Barbé, an Attorney at the Court. This grain comes from his estates."[3] 110 muids of grain was found at Trillebardou; one-third of this came from Châlons and Vitry, the rest belonged to residents.[4] At Meaux, similar conditions prevailed.

In the Seine Valley, the principal resident grain dealers affirm persistently that the grain they handle comes from their farms. "Sansoy of Provins said that he was not a merchant, that he had not purchased the grain in his possession, it was the product of his estates for several seasons. He declared that he had refused no offer made by the factors of merchants of Paris. Since the preceding harvest he said that he had sold about one hundred muids, Paris measure, and that he still had about 150 muids."[5] In this vicinity, too, there was a gentleman named

[1] Bib. Nat., Fr. 21641. 30 Oct. 1660. La-Ferté-Gaucher.

[2] *Ibid.* 190. Oct. 1660.

[3] *Ibid.* 204. 30 Oct. 1660. Procès Verbaux.

[4] *Ibid.* 190. Oct. 1660.

[5] *Ibid.* 210. 2 Nov. 1660. Provins. Many other affirmations that the grain comes from their own estates.

Chenoist, who had 500–600 muids in his château.[1] At Provins, there were three or four individuals engaged in a regular granary trade, but the transition was becoming marked even in 1660, and it is difficult to disentangle the old and the new. It is evident, however, that the granary trade had been considerable, and it must have been the characteristic form of trade in the sixteenth century.

In the Valley of the Oise the commissaries found conditions somewhat different. The essential feature is indicated by their mode of stating the quantity of grain found. "In the granaries of Noyon, belonging to merchants trading with Paris, was found 2180 muids of wheat and *méteil*."[2] In the Marne and Seine towns the granaries generally belonged to the residents who sold in the granaries to merchants of Paris. Here at Noyon the merchants bought on the market, and then stored the grain until it was advantageous to ship. The market was supplied with reference to this demand. "Each market day grain came in from Santerre, Vermandois, Artois, and Flanders, especially from Brussels, Arras, Bapaume, Perronne, Saint-Quentin, Ham, and other places. More than one hundred muids arrived for each market."[3] This estimate seems high, but it is confirmed by figures of 1700, giving the arrivals at Noyon of grain from other generalities.[4]

Grain Arriving at Noyon from other Generalities

		Quantities Paris muids	Generality of export
1700	May	182	Haynault, Flanders, Amiens.
	June	131	Amiens.
	July	142	Amiens, Flanders.
	August	62	Amiens.
	September	79	Amiens.
	October	80½	Amiens.
	November	62	Flanders, Picardy.
	December	69	Picardy, Flanders.

[1] Bib. Nat., Fr. 21641. 210. 2 Nov. 1660. Provins.

[2] A mixture of wheat and rye, or wheat and barley. Bib. Nat., Fr. 21641. 190. Noyon.

[3] *Ibid.* 190.

[4] G[7]. 513. Estat des Bleds arrivés dans la Gén. de Soissons. Letters of Sanson, 7 Juin, 6 Juillet, 8 Sept., 8 Oct., 7 Nov., 5 Dec. 1700, 5 Jan. 1701.

Besides this foreign grain, much would come to the market from the immediate vicinity, so that we may accept the figures of the Lieutenant General. Pont-Sainte-Maxence was another important shipping point on the Oise, and there the trade was carried on in much the same manner as at Noyon. The commissioners report that "they summoned one Pierre Carabin, a grain porter. He said that some of the bourgeois and residents of the town bought grain on the market to sell to merchants who had granaries and engaged in trade with the town. At times, too, the bourgeois sold to persons of Beaumont, Creil, or other places. The Widow Chevalier and one of her sons are engaged in this trade at Pont-Sainte-Maxence. They buy daily at Pont, and in the environs, to sell again later. They have long had great quantities stored in their houses and granaries. The dearth at Pont was caused by the purchases made by the Widow Chevalier and others. They took up all the grain exposed on the market to hoard it and sell later."[1] The prosecuting attorney of the town (Le Procureur du Roi) confirmed this statement. Most of the grain coming to market was purchased by merchants resident in the town or coming from Beaumont, Creil, and other places.[2] There is reason to believe that the trade at Soissons was conducted on a similar basis before 1660, but there is little precise evidence. The market was completely disorganized by the new commercial practices, but the merchants had apparently been buying on the market up to that time.

The evidence that these conditions had existed throughout the sixteenth century is not very considerable. The most definite statement is made by the Lieutenant Civil of the Châtelet of Paris. At a general assembly at the Hôtel de Ville, September 13, 1565, he says "that he has been in Champagne recently and knows that there are large quantities of grain stored in the châteaux, and in some of the towns."[3] This does not state definitely that the granaries were the usual source

[1] Bib. Nat., Fr. 21641. 235. 2 Nov. 1660. Pont-Sainte-Maxence.

[2] *Ibid., eod. loc.*

[3] *Reg. du Bureau,* V, 519–520. 13 Sept. 1565.

of supply, but it indicates that the granaries of landlords and tithe owners were even then a considerable factor in the trade. Aside from this statement, there is evidence that the sixteenth century trade was very closely associated with a few of the river towns. In 1565, the Parlement of Paris issued a special ordinance authorizing "all persons to buy grain in the towns and villages of the vicinity: even in Châlons, Château-Thierry, Meaux, Provins, Melun, Étampes, and others." [1] In September of the same year, the Provost of Merchants sent H. Simon to Nogent, Pont-sur-Seine, Troyes, Vitry, Châlons, Épernay, Châtelnaudry, Meaux, and other towns in Champagne and Brie. The exact character of the mission does not appear, but it was primarily an effort to secure permission to buy grain in these towns.[2] In 1585, commissioners were sent up the Seine to Pontz, Bray, and Montereau-sur-Yonne, to have grain shipped to Paris. [3] Two years later the municipal officials ask the King to write to the Governor of Champagne and Brie, bidding him "to permit the shipment of grain from Châlons and Vitry, where it is abundant." [4] The concentration of trade in the towns and the occasional statements that great quantities were to be found in the towns, both point to the granary trade.

This was the simplest form of wholesale trade. In the Saône Valley, whence we have abundant evidence for the sixteenth century, the granary trade was the characteristic form. It was transformed there somewhat earlier than in the Seine Basin, as the supplies were not so large and better ways of bringing the supply to market had to be found. This granary trade was essentially passive; the owners made no effort to seek the market; if the merchants did not discover them, they could wait until dearth came. Prices would rise, and the effort to secure supplies would bring merchants to the doors of the granary, prepared to pay good prices. The abundance of the total avail-

[1] Delamare, *op. cit.*, II, 1007.

[2] *Reg. du Bureau*, V, 517–518. 10 Sept. 1565.

[3] *Ibid.*, VIII, 437. 2 Avril 1585.

[4] Delamare, *op. cit.*, II, 1011. 3 Juillet 1587.

able supply in the Seine Basin was so great that even this cumbersome and crude system was adequate for a century and a half. It is this relation to the fundamental feature of trade in the Seine Basin that affords the best ground for our surmise. Long continuance of the granary trade would be possible only in a region where supplies were, on the whole, somewhat in excess of demand. This granary system was still perceptible in 1660; the whole of the preceding period was characterized by lack of pressure on the supply; so it is by no means too much to infer that the granary system, which would have been so well adapted to the conditions of the sixteenth century, was in fact the characteristic mode of marketing.

The absence of real pressure upon the supply of the Seine Basin is most clearly indicated by the existence of a sporadic export trade to foreign countries. It will be remembered that the surplus of the Seine Basin during the fifteenth century went to Rouen or to foreign ports through Rouen. The sixteenth century witnessed the delimitation of supply areas for Rouen and Paris. The most unfortunate effect of this upon the producing regions of the Parisian area was the reduction of the demand, and so considerable a reduction that there was apparently a real surplus. This could find a market only on the Lower Seine at Rouen, or at the coast ports on the Somme, particularly Saint-Valery.

In February, 1501, a general assembly was held at Paris. The whole subject was canvassed, and the meeting finally decided "that action should be taken to prevent the exhaustion of Santois, Beauvoisis, and neighboring provinces, by foreign export down the Somme." Then the Échevins ask the Parlement to issue letters to the Baillis of Senlis, Amiens, Vermandois, and to the Sénéchal of Ponthieu, ordering them to prevent the export of grain abroad by way of the Somme.[1] In 1508 we hear that "the merchants go up to Santerre to buy all the grain they can, and then ship to Rouen by way of the Seine."[2] A month later the merchants complain of the prohibitions at

[1] *Reg. du Bureau*, I, 53–54. 20–27 Fev. 1501.

[2] *Ibid.*, I, 148. 23 Fev. 1508.

Paris. They say that there is no more danger and that the prohibitions should be removed. The Échevins finally decide to allow the merchants to export grain up or down the river, if they agree to place half of their grain on sale at Paris.[1] There are other indications of this foreign trade which will be noted in another connection; it is sufficient here to note the movement. There is this elusive trade to foreign parts, generally causing apprehension and restrictive regulation at Paris. It continues spasmodically despite prohibitions, because the Parisian demand was not great enough to carry off the whole supply.

The possession of this abundant supply renders the history of the Parisian trade in the sixteenth century dull and uninteresting. There is no active development of organization, no serious difficulty in time of dearth, so that even in the sources the trade leaves little trace. The second quarter of the following century, however, sees the beginning of a change. The surplus supply was then required by the growing needs of the city. The merchants were extending their commercial connections. New means of securing supplies were needed. The old passive granary trade, which had maintained itself during the quiet years of the preceding century, was now beginning to prove inadequate for the demands of the growing trade. The grain trade acquired new vitality, new importance, and new interest. A period of active development begins, which carries us rapidly from conditions that are purely medieval to conditions that are almost modern.

What then was the occasion of this pressure upon the supplies of the Seine Basin that changes the appearance of the trade so fundamentally? There are two factors that might increase the pressure on the mercantile grain supply: actual growth of population; dependence upon the markets of sections of the metropolitan population that had formerly secured grain independently of the markets.

The growth of Paris previous to 1789 cannot be accurately traced. The population of the city seems never to have been

[1] *Reg. du Bureau*, I, 150. 23 Mars 1508. In this connection the loss of the municipal records of Paris is a real misfortune.

accurately known. The conventional figure of 600,000 persons appears in the documents throughout the seventeenth and eighteenth centuries. It is not the highest figure given at the close of the eighteenth century, but it is accepted even then as the conservative estimate. In short, the statistical attempts are worse than useless, they suggest a stationary condition that certainly did not exist at any time in the course of those two centuries. No conception of the rate of growth can be formed from the data now available, but in many respects this numerical side of the question is by no means its most significant aspect. The periods of most active growth are of most considerable importance, and these can probably be inferred from the material expansion of the city. Maps of the city are extant which exhibit the gradual extension of habitation, and the studies of the topography of the old city inaugurated by Baron Haussmann supplement the evidence afforded by the contemporary maps.[1]

Until the middle of the sixteenth century the city was contained within the walls: on the right bank these followed the line of the *Grands Boulevards* of today; on the left bank the walls began at what is now the *Bibliothèque Mazarin*, then the Porte de Nesle, and formed a rather narrow circuit which included the University quarter. The Porte Saint-Michel, which was the point in the circuit most distant from the river, was only a little beyond the Sorbonne, on the street which is now the Boulevard Saint-Michel. After 1550 there was a distinct tendency to build outside the walls. Three faubourgs developed: the industrial faubourgs on the right bank, outside the Porte Saint Denis, and the Porte Saint Antoine: the fashionable Faubourg Saint Germain, on the left bank. Edicts were issued in 1554, 1587, and in 1627, 1632, and 1648, forbidding the erection of buildings outside the walls without special permits; but the movement continued in ever-increasing volume. The close of the sixteenth century witnessed a rapid extension

[1] *Histoire Monumentale de Paris. Topographie du Vieux Paris*, 6 vols. See especially vols. iii-vi. The general account given here is based on material in vol. iii, pp. 7, 127 ff.

of the faubourgs. New streets were cut, roads were declared to be streets, and the corner lots were quickly taken for building sites. The movement in the industrial suburbs is not traced in detail, but the development of the Faubourg Saint Germain can be followed as closely as the most ardent antiquarian could desire. The first generation of the seventeenth century brought ten religious houses to Paris from various provincial towns.[1] All the new congregations established themselves in the Faubourg Saint Germain. Nobles who had formerly remained on their estates came to Paris and built in the Faubourg. During the reign of Louis XIV this growth of the city continued. Saint-Sulpice, the largest parish church in the city, was begun in 1643, to provide adequate facilities for the constantly increasing number of parishioners established in this new quarter outside the walls. The nobles and higher clergy came to Paris in greater numbers, attracted by the court and the intellectual fascination of the great capital. The industrial development of the city is less easily followed, but the growing commercial importance of Paris in the seventeenth century suggests that the concentration of the special industries of the capital was increasing. The city seems to have begun to expand in the middle of the sixteenth century, growing slowly until the death of Louis XIII and then increasing more rapidly, until in 1715 it was unquestionably the first city in the kingdom.

The other factor in the development of pressure upon the commercial supply will be suggested by an estimate of the consumption of Paris in 1637. According to this account 1600 muids of grain were consumed each week. 800 muids were brought to the markets of the city as bread; 450 muids came to the Ports and Halle as grain; 350 muids were used by the religious houses, who received it from their farms or purchased it privately outside of Paris.[2] Almost one-fourth of the supply

[1] *Topographie de Paris*, III, 135. 1602, Frères de la Charité; 1605, Petits Augustins; 1622, Bénédictins de Calvaire; 1626, Maison des Jeunes Filles; 1630, Monastère du Precieux Sang; 1633, Jacobins, Augustins de Laon; 1634, Établissement Hospitalier; 1635, Chanoinesses de Saint-Sépulcre; 1636, Bénédictins de Saint-Liesse; Religieuses de Saint Nicholas de Tulle, etc.

[2] *Mémoires des Intendants sur les Généralités: Paris*, p. 657.

of the city did not enter into the trade at all. Besides the religious houses, many of the nobles and the wealthy bourgeois procured their own supplies in the country without any contact with the trade. Obviously a change in these habits, an abandonment of this private buying would swell the volume of trade in the hands of the merchants. If the merchants were to buy in the same place as the private individuals or the religious houses, it would affect the trade slightly, but they would probably buy where they were accustomed to, and the change in the trade might be of importance. An increase in the volume of the trade handled by the merchants would tend to develop new forms of commercial organization even if the actual demand of Paris remained stationary.

After 1625–30 the Parisian grain trade begins to develop new practices which are largely the outgrowth of the increased pressure upon the supply. The changes are not especially significant in years of abundance, but the dearths of the period seem to exert some influence upon the organization of the trade. Even the moderate scarcity of the years 1626, 1630–31, 1643, and 1649 was probably not without effect. The full extent of the changes cannot be measured. There were official inquiries, but such papers as survive afford little information, and, in the absence of the full reports of the commissaries, it is idle to speculate upon the conditions of that period.[1] Some of the Procès Verbaux of these numerous commissions might be found among the papers of the Châtelet; those submitted to the municipality were destroyed with the Hôtel de Ville. The evidence available thus represents but a small part of the testimony actually taken, and under these circumstances it is necessary to avoid definite conclusions. There is, however, a little evidence of "country buying." At a general assembly at Paris in 1630, Sr. Perrot says that "the merchants have created

[1] See Delamare, *op. cit.*, II, 372 and 1020. Comm. of 14 Dec. 1630. Bib. Nat., Fr. 21641. 145. 12 Jan. 1631. Commissions. Bib. Nat., Fr. 21635. 38. Arrêt du Parl. 6 Mai 1626. Commissioners sent to Chartres, Soissons, and other places. H. 1803. iii^c^lx; H. 1806. l; H. 1806. iiii^c^xlvii and vi^c^xi. Reg. du Bureau. Commissions of the Échevins, 1631, 1643. Bib. Nat., Fr. 21635. 46. 26 Jan. 1649. Comm. by Parlement of Paris.

the high prices, by going among the farms and paying more than the peasants expected." [1]

The testimony of various grain merchants taken at Paris shows clearly that the granary purchases were still the basis of the trade. Nicolle Euchève says that her husband is "at Vitry-le-François shipping oats and rye that he bought there of merchants of Châlons." [2] Louise Duquesnoy says that "she has at Châlons 500 setiers of wheat and 250 setiers of rye, which was bought for her by Husson Ruche, her agent at Châlons." Hughes de Cloos "has a boat-load at Noyon, ready to be shipped, and 400–500 setiers of rye at Châlons. All this grain was purchased by his factor, Pierre Marchand, who lives at Châlons." Bissart Tirant "has sixty muids in granaries at Fîmes and Soissons. It has all been bought within the last three weeks by Combray, his factor at Fîmes." "Pierre de Clerc has 600 setiers of grain at Châlons that was purchased for him by Arras, his factor at Châlons." All the principal merchants buy through resident agents, and apparently most of the purchases are made in granaries. But some of the merchants were probably buying in the country. "Nicolle Regnault says that her husband is in France [3] to ship grain that he has bought there within the last three days." "Isabelle Labbé says that her husband has a boat-load of grain on the Marne. She does not know the quantity, but her husband bought it in France." Similarly, "Marguerite Froissart says that her husband has a boat-load of grain on the Aube, about sixty muids in all. Her husband bought part at Soissons, but she does not know where he bought the rest. He has some grain at Lizy." [4] The vagueness of this information is suspicious; when the towns are not clearly indicated it generally means that the purchases are made in the country. It is quite possible, too, that the resident factors should have sought supplies outside the town granaries. Later,

[1] Delamare, *op. cit.*, II, 368. 12 Dec. 1630.

[2] Bib. Nat., Fr. 21641. 136–142. All the testimony is from this document. "Assemblée en la Chambre Saint-Louis pour les Bleds." The witnesses are grain merchants.

[3] *I. e.* the Marne towns below Meaux.

[4] All citations from the same Procès Verbal.

the resident factor is generally engaged in systematic "country buying," so that it is possible that the merchants were covering up unpopular practices by feigning ignorance of where the factors made their purchases. The subject is hopelessly obscure.

In 1660, doubt is no longer possible. The merchants began to buy extensively in the country, and by their energetic canvass of the farms the local markets were seriously affected. An anonymous memoir describes these practices. "One Godet, merchant at Châlons, first made prices rise by his canvass of all the granaries in the town, and by his trips in the environs among the laborers. He spread false rumors, and also bought large quantities. At the same time, Tixerand senior, merchant and *Élu* of Vitry-le-François, made a circuit of the granaries of the town and scoured the surrounding country. He forced prices up to such a point that the municipal officers have prohibited exports. Four merchants of Paris have gone to La Ferté-sous-Jouarre where they made their agreements. The same day they left the place and spread through the country, making prices rise without buying very large quantities."[1] Around Soissons this "country buying" was not regarded as a novelty, so that our surmises in regard to the "country buying" after 1630 would be confirmed. "Nicole Gigue, laborer at Soissons, said that the merchants and inhabitants of Soissons *always* (de tout temps) bought grain in the country, up as far as Pontavert. They ship the grain down to Soissons in boats, unload the grain, and store it in their houses or granaries." Henriette Violette, widow of a miller at Soissons, testifies to the same facts.[2] At Mary-sur-Seine, one Lefavre showed the commissaries a granary containing twenty muids. "He said that he sent a boat to Paris every week. The last went the preceding Saturday. The grain we saw had been bought of peasants within eight or ten leagues. It was brought to Mary in carts." They visited the house of Romain Gray, the factor of Audiger of Paris. Gray was not at home. "His daughter

[1] Bib. Nat., Fr. 21641. 173. Mémoire, 1660.

[2] *Ibid.* 363. Procès Verbal, 7 Oct. 1660.

said that he had been in the back country for three days, buying grain, and that he was likely to be away another week." [1] Along the Seine, at Montereau and in the back country between the Seine and the Marne, there was much "country buying." Louise Pigre, widow of the notary of Montereau, said "that Nepveu, who is the agent of the Widow Rousseau, buys in the market at Montereau and of the peasants for six leagues around." Another witness says: "He has been buying among the peasants for the last month, so that he has affected all the markets. Almost nothing comes to market. One Lavallé has also been among the peasants buying their grain." [2] The *Courier* of Champagne reports "that five or six merchants of Paris are riding post through the country." [3]

This development of energetic canvassing was fatal to the local markets. Their supplies were sapped. The peasants sold to the wholesale merchants in the farms, without taking the trouble to bring the grain to market. The market-place was bare. When grain still came to the local market the wholesale merchants appeared and bought it up, if a popular revolt did not force them to beat a hasty retreat. The full significance of the "country buying" is revealed only in the dearths of 1693, 1698, and 1709. The practice did not affect all regions alike but everywhere the old modes of marketing were seriously disturbed. This opened the way to reorganization which in some places was significant, in other places, of little moment.

The destructive aspect of this new phase of the grain trade was most conspicuous in the Beauce. There the result was disorganization of the many little markets and a gradual concentration of the trade. In the early seventeenth century the trade from the Beauce fell into two general divisions; Étampes was the principal market on the eastern side, and on the western side Chartres was most important. "Some of the grain from Étampes was sent to Paris in small boats as late as 1670, but the completion of the paved road from Étampes to Paris ren-

[1] Bib. Nat., Fr. 21641. 197. 10 Oct. 1660. Procès Verbal.

[2] *Ibid.* 261. 31 Juillet 1660. Procès Verbal.

[3] *Ibid.*, Testimony of Françoise Viaret and of Louise Martin.

dered the land route superior.[1] In those days there were thirty to forty boats in the port of Étampes, especially adapted for the navigation of that river. They carried ten muids each, and scarcely sufficed to handle the trade with Paris. . . . Some grain was sent to Paris by the carters." [2] But although Chartres and Étampes were the principal markets of these sections many other markets were in direct connection with Paris. In the direction of Chartres, we hear especially of Dourdan, Houdan, Montfort-l'Amaury, Rambouillet, Épernon, and Nogent-le-Roy.[3] In the direction of Étampes, Corbeil, Melun, and Montereau were most important. "In those days, no merchant of Étampes sent grain to the market of Montlhéry, nor to other markets. They shipped directly and uniquely to Paris. The towns of Sens, Montereau, Melun, and Corbeil likewise shipped directly to Paris. Now all the merchants of Étampes have two or three granaries at Montlhéry, and the merchants of the other towns have recognized that the markets of the towns near Paris are most advantageous because of the presence of the bakers. Latterly, the bakers have been possessed of more capital, and have canvassed the markets, buying at any price. They do not make much profit on their bread unless grain is dear, so they do not higgle over prices. . . . In these markets of the country there are great numbers of men called *blatiers*, who bring in grain on horses and mules. On market days there are 400–500 of these animals at Montlhéry, all loaded with wheat, oats, and barley. The *blatiers* are villagers who cultivate no land but spend all their time in scouring the country." [4] This concentration of trade at Montlhéry was not only bringing together the grain from the eastern side of the Beauce, it was also drawing from the vicinity of Chartres, thus tending to bring to one market the whole trade of the Beauce

[1] G7. 425. 5 Sept. 1685. Mémoire de Menars sur l'Élection d'Étampes.

[2] Bib. Nat., Fr. 21643. 354. 8 Sept. (1698). Mémoire sur les désordres qui se commettent es environs de Paris.

[3] *Mémoires des Intendants sur les Généralités: Paris*, p. 659. Notices sur les marchés dans les environs de Paris. 1686.

[4] Bib. Nat., Fr. 21643. 354. 8 Sept. (1698). Mémoire sur les désordres qui se commettent es environs de Paris.

with Paris. "The market at Montlhéry is one of the most important for thirty leagues around. The farmers of Yenville (Janville) and of Chartres bring in such great quantity every Monday that there are actually as much as four or five hundred muids on the market."[1] The market at Montlhéry, in 1699, thus handled about twice as much grain as the Halle at Paris, a striking development for a market that is not even mentioned in the memoir of 1686 on the grain markets supplying Paris. Much grain still went to Paris direct from the minor market towns, but there is clearly a significant concentration of the trade.[2]

The volume of trade passing through Montlhéry, the number of bakers, merchants, and *blatiers* buying and selling, led to speculative purchases. The grain trade attracted all types of speculators; some sought to gain by scouring the country, buying outside the markets, others confined their attention to operations in the town. In all this ferment of speculation the markets fared badly, Montlhéry no less than the minor local markets. At times, the distress took the form of inexplicably high prices; at times, the markets were ill supplied with grain. Then, quite frequently, the markets were unusually well supplied. This extraordinary confusion makes the trade of the Beauce very difficult to understand, but despite the great variety of reports, it is quite evident that the system of marketing was changing rapidly.

The canvass of the farms by merchants and *blatiers* is reported from all sides. "The merchants of Paris . . . have been to Janville and Chartres among many of the farms. They have bought or contracted to take all the grain of that section, so that only 20–30 muids has come to Montlhéry since 29 January (1699)."[3] Desperrières writes from Chartres, "it is necessary

[1] Bib. Nat., Fr. 21644. 6. Mémoire sur les Bleds. — Undated (1699).

[2] Desperrières, in a letter of 18 Dec. 1698, from Chartres (G^7. 419) comments on the old trade from the Pays Chartrain. He speaks of the movement from Nogent and Chartres to Houdan and thence to Mantes. He does not feel quite sure of the destination of the grain, however, and seems inclined to think that it goes down the Seine to Rouen.

[3] Bib. Nat., Fr. 21644. 6. Mémoire sur les Bleds. (1699.)

to prevent the merchants from buying in the farms and houses of the peasants."[1] From Melun, we hear that all classes "are engaged in the grain trade: magistrates, all kinds of merchants, and even artisans. Some, doubtless the well-to-do, or the most avaricious, buy in the barns of the peasants."[2] Bouville says that he is informed that "many of the merchants are buying of the métayers."[3] In the vicinity of Limours there are rumors of the same practice. The collector of that town is said to be forming granaries: "for the last two weeks carts loaded with grain have been met at night on all the roads leading to Limours and Chevreuse. Several persons of Rambouillet are doing likewise, and it is said that they buy of the peasants on the farms."[4]

But this "country buying" was only one of the changes in the Beauce. The larger market towns witnessed an appearance of speculative buying that caused much apprehension. The officials were at a loss to know how this new phenomenon should be treated, but they were thoroughly convinced that it was dangerous. "I have been told," writes one De Poix, "that three-quarters of the 1200 setiers brought to Paris in the last fortnight from the Beauce was not sold on the markets, at market prices in accordance with the ordinances. It is sold at prices made outside the markets, at the inns and cafés. The peasants exhibit samples in their handkerchiefs or in their pockets, and higgle with the merchants over their cups. The prices are concluded, then they separate to go to the market, where they meet again. They open the sacks and make believe to run the price up to the figure agreed upon. The grain is measured and is then carried off in carts, or on the horses and mules brought to town by the buyers and the millers. The bourgeois and the peasantry who come to buy are seriously inconvenienced, as they cannot secure grain and are forced to return to their homes empty-handed. Meanwhile these buyers and market

[1] G[7]. 419. Chartres, 18 Dec. 1698. Desperrières à Bouville.

[2] Bib. Nat., Fr. 21643. 457. Melun, 16 Dec. 1698. Parry à (Delamare).

[3] G[7]. 419. Orléans, 4 Dec. 1698. Bouville au C. G.

[4] Bib. Nat., Fr. 21645. 88. Extrait d'une lettre écrite de Villepréaux. (1699.)

speculators send out into the farms, and carry away stealthily grain for which they have contracted on the basis of samples, in addition to what they have bought on the market."[1] In this manner the wholesale traders managed to secure the larger part of the supplies of the region without entering into public competition with each other or with the local demand. Incidentally, an important departure from the old system appeared in the buying by sample.

At Montlhéry, this type of extra-market dealing is found in conjunction with other irregularities whose character is not very clear. "When the farmers see that grain is dear, they carry samples of grain to market in their pockets. They show these samples to the bakers from Paris, and make their sales on this basis. The bakers then send their millers to the farms and carry off the grain at their convenience. One miller at Juvisy, named Conart, has shipped as much as fifty muids of grain in one day, on behalf of bakers of Paris."[2] At Montlhéry, also, the bakers at times engaged in curious speculative attempts to manipulate the market. "The bakers of Montlhéry and Linas go every Saturday to the market at Dourdan, but instead of buying what they need for a week or two they form granaries there. They ship from these granaries to Montlhéry, where prices are high. To further their ends they make heavy purchases at Dourdan on Saturday, the market day, making prices rise by their operations, and as the market at Montlhéry on Monday is influenced by that at Dourdan, the bakers are able to dispose of their grain at Montlhéry at a considerable advance in price. Then, too, the wealthier farmers of the environs of Montlhéry, for three or four leagues around, come regularly to market on Monday without bringing a single bag of grain. They watch the course of the market, and almost every time they buy grain of the farmers of the environs who cannot hold their grain, but are forced to sell even before it is threshed. These sales are made on the basis of samples, which the farmers

[1] Bib. Nat., Fr. 21644. 301. Paris, 13 Jan. 1699. De Poix.

[2] Bib. Nat., Fr. 21643. 356. 8 Sept. 1698. Mémoire qui marque les désordres qui se commettent es environs de Paris.

carry in their pockets. The sellers agree to deliver the grain as soon as it is threshed. This goes on every market day, and it contributes much to cause high prices, because the grain is not brought to market by the owners as soon as it is threshed, but is diverted into granaries. Many farmers have thus come to market regularly without bringing any grain to be sold." [1]

At Chartres, the other considerable market in the Beauce, the same intensity of speculative buying appeared, but the accounts are not so detailed. There was much canvassing of the farms in the neighborhood, and in the town itself every one was engaged in the trade; "from the richest to the poorest," all had caught the fever, even "the porters of the market-place and their wives. They are all buying and selling. The well-to-do peasants, who have grain of their own still unthreshed, buy daily on the market. They form granaries and trade both on the markets of the neighborhood and on the town market. I have been assured that among all the traders there are no more than three or four hundred muids of grain." [2]

At Nemours, everything was on a smaller scale, but the general aspects of the situation were the same. "Several merchants," writes an anonymous correspondent, "have purchases made for them by secret agents and then they sell again immediately at higher prices. Most of the merchants come to market before the appointed hour and make secret agreements in regard to prices with the carters who have grain to sell. The latter keep their sacks closed all through the market, and when it is over they deliver the grain to the merchants. Some merchants stop the peasants in the streets before their houses; others seek them in the cafés and inns; others go among the farms, scouring the rural districts." [3] In short, there was no longer any organized market at Nemours.

In this confused picture of the destruction of the old market system in the Beauce is revealed the full meaning of the pressure

[1] Bib. Nat., Fr. 21643. 356. 8 Sept. 1698. Mémoire qui marque tous les désordres qui se commettent es environs de Paris.

[2] G[7]. 419. Chartres, 18 Dec. 1698. Desperrières à Bouville.

[3] Bib. Nat., Fr. 21645. 333. Extrait d'une lettre écrite de Nemours, 1699.

which began in the last years of Louis XIII. The increased intensity of commercial demand destroyed the traditions of a century and a half. The transition is difficult to follow because it leads to so little that is definite. There is a concentration of trade at Montlhéry that is really significant, but the new market is not based on any definite regulations. It is the creation of commercial convenience, and disappears in a large measure amidst the confusion of the period. The trade flows through Montlhéry, indeed, but there is no well-organized market. The inadequacy of the old system is proved, but nothing new supplants it. The markets exist in form, without any of the regularity that secured for the buyers and sellers the comprehensive competition that should be found on a market. The merchants buy freely in the cafés and inns; supplies no longer appear in full on the market; the farmers are content to bring samples to market; the merchants, too, scour the countryside, buying in the farms, so that the peasants no longer come to market with their wonted regularity. In short, the problem of marketing appeared in all its complexity; all the dangers and disadvantages of the chaos were perceived more or less clearly by the administrative officials; the solution of the difficulty was, however, beyond them. They were naturally inclined to enforce the old regulations, but the inexpediency of such measures was quickly revealed and the attempt was abandoned. In this section of the Seine Basin the disorganization of the markets produced no helpful results; no new forms were developed that promised any improvement in price-making and distribution.

In the Valley of the Oise the disadvantages of the prevailing methods of the wholesale marketing appeared, but not in such an exaggerated form that thorough reorganization of the system became necessary. Nothing could better illustrate the inertia of institutions. No far-reaching change took place until the old system became impossible. The old market was seriously affected; the wholesale trade became quite independent of the town market, and finally encroached upon the supply coming to the town, but despite all the difficulties of the case, nothing was done to organize the trade on a new basis. The general aspects of the trade at Soissons underwent little change in the course of the latter half of the seventeenth century; the character of the marketing in 1660 is typical. Conditions in the town itself are described by the Procureur du Roi. "The merchants trading with Paris and other inhabitants do not allow the grain to come into town for the market, but go out to meet the carters. They buy secretly not only outside the town but even in the streets. This impairs the market so that generally only three or four muids are offered for sale."[1] But much grain was bought in the country, either on the farms or in granaries of landlords. Thus, Claude Archin had eighty muids of grain "which he had bought from day to day of the peasants of the country and others."[2] Another merchant has 300 muids in the granaries of the Abbey of Saint Jean des Vignes,[3] part of which was probably bought of the Abbey. In another granary eighty muids were found: the product of the dues of "Lestrage," which had been farmed out by the *Lieutenant Particulier* of Soissons.[4] Another granary had been filled with grain brought in within the last three weeks from Fer-en-Trétenois.[5] Antoine l'Évêque had 240 muids of wheat, 60 muids of mixed grain, 40 muids of rye, 30 muids of oats, which he had bought from time to time in the town of Soissons or in the neighborhood. In partnership with Audiger and Le Vaux, he had bought about 900 muids of grain of the Maréchal d'Estrées. Part of this was in the Château at Soissons, part at Crèvecoeur; and what had not already been shipped to Paris was still in the Château.[6]

The wholesale trade had thus taken control of practically all the supplies of the region; what the merchants did not themselves buy in the country was bought by them or by bourgeois as soon as it reached the town. The town was necessarily

[1] Bib. Nat., Fr. 21641. 250 and 254. 6 Nov. 1660. Dépositions du Procureur du Roi and du Sr. Martinet.

[2] *Ibid., sous nom* "Claude Archin."

[3] *Ibid.*, déposition de la femme de Danré.

[4] *Ibid.*, déposition d'Antoine Martinet.

[5] *Ibid.* 250 ff. 7 Nov. 1660.

[6] *Ibid.*, testimony of Antoine L'Évêque.

dependent upon the wholesale merchants, since its supplies were largely derived from their granaries. The position of the town was insecure, but the consequences of the domination of the trade by the wholesalers were not necessarily serious. The merchants were left to do very much as they pleased for long periods. In 1660, there was some complaint about the failure to enforce the ordinances. The principal judicial officers were said to be interested in the trade, so that they purposely refrained from enforcing the regulations.[1] At all events, the trade continued on this illegal basis throughout the remaining years of the century. In 1670, the merchants even had the courage to claim exemption from market dues on the ground that their trade did not pass through the town market. They declared that 20,000 muids were shipped annually to Paris, and they implied that most of the grain was bought outside the town.[2]

The danger of this domination of the wholesale trade appeared in 1684, when the intensity of the Parisian demand caused an extraordinary rise in prices. Soissons was threatened with dearth by the extent of the shipments to Paris. The Intendant writes: "Wheat, which was worth only 20–22 écus per muid last year, rose to 38 écus in June and July, and now, September 1st, grain is worth 46 écus, — a figure never before reached at this season of the year. These high prices have caused general consternation, and the common people murmur. . . . I have just sent the Échevins an ordinance, which requires the merchants to take turns in supplying the markets. Measures have also been taken to prevent prices from exceeding prices at Paris. No sales may be made to merchants of Paris, so long as any individuals desire to buy at retail to supply their wants." [3] The principle involved in this ordinance was important but no reorganization of the trade was effected. The town of Soissons was protected; the proper relation between the wholesale and the local trade was established by an administrative order, and

[1] Bib. Nat., Fr. 21641. 250 ff. 6 Nov. 1660.

[2] H. 1822. Reg. du Bureau, clxii. 1670.

[3] Boislisle, *op. cit.*, I, 28, 107. 1 Sept. 1684. Le Vayer. G[7]. 510. 1 Sept. 1684. Text of the Ordinance enclosed with letter. Godard: *Pouvoirs des Intendants*, p. 313 n., cites the Ordinance.

yet there was no progress toward the development of machinery to do automatically what Le Vayer was obliged to compass by ordinance. The Intendant had to act as "Deus ex machina"; fortunately, his discretion and insight enabled him to conduct himself creditably. The adequacy of the expedient as a safeguard against the disorders of the chaotic wholesale trade assured the persistence of the old conditions.

In 1693–94, there was a repetition of the experiences of 1684. The point of view of the Parisian authorities was altered by their interest in purchases made for the government in Soissons. The correspondence is largely filled with this affair, but the general conditions do not appear in the letters. Incidental information, however, shows that the wholesale merchants were engaged in the usual operations. Delamare writes: "Twenty merchants of Neuilly-Saint-Front are buying up all the grain, forming granaries, and selling to merchants of Paris." [1] An anonymous correspondent writes from Compiègne, one "France bought on the market through secret agents, but he was discovered, and the two women buying for him were arrested. . . . The merchant then went to Gillecourt, a village near Crépy, buying there in the farms, for twenty sous per sack more than the market price. Since that time, all the farmers for five leagues around take their grain to him. He has relatives here who receive his purchases and declare that it is from rents." [2] At Soissons there was much apprehension, and Bossuet admits that the supplies of the province are small. He feels that it will be necessary to control the trade with care, if exhaustion is to be avoided.[3] On the whole it is probable that the conditions were the same as in 1684. This much at least is certain; the wholesale merchants were again made responsible for furnishing the local market. Bossuet says: "according to an old regulation the maire and échevins for the last two months have required the merchants to place a fixed quantity of grain on sale

[1] Bib. Nat., Fr. 21643. 270. Note by Delamare, 1684.

[2] Bib. Nat., Fr. 21642. 275. Lettre anonyme de Compiègne à Mme. l'Abbesse de l'Hôtel Dieu de Paris, 1693–94.

[3] G^7. 1632. Soissons, 13 Juin 1693. Bossuet.

in a specified place. They set the price at some figure slightly below the current price, and the grain is sold to the poor artisans in the presence of échevins." [1] The measure of Le Vayer was not reproduced in its fulness, although the practical effect of the ordinances may well have been similar. The wholesale trade amassed such quantities of grain in the town that it was hardly possible for the town to suffer serious inconvenience. The rural districts were much more likely to feel the pressure of the dearth, and they were not assisted by the supply brought to the market at Soissons by the wholesale merchants. The peasants and villagers had no means of protecting their interests except open violence, and the stopping of carts and of grain boats was not an efficient means of securing reorganization of the trade. The comparative security of the town made the officials indifferent, except in times of crisis when their empirical expedients remedied the trouble that lay at their door, without in the least removing the fundamental cause of the disorders.

This intensification of the distress in the rural sections appeared strongly in 1697 and 1709. Apprehension was aroused by heavy shipments towards the north, in part designed for the army, but in part private trading ventures. The incident is not described clearly by the Intendant and most of the details are not relevant. It is worthy of note, however, that the violence was most considerable in the smaller towns, Genvry, La Fère, Haut, Marle, and Chaulny. There was trouble at Noyon, also, but less violence.[2] In 1709 the difference between the distress in the towns and in the country is still more clearly marked. At Soissons it was primarily a matter of high prices, extraordinary prices, to be sure, but grain could be bought. "Prices went up a pistole per muid at the last market," writes d'Ormesson, March 1, 1709, "and merchants who have come up from Paris this last week have bought in the granaries of bourgeois at 52 écus per muid of Soissons.[3] In the next five

[1] G^7. 1632. Soissons, 3 Oct. 1693. Bossuet, avec reponse du Sr. du Pile en marge.

[2] G^7. 572. Soissons, 11, 12, 13, 15 Juin 1697. De la Houssaye.

[3] Twenty-two écus was an ordinary price, see *supra*. G^7. 1650. Soissons, 1 Mars 1709. d'Ormesson.

weeks, 805 muids of wheat and 57 muids of oats were sent down to Paris, notwithstanding the high prices.[1] In the six weeks preceding April 18, nearly 2000 muids were shipped to Paris from Soissons, without counting other ports on the river. Evidently the rate of export increased rather than diminished. But no word of distress in Soissons. D'Ormesson fears for the province as a whole, and declares that any attempt to draw grain from Soissons for the army is likely to provoke popular violence. The Bishop writes that the village markets of the back country are in many places entirely without supplies and without hope of securing any grain, unless the grain purchased by merchants of Paris is placed on sale. Fère-en-Tarlenois, Braine, Vailly, Coucy, and Attichy are mentioned particularly, but the distress was probably not confined to those villages.[2] The country districts thus suffered most severely from the disorders of the wholesale trade, but the relative indifference of Soissons left the trade unreformed.

As in the Beauce, there was much distress and chaos, but it did not happen to take a form that led to practical results. Empirical expedients and the comparative security in the larger towns on account of the swelling volume of the trade made it possible for the towns to tolerate the informality of trade that was contrary to the interests of the back country and of Paris. At Noyon, circumstances were tending towards the establishment of a wholesale market, but the tendencies fell just short of definite results. The stream of *blatiers* coming into town from day to day might easily have led to the development of an informal wholesale market such as appeared at Bray. But something was lacking. The volume of trade was not great enough. The opportunity of selling privately to the merchants and bourgeois was too alluring. The trade may have been too irregular. At all events, the apparently significant tendencies at Noyon came to nothing. Unquestionably an impor-

[1] G⁷. 1647. Bleds chargés à Soissons pour Paris depuis le 6 Mars jusqu'au 13 Avril 1709.

[2] G⁷. 1650. Soissons, 25 Avril et 4 Mai 1709. Évêque de Soissons: Attichy, 12 Mai 1709. Marillac.

tant factor was the absence of severe pressure of Parisian demand. Supplies could be secured elsewhere in case of need, and the dependence upon Soissonnais was never very great. It was an occasional source upon which little reliance was placed. Consequently, purchases in Soissons were generally curtailed before the region was very seriously affected. The metropolitan demand was sufficiently intense to exhibit the possibilities, but it never pressed beyond that point. The history of the trade there is for this reason peculiarly tantalizing; it presents the problem, but the problem never seems to need a complete solution.

III

The First Wholesale Market

In the Valleys of the Marne and Seine, the history of the trade is more significant. The general forms of market organization in 1660 were very similar to the forms in the Oise Valley. The larger towns were quite as indifferent to the welfare of the back country. But these regions were the primary source of water-borne supply, the reliance of Paris; Paris was consequently ready to take an active part in the regulation of the trade throughout this section. The interest of Paris, too, was never asserted without regard to local conditions. The efforts of Parisian officials were ever directed towards finding some means of reconciling all the conflicting necessities. The pressure upon the sources of supply was more persistent in time of stress, and there was a distinct attempt to regulate the trade from the broad standpoint of the general welfare of all sections. The pressure led to new forms of market organization; the far-sighted administrative officials were alert and ready to seize upon a solution of the ever-present problem. The history of the trade on the Marne and Seine consequently led to definite results. The first wholesale markets appeared.

In the Valley of the Marne, the abundance of the available supply rendered administrative control relatively infrequent. Information is inadequate, and there is every indication that the market system developed less rapidly than in the other parts of the Seine Basin. The indifference of the resident merchants persisted longer than elsewhere, both in their dealings with the wholesale merchants and with the *blatiers*. At Châlons, the granaries were doubtless the basis of the wholesale trade, as has been stated in a previous chapter, but the mode in which these granaries were filled is a matter of importance. In the early period, rents in kind were the most important source of supply. In 1660, this was no longer true. Magdelaine Goudouin says that *blatiers* from Lorraine brought great quantities of grain to the town.[1] Probably this *blatier* trade was quite extensive even then, so that grain came to the town in that way from the vicinity as well as from Lorraine. The *blatiers* doubtless sold their grain on the market to the bourgeois, and the well-to-do had an opportunity to increase their stores by judicious purchases on the market. Trade on the Marne was thus very considerable even in those years which mark the beginning of active development in the Oise Valley or on the Upper Seine. But both at Châlons and at Vitry it was the dull granary trade, — apathetic, inert, manifesting none of the feverish effort to secure the maximum profit that characterizes modern trade.

The "country buying" that was so wide-spread in the Seine Valley in 1660 did not appear on the Upper Marne until 1694. That great dearth indeed marked the beginning of the transition from the old market system to the new. The merchants of Châlons began to devote more attention to the business; instead of waiting for the grain to come to them, they made an active canvass of the country. The region between the Marne and the Seine offered the greatest supplies, and although there was some competition with merchants who worked up from the Seine, the traders penetrated to Arcis-sur-Seine. In January, 1694, "Lorinet and Clement, merchants at Châlons, came to Arcis four or five times. They bought and shipped great quantities of grain which they said were destined for the king's store houses. After the grain had been measured and put in

[1] Bib. Nat., Fr. 21641. 357. 4 Nov. 1660. Testimony of Magdelaine Goudouin.

sacks, it was left for 6–8 weeks in the granaries at Arcis." The witness, a measurer, said that "he had no idea of the quantity secured by the merchants, but every trip occasioned the shipment of 20–30 wagon-loads." [1]

Some grain went to Vitry from Arcis, most particularly grain purchased by one Guidor, a merchant of Nogent-sur-Seine. He shipped ordinarily to the Seine ports, but at times sold grain to merchants at Vitry.[2] Roger, a merchant of Vitry, also made purchases in this vicinity, notably "of a couple of *blatiers* who lived at Aunay. These *blatiers* bought of the peasants in the farms, and sold to the various wholesale merchants at Arcis." [3]

But the direct buying in the distant villages by merchants of Châlons and Vitry was relatively unusual. There was considerable trade in the hands of *blatiers* who bought on the Aube and sold at the Marne ports. This was quite as new as the direct "country buying," and much more important. In 1630, the Aube Valley sent its grain directly to Paris;[4] in 1694, the direct trade with Paris was still notable. The commissioners said that there were three classes of merchants at Arcis-sur-Aube, "the merchants who traded directly with Paris, Piot and Thomas; merchants limiting their operations to Arcis itself, buying and selling in the town; persons who acted as agents of Parisian merchants." [5] But the *blatier* trade with the Marne ports tended to carry the grain to the larger entrepôts. "*Blatiers* who come from neighboring towns buy a considerable portion of the grain on the market, and even buy of the merchants of Arcis. They sell later in the markets of La-Fère-Champenoise, Vitry, Châlons, and other places where wholesale merchants buy." [6] Jean Barbaron, one of the witnesses, describes the

[1] Bib. Nat., Fr. 21643. 239. 1 Août 1694. Arcy-sur-Aube. Testimony of Jean Barbaron.

[2] *Ibid.* 239. 1 Août 1694. Charles Dedet.

[3] *Ibid.* 248v. 2 Août 1694. Pierre Hughes. *Ibid.*, 247. Marion, factor of Faure, testifies to the same facts.

[4] Bib. Nat., Fr. 21641. 136. Testimony of Marguerite Froissart, 16 Dec. 1630.

[5] Bib. Nat., Fr. 21643. 194. 30 Juillet 1694.

[6] *Ibid.* 194. 30 Juillet 1694. Procès Verbal, Arcis. General statement of the result of the inquest.

operations of Piot and Thomas in detail. He speaks of their shipments to Paris, "they shipped four or five boat-loads of grain to Paris during the last year. Under this pretext they scoured the country, buying in all the farms and villages around Arcis. They brought this grain to their granaries in the town. But he has observed, of late, that they sold to *blatiers* of Épernay, La-Fère-Champenois and other places, instead of shipping to Paris."[1] The smaller resident merchants were even more dependent upon the *blatiers*, if we may trust the report of Claude d'Ossé, the Surgeon. "The merchants who have less capital than Piot and Thomas buy the grain that is brought to the market at Arcis by the peasants. This they store in granaries and sell later to *blatiers* who come to buy."[2] The Aube Valley trade was gradually drawn towards the larger shipping ports of the Marne. The resident merchants who had previously been engaged in trade with Paris were assuming the functions of collectors for the Marne towns, assisted by the numerous *blatiers* who were carrying grain from market to market. The growing volume of this *blatier* trade rendered unnecessary special efforts on the part of the merchants of the Marne towns. The passive attitude toward supply was, on their part, the more characteristic even in these closing years of the century.

There was some "country buying" in this region in 1697–1700 and in 1709, but it was quite inconsiderable in comparison with the extent of the granary trade, and it was largely the work of Parisian merchants or local merchants who resided in the small towns. The merchants of Châlons and Vitry remained indifferent to the trade outside the town.

In 1697, Larcher speaks of trouble from "country buying" on the frontier of Champagne. "There are many merchants and *blatiers* in these cantons, who are carrying grain away from the villages by night as well as by day." But this was for export over the frontier at Mézières.[3] In 1699, we hear that Sr. Peraud,

[1] Bib. Nat., Fr. 21643. 239. 1 Août 1694. Jean Barbaron.

[2] *Ibid.* 239. 1 Août 1694.

[3] G^7. 227. Châlons, 17 Nov. 1697. Larcher.

Procureur at the Baillage of Châlons, had formed several granaries, at Pontavert, Châlons, and other places. He was said to have scoured the whole countryside for grain.[1] In 1700, Pomereu made a careful investigation and reports "that some of the merchants of Châlons who trade with Paris are suspected of buying grain in the farms instead of on the markets."[2] In regard to merchants of Vitry, he is even more doubtful of the reliability of general reports: "there are some who are suspected of taking up grain in the country districts, but these accounts are vague rumors without any proof."[3] But there were instances, particularly on the frontier, in Rethelois, where an anonymous correspondent complained of the practices of one Mme. Perart of Châlons, apparently with real foundation. Of this woman Pomereu writes: "she and her husband who live here, together with a brother-in-law at Charleville, have been engaged in a very considerable grain trade for several years. They buy everywhere and most of the shipments are said to be destined for Paris."[4] With due allowance for these individual exceptions, it is evident that the trade was characteristically centered in the towns, Vitry and Châlons.

Detailed evidence of the handling of grain at Châlons does not appear. The one precise statement in regard to the mode of buying is found in the declarations of a number of grain merchants in 1698. De Vige, one of the principal merchants, says that in the course of the preceding month he bought 150 setiers of grain of *blatiers* who brought it to his door.[5] Very likely this was a typical mode of buying. It is in keeping with the character of the trade, an outcome of the apathy of the merchants and of the desire of the *blatiers* to sell their grain without waiting for the regular market day.

At Vitry, the trade was certainly of this type. The granary was the basis of all trading, both of buying and of selling. There

[1] H. 1837. Reg. du Bureau, 202. 9 Mars 1699.

[2] G7. 229. Châlons, 13 Nov. 1700. Pomereu.

[3] G7. 229. Châlons, 18 Nov. 1700, Pomereu.

[4] G7. 229. Chalons, 22 Août 1700. Pomereu and enclosure from Rethel, 18 Août 1700. See also G7. 1642. Châlons. 13 Fev. 1709. Harouys.

[5] G7. 228. Châlons, 2 Oct. 1698. Larcher.

was some "country buying," but it was not very wide-spread.[1] In 1694, we get brief indications of the character of the trade in the town. The Provost says: "the country people are accustomed to carry their grain directly to the merchants to whom they sell, and from whom they frequently receive loans."[2] These customs were rudely disturbed by the agent of the Provost of Paris who endeavored to enforce the old market regulations, requiring that all grain be sold on the market.[3] The result of this was a complete cessation of trade at Vitry. "In two months, scarcely enough grain came into town to load one boat . . . the peasants and *blatiers* went to Châlons or to Troyes where the trade was free."[4] Trade was reëstablished at Vitry only by the publication of an ordinance permitting "peasants and country people to bring their grain to town, and to dispose of it as they see fit, permitting merchants to buy freely, except from twelve o'clock of the day before market day to noon of the following day."[5] Nothing could show more clearly that the *blatier* trade had grown to such an extent that grain was coming every day and that the *blatiers* were selling to the merchants in their houses. The old market regulations could no longer be enforced. The wholesale trade had become concentrated in the town; there was little "country buying," but there was no organized wholesale market.

Fortunately, however, we are not obliged to depend solely upon these inferences. The trade of Vitry is comprehensively described in a letter from Pomereu that leaves nothing to be desired. "There are ninety-two grain merchants who have registered in the Baillage of Vitry. Only thirty ordinarily trade personally with Paris, the others assist them when they have not enough to fill a boat, for it is always possible to buy

[1] In addition to the statement of Pomereu in his letter of 18 Nov. 1700, see G^7. 1630. Vitry, 11 Nov. 1693, where three women are accused of buying in the farms.

[2] Bib. Nat., Fr. 21643. 48. Vitry, 19 Dec. 1694. Le Bel, Prévôt à Vitry.

[3] G^7. 1635. Also Bib. Nat., Fr. 21643. 19. 19 Oct. 1694. Ord. de Le Blanc, Comm. des Prévôt des March. et Échevins de Paris.

[4] Letter of Le Bel, see note (2).

[5] Bib. Nat., Fr. 21643. 26. Vitry, 15 Dec. 1694. Ord. du Prévôt.

enough in their granaries to complete the consignment. They all buy part of their grain in the markets, but they are also accustomed to receive at their houses the peasants and other people who bring them samples of grain. They trade on the basis of these samples and fix the price. Then the peasants deliver at the granaries the quantity agreed upon without bringing the grain to market. This is not strictly in accordance with the ordinances, but the usual regulations are very properly suspended, as the grain purchased in this manner is destined for the provision of Paris."[1] Clearly the general conditions of trade were what they had been in 1694. The town was frequented by the peasants and *blatiers* of the immediate neighborhood and from Lorraine. The volume of trade thus concentrated in the town was considerable. In its general aspect it was the same tendency that appeared in the Beauce, in Santerre and Soissonnais, in Touraine, but the effect on the organization of the trade was somewhat different. At Montlhéry, the trade was confined primarily to the market days, there was selling by sample in the cafés as well as on the market, but in some form or other there was a concourse of buyers and sellers, competing with each other. At Noyon, for a time, the *blatiers* flocked into town not only on market day but on other days of the week. The merchants bought on the market, and there seemed to be a possibility of the establishment of a wholesale market. But the merchants did not rest content with waiting until grain came to Noyon; they persisted in working up into the supply regions to buy on the tributary markets. Whatever came to Noyon was quickly purchased, but there was no reliance upon the *blatier* supply. Here at Vitry, and probably at Châlons, the abundance of the available supply rendered the merchants less enterprising. They were quite willing to wait for supplies to be brought to town, but the combination of general sluggishness and the long-established custom of buying in granaries

[1] G^7. 229. Châlons, 18 Nov. 1700. Pomereu. This letter is in unusually bad condition. It has suffered from book-worms, dampness, and dirt, so that some words are entirely missing. The last line or two of my citation is somewhat conjectural, though the general meaning of the original is clear.

resulted in informal dealing in the houses of the merchants. The concentration of trade needed for the establishment of a market was present, but the assembling of buyers and sellers did not accompany the other feature of the market.

In the Seine Valley, the combination of circumstances was more felicitous. The trade of the region was remarkable, even in 1660, for the enterprise and vigor displayed by the merchants. If the available supply was not as great as that of the Marne, the inherent difficulties merely served to stimulate the merchants to greater efforts. This feverish energy of the wholesale merchants was communicated to the *blatiers*, and the widespread endeavor to realize the anticipated profits of the trade gave it a briskness that is very modern. This difference in the temper of the traders, combined with the gradual tendency towards concentration, led to the formation of a real wholesale market at Bray.

The early appearance of "country buying" in this region has already led to some study of conditions in 1660. The activity of the merchants in these districts has received considerable attention. The "country buying" around Montereau by Nepveu, Lavallé, Le Brie, and other factors of Parisian merchants, the formation of granaries in the towns for convenience in shipping, the legal recognition of this irregularity, by the acknowledgment that grain passing through a town in such a manner need not pay market dues, all this has been discussed. The significance of the change is somewhat concealed by the persistence of the granaries in the shipping towns. There is a wide difference between the granary formed in the town by purchases on the market, and the granary formed by grain purchased in the country.

When the trade quieted down after the dearth of 1663, the merchants became less active in their operations in the country; the *blatiers* were able to take advantage of the opportunity left by the merchants. The Seine towns witnessed an increase of the market trade, especially at Bray. There was an approximation to conditions on the Marne. The town granaries of merchants and bourgeois were filled by this *blatier* trade, but the enterprise of the merchants led to active buying from the *blatiers*. They sought out the *blatiers* instead of waiting for the *blatiers* to come to their houses. This resulted in the establishment of a wholesale market. The *blatiers* naturally came to the Halle, the merchants sought them there, and bought freely every week-day, whether it was a market day or not. There was thus a concourse of buyers and sellers, who were assembled not for local but for wholesale trade. The limitations of the local market regulations were no longer in force, and the trade was continuous instead of being intermittent.

The date of the change cannot be ascertained with accuracy. The first descriptions of this custom come from the year 1694, when the practice is said to be the customary form of the trade, interrupted for the two years preceding by the "country buying" of Jean Roger and his factors. Doubtless the custom took form gradually between 1680 and 1690. Even in 1692, the market at Bray can hardly have presented the definite form suggested by Delamare's account, in the *Traité de la Police*. The careful statement of Pierre Philipon presents all the irregularities and qualifications that must be added to the sharp, clear-cut description of Delamare: "Every Friday," says Philipon, "the grain market is held at Bray. It opens at eight o'clock for the bourgeois and for the bakers, and when they are all supplied the merchants are allowed to buy. Between Martinmas and Easter the peasants bring grain to Bray every day, whether it is market day or not. They carry their grain to the Halle *or* to the houses of individual merchants, and sell to such persons as present themselves. In years of plenty, the peasants brought such a great quantity that all who were engaged in the trade could buy what they wished, but for the last two years grain has been dear. Much less has come to the market, as the peasants of Brie have become accustomed to carry their grain elsewhere. Almost no one has come to Bray save the peasants and *blatiers* from Burgundy who have continued to come every day of the week."[1] Thus we must

[1] Bib. Nat., Fr. 21642. 311 ff. 20 Juillet 1694. Inquest at Bray, testimony of Pierre Philipon.

not think of this informal wholesale market at Bray as a definite, comprehensive system; much of this *blatier* grain was sold to the merchants at their granaries just as at Vitry. Possibly the proportion of grain sold in that manner was really considerable. At all events, the trade was very unstable, changing its form considerably under the pressure of rather slight circumstances.

In 1693–94, the customary mode of buying was completely disorganized, primarily by the energetic efforts of Roger and his partners to secure control of the grain in the Seine Valley. With agents in most of the important ports and what was then a rather large capital, Roger had his agents buy extensively in the farms and in the towns, urging them to secure the grain at any cost. "Colmet, the Receiver of the Domain, was Roger's agent at Bray. He had acquired control of practically all the grain brought to Bray. His wife, who was engaged in collecting the tolls at the bridge, combined this task with the grain trade. She stopped all the peasants' carts bringing grain to town, talked with the drivers and told them to carry the grain to her house. When it was market day and the peasants were obliged to go to the Halle, Colmet's wife would come and outbid all the other merchants, so that she secured the greater part of the grain, although she paid more than the other merchants had decided to offer. Colmet himself rarely appeared on the market at Bray. He went off on horseback. The witness did not know where he went, but last year, between Martinmas and Christmas, many cart-loads of grain came to Bray in sacks bearing Roger's mark, so that he supposed it was grain that Colmet had purchased in the farms."[1] Other witnesses said confidently that Colmet bought extensively in the country. The resident merchants were equally guilty of this "country buying." Étienne Musseau says: "the merchants of Paris buy in the farms whenever they are in the region. The merchants of Bray do likewise, especially Gaillard, who is factor of Thomas Viard of Paris. He has never seen Gaillard buy grain on the market, although he carries on a very large trade in the neighborhood, and has

[1] Bib. Nat., Fr. 21642. 311. 20 Juillet 1694. Pierre Philipon.

granaries at Donne-Marie and at Vimpelles. Colmet, agent of Roger, also buys in the country of the peasants, so that very little grain comes to market." [1] The Notary gives a more detailed account. "The officials at Bray wished to stop these abuses. They ordered the peasants to bring their grain to the market, and required the merchants to buy there, but this regulation was not observed for more than six or eight markets. The merchants began to scour the country again, asserting that they had received permission to buy in the farms. . . . In the streets of the towns, Colmet's wife and other merchants stopped the peasants on their way to market, prevented them from proceeding to the Halle, and even forced them to sell their grain on the spot. After such purchases the merchants frequently divided the grain between them, and at times with much heat and quarreling. Each tried to out-bid the other, and the peasants said that they could sell their grain for whatever they wished, so great was the eagerness of the merchants to secure it." [2]

The incipient wholesale market was thus disorganized shortly after the custom had become established. Even after 1694, the old custom did not reassert itself at once. The disorder continued through 1699. "For five or six years," says Louis Cajon, "the peasants have ceased to bring their grain to town for the regular market. They also have ceased to unload at the Halle. Instead, they carry the grain directly to the merchants, who buy on the bridge or in the streets and have the grain delivered at their houses. Pierre Blot, Lamy, Cottereau, de la Noue, the widow Chaillot, and Philippe de Billy, grain merchants, stop the carts of the peasants on the bridge, examine the samples, bargain, bid against each other, quarreling and becoming so excited that they are almost ready to fight." [3] Nicolas Amant tells the same story. "The peasants frequently bring grain to town on all days of the week except feast days. They have come more frequently for the last six weeks than

[1] Bib. Nat., Fr. 21642. 311. 20 Juillet 1694. Étienne Musseau.

[2] *Ibid.* Ed^me^ Mercier.

[3] Bib. Nat., Fr. 21643. 317. 3 Jan. 1699. Louis Cajon.

previously. At the same time, la Noue, Jacques Sennené, Cottereau, Lamy, Philippe de Billy, and the widow Chaillot go out to meet them at the bridge. They stop them, examine the samples, and bid against each other." [1] If this were all, the tendency towards a definite wholesale market would be very clear. We have a real competition among the merchants, and it is of little moment whether they meet the grain at the Halle or on the bridge. There is a concourse of buyers and sellers. Bidding on the lots of grain is animated. Speculation is rife. Prices rise beyond the usual local figures, so that this active wholesale trade causes great apprehension. Doubtless the existence of this trade in the town induced Delamare to insert in his *Traité de la Police* the description of the daily market at Bray. His knowledge of the facts was extensive, since these inquests were made by him personally, or by officials in close touch with him. But it is necessary to recognize clearly the qualifications that must be added. The trade which still comes to town during these years is only part of the trade.

A remarkable change had taken place in the attitude of the *blatiers* and country people. Colmet says that "for four years or more the peasants in the vicinity of the town, who became wealthy during the dearth, have no longer brought their grain to the Halle at Bray, but have waited for the merchants to come to them. They even refuse to sell except in the late season, and then only if the season offers special advantages. If the merchants do not offer the prices they expect, these peasants hold the grain over until the following year. This avarice reduces the market of Bray to a few muids of grain, although formerly the peasants brought in 40–50 muids." [2] At all events the merchants of Bray bought freely in the farms. La Noue had "an agent at Goix, named Rizon, another at Vimpelle, and two or three others in different places. They do nothing but run from farm to farm, buying up all the grain they can lay their hands on. When one of them has five or six cart-loads,

[1] Bib. Nat., Fr. 21643. 317. 3 Jan. 1699. Nicolas Amant.

[2] *Ibid.* 317. 3 Jan. 1699. Jean Colmet.

he sends it to de la Noue at Bray or to a granary that de la Noue has at Port-Moutain." [1]

Granaries were formed even in the back country. At Plessis-Saint-Jean, one Châtelain bought extensively of peasants, personally and by agents. An inn keeper at Montigny acted as agent. All the grain was amassed in granaries. Châtelain sold only by sample, and in the late season when prices were high.[2]

In this chaos of speculation it is difficult to see anything sufficiently precise and permanent to be of significance. Even our wholesale market is pretty elusive. But it was its appearance, even with this extreme disorder, that gave Delamare the idea of a legally established wholesale market, which he applied at Vitry with such success in 1709. The zeal of the merchants in the Seine Basin was too keen to enable any regulation to survive a period of dearth, but the relative quiet in the Upper Marne Valley gave administrative regulations a better chance of survival. In all probability the tendencies towards order would establish themselves in the ordinary years, even at Bray, but the real significance of the wholesale market is in our period limited to Vitry.

The conditions of trade there previous to 1709 have already been described. The history of the year 1709 turns upon the experience of Delamare in the Seine Valley in 1694 and 1699, when he drew up the inquests which we have just considered.

The marked contrast between the trade at Vitry and Châlons and the trade at Bray is explained by Delamare's letter of August 14, practically the first report sent back to Paris: "I perceive that most of the grain in this province is in the hands of the wealthy bourgeois and officials. The resident grain merchants are well-to-do, but few of the merchants from Paris are rich or capable of carrying on a large trade. They buy here on credit. The sellers are not under any necessity of selling,

[1] Bib. Nat., Fr. 21643. 317. 3 Jan. 1699. Louis Cajon, also Nicolas Bridon.

[2] *Ibid.* Several depositions following the deposition of Jean Colmet.

and do so only when they find it convenient. The buyers have little ready money, but they pay what the residents ask. The credit they are obliged to give forces them to increase the price enough to give them interest on their money. Would to God that they might cease to give credit! If they came themselves to Paris, we would have our grain cheaper. It would pass through two hands, whereas now it passes through three or four hands." [1] The extraordinary feature of the trade of Vitry, however, is the importance of the granaries formed from rents. "The officers and notable bourgeois who live on their rents, even the farmers of the ecclesiastical estates and others who receive rents in kind, have always had complete freedom to form granaries. In many cases their tenants are required by their leases to deliver at Vitry the grain turned over in payment of rent." [2] But most of these persons were not very wealthy. "All the property of the residents of Vitry is land, and their income is paid in kind. What they now have in their granaries is the product of seven or eight years' rents on which they had realized nothing. Lately, most of them have been selling, but there are only five or six families that could really be called rich. The others have very moderate fortunes or are actually poor. All have some domains, however, both rich and poor, so that the grain is distributed among such a number of families that no individual has been able to secure large profits." [3]

But the trade of Vitry was not entirely based on these rents. The situation of the town, practically at the head of navigation on the Marne, attracted a considerable volume of trade; not only the grain of the neighborhood came thither, but even grain from distant sections outside the Baillage, especially Lorraine and Bar. This grain was purchased by the resident merchants or by the bourgeois. It is the trade that is described by Pomereu in 1700. Since that time, however, some merchants had moved out to the suburbs so that

[1] Bib. Nat., Fr. 21647. 62. Vitry-le-François, 14 Août 1709. Delamare.

[2] *Ibid.* 21650. 246. Observations pour la police des grains à Vitry.

[3] Boislisle, *op. cit.*, III, 267, 693. 5 Fev. 1710. Delamare.

they might the more easily secure the grain brought in by peasants.[1]

The trouble at Vitry was not lack of grain. Delamare had been sent up from Paris to prevent the merchants from holding back their shipments. He began by visiting the granaries and by urging the merchants to forward considerable consignments to Paris. "These shipments," he says, "stimulated trade, and divers foreigners arrived at Vitry with grain in carts or on pack horses. I spoke with them and assured them of my protection, I even permitted them to sell daily in the public square, which had never before been done."[2] These foreigners were the Lorraine *blatiers* who had formerly sold their grain to the merchants in their houses. In 1709, the merchants had begun to stop these *blatiers* in the streets or on the roads outside the city, so that Delamare had granted them full permission to sell on the public square. This provision attracted more trade, and "prices fell. . . . The people were very much pleased, but the rich bourgeois and merchants were much put out. They endeavored to harass the Lorrainers and other foreigners, refusing to make any offers for their grain. The foreigners came to find me, and I enabled them to sell their grain at a satisfactory price. They are coming in daily. It is one continual stream of convoys from Lorraine, Bar, the Bishoprics of Toul and Verdun, some from Alsace, and I have even been told that some are *en route* from Franche Comté."[3] The increasing volume of trade spread dismay among the merchants, who had expected prices to rise from a continually increasing scarcity. Delamare feared intrigues and was anxious to establish trade on a basis that should be so satisfactory to the *blatiers* that they would continue to come. To this end, he issued the ordinance of 21 October 1709. "All grain which has been despatched to Vitry and all grain *en route* shall be brought to town and placed on sale in accordance with the ordinances and police regulations. Peasants and other persons

[1] Bib. Nat., Fr. 21650. 246. Observations sur la police des Bleds à Vitry.
[2] Delamare, *op. cit.*, 2d ed., III, Supp. p. 39.
[3] Bib. Nat., Fr. 21647. 129v. Vitry, 20 Oct. 1709. Delamare.

living within three leagues of the town shall expose and sell their grain at the Halle on Mondays, Thursdays, and Saturdays. All other persons shall expose and sell their grain on the Square in the center of the town on all days of the week save Sundays and feast days. No one shall go out to meet the grain entering the town."

"No one shall sell grain except at the Halle or on the Public Square."

"The market at the Square, which is to be held daily except on feast days, shall be open to peasants and foreigners, who may expose their grain as soon as they arrive, and sell at all hours of the day. On the Square, all persons may buy: the people, the bourgeois, the bakers, and merchants, save that the first hour shall be for the bourgeois and country people who have need." [1]

This is the first attempt to organize a regular wholesale grain market. The local demand is legally given the freedom of the wholesale market, but in practice it is not likely that many local purchases were made on the Square. The habit of marketing on fixed days was too inveterate to be quickly supplanted by new modes of buying. The market on the Square with its wholesale supply was devoted almost exclusively to the wholesale trade. Even on market days, the wholesale market was independent of the town market at the Halle. The wholesale trade, which had existed so long without any definite organization, the haphazard buying in granaries, the energetic scouring of the country, the disorderly bargaining with the carters outside the town gates or in the streets, — all this chaos had at last been supplanted by an orderly daily market with a steady inflow of supply and a comprehensive representation of the wholesale demand.

Another feature of improved market organization appeared at Vitry in these years of dearth. There was a striking tendency towards the distributing market, the market that does not collect merely for itself and a single line of export trade, but gathers together the supply of a whole region and then dis-

[1] Delamare, *op. cit.*, 2d ed., III, Supp. pp. 39–40.

tributes the abundance of one section among the towns and villages that are inadequately supplied. An illustration will make this distinction clearer. The characteristic feature of medieval trade was the independent exploitation of the supply region by all the towns whose provision was not assured near at hand. In the neighborhood of Vitry the conduct of the Lorraine *blatiers* illustrates the point. In 1660 some of these Lorraine *blatiers* were not satisfied with prices at Vitry and passed on to Châlons.[1] They endeavored themselves to find the most advantageous market in the whole region, rather than to sell at a central market whence the surplus was sent to the localities in need. In 1710, a similar incident occurs; a group of Lorrainers passes on to Rheims instead of selling at Vitry. Delamare was disturbed by this tendency, but he wrote with great satisfaction a few days later: "The *blatiers* passed through Vitry last Monday, on their way back from Rheims, and one of them came to see me. He confessed that they had sold their grain for less than they were offered here." [2]

But this manner of supplying the towns of Champagne was not at all general in 1708–09. For the most part the grain came direct to Vitry and was then distributed according to the needs of the Parisian or of the local trade. The combination of metropolitan and local trade at Vitry is not as striking as it might be, because the towns of Champagne were seeking barley, which did not enter very considerably into the Parisian trade. It is nevertheless significant that much of the barley consumed in Champagne in 1709 came from Lorraine to Vitry, where it was purchased by agents and merchants of the neighboring towns. This movement had begun in December, 1709, when Delamare arrived at Vitry. The deputies of Rheims had bought wheat and barley in large quantities, but he forbade the shipment of the grain. They would have had a right to carry off this grain if they had bought on the markets, but they had bought in the granaries, and in granaries of Parisian merchants. "Such

[1] Bib. Nat., Fr. 21641. 357. Châlons, 4 Nov. 1660. Magdalaine Goudouin.

[2] *Ibid.* 21647. 156. Vitry, 19 Jan. 1710. Delamare. See also Fr. 21648. 79. Vitry, 17 Jan. 1710. Delamare.

grain constitutes a part of the supply of Paris and may not be diverted to any other destination."[1] Later, Delamare was less disposed to enforce the strict regulations in regard to the Parisian supply. In May, 1710, he writes: "The great exports from this province for the army in the Low Countries and for the fortresses, and the continual passage of troops have created more or less dearth, especially in Upper Champagne where the harvest was light. A prodigious crowd of poor people comes to town every market day to purchase barley and bread. The townspeople regard this with apprehension, but the Lorraine *blatiers* are just now bringing more barley than wheat so that they have been a great assistance to us."[2] A couple of weeks later, "the town of Épernay sent a deputy to buy barley. He came to me and asked permission to buy a few loads on the market. I did not feel justified in refusing permission to buy, after the townspeople were provided. So long as we have such supplies of this grain as we have had in the past, I am sure that it will not be wise to refuse permission to the neighboring towns. This extra trade encourages the Lorrainers and constantly attracts more. The assistance given the towns makes them less inclined to seek our wheat."[3] A month later he says: "The inhabitants of Upper Champagne continue to depend upon us for their subsistence. I see that they are given all the barley they desire. The foreigners are bringing such great quantities that we have enough for the town, and for these poor country people."[4]

This dependence upon Vitry was not unusual, although we seldom have so detailed a description. In 1708, Harouys, in a general report upon the trade of the province, says that Rheims, Épernay, and the frontier towns Sedan and Mézières have to come to Vitry for wheat.[5] Vitry was thus beginning to serve as a general distributive market. Grain came in from a wide area and was divided between Paris and the parts of the

[1] Bib. Nat., Fr. 21647. 145. Vitry, 27 Dec. 1709. Delamare.
[2] *Ibid.* 21648. 17. Vitry, 8 Mai 1710. Delamare.
[3] *Ibid.* 21648. 25. Vitry, 30 Mai 1710. Delamare.
[4] *Ibid.* 21647. 198. Vitry, 11 Juin 1710. Delamare.
[5] Boislisle, *op. cit.*, III, 73, 226.

province that were not naturally well supplied. The larger function of the wholesale market appeared as well as the definite regulations of the market.

In the producing regions supplying Paris there was one feature common to all. On the Oise, on the Marne, and on the Seine, in the Beauce, even in the Loire Valley, there was a marked concentration of the wholesale trade. In each region one or two markets gradually attracted all the trade. The wide and complicated ramifications of the sixteenth century trade were simplified. In 1709, Paris was practically supplied from the markets of Noyon, Soissons, Vitry, Châlons, Bray, Montlhéry, Chartres, and Saumur. At Vitry and Bray, definite wholesale markets were taking form. The idea could easily be applied to the other great market towns. Once that step was taken the worst of the troubles of the grain trade would be overcome, but some difficulties still remained. These were more intimately connected with Paris herself, and with the grain in transit.

IV

The Parisian City Markets

Wholesale price-making at Paris was quite as crudely organized as in the provinces. There was no systematic competition, no correlation of the conditions existing in the different supply areas. This indefiniteness created uncertainty which could easily generate a panic in times of stress. The inadequacy of market machinery had the further consequence of inviting speculative operations on the part of the grain merchants.

There was no single, comprehensive, wholesale grain market at Paris. Each of the three principal sources of supply had a separate market. The Port de Grève, near the Hôtel de Ville, on the quai opposite the Isle Saint-Louis, was the mart for all grain coming down the Seine or Marne. The supplies from Soissons, Noyon, and from the Lower Seine arrived at the Port de l'École, the quai on the right bank near the old Louvre and the church of Saint-Germain-l'Auxerrois. The Halle au Blé, opposite Saint-Eustache, on the site of the present Halles, was the market for the overland grain. These three markets received practically all the grain that came to the city. But a large portion of the supply of food stuffs never entered the city in the form of wheat. In 1637, one-half the total supply came in the form of flour. The grain from which this was made was bought by bakers on the markets of the environs. The concentration of trade in the seventeenth century brought much of this bakers' buying into touch with the general trade at Montlhéry, but many of the smaller markets were still important, especially on the Marne in the vicinity of Meaux; on the Seine, near Corbeil and Melun; and in the section of Brie nearest the city, Rozoy, Brie-Comte-Robert, and other markets.

The operations of the bakers in the environs in the latter part of the seventeenth century were very extensive. They appear in few of the records, but the inquiries of Delamare in 1699 reveal the general character of their activity. From Lagny he writes: "The bakers from the Faubourg Saint-Antoine scour the countryside, buying in all the farms. Some send their grain to the mill at Noisel, a league from the town, and then ship by river to Brie-sur-Marne, where they go for it with carts. Others ship at the village of Javelins, two leagues from Lagny, a false port used to conceal their operations. Some use the port of Trillebardou and send the grain down to Saint-Maur. The town market has consequently been quite deserted for eighteen or twenty years. The peasants do not come to town with their grain, and if it were not for eight or nine petty merchants who buy of the peasants and bring grain to market, it would frequently happen that there would be no grain on the market." [1] Further investigation by Delamare produced a list of names of the principal persons engaged in the trade at Lagny. He found six bakers of Paris buying regularly in the farms; six factors of merchants and bakers of Paris; and thirty or forty peasants who were most frequently visited by the Parisian bakers and merchants.[2] Very much the same troubles appear

[1] Bib. Nat., Fr. 21645. 49. Lagny, 19 Fev. 1699. Delamare. Letter, with copy of depositions of witnesses.

[2] *Ibid.* 75. Lagny, 1699. Delamare's notes.

at Brie-Comte-Robert. "The peasant proprietors and farmers have ceased to bring their grain to market, coming instead with samples in their pockets. The bakers and the merchants who buy conclude the bargain on the basis of the samples and then go to the farms for the grain." [1]

The wholesale trade of the city was not really visible even at Paris; the quantities held by the bakers could never be ascertained. The importance of this element of uncertainty doubtless increased in the course of the eighteenth century, but even in 1700 it was a serious complication. To this element of difficulty must be added the indefiniteness arising from the absence of concentration in the sale of bread. The bakers sold directly in the retail markets of the various quarters, so that the trade was an absolutely incalculable factor. Grain thus appeared on three independent markets; bread and flour on sixteen different markets, seven of which were really of first-class importance.[2] Speculative dealing that had already begun in some of the producing regions was vigorously and successfully suppressed at Paris. There was no bond of unity between the numerous markets engaged in the grain trade.

At Paris, indeed, the conservatism of the period was strongest. New ideas worked in only with the greatest of difficulty. The active buying and selling among merchants without displacement of the grain was not permitted. Such regrating was frowned upon with all possible severity. The wholesale merchants at Paris sold on the ports to bakers,[3] and to the well-to-do bourgeois who accumulated stores for their use and had the grain ground as their needs demanded. It was all, in a sense, retail trade. The retail buyer was ill-informed, careless of minute differences of price, and relatively unskilled in the technique of buying. But in addition to the ignorance and incapacity of the buyers,

[1] Bib. Nat., Fr. 21643. 211^{v}. 13 Juillet 1694. Procès Verbal. Testimony of Étienne Lesueur. See also a memoir on the market at Tournan in 1699, Bib. Nat., Fr. 21645. 576.

[2] Coin de Saint-Paul; Place Maubert; Marché Neuf; Faubourg Saint-Germain; les Quinze Vingts; le Marais; Quai des Grands Augustins. See G^{7}. 1659. Reports of d'Argenson, 1709–10.

[3] See especially G^{7}. 1659. Mémoire du 30 Nov. 1709 sur Le Port de Grève.

the efficiency of the grain markets was seriously affected by one of the regulations to which the merchants were subjected. The elasticity of the market was impaired by the restrictions placed upon the liberty of the merchants to raise prices. Each boat-load of grain was regarded as a unit, although the boats contained 30–40 muids (150–200 bushels). The whole load must be sold at the opening price or at a lower figure. Sales were frequently very slow, so that portions of many boat-loads would be on sale at the same time. Whatever grain was held thus could not be influenced by any conditions which would cause a rise in prices. Furthermore, any grain arriving on the port must be placed on sale; the merchants were not allowed to remove the grain to granaries unless it had been damaged by water so that special treatment was necessary. All these circumstances aggravated the general defects of the market system of Paris. Unprofessional buying of a retail, rather than wholesale, character, absence of responsiveness to changes in demand, regulations distinctly hostile even to the honest interest of the merchants, — everything tempted the merchant to play upon the weakness of the metropolis, in the hope of realizing the gains which a better organization would have permitted within the limits of the law.

The efforts of the merchants to hold back their consignments of grain were the outcome of the regulations in regard to sale. If a boat arrived when the market was dull, the merchant suffered not only from a slow sale, but also found himself deprived of any hope of benefiting from an improvement in the market. The low prices of the dull period would be the maximum that could be realized upon that grain. What wonder that the merchants formed granaries just outside of Paris, that they devised expedients for delaying grain in transit, that they devoted themselves to a careful study of the idiosyncrasies of the Parisian market! Driven to such measures in pure self defence, they were not slow to discover the vast opportunities for gain afforded by the inadequacy of the market organization and by the extraordinary invisibility of the wholesale supply.

The investigations of 1660 were first directed against these entrepôts, and with great success. Quantities of grain were found and sent to Paris to relieve the distress. The Procès Verbaux contain long lists of visits to granaries. "The wife of Sebastian Toussaint said that her husband was not at Trillebardou. She opened a granary containing thirty-four muids of wheat, which had been brought down from Châlons and Vitry." [1] In some cases the declarations give the date of purchase. At Meaux, for instance, one of the dealers said that "the grain had all been bought at Châlons about two years ago." [2] Entrepôts of up-river grain were found at Trillebardou, Meaux, Mary, La-Ferté-Gaucher, La-Ferté-sous-Jouarre, and Lizy.[3] Some of the grain had been kept in store for five or six years, but that was probably exceptional. The same abuse evoked complaints throughout the rest of the century. In 1684, the Provost of Merchants says that the merchants "place their grain in granaries and entrepôts in various towns on the river by which the grain is brought to Paris. They consult with each other and agree to ship small quantities from these towns to Paris. They even delay the boats in transit, so that the ports shall not be abundantly supplied. They seek to assure themselves unjust gains at the expense of the public." [4] In 1698, the Provost issued summons to one François Marin, Measurer and Merchant of Meaux, "who has recently purchased thirty muids of wheat at Vitry, to be carried into Meaux and to be mixed with grain from France and Brie, before being brought to Paris." [5] In 1700, commissioners were sent to Château-Thierry to secure the shipment of grain delayed in transit. For some reason or other, the Procès Verbal of the commission was copied into the Registers of the city, so that it has survived. In this instance about 300 muids of oats had been sent down from Châlons to Château-Thierry. The report is significant

[1] Bib. Nat., Fr. 21641. 194. 7 Oct. 1660. Procès Verbal à Trillebardou.

[2] *Ibid.* 205. 29 Oct. 1660. Meaux.

[3] *Ibid.* 289 and 298. Originals, signed by the Commissioners and witnesses. Oct. 1660.

[4] H. 1830. Reg. du Bureau, lxix. 14 Sept. 1684. Commission to Bon Rislé, huissier, to open granaries. The municipal records probably contained the reports of the commissioners. See also H. 1831. Reg du Bureau, 923. 30 Juillet 1688.

[5] H. 1837. Reg. du Bureau. 28 Août 1698.

chiefly because it reveals the manner in which the legal requirements were evaded. To prevent entrepôts, boats arriving at the ports were required to exhibit way-bills (*Lettres de Voiture*) stating the place where the grain was shipped and the destination. If this ordinance could be enforced, the entrepôts could not be formed. But the regulation was of no practical importance. The merchants shipped from the up-river ports without taking way-bills, by necessity working in confidence with the local officials. As the local officials were themselves engaged in the trade, the difficulties of getting off without way-bills were reduced to a minimum.

Practically none of these boats sent down to Château-Thierry were accompanied by way-bills. Le Lieurre, who received them at Château-Thierry, said that " he did not know whence they had been shipped, but that the boatmen were from Châlons. The boats were addressed to him by Pouillot, a factor at Châlons, and orders had been sent to unload the boats and store the grain in granaries. He could not say to whom the grain belonged, as there were no way-bills (*Lettres de Voiture*).[1] Another consignment arrived while the commissioners were on the spot, so that they were able to get detailed information from Barbier, the boatman. He said that he had brought six boats down six weeks before. They contained 100 muids of oats, which he had taken aboard at Thou-sur-Marne, four leagues above Châlons. Charles Pouillot, factor for Collinet of Châlons, had the grain loaded. The grain belonged to Collinet of Châlons (a merchant trading regularly with Paris). There were no way-bills because the oats were not destined for Paris, but merely a note from Pouillot addressing the consignment to Robert Fournier, a measurer at Château-Thierry."[2] All these incidents are significant: the shipment from a little village outside Châlons; the absence of way-bills; the evasive explanation of the informality in shipment. They explain the persistence of the entrepôts on the Lower Marne, despite the constant efforts of the Provost of Merchants to stop the delays in transit.

[1] H. 1839. Reg. du Bureau, 10. 23 Août 1700. Testimony of Le Lieurre.

[2] *Ibid.*

The final shipment from the lower Marne towns was a simple matter. Those towns were all important shipping points for the grain of the vicinity, most of them busy trading ports with granaries of resident merchants, and there was the additional facility of weekly or semi-weekly freight boats. Consequently the entrepôt trade could easily be concealed under cover of the normal trade of those towns.[1]

The wholesale supply of Paris was thus rendered invisible by an extraordinary combination of circumstances. In the producing regions, the trade was largely independent of markets. In some places the trade was carried on in the granaries, while in other places the merchants scoured the countryside, buying in the farms. In either case, the grain never came into general view. At Paris, the wholesale traders were obliged to engage in what was practically retail trade. Such few advantages of concentration as were secured in the producing regions were nullified by the multiplicity of city markets. The bakers added to the confusion by procuring a portion of their supplies in the immediate vicinity of the city, buying in small quantities on local markets, or canvassing the farms with the same energy that was displayed by the merchants in the more distant producing regions. Lastly, the difficulties of disposing of grain advantageously at Paris gradually led the merchants to form entrepôts nearby, from which they could bring grain to the ports at short notice. It is difficult to imagine a more completely invisible supply.

This invisibility and the sense of insecurity it engendered caused constant apprehension in the metropolis. Even in these days of agitation against great corporations, the intensity of feeling of the seventeenth century Parisian can hardly be understood. His outpourings on the subjects of monopoly and regrating are likely to excite little besides derisive comments on the obsolete economic thought of the time. But a sympathetic comprehension of his actual situation leads to the recognition that there was some reason for his panicky fears and his

[1] See the Procès Verbaux of Delamare in 1699 at Meaux, La-Ferté-sous-Jouarre, and Lizy. Bib. Nat., Fr. 21645. 29, 92, 158.

suspicious hostility to the merchants. All classes were so sensitive to the least sign of danger that the instability of the Parisian markets was doubtless much increased. It was this deep-seated apprehension that yielded a ready credence to the legend of the *Pacte de Famine* in the latter eighteenth century. Then, as in 1709, the source of all trouble was inadequate market machinery.

CHAPTER III

The Chambre d'Abondance at Lyons and the Wholesale Merchants

The history of the trade that developed around Lyons differs in one important feature from the history of the Parisian trade. In the Seine Basin the sources of supply were numerous and fairly well utilized from an early date; the relative abundance rendered official interference less conspicuous. The trade was allowed to develop according to the play of circumstances. The Lyonese trade followed a very different course. The supply of grain available was barely adequate even in years of ordinary fertility. Every dearth caused a panic, both in the producing regions, and in the city. All were convinced that the supply was inadequate. This feeling was intensified by the incomplete knowledge of the relative importance of the possible sources of supply. The most favorable regions were the last to be systematically exploited, and then, instead of drawing supplies regularly from every possible source, the merchants endeavored to purchase in one region all the grain needed by the city. There was little of the concurrent utilization of the many sources of supply that is so striking in the Seine Basin. Lastly, the officials left the merchants too little freedom. In critical moments the provincial officials stopped the trade absolutely, or at least assumed complete control of all movements of grain. The municipal officials endeavored to encourage the merchants, but they frequently apprehended serious deficiencies and then engaged in trade on the account of the city. At such times, the Consuls intended to force the merchants to sell at lower prices, and actually sold the municipal grain at cost. But these ventures generally resulted in severe losses, and the good intentions of the Consuls were misrepresented. The losses attracted public attention, and the merchants, who suffered from competition with the municipality, were not slow to spread rumors of underhand practices. They suggested various methods by which private gains might be secured at the expense of the public. All these differences may be traced to the normal excess of supply in the Seine Basin, and to the bare adequacy of the supply available for meeting the necessities of Lyons.

The organization of the trade at Lyons was less advanced. At Paris even in the thirteenth century, there were wholesale merchants trading in distant sections and bringing grain to Paris by water. At Lyons, there was no wholesale water-borne trade even in the early fifteenth century. The trade in the Rhône Basin never achieved the degree of organization found at Bray and Vitry in 1709. The simple local market persisted longer at Lyons, and the wholesale trade was less highly organized. In addition to this element of connection with early types of marketing, the emphasis upon early forms is intensified by the possibility of treating the sixteenth century at greater length. The history of that period in the Seine Basin seems to have been relatively uneventful. At all events, the records are inadequate, especially when compared with the richness of material for the late seventeenth century. In the Rhône Basin, the sixteenth century was a period of significant development, and the records have survived practically intact, so that the gradual rise of the wholesale trade can be traced in considerable detail. Then too, the seventeenth century leads to so little that is new that the interest in Lyonese development lies rather in the point of departure than in the final result. Every feature of the Parisian trade carried our attention forward to the creation of the modern market system. Every incident in the history of the trade of Lyons carries us back to medieval conditions.

The specific problems of the grain trade at Lyons were due in great measure to the physical characteristics of the region. The situation of Lyons is truly magnificent, but the nature of the advantages of the location entails disadvantages which have exerted a great influence upon the history of the city. The rough mountainous character of eastern France necessarily gives great prominence to the depression between the Saône and the Jura, which continues for a short distance below the junction of the Rhône and the Saône. The many advantages offered by this strip of fertile plain, in the midst of the numerous ranges of mountains, inevitably created an important settlement at the junction of the rivers, — the point which commanded the whole plain, and in addition possessed the advantage of a good road over the mountains to central France. Lyons was the natural entrepôt for all the trade between Italy or Germany and Central or Northern France. The mountainous character of the region produced a concentration of trade that would not have developed without some such compelling circumstance. The excellence of the site of Lyons is due to this isolation between the Massif Central, the Alps, and the Jura. But despite the brilliant commercial development founded upon this unique position, the permanent welfare of the city could be assured only by some more lasting source of wealth than the Italian trade that was poured into France through Lyons in the sixteenth and seventeenth centuries. The silk trade encouraged manufacturers, and an industrial development began of which the Lyonese had great hopes. But then the disadvantages of the situation of the city became apparent. The configuration of the region hampered industrial development; great concentration of population was impossible because of the limited food supply available in the relatively infertile Rhône Basin.

The available supply of grain was small not only in the immediate vicinity of Lyons, but also in the more distant regions whence grain could be procured without prohibitive cost. The plains near the city are exceedingly narrow. Opposite the city, the foot hills of the Jura are scarcely fifteen miles distant. Below the junction of the rivers, the hills approach more and more closely so that the identity of the plain is soon lost. Above Lyons the plain is wider and extends north up the Saône Valley with little serious interruption, but Lyons could not rely upon that region, since the Saône towns drew their support from the upper reaches of this plain. The rougher districts were hardly more than self-sufficient, and at times they were even dependent upon Lyons. Lyons was thus actually confined to the region within thirty or forty miles of the city. Bresse,

Bugey, and a corner of Dauphiné furnished the excess supply available in the immediate vicinity.

The difficulty of securing abundant supplies in the immediate vicinity led to a determined effort to discover reliable sources of supply elsewhere, but this was no simple matter. Grain could be secured on the Lower Rhône in small quantities, both in Languedoc and in Provence. There was ordinarily a small surplus in Auvergne, in the vicinity of Clermont-Ferrand. A more considerable supply could be found in Burgundy and Bassigny. But each region presented some special difficulty. The swift current of the Rhône made transportation from Languedoc and Provence costly and difficult. The surplus of the Lower Rhône too was not very large, and official opposition combined with these uncertainties to prevent the development of regular trade between Lyons and the Lower Rhône. From Auvergne, transportation was costly, as much of the journey was overland from Roanne to Lyons. Burgundy was the most favorable source of supply, but the principal producing sections were far from the river, and grain was not collected in the river towns until the activity of the Lyonese had started a movement of trade in that direction. These difficulties checked the development of trade. The merchants hesitated to embark in the risky venture of buying grain in Languedoc, Auvergne, or Burgundy, though the Consulate endeavored to encourage private enterprise. These three features are characteristic in the history of the Lyonese trade: scarcity of grain, timidity of the private merchants, municipal participation and stimulation of trade.

The Parisian trade had begun to assume considerable proportions before the records became sufficiently elaborate to furnish any indications of its character. At Lyons there is no such "pre-historic" period. The grain trade first appears in the records in the late fourteenth century, but unlike the *Livre des Métiers* of Étienne Boileau, these documents suggest the utmost simplicity of trade. At Lyons, the earliest material easily available is to be found in the Letters Patent and Letters Close, a much less fruitful source of information than guild statutes. Letters Close were issued in 1386 by the Governor of Dauphiné to the Castellans of Vaulx, Saint-Symphorien-d'Ozon, Pusignan, Mézieux, Colombier, and other places, ordering them to allow the citizens of Lyons to carry off their rents in grain.[1] The right of Lyons to draw supplies from the plain was thus recognized at an early date, despite the complications caused by the provincial boundary. This is the theme of all the early letters. In 1415, the ecclesiastical consistory of Dauphiné was required to authorize inhabitants of Lyons to transport grain from Dauphiné to Lyons. The complaints of the Lyonese were occasioned by the difficulties experienced in carrying to Lyons tithes, cens, and other payments in kind.[2] A couple of years later the subject was canvassed more thoroughly by the Consuls at Lyons and the Governor of Dauphiné. The Consuls asserted that citizens of Lyons were not allowed to bring to the city the rents that accrued in Dauphiné.[3] This narrow limitation of rights is striking, and although it is easy to infer too much from what is left unsaid, it is none the less remarkable that there was no reference to grain merchants or to trade between Dauphiné and Lyons. In 1432, the charter of the Governor of Dauphiné permitted ordinary trade: "the inhabitants of Dauphiné shall be allowed to sell their grain in Lyons, and the inhabitants of Lyons may procure grain in the province."[4] This is clearly the last phase of the struggle to obtain full trading rights in the plain to the east of Lyons. The limits of the region are indicated by the letter of 1386, and although the later measures bear no restriction, it is fairly certain that active trade was limited to the small area between the foot hills of the Jura and the Rhône. The most significant aspect of this episode is the suggestion of a very simply organized trade. The people of Lyons evidently drew most of their grain from the immediate vicinity and much of it was the product of their own estates. Gradually, regular trade with this corner of Dauphiné became necessary. The city was small and the mechanism of the grain

[1] Lyon, Arch. Mun., AA. 78, 18. 10 Dec. 1386. See also AA. 77, 11. 4 Sept. 1379, similar letter by Carolus de Bouillé.

[2] Lyon, Arch. Mun., Chappe IV, 381, 1. 6 Nov. 1415.

[3] *Ibid.*, 381, 2. 1417. Divers Lettres.

[4] *Ibid.*, 381, 4. 21 Sept. 1432.

trade very rudimentary. Probably there were no merchants engaged in bringing grain up or down the river. The market was supplied by the *blatiers* and peasants of the plain. In 1460, we find the first reference to grain markets at Lyons. Prohibitions in Forez led ultimately to Royal Letters Patent addressed to the Bailli of Mâcon and the Sénéchal of Lyons: "Prohibitions have recently been issued in Forez and Beaujolais, so that the merchants and other persons of those provinces have not dared sell their grain to our subjects of Lyons. . . . The merchants and inhabitants of Lyons have consequently been unable to engage in trade with those of Forez and Beaujolais, as they are wont. This has caused the price of grain to rise at Lyons and in Lyonnais. . . . For these reasons we order you to permit all merchants of Lyons and Lyonnais to export from Forez and Beaujolais grain already purchased or to be purchased."[1]

If this was the only evidence to suggest a very simply organized trade, I should hesitate to characterize the first half of the fifteenth century in this manner. Charters are a particularly unreliable basis for conclusions since there is so much chance involved in their preservation. Large numbers have been lost, and there is no reason to infer that the decimation of such material has been governed by anything but blind chance. The charters cited, however, are only a small portion of the material on which inferences may be based, and, where there is so little tangible evidence, it is necessary to read it in connection with evidence of a later period. In the history of the Lyonese grain trade the first important mass of material appears in 1481, as the result of municipal attempts to secure grain. The incident is significant not only in its general character but in its date. It is an indication of the beginning of the rise of Lyons, and helps to explain both the simplicity of organization in the grain trade before 1450 and the energetic efforts of the municipality at the close of the century. The fairs of Lyons were established in 1463; the first important patents to the silk weavers were granted by Louis XI; at that time, the Italians began to come

[1] Lyon, Arch. Mun., Chappe IV, 381, 6. 3 Juin 1460.

in considerable numbers. None of these elements in the commercial growth of Lyons were of great importance in the latter half of the fifteenth century, but all these little facts suggest that this was indeed the period when the great expansion of the city began. The small provincial town was beginning to expand. Development of new sources of food supply had become a pressing question.

In 1481, the Consuls undertook to purchase grain directly; there was scarcely any reference to merchants, and no reference to regular grain merchants. There is no indication that there was any regular trade with distant sections. Apparently this municipal undertaking was a bold pioneer enterprise. It was essentially the work of merchants engaged primarily in other lines of trade. The project was sketched in full at the first meeting that considered the subject. On the fifth of August, 1481, " all the councillors assembled to consider the grain supply, and to prevent the city from suffering any inconvenience. Humbert de Vary was summoned to attend and join in the deliberation. . . . It was finally decided to send to the king in order to get permission to procure grain in Languedoc, Dauphiné, and the Beauce, and if possible to secure exemption from tolls. Furthermore, it was decided to receive in the name of the town such monies as might be subscribed for the purchase of grain. The price should be fixed by the councillors to yield the profit deemed expedient. This done, it was decided to send Taillemand to Moulins on the morrow, as he reported that grain had arrived there. He shall forward grain promptly to the city, and shall also endeavor to discover if grain can be bought in the Beauce. He shall consider whether it would not be well to buy as much as 2000 ânées.[1] One Papillon of Moulins has said that he would be willing to be party to a venture of 1000 francs, if Taillemand would make him a loan, so the latter was asked if he would engage in the venture. He said that he was already in partnership with Papillon." [2] These last lines suggest

[1] The ânée is equivalent to $6\frac{1}{2}$ bushels English measure.

[2] Lyon, Arch. Mun., BB. 352, II, Actes Consulaires. 5 Août 1481. The MS. is difficult, and the reading of the last two lines is somewhat uncertain. The

a mercantile undertaking independent of the project of the consulate, but this is the only reference to distant purchases by private individuals. The proposal to get special Letters Patent from the King led to the specific description of the regions whence supplies were to be derived. The proposal to buy in the Beauce also appeared in the instructions to the agent of the municipality. On the whole, the scheme has the appearance of being the result of deliberations by merchants who think of buying grain, in this time of need, in the provinces to which their trade carries them. The trading connection with Orleans and Paris suggested the Beauce. The frequent trade at the fair of Beaucaire of Avignon suggested purchases in Languedoc. The great distance to which they propose to send indicates a perception of the futility of relying entirely upon the grain in the immediate vicinity of Lyons. Neither the plain to the east of the city, nor the parts of Forez and Beaujolais frequented by the petty merchants, could suffice for the growing needs of the city.

The municipality at first endeavored to direct the purchases itself. Humbert de Vary, who was acting as an agent for the Consuls, bought 1500 ânées of grain at Orleans and other places in that region, early in September. Just as he was ready to have the grain shipped, prohibitions were issued. At this juncture the expediency of securing Royal Patents was revealed. The envoy at the Court reported that the King had issued the Patents desired, and the Consuls at once forwarded the documents to Orleans.[1] But the Consuls found the details of the undertaking burdensome, particularly when the grain had arrived and it became necessary to distribute the municipal supply by selling grain and bread in the small quantities needed by individuals.

These aspects of municipal purchases were probably responsible for the final organization agreed upon at the meeting of October 28th. It was then resolved that the city "would

Archivist kindly revised my transcript. This volume of the registers contains the notes taken during the meetings, and the record is at times influenced by the hurry of note-taking.

[1] Lyon, Arch. Mun., BB. 352, III. 22 Sept. 1481.

entrust the matter to four well-intentioned citizens who were skilled in such affairs. These persons should make the purchases, arrange for the payments, and do all other things that were necessary. In order that the notables who had loaned funds should be protected by a more complete guarantee, the Consuls summoned the wardens of the guilds and other notables." This Assembly agreed to all the propositions of the Consuls, and gave them full authority to establish the commission of four to handle all details of the purchases.[1] "The commissioners purchased large quantities of grain in the name of the town, procuring such supplies that the city and vicinity were maintained in abundance for the greater part of a year in which they would have suffered severely without this aid. . . . Between Christmas 1481 and July 1482, the commissioners distributed about 3300 ânées of grain: 1000 ânées as raw grain, 2300 ânées in the form of bread."[2] The operations of the municipality were, thus, of great importance at the time. Very likely grain had never before been handled at Lyons in such quantities. The Consuls had shown what could be done in the wholesale grain trade, and although their object was primarily to meet immediate needs, the desire to stimulate private effort was doubtless present.

The energy of the consulate seems to have roused the merchants of the city to a realization of the possibilities of the grain trade. The next twenty years were marked by the appearance of wholesale grain merchants. In 1489, there is an interesting indication of the rapidity with which the city was becoming accustomed to dependence upon more distant sources of supply. The bakers complained that the shipments from Burgundy, Dauphiné, and Dombes had been stopped by local prohibitions. They protested against this interference with *long established custom.*[3] Ten years later the merchants were more definitely established. Several merchants offered to supply the city with grain "at six 'blancs' (sic) per ânée above cost," if the city

[1] Lyon, Arch. Mun., BB. 19, 138. 9 Août 1489.
[2] *Ibid.*, Chappe IV, 381, 10.
[3] *Ibid.*, BB. 19, 138. 9 Août 1489.

would guarantee them against loss.[1] The Consuls agreed to this proposition. A year later, there was dearth in Lyonnais, Dauphiné, and Bresse. The Consuls decided to ask permission to export 5–6000 mines from Burgundy. The register is not explicit, but it implies that the grain was to be bought by merchants, although the municipality undertook to obtain the necessary permits.

In these twenty years, the outward aspect of the grain trade was completely transformed. Before 1481, there is no evidence of wholesale trade. The city was supplied by peasants from the plain, and to some extent by small quantities of grain drawn from Forez and Beaujolais. There is nothing to suggest acquaintance with more distant sources of supply, nothing to suggest the presence of wholesale merchants, nothing that could properly be called wholesale trade. In the distress threatening in 1481, the Consuls resolved to make purchases in distant regions. Certain merchants were commissioned to buy grain and manage the undertaking. There was no perception of the best sources of supply, but large quantities of grain were bought primarily in the Beauce and in Auvergne. Then the merchants turned their attention to the grain trade. In 1489, dependence upon Burgundy was declared to be an "immemorial" custom. The merchants who had thus extended the scope of the Lyonese food supply, however, were probably not professional grain merchants. The venture in grain may well have been an incident among other transactions. But wholesale dealing in grain had begun and there was some knowledge of the regions where grain could be found.

In 1500, the fear of dearth led to the organization of a Bureau to buy grain on account of the municipality. This measure was taken in December and the experience of 1481 was evidently still fresh in the minds of the Consuls. Four persons were named "to act as bursars and to act as sureties for the sums subscribed." Two of the persons named failed to appear on the following day to accept the office, and after a short interval their places were filled.[2] There was thus a commission with

[1] Lyon, Arch. Mun., BB. 24, 176. 3 Août 1498.

[2] *Ibid.*, BB. 24, 289, 290, 298. 18, 19 Dec. 1500; 15 Fev. 1500–01.

practically the same powers as the commission of 1481, but the presence of a body of wholesale grain merchants altered the situation fundamentally. The municipal Bureau could not proceed with the complete independence that was not only possible but necessary in 1481. The merchants rendered direct purchases by the commissioners less necessary, and the municipality scarcely needed to do more than procure Letters Patent from the King. This step indeed had been taken before the commission of four was chosen. The King was asked to grant patents for the export of grain from Burgundy, Bassigny, Champagne, Franche Comté, Languedoc, and Provence — a most comprehensive catalogue of all the possible sources of supply.[1] The Patents arrived at Lyons early in January, and then there was a most interesting recognition of the changed conditions of the grain trade. "To proceed to the execution of the said Patents, the Consuls summoned the *principal merchants, who are accustomed to buy grain in the Duchy of Burgundy, Bassigny, Champagne, and the County of Burgundy.*" Then the various merchants were asked what amounts of grain they would agree to buy. "Pierre Prestreau offered to bring 100 charges of grain to Lyons. Thibaut Canis said he would buy 500 charges in Burgundy. Jehan Combe, a baker, offered to secure 500 charges in Bassigny." "Benoit Panthier agreed to bring 300 ânées from Burgundy within a month, and 300 more before Easter."[2] When the merchants made agreements of this type, the city issued passports to them addressed to the officials of the producing regions. The activity and number of merchants seems to indicate a remarkable rapidity of development.

Despite the complications introduced by the presence of merchants, the municipal commission made purchases in the name of the town. February ninth, the Consuls ordered "that Pierre Renard should send a trustworthy man to Roanne, on the morrow, to find out how much grain there was in that town,

[1] Lyon, Arch. Mun., BB. 24, 288. 11 Dec. 1500.

[2] *Ibid.*, BB. 24, 292. 5 Jan. 1500–01, and 19 Jan. Quarnet et Papier fait pour tenir raison de la traicte des Bleds que le Roy a octroyée à la Ville. See also the deliberations of the Consuls, 7–8 Jan., p. 293.

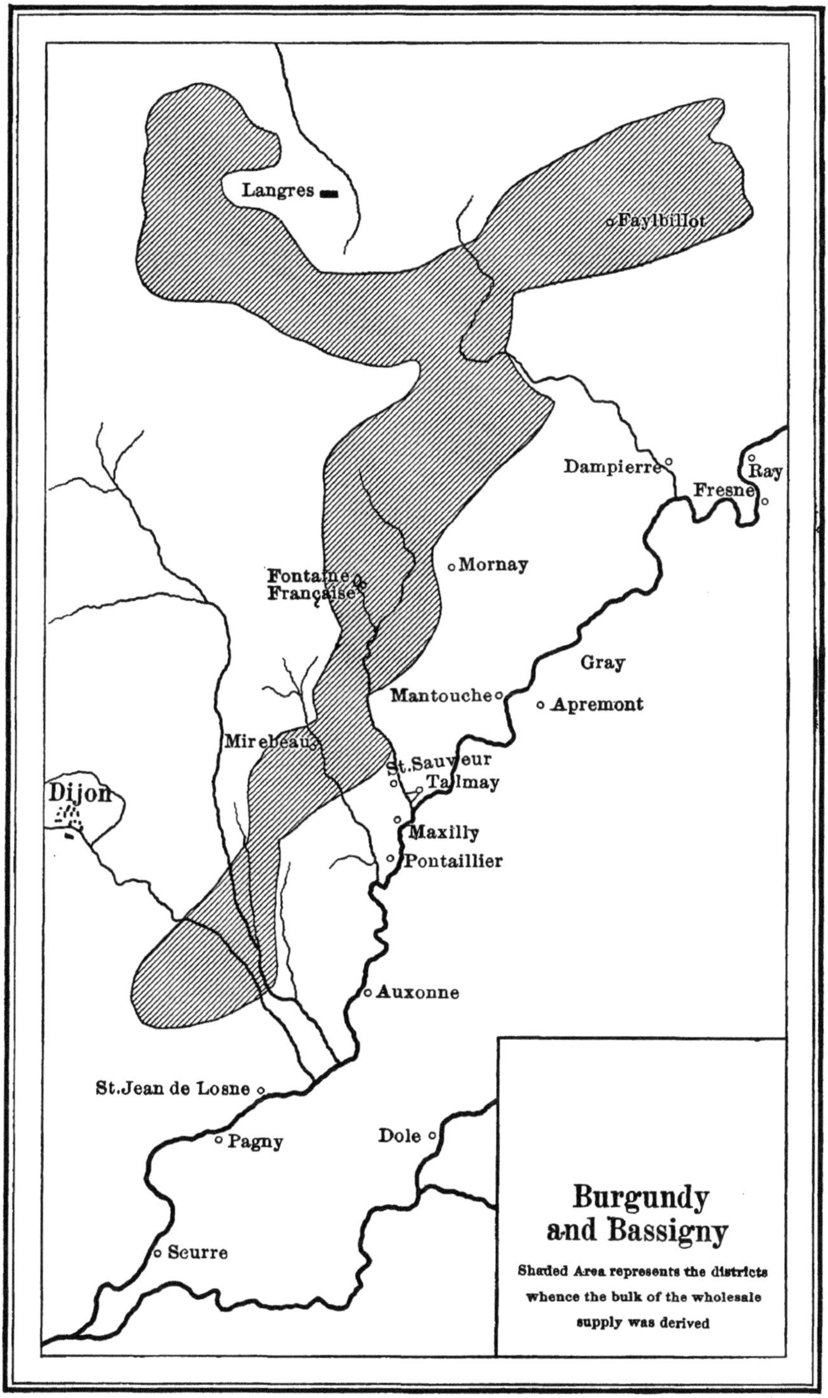

Langres
Faylbillot
Dampierre
Ray
Fresne
Mornay
Fontaine Française
Gray
Mantouche
Apremont
Mirebeau
St.Sauveur
Talmay
Dijon
Maxilly
Pontaillier
Auxonne
St.Jean de Losne
Pagny
Dole
Seurre
Burgundy and Bassigny
Shaded Area represents the districts whence the bulk of the wholesale supply was derived

and to buy 400 ânées at any price that it is necessary to pay."[1] A week later, Pierre Renard was ordered "to go to Burgundy to buy grain in the name of the town."[2] He was instructed to buy freely according to his judgment. The Consuls also had grain purchased in Languedoc. The agent in that section, however, interpreted his instructions too liberally, buying 3000 ânées at a cost of 12,000 francs. The Consuls were unable to furnish this sum, so the grain was turned over to one of the merchants.[3] Other contracts in Languedoc and Provence to the amount of 1600 écus (4800 francs) were accepted by the Consuls. The function of the four commissioners is not very clear. Their commission had given them full authority, but the Consuls retained the control of the grain trade. The organization of the commission had followed the precedent of 1481, but the difference in conditions was soon perceived, and the Consuls found that they could easily attend to all the details of the trade. In July, 1504, a commission of six persons was organized "to procure a fund of 10,000 francs, to send to court and to the Governor of Burgundy to secure Patents for the export of grain."[4] This commission did not make any direct purchases, but contracts were made with merchants to guarantee them against losses due to a fall in prices.[5] The municipal efforts were not important, and the merchants were left to their own devices. In reality, municipal trading of the type that appeared in 1481 was obsolete even in 1500, and the increased activity shown by the merchants rendered encouragement superfluous. It seemed as if the stimulus given the wholesale trade had been so completely successful that the municipality could cease to concern itself with that matter.

But there was still a need for some encouragement and control. The merchants were only too willing to receive aid, and guarantees against loss and passports could advantageously be offered to merchants who were willing to undertake the trade. The

[1] Lyon, Arch. Mun., BB. 24. 9 Fev. 1500–01.
[2] *Ibid.*, BB. 24. 17 Fev. 1500–01.
[3] *Ibid.*, BB. 24 (304). 15 Mars 1500–01.
[4] *Ibid.*, BB. 24, 466. 29 Juillet 1504.
[5] *Ibid.*, BB. 24, 466v. 12 Août 1504.

years 1500–1504 had witnessed the opening up of great prospects. The trade awoke to a full consciousness of all the sources of supply, and no region was too distant to tempt the merchants. Languedoc, Provence, Beauce, Burgundy, Bassigny, Champagne, Franche Comté, all held out hopes to the Lyonese. But this extraordinary extension of the trade was not permanent. The merchants possessed a very inadequate knowledge of the relative advantages or the extent of the supply available in these regions, and hopes of great gains faded gradually before the obstacles that were revealed by bitter experience. But a full knowledge of conditions in the producing regions was gradually obtained.

This resort to the distant regions of the Rhône Basin was probably irregular during the early sixteenth century. Supplies were ordinarily secured nearer the city, but in case of need merchants were ready to buy in Burgundy or Languedoc. The first fifty years of the century are interesting by reason of the gradual development of regular dependence upon Burgundy. The regions near the city were still utilized in part, particularly the plains of Dauphiné and Bresse. But while the other sections gradually lost their importance, the wholesale merchants turned their attention more and more definitely towards Burgundy. The trade developed a distinct organization in the Saône towns, and with the gradual improvement of the system of marketing, the resources of Burgundy became steadily more available. In 1529, Burgundy was not mentioned in the sources of supply enumerated by the witnesses examined by the Governor of Lyonnais, to discover the cause of the high price of grain. "The high prices are due," they said, "to the prohibitions which have been issued in the neighboring provinces, Dombes, Beaujolais, Forez, Vivarais, Auvergne, and Velay, which generally supply Lyons. Grain is generally brought from these provinces to Lyons, but none has come recently on account of the prohibitions."[1] Merchants were busy in Burgundy, but they were not buying for Lyons, and it is hardly likely that they were

[1] Lyon, Arch. Mun., Chappe IV, 381. 21 Oct. 1529. Procès Verbal fait à Lyon par Pomponne de Trevoux, Gouverneur ez Pais de Lyonnais.

Lyonese. In February, 1527, Genoa purchased 1500 mines of grain in Burgundy.[1] A month later the Consuls permitted the Commander of the Knights of Saint John to carry 164 ânées of grain down the river from Burgundy.[2] A year later the Consuls were disturbed by the quantities of grain passing the city, so they sent a deputy to the Governor of Burgundy asking him to require the merchants to leave one-third of their grain at Lyons.[3] This proposal seemed to meet with little success for in May the same fears appear in the deliberations. Jehan Charreton asked for permission to carry 700 mines of grain down the river. He said that it was purchased in Burgundy and Champagne, and that it was destined for the Grand Master of Rhodes. It is pretty clear that the Consuls disliked to issue the permit, but Charreton exhibited Royal Patents and they dared not interfere.[4] The general question was discussed for a while but no decision was reached. A week later, a merchant from Provence came down the Saône with 1200 ânées of grain destined for Arles. He had Royal Patents, but the Consuls persuaded him to sell part of his grain at Lyons.[5] The shipments from Burgundy to the lower river were possibly heavier than usual in 1528, but it was not an infrequent phenomenon [6] and it does not suggest an explanation of the omission of Burgundy from the list of sources of Lyonese supply. Lyons was able to do without Burgundian supplies in ordinary years, and the Burgundian surplus was disposed of elsewhere.

The slow development of Lyonese trade in Burgundy was primarily due to two factors, the slow growth of the demand of Lyons and the difficulties of trading in Burgundy. Of the two, the absence of organization in the producing region was undoubtedly the more important, for the moment that facilities be-

[1] Lyon, Arch. Mun., Chappe IV, 381, 17. 15 Fev. 1527.

[2] *Ibid.*, Chappe IV, 381, 17 bis. 15 Mars 1527.

[3] *Ibid.*, BB. 47, 15. 30 Avril 1528.

[4] *Ibid.*, BB. 47, 16. 7 Mai 1528. Chappe IV, 460, 3. The Royal Patents mentioned in the registers.

[5] *Ibid.*, BB. 47, 19. 14 Mai 1528.

[6] *Ibid.*, Chappe IV, 393, 33. 16 Fev. 1539. Dijon, Arch. Mun., G. 256. 24 Jan. 1539–40.

came greater in Burgundy the less favorable sources in Auvergne and Velay would be abandoned. It was not essential that the demand of Lyons should greatly increase. The advantage of trading with Burgundy was not only a matter of quantity but also a matter of transportation to Lyons. These basic factors, however, were of little avail in the early sixteenth century, as the grain was not collected in Burgundy with reference to the Lyonese trade. It was not easy to find, and the most fertile regions were far from the Saône, so that even when the merchant had secured his grain, he must needs arrange for land transportation in a province where he was not familiar with the routes or the carters.

From the point of view of the Lyonese, the most serious difficulty was the absence of any considerable supplies in the river towns. It is hazardous to assert that there was, at that time, no movement from the back country to Auxonne, Maxilly, and Saint-Jean-de-Losne, but it is quite certain that such movements were inconsiderable. In 1505, the Échevins of Dijon mentioned a rumor "that several carters had passed carrying grain to the Saône."[1] The next day they issued an order to pay a gratuity to a peasant who informed the proper officials that grain was passing (Axsery) on carts toward Saint-Jean-de-Losne.[2] In 1509, the implication was less direct. The Échevins complained of high prices, of markets that were inadequately furnished; all the troubles were attributed to the export of grain from the vicinity under the cover of darkness.[3] In 1531, granaries are mentioned at Auxonne, but they were based on the revenues of estates.[4] The towns were used as shipping ports, but the merchants were obliged to buy in the back country. Thus, in 1529, the Mayor of Dijon induces one of the Lyonese merchants to sell one-half the grain collected at Saint-Pierre-de-Massilly. "The Lyonese merchants, who were two in number, said that they had only 100 mines of grain, which they

[1] Dijon, Arch. Mun., G. 258. 12 Juin 1505.
[2] *Ibid.*, G. 258. 13 Juin 1505.
[3] *Ibid.*, G. 258. 1509. Mémoire contre la Chereté.
[4] *Ibid.*, G. 260. 27 Mai 1531; 3 Jan. 1532.

had bought in divers places — Lorraine, Champagne, and elsewhere."[1]

In reality the Burgundian trade was very loosely organized at this time. Dijon and Langres were the only towns where there was much trade in grain. There were merchants in both places, but even in these towns the wholesale trade was largely a matter of sales in the granaries of the landlords.

The local merchants of Burgundy were essentially merchants of the earlier type, persons buying on the local market, hoarding, and selling when prices rose. They engaged in the movement of grain only to a slight degree, although they did buy in country granaries. The Échevins of Dijon mention such merchants in 1509. "There are several wealthy merchants here engaged in engrossing, despite the ordinances."[2] In 1539, the Lieutenant of the Bailli of Dijon issued an ordinance against "merchants and other persons who go daily to the market towns, where they buy grain and form granaries."[3] The Lieutenant of the Governor also took measures against merchants, "who have bought grain in the markets in order to form hoards. . . . or who have bought or given earnest money for the grain of nobles or of other persons." He ordered that any grain in excess of private needs should be straightway sold on the public market.[4] The scale of the operations of these merchants of Dijon is not very clear, but the information about the merchants of Langres gives some idea of the magnitude of their business. We have this note of a single transaction: "Jehan Gastebois, merchant resident at Langres, acknowledges the receipt of 2172^{ll} from the agents of Dijon, in consideration of divers consignments of grain, viz: — 120 mines @ $6^{ll}\ 5^{s}$; 160 mines bought by them of me and of Nicholas Hendelot, merchant at Langres" etc.[5] The merchants of Langres probably secured

[1] Dijon, Arch. Mun., G. 258. 11 Mai 1529.

[2] *Ibid.*, G. 258. 1509. Mémoire sur les Bleds.

[3] *Ibid.*, G. 256. 15 Jan. 1539. Ord. du Lieu. du Bailli de Dijon.

[4] *Ibid.*, G. 264. 14 Mai 1539. Copie d'une Ordonnance du Lieu. du Gouverneur. See also G. 256. 1, 18, 22 Oct. 1535. Ord. du Lieu. du Bailli de Dijon.

[5] *Ibid.*, G. 263. 26 Juillet 1532. G. 263. Compte des Bleds achetés pour la Ville de Dijon suivant l'Ordon, du 17 Mars 1531–32.

their grain by purchases on the markets and in country granaries. The merchants at Dijon doubtless handled quite as large a trade as the merchants of Langres. On the whole, it is not too much to assert that we find at this time the beginnings of the local wholesale trade.

The merchants, however, controlled only a part of the trade. The granaries of *rentiers* were probably a more important factor than the granaries formed by merchants. These hoards formed of rents in kind were not necessarily located in the towns. In many cases, the grain was stored at least temporarily in the country. The significance of this form of hoard is not much influenced by its location, though it was naturally much easier to deal with the persons who had town granaries.

The extent of these granaries was revealed by the efforts of the Échevins of Dijon to secure supplies in times of distress, Visitation of granaries was the most obvious and most successful provision against dearth. This was the first step taken in 1529. The Échevins decided that "it was necessary to know who had granaries in the town and in the country." It was proposed to buy grain in the name of the town, and without any inquiry "they resolved to speak to M. de Firloix, Madame d'Agen, M. Joigny, Maître Gerard Benigny, factor of the Admiral, Sr. Valrien, Thomas Mathus, M. des Barres, Antoine C — (?) and MM. de Saint Esleu (?), all of whom are said to have granaries in the town."[1] These were the people whose granaries were so well known that it was a matter of common knowledge. The next day other granaries were reported, notably those of Mlle. de Maillotz, who had 60 mines at Dijon, and 60 mines at Chevigny.[2] In June, one of the Échevins reported that he had purchased grain in the granaries of the Admiral at Mirabel, Beaumont, Charmes, Rouvre, and Fontaine-Française.[3] Other granaries were mentioned.[4] In 1531, it was the same story, though there was more buying at Langres and the importance

[1] Dijon, Arch. Mun., G. 258. 26 Avril 1529.

[2] *Ibid.*, G. 258. 27 Avril 1529. The names are difficult to read.

[3] *Ibid.*, G. 258. 7 Mai 1528; 19 Juin 1529.

[4] *Ibid.*, G. 259. Compte des Bleds achetés en 1529.

of the clerical granaries was emphasized. The memoir mentions only the quantities that are still to be shipped, but even these are considerable. From the Dean of Langres, 60 mines were to be received; from M. l'Official of Langres, 40 mines; from M. André Bobinet, prebend, 18 mines; 50 mines at Givey in Montagne were still to be paid to the Dean of Langres." [1] Lay granaries were visited at Rouvre, Breteniers, Thorey, Saulon, La Chapelle,[2] Montigny,[3] and Vauldrimont.[4] Another interesting phase of the purchases made by Dijon in 1531, was the buying of grain that was stored in the villages of Bassigny by merchants of Langres: 61 mines were bought of Jacques Benné, merchant at Langres, to be delivered at Cogirnon near Chalindrey in Bassigny. Other merchants of Langres agreed to deliver grain at Chassigney, Prangey, Chaume, Mormand, Troichaud, Rozet, Trouchoit, Monteycourt, Bellême, and Saint-Maurice.[5] Most of these little places can hardly be identified today, but it is necessary to call attention to the extent of this practice. The grain was very slightly concentrated. Despite the appearance of merchants at Dijon and Langres, the grain remained in the villages until it was hunted out by the merchants or until the absentee landlord decided to sell the accumulated rents of his estates. There was little or no movement of grain. It required a great effort to amass any considerable quantity, and if it were not for the size of some of the granaries, it would have been well-nigh impossible to collect a large quantity. The resources of the province were great, but they could not be easily utilized because of the absence of organization of the wholesale trade.

When the Lyonese merchants first came to Burgundy they generally went to Dijon, but the municipal officials disliked to see them buying in the vicinity, and there were various ways of passing them on to other regions. Even the agents of Dijon

[1] Dijon, Arch. Mun., G. 258. Mémoires des Restes des grains qui sont à venir des achapts faits par la Ville de Dijon depuis le carême derrenier passé. 1531.

[2] *Ibid.*, G. 261. 9 Fev. 1531.

[3] *Ibid.*, G. 260. 3 Juin 1531.

[4] *Ibid.*, G. 260. Pentecôte, 1531.

[5] *Ibid.*, G. 263. Compte des Bleds achetés pour la Ville de Dijon suivant l'Ordonnance du 17 Mars 1531–32.

at court endeavored to dissuade the Lyonese from attempting to buy in Burgundy. "Much better terms could be made with the merchants of Champagne and Bassigny," they said.[1] This unwillingness to encourage purchases around Dijon undoubtedly added to the difficulties of the Lyonese. Supplies were unquestionably to be had in Bassigny, but transportation was difficult and the trade in Bassigny was not concentrated even to the degree that the trade of Burgundy was concentrated at Dijon. In these conditions, we have the explanation of the slow development of Lyonese trade in Burgundy. The trade had too little connection with the Saône towns; the importance of local and town granaries made it difficult for a stranger to engage in the trade; the jealous regard of Dijon for the supplies of Burgundy generally obliged the merchants to push on to Bassigny where all the difficulties were increased.

Despite the obstacles in the way of regular trade, the Lyonese merchants travelled up to Burgundy in continually increasing numbers, so that in 1557 Burgundy was called "the nurse of Lyons and Lyonnais."[2] It was at this period that the influence of this persistent buying began to appear. The gradual development of trade with Lyons attracted trade to the Saône towns, and in 1556 the transition, which ultimately produced a complete reorganization of trade in Burgundy, was well under way. Dijon and Langres lost much of their importance, and Auxonne, Talmay, Maxilly, and Saint-Jean-de-Losne became the centers of an active trade drawing from Burgundy and Bassigny for the support of Lyons.

Our information, in 1556–57, is derived from letters written by the Deputies sent to Burgundy by the Consuls of Lyons. The first letter indicates nothing new. They were shipping grain at Auxonne and visiting granaries in Burgundy, Bassigny, Lorraine, and Franche Comté.[3] In the letters of the following

[1] Lyon, Arch. Mun., AA. 101, 12. Paris, 15 Jan. 1528–29. Laurencin.

[2] *Ibid.*, Chappe IV, 339–340. Procès verbal faite par Mre. Jehan de Fournel. Conseiller du Roy, Lieut. Gen. en la sénéchaussée et siège présidiale de Lyon, 10 Fev. 1556–57.

[3] *Ibid.*, AA. 32. Auxonne, 27 Mars 1556. Guimbre.

year indications of change appear. There are references to merchants resident in the river towns. This addition to the trade from Bassigny to the Saône caused a pressure upon means of transportation that enabled the carters to charge two or three times the ordinary rates. "There is a rumor in these parts," writes the Deputy, "that Dutenot, Craignat, and Mascoyer are going to ship more than 3,000 mines of grain. The merchants of Auxonne and Guillaume Imbellot of Châlons-sur-Saône have also shipped great quantities."[1] "The carters are so persistently sought out by these merchants of Auxonne, Dijon, Beaune, and Châlons that it almost impossible to get hold of any."[2] "Mascoyer and Oudelot sent out three men to find carters, but the best they could do was to secure a promise of twelve or thirteen next week, and if Oudelot were not Capitan of the carters of the Commissariat he would not have been able to compass more. His position enabled him to secure others, and the shipment of the grain has begun."[3] "The carters have at last banded together after having been beaten by the agents of Mascoyer, as well as by those of Dutenot and Arginot, and by the agents of the merchants of Auxonne and Beaune. The carters now ask forty sous for what they used to do for fifteen sous, and for the trip from Bassigny which formerly gave them 35 sous, they now ask 3^{ll} 15 sous (75 sous)."[4] The trade was rapidly losing the apathy of the earlier period, and it was beginning to move to the Saône towns to meet the Lyonese merchants.

The development of the trade of the river towns proceeded steadily and in 1581 there were active merchants in all the more important towns, collecting grain to sell to the Lyonese. It is unfortunately impossible to trace the details of the transition, but the general fact of the change is indicated by the correspondence between the officials of the Saône towns and Lyons. It is in itself significant that there was enough trade to engender

[1] Lyon, Arch. Mun., AA. 32. Langres, 26 Mars 1556–57.

[2] *Ibid.*, Letter of 22 Avril 1557.

[3] *Ibid.*, Letter of 26 Mars.

[4] *Ibid.*, AA. 32. 3 Avril 1556–57.

such correspondence, and the letters are so explicit that it is impossible to escape the conclusion. In January 1581, the Échevins of Auxonne write to the Consuls of Lyons: "The merchants of this town who are engaged in trade with Lyons make complaints of the conduct of a collector who wishes to levy 'Coupenage' on the grain sent to Lyons. . . . You will find that this is important, as it will increase the cost of grain, and some merchants may lose interest in the trade."[1] Later in the same month, "the merchants of Mâcon assembled with the merchants of the Duchy of Burgundy, the Vicomté of Auxonne, and of Bassigny, to secure relief from the extortions of the Reverend Archbishop of Lyons, who asserts a right to levy 'coupenage.'"[2] There are similar complaints from Châlons-sur-Saône.[3] In 1589 a hoard was purchased by Sr. d'Acier of Auxonne and other merchants who were associated with him.[4] The first step in the organization of the wholesale trade had been taken; local merchants had begun to collect grain at the shipping ports on the river.

The municipality exerted an important influence upon this development of the wholesale trade, since the difficulties of marketing in Burgundy, the hesitation between the different sources of supply, the fear of loss, all tended to discourage the merchants. Throughout the century the municipality was constantly assisting and stimulating the merchants.

The most direct form of assistance needed by the merchants was protection against the prohibitions issued by the local officials of the producing regions. This task the municipality discharged easily. There was generally a deputy at the Court, who could at any time secure Royal Patents to cancel the prohibitions issued by the Governors, provincial parlements, or municipalities. Deputies were also sent to the producing regions to secure the repeal or modification of prohibitions, or to assure the execution of the Royal Patents and of the licenses

[1] Lyon, Arch. Mun., AA. 70, 32. Auxonne, 15 Jan. 1581.
[2] *Ibid.*, AA. 72, 35. Macon, 21 Jan. 1581.
[3] *Ibid.*, AA. 70, 91. Châlons, 19 Jan. 1581.
[4] *Ibid.*, AA. 29. Paigny, 5 Nov. 1589. Charny.

issued by the Consuls on the authority of the royal letters. All these forms of control must needs be exercised by the Consuls themselves. There could be no question of creating a Chambre d'Abondance after the plan of 1481.

The great risks of the trade were a more serious difficulty, and did much to deter the extension of private enterprise. This was important even in ordinary seasons when the merchants were trading in Burgundy. In years of dearth, the consequences of this timidity of the merchants furnished more ground for apprehensions. At such times, the Consuls felt that it was necessary to stimulate trade from all possible sources of supply, encouraging buying not only in Burgundy but also in Auvergne and in Languedoc. The risk of such ventures was enhanced by the infrequency of trade, and the actual risk was magnified by ignorance. Conditions in Languedoc in 1529 are typical. Claude de Bourges had been sent to Avignon by the Consuls to stimulate the local merchants, and to buy for the city. He found grain in plenty. The Legate "addressed him to three merchants, M. de Lers, who had about 1000 setiers of wheat, Maître Moreton, steward of my Lord the Legate, who had 1200 setiers, and Sr. Honnorat Plonyer. In all there were 3000 ânées, located near the river, conveniently for shipment.... If prices were high enough, he says, there are plenty of persons who would be willing to send grain up to Lyons. I know half a dozen already, who will ship if they are guaranteed against losses."[1] At Romans, the Maître de le Monnaye tells him that there is plenty of grain, but that it is dear. If trade were free, it would perhaps be possible to buy advantageously, but the merchants will not send grain up to Lyons at the risk of selling at the same price there.[2] At Valence, he found a man who would send grain up to Lyons, if he were guaranteed the price of twenty-eight sous per bichet.[3] There is no evidence that such contracts were made in that particular instance, but such guarantees were freely given by the Consuls. The contracts

[1] Lyon, Arch. Mun., AA. 29. Avignon, 6 Nov. 1529. Claude de Bourges.

[2] *Ibid.* Valence, 26 Oct. 1529. Claude de Bourges.

[3] *Ibid.* Valence, 12 Nov. 1529. Claude de Bourges.

were made and enforced to the letter. In 1544, such an agreement had been made with Étienne Tremblay of Charlieu, who engaged to bring 600 ânées to Lyons from the Beauce. He complained that he had been able to sell only 40 ânées before prices fell, and he claimed reimbursement. The Consuls refused to pay. They declared that he had not kept any of the articles of the contract. The grain had not reached Lyons within the time specified, and he had refused to sell either at the price agreed upon, or at the current price.[1] Somewhat later, the Consuls summoned Robert Tricaut, and asked him if he would go to the Beauce to bring grain to Lyons. They agreed to guarantee a price of twenty-four sous per bichet,[2] but Tricaut refused, and the Consuls finally decided to send him "to Orleans and other places on the road where grain merchants are to be found." He was instructed to secure promises from merchants to bring grain to Lyons, and guarantee them 24–26 sous per bichet at least, and if prices were higher the merchants were to have the surplus.[3] In 1573, the Consuls adopted even more vigorous measures. "Claude Platt, André Mornier, Claude Belleton, François Lobat, and Benoit Montcony were ordered to purchase 1000 ânées of grain for the provision of the city, to prevent the people from suffering want at the end of the season. The merchants replied that they were willing to make the purchases and that they would give their time and use their credit to the best of their ability, but they did not think that the loss should fall on them if the grain were shipwrecked or sold below cost, or if they lost any of the specie which they must needs send to Burgundy." The Consuls agreed to guarantee the merchants against loss.[4] This case was rather involved as the merchants were themselves Consuls, and were thus guaranteeing private ventures with the authority of the town. It indicates the opportunity for transactions that were perhaps of doubtful

[1] Lyon, Arch. Mun., BB. 61, 270. 9 Avril 1543–44. See also BB. 61, 234. 3 Mars 1543–44.

[2] *Ibid.*, BB. 61, 237. 10 Mars 1543–44. Note also of a similar contract with Antoine Bouyn.

[3] *Ibid.*, BB. 61, 240. 14 Mars 1543–44.

[4] *Ibid.*, BB. 91, 52. 17 Fev. 1573.

ethical character. In the same year, an agent was sent to "Dauphiné and Avignon to discover how much grain was available for export to Lyons, and to assure the merchants that the Consulate would guarantee them against loss."[1] Later a premium of two sous per bichet was offered to all "foreign" merchants who brought grain to Lyons during the months of April, May, and June.[2] This type of encouragement may fairly be characterized as an established policy. Such powers must necessarily be exercised by the Consuls themselves. It was not a task to be delegated to a subordinate commission.

But when the Consuls endeavored to extend their activity beyond these limits, when they purchased grain instead of encouraging the merchants, the difficulties multiplied out of all proportion to the results. Direct municipal purchases were made in 1528–29, 1530, 1532, 1544, 1573, and 1580, but the administration of the affair was always hopelessly involved. In 1528, the purchases were not large, but the grain had to be forced on the bakers at the end of the season at a distinct sacrifice, as it had been held too long. A list of the bakers was drawn up and each assigned a fixed amount of grain, which they were required to buy weekly of the Consuls at twelve sous five deniers per bichet. They were ordered to use no other grain while the ordinance was in force.[3] The bakers were bitterly opposed to this action as the price was high. They refused to take the amounts assigned, or, in some cases, took the grain but refused to pay the price, delaying payment indefinitely. All these troubles meant loss to the municipality, and cast discredit on municipal purchases. In 1573, the Consuls ordered the distribution of 100 ânées per week to the bakers, and this time there was less trouble.[4] In 1580, the grain had to be forced on the bakers by measures which caused much ill feeling. The bakers complained of the prices charged for the grain, and of the prices

[1] Lyon, Arch. Mun., BB. 91, 83. 8 Mai 1573.
[2] *Ibid.*, BB. 91, 105. 7 Juillet 1573.
[3] *Ibid.*, BB. 47 & 71. 28 Mai 1528.
[4] *Ibid.*, BB. 91, 87. 19 Mai 1573.

at which they were allowed to sell their bread. Some refused to take the grain.[1]

Another mode of assuring the city against the irregularities of trade was the control of a private granary secured by reason of special favors or by a direct contract. In September 1559, one Tipperaus "offered to store 2000 ânées of grain in the city to be sold at such times, previous to the Saint-Jean, 1560, as shall please the Consuls. In consideration of this agreement, the said Tipperaus was paid fifteen sous per bichet."[2] A more elaborate contract of the same type was made in October of the same year: "Claude Tisserand, merchant and citizen of Lyons, promises to secure and place in granaries before Christmas 2000 ânées of grain which shall be stored at his expense and risk until the Saint-Jean following. He agrees further to sell said grain to the inhabitants of Lyons as the Consuls shall direct, with the understanding that he shall sell at one sou less than the market price if the current price exceeds eighteen sous per bichet, and that in case the price falls below fifteen sous six deniers per bichet, the Consuls will be liable for the difference between the current rate and fifteen sous six deniers."[3]

The policy of the Consuls during this period of growth was a policy of encouragement of private initiative, and of supplementary purchases on the credit of the town. The wisdom of encouragement can hardly be questioned; the trade was in such a condition that the hope of gain was pretty evenly balanced by the risk of loss. Legal obstacles contributed to dissuade the merchants. These troubles could be adequately met by the Consuls directly; the ordinary organization of the city was able to deal with all questions which arose in the fulfilment of this aspect of municipal policy. But the Consuls were never content to stop at this point. The wholesale trade, even with the encouragement of the municipal guarantees, tended to fall below

[1] Lyon, Arch. Mun., BB. 105, 66. 12 Avril 1585. Also GG. Chappe IV, 481. Comptes de 1573. *Ibid.*, BB. 117, 111. 15 Avril 1586.

[2] *Ibid.*, BB. 81, 196. 7 Sept. 1559.

[3] *Ibid.*, BB. 81, 205. 5 Oct. 1559.

the amount required to keep prices within comfortable limits in periods of stress. The Consuls were constantly seeking to reduce prices below the level which the merchants judged necessary to assure a fair hope of profit. To accomplish this purpose, the Consuls were obliged to undertake ventures which were almost certain to involve loss. They placed on the market quantities of grain which lowered prices below the actual cost of the grain.

The expediency of this policy was never very seriously questioned. Criticism was levelled at the details of administration rather than against the policy. At times, there were accusations of fraud. In the period from 1500 to 1580, municipal purchases were not large, but as the community became convinced that some purchases of this sort were desirable, it became equally certain that the Consuls could not advantageously administer the undertaking themselves. At no time between 1504 and 1586 was a commission actually established, as in 1481, 1500, and 1504, but in one way or another it just missed being established. The rise of the wholesale merchants made direct purchases less necessary than they had been in 1481, and the importance of the Consulate in affording encouragement to the merchants tended to put everything related to the trade in the hands of the Consuls. Then, too, there was an unwillingness to recognize the necessity of direct purchases by the municipality. The Consuls were ever hoping to render the private trade wholly adequate. But the experience of the sixteenth century demonstrated both the necessity of some regular purchases by the municipality with the expectation of some loss and the necessity of some subsidiary commission to manage this undertaking.

The idea of a definite and independent Chambre d'Abondance appeared throughout the century, but it was not carried out until the necessity of some regular municipal trade was recognized. The early plans were not adopted because the Consuls could not persuade themselves that direct purchases were more than a temporary expedient of such exceptional character as to make the special machinery of a Commission unnecessary.

In 1528, the first year of serious trouble after 1504, the larger outlines of a Chambre were sketched. "M. Champyer . . . thought that all should contribute a quantity of grain proportionate to their means, so that the poor people should not lack. Four persons should be elected to take charge of the affair. They should be given the list of contributors." The other persons present were of the same opinion, and the Consuls went so far as to draw up a list of contributions, but the commission was not heard from.[1] This Bureau would have been a much less important commission than that of 1481, but it was not unlike that of 1504. Purchases were made by the municipality in 1528, and the mode in which they were made suggests a probable explanation of the view that no special Commission was necessary or desirable. Claude de Bourges, the agent in Languedoc, was sent thither to stimulate private trade by assurances against risk or by promise of definite prices. His purchases for the municipality were certainly only an incident in his commission, and it is quite possible that they were made only when he found it excessively difficult to stimulate individual initiative. He says, indeed, in the letter of November 6: "I declared to the Legate the cause of my journey, . . . the permission to export grain from Languedoc." [2] Similar implications appear in the letter of October 26, from Valence. Evidently the Consuls had hoped that the trade would flow towards Lyons once the prohibitions were cancelled and the merchants excited by the expectation of good prices. This aspect of the policy of the Consuls is more directly revealed by reports of Guimbre, the agent in Burgundy. In April, the Consuls hear that "the merchants of Auxonne and others who have grain complain that their grain cannot be sold, or at any rate has a very small sale on account of the prohibitions." Guimbre writes that the merchants of Burgundy dare not send their grain down to Lyons on account of the prohibitions.[3] Rumors and statements of this type inevitably led the Consuls to attach an exaggerated impor-

[1] Lyon, Arch. Mun., BB. 47, 165. 8 Dec. 1528.
[2] *Ibid.*, AA. 29. Avignon, 6 Nov. 1528.
[3] *Ibid.*, BB. 47, 224. 5 Avril 1529.

tance to the prohibitions. They were slow to learn that there were many other causes which tended to make the wholesale trade less considerable than they hoped. Direct purchases were, in many cases, if not regularly, a last resort, a mode of procuring supplies that was adopted only when the agents had failed to stimulate the local merchants to make shipments.

In 1544, we have some of the commissions of the deputies of the town. They were probably given much the same powers as the deputies of 1528. Antoine Bouyn was sent to Languedoc, Décapelle to Beauce, Charollais, Nivernais, and Bourbonnais, Janot and Guillaume du Mont of Seurre, to Forez and Auvergne. All the commissions were at first drawn up in the same terms: "we have given and give power and authority to . . . to proceed to . . . (Languedoc) . . . and other suitable places to take up grain, and make contracts and agreements with the merchants and other persons to the effect that grain shall be sent to Lyons, in such quantities as he shall deem proper. For the assurance of the price and purchase of the grain, he shall have authority to contract liabilities binding upon us as councillors, and upon the property of the town, and if he judges it expedient he may contract liabilities binding upon us as private individuals and upon our property."[1] The intention is here obscure. The commissioner is charged both with stimulation of private trade and with purchases in the name of the town. The draft was unsatisfactory to the Consuls, and a revised form was issued the next day. Antoine Bouyn was given this commission, which emphasizes the policy of encouragement. "The said Bouyn shall make agreements with such merchants as he shall find suitable, engaging them to ship not more than 10–12,000 ânées of grain. He shall agree that if they cannot sell the grain for a price that is fixed by him, they shall be indemnified for the loss suffered. The merchants shall agree to bring the grain to Lyons at their expense and at their risk, and they shall be

[1] Lyon, Arch. Mun., BB. 61, 214. 25 Fev. 1543–44. The original is obscure in phrasing, especially the words "pour recouvrer des bleds, et illec marchander et convenir avec telz marchands et personnes qu'il verra estre son affaire. Pour fair venir en ceste ville telle quantité des bleds qu'il s'avisera."

required to sell as soon as the grain arrives."[1] The commission to Jannot was of the same character. He was instructed to go to Puy, Riom, Montferrand, Clermont, and elsewhere in Auvergne, to see if he could not come to some agreements with the merchants and other persons having granaries. If he found merchants who were willing to sign contracts, he might engage for the delivery of 6000 ânées, and might guarantee a price of twenty-three sous per bichet.[2]

The effort to confine the deputies to the policy of encouragement is marked. This is more significant when it is considered in connection with the failure of a project for a loan to be used for the purchase of grain. The preceding August, the Consuls had gone so far as to summon an assembly of notables "to find a remedy for the dearth, to form granaries and to find money."[3] The resolution was carried in due form, but there is no record of any meeting, nor any accounts of grain bought outright in the name of the town. The commissions first drawn up for the deputies were revised to avoid a possibility of interpreting them as a grant of power to make purchases. The intention of the municipality is clear. The policy of encouragement and insurance against risk was to be maintained as long as possible, and in that year it was not necessary to resort to direct purchase.

In 1573, we find the municipality not only engaged in direct purchase of grain, but also establishing a commission to attend to the details. The Consuls had purchased 1000 ânées of grain. On February 2, the first instalment arrived. The Consuls then ordered "that the grain should be placed in the most convenient granaries at the Port Saint Vincent, and that Sr. de la Capelle should be commissioned to keep account of the entry and of the distribution of the grain. And because certain bourgeois have offered to lend money to assist the town, on condition of being reimbursed with the money received from the sale of the grain, it has been decided to accept the loans offered. In case the sums subscribed by the bourgeois are not sufficient,

[1] Lyon, Arch. Mun., BB. 61, 216. 26 Fev. 1543–44.
[2] *Ibid.*
[3] *Ibid.*, BB. 61, 113. 17 Août 1543.

2000^{ll} shall be borrowed on the Place to be employed in the payment of the 1000 ânées. To do this, we commission the Councillors Morniers and Démasses, both to receive the loans of the bourgeois, and to borrow the surplus on the Place. . . . The said Consuls agree and promise both in their capacity as Consuls and in their private capacity, to guard the sums entrusted to them and repay each person in full." [1] This special committee of two Consuls possessed many of the duties of the later Chambre d'Abondance, but the Consulate as a body retained direction of all the purchases.[2] In the next few years, there was a growing conviction that the supplies furnished by the wholesale trade were likely to be slightly inadequate. These purchases in 1573 were followed in 1574 by a more formal recognition of the probable necessity of similar measures in the future. The Consuls went so far as to secure Royal Letters Patent granting them full power to make purchases and receive loans.[3] The Patent is so much concerned with the question of provincial prohibitions that it is difficult to decide whether the cancellation of the prohibitions or the grant of authority to form reserves was its principal object. The inclusion of the provisions for the formation of municipal granaries indicated that the idea was occupying a larger place in the minds of the Consuls.

In 1580, the project was again brought forward, and the motives are stated. "Inasmuch as the city frequently suffers from dearth, the Consuls have resolved to establish a general granary which shall always be kept filled, and renewed at regular intervals. With this in view, all the Estates of the town and the inhabitants of the neighborhood shall be invited to contribute to this good and holy enterprise." [4] The conception of a permanent reserve was entirely new, and the proposal signifies an increased lack of confidence in the adequacy of the wholesale supply. The difficulties were in reality two-fold; there was a great possibility that the merchants would fail to bring enough

[1] Lyon, Arch. Mun., BB. 91, 35. 2 Fev. 1573.

[2] *Ibid.*, BB. 91, 82. 7 Mai 1573.

[3] *Ibid.*, Chappe IV, 401, 52. 7 Oct. 1574. Lettres Patentes de Henri III, confirmées par le Duc de Lorraine, 20 Oct. 1574.

[4] *Ibid.*, BB. 105–106. 7 Jan. 1580. Chappe IV, 443, 1.

grain to Lyons, and it was even more likely that irregularity of arrival would subject the town to periods of distressingly high prices. The formation of a municipal granary of moderate capacity would remedy both of these dangers which were at last believed to be inherent in the conditions of the trade. The idea of such a granary managed by an independent commission gained more and more hold on the citizens of Lyons. It was an essentially different conception from the Bureaux of 1481, 1500, and 1504. The main idea of the early commissions was to purchase supplies in distant sections from which there was no regular trade to Lyons. The growth of the wholesale trade had rendered this type of municipal policy obsolete even in 1500 and 1504. The new policy of encouraging individual effort supplanted the policy of municipal purchase and succeeded until the trade ceased to expand. Then the municipality found that some purchases could advantageously be made. It was beginning to be necessary to supplement individual endeavor. It was expedient to form a reserve to protect the city against the irregularities due to the uncertainty of river transport and the temporary delays caused by prohibitions.

The experience of 1586 brought this policy to the point of complete expression. The fulfilment was long postponed, but the conception of the new policy was complete in every essential feature. The gradual pressure by which the Consuls were driven to make extensive purchases is the most significant feature of the episode. In the latter part of March, the Consuls apprehended serious inconvenience from the prohibitions in Burgundy and Dauphiné. The merchants were unable to afford any immediate relief on account of these obstacles, so that a visitation of private granaries was ordered. These were to be opened to provide for the needs of the town until grain could be obtained.[1] Meanwhile, Patents had been obtained from the King, cancelling the prohibitions. The deputies of the town in Burgundy were instructed to enforce these patents; and a deputy was sent at once to Auvergne to secure the passage of the grain held at Roanne.[2] A week later the fear of dearth had

[1] Lyon, Arch. Mun., BB. 116, 63. 20 Mars 1586.

[2] *Ibid.*, BB. 116, 67. 29 Mars 1586.

become more pressing. The prohibitions in Burgundy and Bassigny seemed so dangerous that another agent was sent to the King to obtain fresh Patents to nullify the prohibitions. Then the Consuls began to doubt the possibility of securing supplies from Burgundy in time; the agent to the King was consequently instructed to buy grain at Orleans. "He shall pass through Orleans to see if he can not find some merchant willing to sell 800–1000 muids of grain, to be delivered at Lyons by May fifteenth."[1] April 15, a deputy arrived from Roanne to report that there was a considerable quantity of grain but the prices were high. He was sent back at once with instructions to buy 2000 ânées, and although there was at first some desire to limit the price to be paid, he was finally given carte blanche, for fear that the opportunity of securing the grain might be lost.[2] A week later, the deputies in Burgundy were sent instructions to buy 3000 ânées or more anywhere they could and at any price.[3] The Consuls had given up all hope of securing adequate supplies from the merchants. The prohibitions might be removed, but the delays incident to getting private ventures under way would render this resource of no avail. The city needed grain at once. The only expeditious means of obtaining supplies was direct municipal purchase, and the Consuls did not hesitate. Their efforts were successful. The first serious realization of danger appeared on April fourth. On May tenth,[4] the first instalments arrived from Burgundy. Municipal purchases continued till the harvest.[5]

The prohibitions in the provinces gave the crisis a severity that was distinctly abnormal, but the inadequacy of the private trade, so powerfully impressed upon the Consuls, was real. The volume of trade might at any time fall below the amount needed by the city; prohibitions, ice on the river, mere timidity on the part of the merchants might cause a temporary but prolonged scarcity. The absence of a large supply close at hand

[1] Lyon, Arch. Mun., BB. 116, 68. 4 Avril 1586.

[2] *Ibid.*, BB. 117, 113. 15 Avril 1586.

[3] *Ibid.*, BB. 117, 119. 22 Avril 1586.

[4] *Ibid.*, BB. 117, 134. 10 Mai 1586.

[5] *Ibid.*, BB. 117, *passim*. Chappe IV, 411, 60 bis. Paris, 19 Juin 1586.

exposed the city to dangers from irregularity that were no serious menace to cities like Paris and Rouen. The crisis in 1586 was phenomenal; it resulted in a remarkably precise formulation of all the ideas that had been in the air since 1573. May 13, 1586, a general assembly was summoned to consider a plan drawn up by the Consuls to prevent the recurrence of the difficulties experienced so frequently.

In the opening speech, Mandelot, the Governor of Lyonnais, stated the motives which impelled the Consuls to call the meeting. He laid great stress on the feeling that private trade was at times unable to meet the needs of the town. "Even the Consuls," he says, "have recently had great difficulty in securing grain, on account of the severity of the dearth throughout France. To prevent the recurrence of such distress in the future, the Consuls have decided to empower six notable bourgeois to buy grain after the harvest. Their purchases shall be stored in a public granary, to succor the people in time of famine."[1]

The remarkable feature of this proposal, however, was the extraordinary completeness of the provisions for the organization of the Commission. "The Commission shall have the title Intendants d'Abondance and shall promise the Consuls to buy or have bought, after the harvest of the present year, such quantities of grain, wheat, rye, and lentils, as the Consuls and the Intendants shall deem expedient. They shall make these purchases in Beauce, Sologne, Nivernais, Bourbonnais, Auvergne, Charollais, and other neighboring regions. *As far as possible they shall refrain from purchasing grain in Burgundy, in order not to curtail the opportunities of the merchants to engage in the trade which they ordinarily pursue in Burgundy and Bassigny.* Likewise the said Intendants shall make no purchases in the government of Lyonnais, nor in the Pays de Dombes, since the bourgeois, citizens, and other inhabitants are accustomed to make provision for their families by purchases in these regions.

[1] Lyon, Arch. Mun., BB. 116, 89; 117, 140. 13 Mai 1586. Assemblée en l'Hostel Commun de la Ville de Lyon. The wording of the speech is condensed.

"The Intendants shall provide for the shipment of all grain bought in pursuance of their orders, and shall store it in granaries of which they shall hold the keys.

"The Consuls shall entrust to the Intendants not more than 20,000 écus soleil in specie, drawn either from the personal fortunes of the Consuls or from sums borrowed by them on their own credit. In acknowledgment of this sum, the Intendants in their own names shall deliver receipts to each of the amount loaned, which shall be repaid at the end of the year with the profit of ——% per year, or from fair to fair at the rate of 'change' in this city.

"And inasmuch as it would be advisable to create a larger fund than this 20,000 écus, the Intendants shall exert their influence to borrow the sum needed for the purchases, transportation, and other expenses incidental to the undertaking. For these sums, the Intendants shall give receipts made out in their own name, to bear such interest and profit as they shall agree upon.

"For the transaction of these various affairs, they shall assemble at a regular place of meeting. All six Intendants shall attend if possible, but, in the absence of one or two, the four present shall decide such questions as arise, and their decisions shall afterwards be ratified by the absent members. The duties shall be divided among them, and they shall have authority to commission such agents as they shall find necessary, to make the purchases and supervise transportation. Likewise one of their number shall be particularly charged to keep or supervise the keeping of the cash book and other papers concerning the undertaking.

"The duties and authority of the Intendants shall terminate annually, beginning with the feast of Saint-Jean Baptiste, and ending on the same feast day in the following year. At the end of the year thus indicated, three of the six Intendants shall leave office and in their place three persons shall be elected by the Échevins and the Intendants. These newly-elected Intendants shall discharge the duties of the office for the year, and at its close the three Intendants of longest standing shall leave office, and three others shall be elected.

"At the end of each year, between Easter and the Saint-Jean, the aforesaid grain purchased and stored in the city shall be sold by persons appointed by the Intendants for the purpose, who shall take charge of all the product of the sale, in order to pay the loans from individuals, both principal and interest. . . .

"When the grain has been sold, the Intendants shall render account of their administration to the Consuls, and to the three incoming Intendants. The Governor, the Clergy, the officers of Justice, and other notables may be present, and if it appears by the account that there has been a loss, whether because of sale below cost, or by reason of deterioration, excessive expense of transportation, or loss from shipwreck, fire, violence, theft, or pillage, the Consuls in their private capacity shall indemnify the Intendants and reimburse them immediately after the rendition of the account, without any formal process.

"The sum thus paid by the Échevins to the Intendants shall be distributed and imposed on all the inhabitants of the town, as the Orders and the Estates have expressly consented. Likewise, if it shall please God to grant any profit, it shall belong to the public and remain to serve as part of the fund assigned to the enterprise." [1]

This elaborate attempt to organize municipal purchases was premature. It was the result of an unusual crisis which was somewhat artificial because of the excessive influence of prohibitions. The moment chosen for the establishment of the Chambre d'Abondance was unfortunate; coming at the close of a season, when the municipality had extended its credit for immediate purchases, it proved to be impracticable for the Consuls to turn over the sum of 20,000 écus, provided for in the plan. The six Intendants d'Abondance were duly elected and they endeavored to discharge the duties imposed upon them, but there was no money. At the end of October, they appeared at the Consulate, and said that they had sent into the provinces to make purchases, but that the Échevins had failed to pay the 20,000 écus without which the enterprise could not be pros-

[1] Lyon, Arch. Mun., BB. 116, 89; 117, 140. 13 Mai 1586. One of these registers is the minute made during the meeting, the other is the formal copy.

ecuted. They added that they would be obliged to resign, if the funds were not speedily forthcoming. The Consuls asked for time to consider the subject, but no record of a decision appears.[1] There are no accounts of purchases by these Intendants d'Abondance, so that it is likely that they resigned on account of lack of funds.

There is no more significant commentary upon the nature of institutions and of institutional development than the absence of any municipal purchases for the half century that follows the formulation of the elaborate scheme of 1586. It was not an unprecedented proposal; the origin of every feature of the scheme can be perceived in the history of the preceding decade, and above all in the events of the first four months of 1586. We can rarely trace the gradual development of a relatively new institution with more completeness. Nothing could produce a more convincing impression of permanence and of appositeness, and yet all this structure crumbled and fell to the ground, incapable of supporting its own weight. For fifty years there was no suggestion of a recurrence of such a crisis as that of 1586; no renewal of the project to form a municipal granary. The private trade, which in 1573, 1580, and 1586 had revealed serious incapacity to supply the needs of the city, succeeded for a long period in meeting all the wants of Lyons. When the Consuls finally became convinced that the general wholesale trade was not quite adequate, the trade ceased to cause further difficulty. The problem which had seemed so serious in 1586 apparently ceased to exist for half a century.

The explanation of this curious feature of the grain trade at Lyons is probably similar to the explanation that has been suggested for the persistence of the system of local marketing. There were latent defects in organization which were really inherent in the conditions of the trade, but they appeared only under pressure of unusual circumstances. Some chance incident might reveal the nature of the difficulty long before the pressure of conditions had become sufficiently insistent to require com-

[1] Lyon, Arch. Mun., BB. 117, 233. 31 Oct. 1586. The Consuls were to decide the matter the third of November, but there is no record under that date.

plete reorganization. The solution of many social problems is frequently conceived long before the difficulty has become so pressing that reform is necessary. In this sense, the Abondance of 1586 was a premature solution of the grain trade problems of the seventeenth century. The sixteenth century was characterized at Lyons by the effort to stimulate individual endeavor; the municipality avoided direct purchases as far as possible, and wisely relied upon the supplies procured by merchants. The seventeenth century was characterized by a deepening conviction of the inexpediency of reliance upon the private trade. A fortuitous combination of circumstances in 1586 happened to bring out most of the essential difficulties that characterize the seventeenth century, so that the policy of the seventeenth century was strikingly foreshadowed long before it became a practical necessity.

In 1620, the first indication of renewed trouble in the grain trade appeared. The Consuls were not active, but the judicial officers endeavored to protect the city against want. The expedient adopted was a curious compromise between the policies of encouragement and of direct purchase. The merchants of the city were summoned towards the end of March and ordered "to maintain fixed reserves in their granaries until the month of August. Until then each merchant shall replenish his granaries as he sells, so that the quantity in his possession shall never fall below the amounts indicated in the annexed roll. To free the merchants from any fear of a decline in price which might cause them to lose money, it is also ordered that until the month of August, the bakers of the town shall be required to buy grain of the said merchants, at the price of $12^{ll}5$ sous per ânée for wheat from the Pays de Verdun or above, and 13^{ll} per ânée for wheat from the lower river." [1]

Ten years later, the project for a Chambre d'Abondance reappeared. The Abondance was formed to supplement the efforts of private merchants, especially by endeavoring to procure supplies in regions not generally frequented by the merchants.

[1] Lyon, Arch. Mun., Chappe IV, 427, 3. 27 Mars 1620. Ordonnance de la Sénéchaussée.

The merchants confined their attention to Burgundy, but it was hazardous to rely so completely upon a source of supply which might be rendered valueless by a local crop failure. The natural tendencies in the development of the wholesale trade had been unsound; the advantages of Burgundy were so marked, the disadvantages of the lower river so distinct, that the private merchants gradually neglected entirely the sources of supply which had been utilized for a brief period in the early sixteenth century before the Burgundian trade had become concentrated in the Saône towns. Trade with the lower river might have been stimulated, perhaps, by means of guarantees and premiums, but the delays and indirectness of such procedure were too serious to render such a policy expedient. In 1630, the Consuls frankly adopted the essential features of the Abondance of 1586. The Bureau was charged with making purchases in the regions unfrequented by the merchants and with the formation of granaries designed to secure the city against the dangers arising from the irregularity of the trade.

As in 1586, the project was laid before a General Assembly of the town, but the assembly was much less ambitious than its predecessor. The Intendants pour l'Abondance were appointed for a year only, but their attributions were practically identical with those of the Indendants of 1586, and the constant reference to the meeting of 1586 indicates direct influence. A few men who had attended in 1586 were present in 1630. The chief difference lay in the mode of securing funds. In 1586, the Consuls had agreed to contribute 20,000 francs and private subscriptions were to be solicited; in 1630 a loan was to be raised entirely by private subscriptions, and 30,000 francs were promised at the meeting. There was no provision for any loan from the municipality, so that the financial basis of the Chambre d'Abondance was quite independent of the municipality. The rate of interest to be paid was fixed at $6\frac{1}{4}\%$ and the guarantee against loss was to have an official character, which it possessed actually, but not technically, in 1586. A new provision was added requiring the bakers to buy grain of the Abondance at fixed prices, in order to dispose of supplies left in the granaries at the close of a season.[1] In other respects the articles of 1586 and 1630 were identical.

This Chambre d'Abondance remained active till 1632. It was reëstablished in 1637–38, without any noteworthy change in organization. In 1643, the organization of the Chambre was modified in many details and it was proposed to make it permanent, thus adopting at last the most ambitious element of the plan of 1586. The articles drawn up by the General Assembly were printed and distributed quite widely, and, as the Abondance then became a permanent body, the year 1643 came to be regarded as the date of the establishment of the Chambre d'Abondance. There were some important changes. The number of directors was increased from eight to eleven, and it was provided that the Provost of Merchants and one Consul should be members *ex officio*. In regard to raising of the loan there was a compromise between the plans of 1586 and 1630. "The purchases of grain shall be made with funds subscribed by the Directors of the Abondance and by the Consulate. The Consulate shall subscribe in its official capacity as member of the Abondance, and shall employ the municipal funds." Evidently reliance upon voluntary subscriptions had proved to be inadequate and the loans were given a more official character. The other provisions of previous plans were repeated: the limitation of purchases to distant sections unfrequented by merchants, the interest to be paid on loans, the guarantee against loss, and the regulation that the bakers must buy remainders at prices fixed by the Directors of the Abondance.[2]

The permanence projected in 1643 was really achieved. The accounts are the simplest indication of the persistence of the Chambre. The Archives at Lyons still possess the accounts of the Abondance for the years: 1648–50, 1651–53, 1654, . . . 1667–70, and for each subsequent year to 1713. The Abondance

[1] Lyon, Arch. Mun., GG. Chappe IV, 442–443. (Extrait des Registres Consulaires), 30 Juillet 1630.

[2] G^7. 1633. Imprimé, Paris, 1667. Bib. Nat., Fr. 18599, 429. Imprimé, Paris, 1667.

Lyon, Arch. Mun., Chappe IV, 5 and 6. Several copies. The original minute is, of course, in the Actes Consulaires under the date 31 Août 1643.

was not maintained from 1713 to 1730. But in 1730 it was reëstablished and remained in existence until the Revolution.[1] Some registers of the deliberations of the Abondance have also survived, covering roughly the period 1630–84.[2] The Abondance was thus an important factor in the history of the Lyonese trade after 1643.

If the Chambre d'Abondance is considered solely from the point of view of organization, the year 1643 marks the beginning of the last phase of this form of public purchase of grain. The policy adopted by the Abondance, however, underwent considerable change. The relations with the merchants were very different in 1693 and 1643. It is scarcely too much to say that the real purpose of the Abondance was fundamentally different.

The registers of deliberations for the years 1630–49 show that the policy of the directors was closely related to the municipal policy of the sixteenth century. The Consuls of that period had sought primarily to stimulate the private wholesale trade with Burgundy. In the early seventeenth century the directors of the Abondance were commissioned in part to purchase grain directly in Auvergne, Beauce, and Languedoc, but also to stimulate private merchants to engage in trade with these regions. Lyons needed to have the possibility of recourse to more than one source of supply. The private merchants were accustomed to trade only with Burgundy and it was desirable to induce them to extend the range of their purchases. The stimulation of trade was hardly one of the purposes of the establishment of the Abondance, but in practice it became a definite policy. In fact, the Abondance from 1630–50 adopted the policy of the Consuls of the sixteenth century, although the different aspects of the policy received different emphasis. The Abondance gave much attention to direct purchases. Grain was bought more frequently and in larger quantities than at any time in the sixteenth century. Like the Consuls, they were obliged to secure special Letters Patent from the King to protect their shipments and to safeguard the merchants against the local

[1] Lyon, Arch. Mun., GG. Chappe IV, 481.

[2] *Ibid.*, GG. Chappe IV, 538, 49, 50, 51.

prohibitions. But the directors of the Abondance also made many contracts both with the local and the Lyonese merchants, engaging to secure them against changes in price if the merchants agreed to deliver the grain at Lyons within specified periods. This was the policy of the sixteenth century.[1] Local "foreign" merchants were brought to a consciousness of the possibilities of trade with Lyons; the Lyonese were shown the advantages of making purchases in Languedoc, as well as Burgundy.

In the course of the seventeenth century, there was a distinct development of trade with Languedoc. Auvergne and the Beauce were very seldom visited by Lyonese whether at the instance of the Abondance or on private initiative, since both regions offered few advantages and the difficulties were great. The lower river was more tempting, and it is pretty evident that it was visited more and more frequently. This change was in part due to the efforts of the Abondance to stimulate trade, in part due to the normal development of the wholesale trade. It was this change that altered the relation between the Abondance and the merchants.

The transition cannot be dated with accuracy, but the character of the changes in the organization of the trade can be very clearly traced in the letters of the deputies of the Abondance in Burgundy, 1667–77. In the latter half of the sixteenth century the Burgundian trade had begun to flow toward the Saône towns. Local merchants appeared who collected the grain in the back country and brought it to the river to meet the merchants from Lyons. The organization of this wholesale trade developed steadily, and by the middle of the seventeenth century it was so highly concentrated in the river towns that the Lyonese merchants did most of their buying in the towns. The Lyonese merchant thus tended to become a capitalist who confined his attention to the latter stages of the trade, trusting commission agents or factors with the collection of the grain in the producing regions. The papers of a law suit, in which

[1] Lyon, Arch. Mun., GG. Chappe IV, 538–549. Registres des Délibérations l'Abondance.

the Consuls of Lyons were engaged in 1630, indicate that this capitalistic form of trade was an established practice even then. The Lyonese merchants were buying in Champagne, in Bassigny, and in Burgundy.[1] In most of the towns, the larger merchants were represented by factors. There are traces of partnerships.[2] These and other facts indicate that the conditions we find in 1667–77 may have prevailed much earlier. In all probability, however, there is a change in degree. Even if there were factors and commission agents in the early seventeenth century, it is hardly likely that this form of trade was so important. The conduct of the Abondance in the years 1630–50 shows that the merchants could not then be easily induced to buy on the lower river. Later, when the development of the local wholesale trade had emphasized the capitalistic side of the trade of the Lyonese merchants, they found it easier to turn their capital in any direction. The large mercantile house with its staff of factors and its regular commission merchants could readily develop relations with the local commission merchants of the lower river. The larger scale of doing business was in itself likely to make the merchant more willing to direct his trade to the most advantageous sections.

The letters of 1667–77 show that the trade had reached this stage of development, and they also suggest that the large scale of operations was relatively new. The local merchants were nearly all working on commission for Lyonese merchants. Du Pradt writes in November, 1667, "there are very few merchants here who have not commissions from Lyons. One Fegnet, at Talmay, collects great amounts by reason of his intimate knowledge of Franche Comté and the vicinity of Langres. He works on commission, and has promised not to engage himself on new commissions without speaking to me."[3] Other agents are noted, "one Balan d'Aprémont, who ordinarily

[1] Lyon, Arch. Mun., Chappe IV, 411, 67. Juin–Sept. 1630. Procès entre les Échevins de Châlons-sur-Saône et de Lyon.

[2] *Ibid.*, Chappe IV, 411, 63. 12 Avril 1628. Arrêt de Conseil. . . .

[3] *Ibid.*, Chappe IV, 460, 30. Gray, 10 Nov. 1667. Most of these letters were written by Du Pradt, a deputy of the Chambre d'Abondance, to the Directors of the Chambre at Lyons.

works on commission for merchants of Lyons." [1] The Aigneus, uncle and nephew, "Dugas and his company," and many others are mentioned. The Aigneus worked on a standing engagement with certain merchants, and this contract made such demands on them that Aigneu said he could not undertake to buy a couple of hundred mines for the Abondance, as he did not wish to break with his regular employers.[2] The efforts of these local dealers brought the grain to the river very quickly. In 1671, Du Pradt says that the granaries of the river towns were generally filled by the first week in November.[3] In September, 1667, he says that there is no new grain to be had anywhere, but that there will be an abundance before the end of October.[4] This does not mean, of course, that the whole crop was moved towards the river, but the portion of the crop usually available for wholesale trade appeared in the river towns early, so that the local merchants were well supplied by the first of November, and were ready to ship to Lyons.

The complete ascendency of the local merchants appears most clearly when the grain is followed into the back country. Almost everywhere we meet the merchants of the river towns, rarely Lyonese merchants. The proportions of the trade in the towns attracted many *blatiers*, so that the factors were able to buy much grain on the town markets or in the streets. This appearance of *blatiers* in the towns is indeed one of the most striking features of the period. Writing from Auxonne in November, 1667, Du Pradt says: "from Langres, which is ten leagues distant, much grain comes to this town. At Marsilly and at Talmay, there are many carts loaded with grain." [5] At Gray, in 1669, 120 carters came in during a single week. Arrivals were quite as frequent at Auxonne.[6] But the intensity

[1] Lyon, Arch. Mun., Chappe IV, 460, 30. Auxonne, 20 Nov. 1667. Du Pradt.

[2] *Ibid.*, Chappe IV, 460, 30. Gray, 31 Oct. 1667. Du Pradt. See also *ibid.*, Châlons-sur-Saône, 4 Dec. 1667. Du Pradt.

[3] *Ibid.*, Chappe IV, 460, 30. Auxonne, 8 Nov. 1671. Du Pradt.

[4] *Ibid.*, Chappe IV, 460, 30. Auxonne, 14 Sept. 1667. Du Pradt.

[5] *Ibid.*, Chappe IV, 460, 30. Auxonne, 3 Nov. 1667. Du Pradt.

[6] *Ibid.*, Gray, 22 Nov. 1669. Du Pradt. Auxonne, 25 Nov. 1669. Du Pradt.

of competition among the commission merchants did not always allow the *blatiers* to get to the town market. The rivalry was particularly keen between Dugas and the Aigneus. In December, 1667, Du Pradt says: "Dugas and his associates have 2500 ânées of grain already purchased, and they are still buying, striving to get ahead of the Aigneus who have quite as much as they have. They have agreed several times to divide equally what is brought to town and take it all at the same price. But they break their agreement almost as soon as it is made. Last Tuesday, they nearly came to blows. They pushed prices up to 27 sous 6 deniers per bichet" (15–16 sous was a normal price). Du Pradt could not resist the temptation to enter into the game, so he advised the Aigneus to stop buying in the town. "The granaries of Dugas were full, both in the town and in the country. Dugas would soon be unable to house more grain, and, as he has no commissions, he would have to stop buying. Prices would fall and Aigneu would be able to secure his grain at a moderate figure." [1] The merchants also bought in the back country directly of the peasants. Dugas and the Aigneus were buying in the country in 1667. In 1669, one of the merchants of Lyons was scouring the country buying of the peasants.[2] In 1667, bakers from Lyons were buying in the farms, forcing prices up to extraordinary figures.[3] In 1672, two local merchants were said to be making a round of the country districts.[4] The trade was thus characteristically centered in the river towns. Carters came in from Franche Comté, Bassigny, and Champagne. The merchants bought in or near the towns. Some of the merchants bought in the country, both in the granaries of landlords and of the peasants.[5] From time to time, Lyonese merchants endeavored to compete with the commission agents, and perforce bought in the country.

[1] Lyon, Arch. Mun., Chappe IV, 460, 30. Auxonne, 2 Dec. 1667.

[2] *Ibid.*, Chappe IV, 460, 30. Gray, 22 Fev. 1669, Aigneu aux Directeurs.

[3] *Ibid.*, Chappe IV, 460, 30. Auxonne, 3 Nov. 1667. Du Pradt.

[4] *Ibid.*, Chappe IV, 460, 30. Auxonne, 17 Dec. 1672. Du Pradt.

[5] *Ibid.*, Chappe IV, 460, 30. Gray, 16 Nov. 1669. Du Pradt. "A Rey . . . tous ceus qui se meslent (du commerce des bleds) n'en ont pas 2000 mesures, et c'est la plus grande partie bled de ferme."

On the whole, the trade was in the hands of the commission agents. The organization of the Burgundian trade upon this basis made the Lyonese merchants feel much less closely attached to the locality, and reduced their part in the trade to wholesale buying and selling of the simplest form. This inevitably tended to increase the mobility of their operations. Independently of these causes the scale of buying tended to increase.

In 1693, the Abondance was facing a very different situation from that of 1630. Then, the merchants were disinclined to buy outside of Burgundy. They were accustomed to the narrow routine of their trade, devoting much of their energy to finding supplies in Burgundy. In 1693, they were possessed of more capital. They were free to devote their attention to the larger aspects of the trade, as the petty business of collecting grain in Burgundy was done by the local commission merchants. They were ready to buy in Languedoc and Provence, and quite as well prepared as the Abondance to undertake such a venture. In 1693, the private merchants were buying in Languedoc and Provence even before the Abondance. The Chambre was no longer necessary because the merchants confined their attention too exclusively to Burgundy, or because they were over-cautious and unwilling to incur risks in novel ventures. The Abondance stood in a new relation to the city and to the merchants. What was its influence upon the private trade? Did it still discharge a useful function? The necessity of asking these questions suggests the extent of the change that had taken place. Previous to 1693 the utility of the Abondance was not seriously questioned, and the judgment of the historian confirms the opinion of contemporaries. Before 1693, it is relatively easy to see many good reasons for such a municipal commission. After 1693, whatever our final judgment may be, the Chambre d'Abondance presents a serious question.

Some criticism appears as early as 1683, when the Intendant wrote to the Contrôleur Général: "The Chambre d'Abondance stores grain in large granaries, to insure adequate supplies in time of dearth. If the rules of this establishment were well observed, it would be a great aid to the city, but when people who have inferior grain sell it at high prices to the Abondance, the city gains little and the poor suffer. It is said that the Abondance costs the city 5000–6000 ll annually, although it ought to be no occasion for loss and might even yield a profit. The directors should buy when grain is cheap and sell when it is high." [1] All too frequently it happened that this was just what the Abondance failed to do. They waited until the dearth was perceived and then bought frantically at any price. Consequently their purchases were made while prices were highest and some grain was often unsold when prices had fallen to the normal level. This difficulty arose in part from the unwillingness of the bourgeois to make loans to the Abondance when the prospect of dearth was not immediately before them. Even "if they promised subscriptions many delays in payment might occur which would seriously impair the efficiency of the Abondance." The bourgeois took little interest in the Abondance except in time of crisis.

In the fall of 1693 this indifference to the needs of the Abondance was striking. The Hôtel de Ville had contributed 40,000 livres, the Abondance raised 20,000 livres among its directors, and several bourgeois promised loans amounting to 340,000 livres. But only 70,000 livres of these voluntary subscriptions were paid in, and those who were still to pay objected to placing their funds in the hands of the Consuls, lest the Consuls should apply the loans to some other purpose.[2] The Abondance did not possess resources that would render it independent of the Consuls, and as soon as the Consuls interfered, the Abondance lost much of its slight influence with the bourgeois. The Abondance needed to have larger funds at its disposal; it should not be harassed by delays in payment of subscriptions; and its relation to the Consulate needed to be defined more clearly. Some reform was essential. In the fall of 1693 it was too weak to be of real assistance, but it had sufficient vitality to involve the city in considerable losses. At this time, the sentiment

[1] G⁷. 355. Mémoire sur la Police de Lyon. Août, 1683. d'Ormesson.
[2] G⁷. 1631. Lyon, 19 Sept. 1693. Montgivraut.

of the citizens was favorable to the Abondance; it was not a question of doing away with it, but of a reorganization designed to increase its efficiency.

In September and October, the principal amendment suggested was an increase in the number of Directors. Each Director was supposed to contribute to the funds employed, and the idea current was in favor of adding from twelve to fifteen directors to the nine special directors chosen in accordance with the Regulation of 1643.[1] The Duc de Villeroy opposed this on the ground that "the great number of Directors might cause much trouble. The wisest measures are seldom taken by large bodies, which agree on the course to be taken only with great difficulty. . . . It would be much better to raise the standard of wealth required of each Director."[2] Despite the great influence of Villeroy at Lyons, his criticism had no immediate effect. The Contrôleur Général sent Letters Patent for the increase in the number of Directors, and some attempt was apparently made to organize the work on this basis. The failure was complete. October 20, Montgivraut writes: "your letters on the augmentation of the Directors of the Abondance were received three weeks ago, but nothing has been done. For I do not consider that anything is accomplished by the mere appointment of from twelve to fourteen men, who not only have not been set to work, but who have not even been informed of their appointment. There is not a sou in the chests of the Abondance, and 200,000 francs are still due on the subscription made four months ago. There is no thought of procuring new loans. I am convinced that the lack of funds prevents any active buying; nothing is being done."[3] The failure of these attempts led to new projects for reform of the Abondance, and gradually the wisdom of Villeroy's suggestions became clear. The discussion was lengthy, and week after week passed without any hope of seeing the Abondance in

[1] G7. 1631. Lyon, 19 Sept. 1693. Montgivraut.

[2] G7. 1631. Du camp de Carnière, 15 Oct. 1693. Villeroy, Gouverneur de Lyonnais.

[3] G7. 1631. Lyon, 20 Oct. 1693. Montgivraut.

condition to undertake any active work. The possibility of dearth was constantly haunting the Consuls, and they began an energetic canvass of Languedoc and Provence. Unfortunately, the deputy who was sent to make the purchases for the Consuls proved to be more active than discreet. All the worst features of municipal interference were emphasized, and his conduct exerted a marked influence upon the attitude of the Lyonese to the Chambre d'Abondance. Public opinion which had been favorable became more or less hostile, and there was much severe criticism of all interference with the grain trade.

In previous attempts to supplement the purchases made by merchants, the Consuls and the Abondance had always endeavored not to interfere with the merchants. All the early *règlements* of the Abondance had required the directors to purchase grain only in those regions not frequented by merchants. Everything was done to assist and stimulate private endeavor. In 1693, the Consulate gave every one the impression that it was seeking to drive the private merchants out of business. Whether this was the result of Chaiz's indiscretion or whether the Consuls really had designs against the merchants, we cannot now be certain; but the conduct of Chaiz on the lower river is not involved in any obscurity. Complaints of his arbitrary action appear in September, and continue in increasing volume for the next two months.

A merchant of Lyons writes, 16 September: "I have just received letters which declare that Sr. Chaiz pretends to have orders giving him exclusive right to purchase grain. This has caused us to stop buying. He has forbidden the boatmen under pain of imprisonment to ship grain for anyone besides himself, and this has intimidated the boatmen. Those who had started up river with our grain have stopped on the way, unwilling to proceed, and others refuse to handle our grain at all." [1] A month later, Bérulle, the Intendant at Lyons, reports a mass of rumors and suspicions. "Chaiz not only prevents the merchants from continuing their purchases but even forces

[1] G[7]. 1631. Lyon, 16 Sept. 1693. Jourdan de Grousse, Marchand à Lyon, au C. G.

them to agree to make none in the future. To compel them to obey, he prevents them from shipping the grain already purchased, and obliges them to turn it over to him at the cost price. This conduct estranges the merchants so completely that I fear we shall be without grain. I remonstrate daily with the Provost of Merchants. . . . It is more than a month since any grain has arrived at Lyons. The conduct of Chaiz and of the Consulate is particularly suspicious. Chaiz has gone to Bâville and to Lebret (Intendants of Languedoc and Provence) and has told them that it is your (*i. e.* the Contrôleur Général's) desire that the merchants should buy no more grain, and that the grain belonging to the town should alone be shipped. I have written them to the contrary, but everything at Arles is held up, and Bâville holds four large boats at Pont-Saint-Esprit, so that nothing comes through to Lyons. It would be well for you to write. Although you have ordered the Consulate to do nothing without informing me, they let me know nothing of what is going on, as they do not wish to have anyone spying around or contradicting them. Their only thought is to make profits. If the Échevins prevent the merchants from loading grain, it is simply to harass and discourage them, so as to induce them to turn over their grain to Chaiz at a low price. The Échevins find it very agreeable to sell for 40^{ll} what cost them only 30^{ll}. I should not worry over their profits, if I did not feel that their treatment of the merchants would infallibly result in a scarcity."[1]

The complaints finally had some effect. November 7, the Provost of Merchants, Du Lieu, says that he will recall Chaiz, and that he has already urged him to encourage the merchants.[2] But it is difficult to be sure of the effect of the letter referred to. The exhortation to Chaiz to encourage the merchants apparently reached him about the 18th, and this is doubtless the letter to which the factor of Saladin and Jourdan refers: "I gave Chaiz the last letter of the Provost of Merchants," he says. "Chaiz flew into a rage, saying that he would rather be recalled

[1] G[7]. 1631. Lyon, (24) 27 Oct. 1693. Bérulle au C. G.

[2] G[7]. 1631. Lyon, 7 Nov. 1693. Du Lieu.

than do anything contrary to his duty. He gave a list of all his purchases to Lebret, who gave him permission to ship. Chaiz said that he could not sincerely include our purchases in the list as they were not bought on the account of the city, and as they were to be sold to the bourgeois at high prices. . . . You (*i. e.* his principals) must try to get letters from the Intendant, if you expect to ship any grain from these provinces . . . for the Intendant does not wish to permit the export of any grain except by Chaiz, the deputy from Lyons. If Chaiz had only wished to help us, he need only have said that our grain was for Lyons, and the Subdélégué would have made no trouble. But Chaiz insists on interfering. He has told the Intendant that we merchants must sell to him, and that he alone was to ship. . . ."[1] Towards the end of November, Chaiz was recalled,[2] and the complaints of the merchants on the Lower Rhône were less numerous.

The hostility to the merchants was doubly serious, for the merchants were buying quite as actively as the Consuls. An estimate, drawn up November 24, represents the purchases of the Consuls and the merchants as about equal.[3] The discouragement of the merchants was thus a serious indiscretion on the part of the Consuls, and the incident doubtless explains much of the opposition to municipal interference that comes to the surface in connection with the reorganization of the Abondance

[1] G^7. 1631. Tarascon, 18 Nov. 1693. Meinard à MM. Saladin et Jourdan.

[2] G^7. 1631. Lyon, 28 Nov. 1693. Du Lieu.

[3] G^7. 1631. Lyon, 24 Nov. 1693.

For the Consulate			For the Merchants		
In Granary	2000	ânées.	Saladin & Jourdan	10,000	ânées
At the Abondance	2550	"	Guignier	4000	"
En Route	2500	"	Chapeyron	3000	"
Ready for shipment in Languedoc and Provence	11,600	"	Galdy	3000	"
			Rollin	3000	"
			Others	3000	"
Ordered at Genoa	8000	"			
	26,650	"		26,000	"

See also a memoir of 10 Dec. 1693 (also G^7. 1631). Estimates of arrivals from 10 Juillet–10 Dec. 1693: 14,460 ânées for the Consulate, and 15,809 ânées for the Merchants.

in January, 1694, while all the details were fresh in people's minds. One of the privileges to be given the Abondance was preference in the use of all means of transportation. This awoke vivid memories of the troubles of November, 1693, and Villeroy protested: "I will say frankly that I do not approve of that article. The preference in the right to use boats will be a serious blow to commerce, which is already sufficiently disturbed. I will even say that in my opinion the only way to procure an abundance of grain is to allow private persons complete freedom to bring grain to Lyons. The Chambre d'Abondance by its care and industry may assure lower prices, and properly speaking that is its function, but I am persuaded that a commercial town like Lyons should not limit the freedom of individuals." [1] Bérulle, the Intendant, denies that the Abondance is of any utility. "The trade should properly be left to the merchants, and to them alone. That is a principle in which I firmly believe. To them alone does Lyons owe its food supply, and not in the least to the Chambre d'Abondance. . . . We should not begrudge the merchants their gain." [2] At no previous time do we find such vigorous expressions of hostility to the Abondance. It is due in part to a real change in the relation of the Abondance to the merchants, in part it is a reflection of the antagonisms aroused by Chaiz in November, 1693. On the whole, I am inclined to think that the distrust of the Abondance in January, 1694, was largely due to the indiscretions of Chaiz. The proposed reform evoked opposition, indeed, but the Chambre was reorganized and worked steadily until 1713, — nearly twenty years. In 1699, Villeroy commended the directors for their public spirit and for their services to the city. In short, everything points to the conclusion that the Lyonese still believed that the Abondance was necessary. They still hoped that it would prevent extraordinarily high prices and secure the city against serious dearth. The merchants were certainly no longer in need of encouragement; no new sources of supply remained to be developed or emphasized; the merchants were

[1] Boislisle, *op. cit.*, I, 350, 1273. 14, 17, 22–26 Jan. 1694. Villeroy au C. G.

[2] *Ibid.*, I, 350, 1273. 23 Mai 1694. Bérulle.

quite ready to trade either in Burgundy or Languedoc; the most notable reasons for the creation of an Abondance no longer existed. What, then, was the Abondance supposed to do?

The new regulations for the organization of the Chambre throw some light upon this question. They present a marked contrast to the provisions of 1643. In the plan of 1694, there is no long article providing that the directors shall make all purchases in provinces seldom frequented by the merchants. Emphasis is placed on the mode of procuring funds. "Each one of the (ten) directors shall place 10,000^{ll} in the Chest of the Abondance. He shall receive interest at 6%." [1] This was an innovation only in part as the directors had previously been required to contribute something, though no stated sum was mentioned. The next two articles are more novel and more significant. "The Consulate shall place a fund of 120,000^{ll} at the disposition of the Treasurer of the Abondance, and the Consuls shall not claim interest or restitution of the principal under any pretext whatsoever. This sum is to serve as capital and as gage of surety for the reimbursement of the sums furnished by the Directors and of the sums borrowed by them of individuals. . . . At all times there shall be at least 10,000 ânées in the granaries of the Abondance, and the grain shall be sold each year and replaced." "If the advances of the Consulate are consumed by the payment of interest and by losses, it shall make additional advances." There was provision for the repayment of the Consulate if the gains of the trade enabled the directors to dispense with the loan made by the Consuls. This article, however, was evidently inserted to cover a contingency that was not regarded as at all probable. One other article should be noted: "The Directors shall not engage in the grain trade on their own account, directly or indirectly, during their tenure of office."

The Abondance was thus to have a minimum capital of 220,000^{ll}, increased by possible private loans; but interest was to

[1] My notes are from the copy at the Arch. Nat. G[7]. 1633. Other copies may be found at Lyons, Chappe IV, 450, 15 and in the Série BB. under the date 9 Jan. 1694.

be paid only on half of this capital. The 120,000[ll] advanced by the Consuls was to be regarded as irrevocably spent. In short, the Abondance was not expected to be a financial success. Losses were anticipated. They were indeed an inevitable feature of the Abondance as it was conceived in 1694. It was to do two things: it was regularly to hold grain through the season; it was to take special measures in time of dearth in order to keep prices low. Sales of grain at cost, or even below cost, were certainly regarded by the Abondance as one of its distinctive functions. Both of these duties almost necessarily involved a loss. The grain in store not only resulted in a constant expense for housing and for interest charges, but it must needs be held until the end of the season and it must generally be sold for less than it cost. The directors were not usually allowed to market at favorable moments; only in time of dearth might the granary be drawn down below the 10,000 ânées prescribed. The losses likely to result in time of dearth are easily understood. The directors would begin to buy in large quantities only when prices had begun to rise; they would be obliged to continue to buy until prices at Lyons were reduced to a satisfactory figure.

These features of the policy of the Abondance in time of dearth appear clearly in 1698–99. The prohibitions of Ferrand, Intendant of Burgundy, issued on October 14, and the letter of the Contrôleur Général, showed the directors that no reliance could be placed upon Burgundy. Ferrand had even declared positively that he could not permit the export of more than 9500 ânées, which would enable Lyons to wait for grain from the lower river.

"The Chambre held a consultation immediately, and sent commissioners in all directions to buy and ship grain with all possible expedition. *The high prices caused by Ferrand's prohibitions in no wise deterred the Abondance.* Of the 9500 ânées to be exported from Burgundy, the Abondance took licenses for 3500 ânées and distributed the rest among the charities of the town and the merchants. . . . We distributed to the bakers of the town the 2000 ânées of grain which came from Burgundy, fixing the price at 36 ll. . . . It was deemed expedient not to make the price lower, in order not to discourage the merchants; *and this much more than fear of loss forced us to maintain this policy.* We were not sure that we could do without their aid. The fear of ice and the closing of the river made us anxious, and we realized that the individual merchant is more industrious than a whole company." [1]

The Abondance clearly considered itself bound to furnish Lyons with grain at less than the market price. There was a constant feeling that the high prices of seasons of dearth were in a sense iniquitous and that prices must be brought down. This could be done only by sales at less than ordinary mercantile rates. It is difficult not to feel that the desire for low prices in time of dearth was unreasonable, and that the Abondance is from this time on endeavoring to procure a more abundant supply than could have been secured if all the trade were to yield a profit. Here we find the influence of the location of the city important. The possibilities of procuring food stuffs were limited. Lyons was never destined to become a great metropolitan center, but at the close of the seventeenth century the aspirations of the Lyonese were extensive. At that time the city was certainly of first-class importance, and the Lyonese were anxious for the future of their city. It is perhaps not too much to see in this last phase of the Abondance an indication of the pressure which was destined to limit the growth of the city. The population of Lyons was tending to increase more rapidly than the available food supply would warrant. The endeavor to procure grain at less than the commercial rate was a natural outcome of this pressure. But the efforts were doomed to failure, and in the course of the eighteenth century the Abondance gradually declined, almost in the same measure as the commercial prestige of the city. As Lyons sank into its natural position, the effort to procure grain below cost was abandoned.

[1] G^7. 358. Lyon, 25 Juillet 1699. Le Prévôt des Marchands à Villeroy.

CHAPTER IV

Lyonese Merchants and Dearth in the Producing Regions

The history of the grain trade in the Rhône Basin presents two relatively distinct problems. The more prominent is the creation of a supply area for Lyons. This required municipal encouragement, and even when the private trade had reached a high degree of development the citizens still felt that municipal purchases were necessary to assure reasonable prices. The other problem in the Rhône Basin attracts less attention but it is quite as important and throws more light upon the character of medieval trade and methods of marketing. There was a constant tendency to subject the producing regions to excessive withdrawals of grain, so that there was at times a serious dearth in the rural districts. In time of scarcity, the cities, with their free capital and wealthy bourgeois, could generally secure all the grain they needed. The poverty of the rural sections rendered much of the rural demand ineffective. The grain flowed towards the towns, and if any region suffered it was the country.

This seeming paradox is the fundamental fact in the relation between town and country. The commercial power of the town gave it an advantage that was decisive in seasons of dearth. The mechanism for supplying the city developed faster than the mechanism for protecting the country against the aggressiveness of the merchants. This was true both in the Seine Basin and in the Rhône Basin, but the difference in conditions rendered this feature of the trade less harmful in the Seine Basin than in Eastern France. The abundance of supply in most of the regions tributary to Paris, combined with the number of sources which might be utilized, prevented this pressure upon the country from becoming an actual menace to the welfare of the region. The dread of this contingency was, however, perennial.

In Champagne it recurs again and again, particularly in the regions on the frontier. From Soissonnais we receive graphic accounts of the impending peril. On the Upper Seine there are frequent complaints, especially from Troyes. But the danger is always forestalled. The anticipation is so lively, the means of relief so close at hand, that the ominous forebodings are never realized. In the Rhône Basin, the possibility becomes an actuality. The narrow limitations of supply, the difficulty of resorting to other sources, or of shifting the burden of trade from one locality to another, made the pressure of dearth felt in every section of the Rhône Basin whenever the crops failed to yield the average return. In the Seine Basin the rural districts suffered little from the lack of highly organized market machinery. In Eastern France, the country was in great need of protection from the excessive exports that might be made by the Lyonese merchants.

The source of all trouble was the inexact determination of the surplus above local needs. Both Burgundy and the Lower Rhône had a surplus, and if exports could be confined to this there would be no trouble, but the wholesale markets could not be forced to limit their purchases to the actual surplus. The crudity of market organization made it impossible to obtain any accurate information of the abundance of the harvest, of the amount of exports, or of the grain in the hands of the wholesale merchants but still in the province. Absence of reliable information on these fundamental points would have rendered current prices valueless, even if no other factors were involved. In addition to the ignorance of these conditions, we must bear in mind the influence of the modes of marketing. In the Rhône Basin, there were no true wholesale markets. The trade was not concentrated, except for shipment. There was little active competition among the wholesale merchants. They bought directly in the country, as far as possible, and did their best to avoid competition. Such competition as appears was intensely personal and not wide enough in scope to be properly effective. The wholesale supply was thus so invisible that the current prices did not represent the interplay of all the factors in the grain trade. This characteristic of current prices is most strikingly exemplified in connection with the relation between the local demand and the wholesale trade. These two demands upon the supplies of the producing regions were never formally pitted against each other. Wholesale merchants at times came into competition with the bourgeois of a particular town, but there was no general attempt to estimate the local demand of the whole producing region, nor any attempt to secure a comprehensive representation of the Lyonese demands.

The inadequacy of prices as a basis for the distribution of commodities is the most fundamental characteristic of the medieval market system. In some form, these general facts can be perceived throughout the history of the grain trade, without any important limitation as to time or place. It is the most wide-spread of all phenomena. But in most places the general principle is suggested only by a few brief remarks, or by indications so scattered that effective presentation is impossible. Three incidents, however, in the history of the trade in the Rhône Valley in 1693 and 1709 exhibit clearly what is elsewhere obscure, but everywhere of capital importance. These three episodes thus deserve attentive consideration not only because they are intrinsically interesting, but also because they afford an opportunity of appreciating fully the nature of the curiously tangled web of inter-market relations that prevailed throughout the medieval period and well into the eighteenth century.

I

Languedoc and Provence in 1693

After the harvest of 1693, the merchants and the Consuls of Lyons took measures to secure grain in Languedoc and Provence, as it was soon perceived that the crop in Burgundy was not so large as usual. Private merchants had been buying in the south before the harvest in May and June, but heavy losses on some of their shipments had discouraged them.[1] They hesitated at first to undertake new ventures, but the realization

[1] G7. 1631. Lyon, 6 Juin 1693. Bérulle au C. G.

of conditions in Burgundy roused them to activity and they were soon buying eagerly at Narbonne, Arles, Tarascon and in the other entrepôts of the southern provinces. In September, the merchants were well under way with their new purchases, equipped with licenses from Bérulle, the Intendant at Lyons, to authorize their exports from Languedoc despite the prohibitions.[1] The granting of licenses continued throughout September and October in ever increasing volume.[2] At the end of October, one of the agents charged with buying provisions for the army writes that he can do nothing in Languedoc and Provence on account of the merchants of Lyons who are buying everywhere and monopolizing all existing means of transportation.[3] In Provence especially, the activity of the Lyonese was notable. Chaiz was buying for the municipality, making enemies of all the private merchants by his efforts to prevent the shipment of their grain and to secure their purchases at a discount.

This feverish excitement on the part of the Lyonese caused much apprehension. Early in October, Bâville, the Intendant in Languedoc, ordered a domiciliary visitation to determine the quantity of grain available in the province and the population to be supplied.[4] The results were anything but encouraging. A population of 1,553,271 persons was reported. Nîmes, Agde, Béziers, Narbonne, Carcassonne, Saint-Papoul, and Mirepoix had a surplus of 410,524 quintals, above what was needed for their own consumption. These towns, however, were the principal shipping points in the province and elsewhere there was less than was needed to maintain the population to the next harvest. This deficiency was estimated at 1,741,918 quintals, very considerably in excess of the small surplus of the shipping points. Besides these statistics the commissioners made various observations in the text of their report. Of the dioceses of Uzès and Mende, they say: "The merchants of

[1] G^7. 1631. Lyon, 17 Sept. 1693. Bérulle.

[2] G^7. 1631. Estat des Passeports donnez pour les Bleds de Lyon, 15 Sept.–10 Oct. 1693. The diversity of measures makes the calculation of totals more burdensome than is worth while.

[3] G^7. 1632. Paris, 30 Oct. 1693. Signature illegible.

[4] G^7. 1631. Narbonne, 5 Oct. 1693. Le Franc de la Grange.

Lyons have carried off more than 20,000 quintals from the diocese of Uzès alone, and, although the diocese suffers, it will be able to get along with the chestnuts which are gathered there. But the situation is different in Mende. The supplies there will last only till April.

"Only in one part of Vivarais was the harvest tolerably good. In the rest of the diocese it was utterly inadequate. But there was a good crop of chestnuts, and as M. de Bâville took care to prevent exports, and some grain was sent up from Nîmes, and Upper Languedoc, it is hoped that the diocese will be able to subsist.

"The dioceses of Lodève and Saint-Pons scarcely ever produce enough grain for the maintenance of their inhabitants, who seek markets in the provinces of Narbonne and Béziers, where there is ordinarily enough to supply their wants.

"Castres, Lavaur, Alby, and Montauban have not witnessed so poor a harvest in many years. Some assistance can be sent from Saint-Papoul and from Carcassonne, but it can hardly be commensurate with their needs. . . ."[1]

Two months later, Bâville writes from Narbonne: "so large a number of poor come from Rouergue and Auvergne, singly and in families, that it is scarcely possible to provide for them. Their faces show that they abandon their homes rather on account of extreme misery than from any spirit of disorder and brigandage. The misery is greatest in the dioceses of Saint-Pons, Alby, Castres, and Mende. There is no grain, no money, and the dioceses have no credit."[2]

In Languedoc, then, the Lyonese merchants succeeded, during the fall, in depleting the reserves at the shipping points which otherwise would have served for the maintenance of the dioceses which had lacked. These dioceses, however, stood in no different relation to the markets in the shipping points, than Lyons. Consequently, the first merchants to arrive could purchase the available grain. The Lyonese were sure to arrive first,

[1] G^7. 1631. Procès Verbaux sur la Recherche des Grains dans Languedoc, 1693.

[2] G^7. 1631. Narbonne, 5 Dec. 1693. Bâville.

as the dioceses nearby could maintain themselves for a short time and ordinarily came down to Narbonne and the other coast ports only in the spring and early summer. The trade, if left to itself, would inevitably result as it did in 1693. This exhaustion of the province was the logical and inevitable result of the lack of organic interdependence between the various local markets of the province.

In Provence, the effect of the Lyonese purchases was less serious; there was constant apprehension, but the province was saved by relatively good crops in the interior, where the grain was not so convenient for shipment to Lyons.

Notwithstanding considerable imports from Languedoc, Provence, Burgundy, and Morocco, Lyons was not very easily supplied. In the latter part of May, 1694, Bérulle writes that there is only grain enough in the city to supply its wants for four days. Large shipments, however, were on their way up stream, and on June 12, the markets of Lyons were filled to overflowing.[1]

II

Burgundy in 1709

In 1709, we find that the endeavor to supply Lyons affects both Burgundy and Languedoc seriously. Unfortunately, there is no one in Burgundy so completely in touch with every detail as Bâville in Languedoc. The story of the troubles in Burgundy does not come to us, therefore, with his clearness of insight and masterly knowledge, but if we read between the lines, piecing together the scattered information that flows in from intendants, mayors, bishops, and private individuals, the general outlines of the narrative may be perceived.

Trouble began soon after the harvest of 1708. The first reports came in from Franche Comté whence much grain was generally shipped to the Saône towns. "The light crop," writes an official of Besançon, "has obliged us to employ all our powers in maintaining supplies in the public markets. But we have encountered many obstacles, through the great shipments made

[1] G7. 1633. Lyon, 23 Mai 1694. Bérulle. Lyon, 12 Juin 1694. Bérulle.

by Lyonese merchants. They have already exported 40,000 sacks, and the shipments continue without interruption by reason of the Order in Council of September 22, which permits the transportation of grain from one province to another. . . . More than thirty commission merchants have come from Lyonnais. They are now contracting for all the grain in the province. Prices have doubled, and if their contracts are executed in their entirety, we shall be reduced to famine." [1]

A merchant, who had contracted to deliver 15,000 sacks of wheat at Auxonne for the army, gives a more general account of conditions in the area supplying the same towns. He went up into Lorraine, October 10, and was much surprised to find a wide-spread apprehension of dearth of grain. "The bakers of Nancy were scouring the countryside, for six and seven leagues around, offering 6–7 livres of their money per rezal. . . . Such as had any grain to sell had closed their granaries as soon as the rumors of dearth became current. The panic spread to all the towns and villages of Lorraine, especially along the frontier of Champagne and Franche Comté, where there are more than fifty villages whose crops were completely ruined by the hail. The inhabitants have assembled in bands and prevented the shipment of grain purchased by the merchants of Auxonne. They cut the sacks and handle roughly those who are sent to ship the grain." [2]

One of the directors of the Chambre d'Abondance also describes the unusual conditions existing in Burgundy. Writing from Gray, August 30, he says: "Yesterday I passed the day at Maxilly and Talmay where there are great entrepôts of grain coming from Langres, but I found no one who would sell. They say they have none. I commissioned Pottier of Auxonne and Christianot of Maxilly to make a tour of Bassigny in secret, to see what they can find. However, there is little hope of

[1] G[7]. 1644. Besançon, 16 Nov. 1708. Vicomte, Mayeur. Lieu. Gén., et Échevins de B.

[2] G[7]. 1645. Mémoire présenté par Sebastien Maréchal à M. de St. Contest concernant le traitte de 15,000 sacs de froment, qu'il s'est obligé de fournir à Auxonne dans le fin de Dec. 1708.

getting any grain from the section before All Saints'. All we can do is to give commissions to trusty merchants to buy what they can along the Saône or in Franche Comté." [1]

Prohibitions had been issued by the Intendants in the months of July and August. There had been extensive purchases for the army, which had consumed the ordinary reserves, and on the crop failure their apprehension increased almost to the point of panic.[2] The incident furnishes an interesting illustration of the inadequacy of the market system. The supplies of the province were already seriously depleted, but nevertheless the merchants were no less eager to buy. The Intendant Pinon puts the matter very tersely in his letter of September 7. "The dearth which you fear at Lyons is already present in this province." [3] But Lyons was soon reduced to desperate straits. Ravat writes from Lyons, October 9: "Including what we have received from Burgundy, we have only 5000 ânées of grain. We need 1400–1500 ânées per week. We are not allowed to ship freely from Languedoc and Provence. Lyonnais and Beaujolais have no grain, and are on the verge of lacking bread." [4] Despite the seriousness of the situation at Lyons, the cities of Burgundy were no better off. The people at Dijon were on the point of breaking out in a bread riot, and the officials tried to calm them by renewing the old prohibitions.[5]

The panic, which was imminent throughout the fall and winter of 1708–09, finally broke out in the spring. The officials had arranged for limited shipments to relieve Lyons, but the people took the law into their own hands. Burgundy became a scene of violence and disorder which swept away the last vestige of organized trade.

[1] G7. 1645. Gray, 30 Août 1708. Perrin, Direct. d'Abondance à Ravat. Enclosed by Ravat in his letter of 7 September.

[2] Lyon, Arch. Mun., Chappe IV, 453, 20. Mémoire pour être envoyé à M. d'Argenson. Oct. 1708. This gives a brief account of the year preceding the date.

[3] G7. 1645. Bourg en Bresse, 1708. Pinon.

[4] G7. 1645. Lyon, 9 Oct., 7 Sept. 1708. Ravat, Prév. des Marchands.

[5] G7. 1641. Dijon, 1 Dec. 1708. Bouchu. Prem. Prés. du Parlement de Bourgogne.

"The fury of the people burst all bounds when they learned of the ordinance providing for the passage of the grain of Tremville, destined for the Abondance of Mâcon, and of some belonging to private merchants. It is said quite openly at Pontaillier and Auxonne that all grain will be stopped without distinction. The orders of the Intendant are disregarded. At Auxonne, the town guard and other troops were called out to stop the grain boats coming down the river. At Pontaillier, the grain of the Abondance de Lyon was seized and distributed to the people at a set price."[1] Similar violence was directed against the grain boats at Maxilly, Mantouche, and Gray.[2]

Around Dijon, the dearth had become actual famine. Commissioners of the Parlement of Dijon report, April, 1709, that "the peasants in the greater part of the province are already reduced to living on the bushes and herbs growing wild in the fields. They eat horses and other animals that have died of disease. In nearly all the towns and villages, the people are in revolt against the municipal officers and threaten to burn and kill the few inhabitants who have any property. In many places armed bands of peasants stop the convoys of grain destined for the sustenance of the towns."[3] Three days later, the market at Dijon was so scantily furnished (only 100 measures) that bread could hardly be had of the bakers. The President of the Parlement resolved to send out four companies of infantry to procure grain.[4]

Despite all this, mark the attitude of the Lyonese merchants. "Scarcely was the edict registered prohibiting the assemblies designed to interfere with the grain trade, than the merchants from Lyons came in great numbers to Saint-Jean-de-Losne and carried off all the grain. This may be the occasion of a great outburst of violence. . . . They give no heed, however. Several villages are reduced to frightful extremities; the inhabi-

[1] G7. 1645. Auxonne, 31 Mars 1709. Rude, Voiturier des Blés.

[2] G7. 1645. Lyon, 9 Avril 1709. Ravat.

[3] G7. 1641. 22 Avril 1709. Rapport des Commissaires du Parlement de Dijon.

[4] G7. 1641. Dijon, 25 Avril 1709. De Migieu.

tants maintain life only by eating boiled herbs and roots. Children of four or five years, for whom the mothers have no bread, feed in the fields like so many sheep." [1]

Langres, in the center of the main source of supply, was barely able to maintain itself through the spring months. "No longer able to draw any grain from the country, the bourgeois were obliged to furnish the markets and support the people from the month of February to the present time (July 1). Their charity and zeal for the public welfare have compassed so much, that although they ought to have closed their granaries to inhabitants of the country and reserved them for the townspeople, nevertheless they have continued markets for the country people two days of the week. Grain is furnished only to those who have a certificate of indigence from their curate. These markets have prevented the country people from dying of starvation, but they have drained the town of oats, and the wheat is nearly consumed." [2]

Upper Burgundy, the Saône towns, Dijon, and Langres were pretty well drained. The situation was even more serious in Lower Burgundy, Mâconnais, and the territory around Châlons-sur-Saône. Inadequately supplied by the vicinage, these towns generally secured some assistance from Upper Burgundy, but the Lyonese trade was about the only trade permitted at all during the year 1708–09, so that the distress was intense along the river between Lyons and Upper Burgundy. Curiously enough, the officials in these towns were under the impression that Lyons was superabundantly supplied. "We see numbers of boats pass, carrying grain for the Abondance at Lyons," writes the Bishop of Mâcon. "I checked a crowd of peasants who wished to stop the boats and buy of the boatmen, but I cannot promise to restrain them in the future. I know that the granaries of the Abondance at Lyons are full of grain, and it is trying to see them making reserves beyond their needs, when we are in actual want. . . . The peasants flock

[1] G[7]. 1641. Dijon, 4 Mai 1709. Quarré, Proc. Gén. au Parlement de Dijon.

[2] G[7]. 1643. Mémoire sur l'état Présent de la Ville de Langres, envoyé 1 Juillet 1709. Signé par M. L'Évêque et tout le corps de la Ville.

into town in crowds, seeking to buy grain. Frequently they are obliged to return without any." [1]

The other side of the story appears in a letter of Ravat, the Provost of Merchants at Lyons: "In Burgundy and along the Lower Rhône, it is just as if we were in hostile territory. Our grain is violently seized without any formality. The boatmen are attacked by armed men, who threaten to kill them if they offer the least resistance." "The needs of the city become daily more considerable, by reason of the peasants who flock in from all sides under the pretext of bringing a little butter or garden truck for sale. They eat their fill of bread and carry away as much as they can conceal from the guards at the gates." [2] A month later, — "We have put everybody on rations of a pound of bread per diem, and to make the breadstuffs last longer we have ordered every one to eat black bread. We no longer separate the bran from the flour." [3]

In the river towns, however, the distress of famine was increased by the lawlessness and brigandage which became general in April and May. At Auxonne, a crowd assembled about a merchant, whose life was saved only by a squad of soldiers. Somewhat later, all the grain merchants of Auxonne left the town for fear of being assaulted. The most graphic accounts appear in the letters of the Bishop of Châlons. He has a somewhat different explanation for some of the phases of the distress, but the difficulty of obtaining exact information is such that it is impossible to go beyond the statements made.

"There is great distress in this province," he writes April 12, "not on account of scarcity of grain, however, for that has existed for several years. The source of trouble is the avarice and hardness of the engrossers. Perceiving that the harvests were light, they bought up nearly all the grain, and guard it like so many dragons. The price is already high, and will double shortly, if the cupidity and avarice of these engrossers is not brought within bounds. Practically all persons of means

[1] G⁷. 1641. Macon, 5 Avril 1709. Évêque de Macon.

[2] G⁷. 1645. Lyon, 11 Avril 1709. Ravat.

[3] G⁷. 1645. Lyon, 25 Mai 1709. Ravat.

of all ranks and conditions have turned grain merchants within the last two months in order to profit by the distress of the people. Under pretext of not allowing the shipment of the grain in the villages, the peasants have taken arms. In some places, seditious spirits without honor or property have placed themselves at the head of these peasants, and lead them around, breaking into granaries to steal and pillage. They sell on the markets what they have stolen. Others infest the roads, crying and begging for bread, often demanding it with threats of violence. Throughout the country districts there is no security for one's purse or for one's life. The poverty of individuals is such that they cannot sow even the lesser grains, as they have none, nor any money to buy. The miserly engrossers wish to sell at seven and eight livres per bushel what we used to buy at eight or ten sous. We have issued an ordinance in this town requiring all the lesser grains to be brought to market within the next fortnight, to be sold at a reasonable price. . . .

"One other thing that does much to increase the misery is the pretext of the necessities of Lyons. That town has twice as much grain as it can use for several years. The granaries of the Hospital and of the Abondance are full. The only distress there was during the closing of the Saône to navigation by the ice. Since then, when all the river towns were resting on the assurance that they had an abundance of grain for several years, Lyons, which does not lack people who seek only their personal gain, has carried off all the grain in Bassigny, on the frontier of Lorraine, and in Burgundy. . . . Meanwhile, all the towns and villages of Burgundy suffer. The poor, unable to secure grain or bread, take whatever they can lay their hands on. The peasants leave their villages, and crowd into the towns, which close their gates in order not to increase the number of paupers.

"There is a little town called Seurre, noted for the rebellions in the wars of 1640–50, and for similar disorders in 1694. The well-to-do have turned 'pirattes de bled.' They scour the country for four or five leagues, taking everything on land or on the rivers. One of those who are most active has a band of 100–120 men, with a train of wagons. They break into the châteaux where there is grain, and carry off whatever they find on the rivers Saône and Doubs. All is carried to Seurre, where they have more than 15,000 bichets. If the war breaks out in the provinces, town against town, and the peasants all in arms, these disorders can end in nothing short of a general insurrection." [1]

"There is no grain on the markets of the towns. The towns that wish to procure supplies from outside can obtain them only by means of escorts of 100–200 men. The peasants are massed on the highways to prevent the shipment of grain from their villages, and the strongest carry off the grain. It is the beginning of a Civil War. The Intendant has ordered that all grain shall be carried to market, but little comes. Yesterday there were only eight bushels for 300–400 peasants who were complaining of the famine. The inhabitants of Macon, not wishing to take the risk of going after grain, have spread hand bills through the country for five or six leagues around offering to pay 100 francs per bichet. Despite the fact that the Lyonese have carried off more than 300,000 bichets in the last eight months, they are still scouring the country around the Saône and Doubs, offering 25–30 écus." [2]

"At Chauvort, a little village a quarter of a league from Verdun, and three from Châlons, there was a young man, Jean Baptiste Bret, formerly a grain merchant. He ruined himself by his misconduct and is now trying to redeem his fortune at the expense of the countryside. He has taken advantage of the general misery, to practise brigandage. With his band of followers he goes to the houses where he knows there is grain, carries it off by force, pays for part of it at such prices as suit his fancy, orders his men to take the rest under the pretext of pressing necessity, although most of his band are really engaged in the grain trade like their leader. At the least resistance they batter in the doors. All the honest people have already abandoned the town, on account of this violence. One of the

[1] G[7]. 1641. Châlons-sur-Saône, 12 Avril 1709. Henri, Évêque de Châlons. See also the letter of 8 May 1709 for further details about Seurre.

[2] G[7]. 1641. Châlons-sur-Saône, 21 Avril 1709. Henri, Évêque de Châlons.

Échevins, after resisting for quite a while, finally joined the band, and now boasts that he will soon be at the head of five hundred resolute men. He swears that he will make himself more feared in Burgundy than Cavalier was in the Cevennes." [1]

The letters of the Bishop of Châlons seem to be rather ill-informed in many respects; he has no accurate conception of conditions at Lyons, or of the extent of exports to Lyons, but his general impression of the cause of the trouble in Burgundy is probably true. It is hard to believe that there was really less grain in Burgundy in April and May, 1709, than was needed by the inhabitants. The closing of the granaries and the complete abandonment of even the old market system are quite enough to account for all the disorder. Yet, it is difficult to see how the crisis could have been met. The necessities of Lyons and the supplies sent to the royal granaries created a demand that led inevitably to the feverish speculation and disorganization of the markets. Lyons certainly did not secure any more grain than was barely necessary for her sustenance. The crisis revealed in startling clearness the necessity of closer organization of the trade.

III

Languedoc in 1709

In Languedoc there was more calm. The different factors can be traced more clearly, and the repression of the panic removed the distorting elements of violence and disorder. The harvest of 1708 in Languedoc was better than the average; distinctly good in Lower Languedoc, it was only slightly less abundant in the more fertile Upper Languedoc.[2] These reassuring crop prospects attracted a considerable trade to Languedoc. The Genoese came, as usual; the Lyonese also appeared, as in 1693; some grain passed from Upper Languedoc to Guienne. The fertile area in Languedoc thus shipped in three directions. The magnitude of the exports contemplated soon gave Bâville reason for serious apprehension. The Genoese were planning

[1] G⁷. 1641. Chauvort, 3 Mai 1709. P. Lebault.

[2] G⁷. 1644. Montpellier, 5 Août 1708. Bâville.

to buy 40,000 quintals, and by August 18 had sent 60 ships to Agde and Cette. The dearth in Guienne and Provence was then known. Bâville proposed that prohibitions of foreign export be used.[1] A week later, he reported that the Genoese came in increasing numbers. Without waiting for orders from the Contrôleur Général, he required them to get permits from him for the export of grain, and on his own authority limited exports temporarily to 1000 setiers.[2] The magnitude of the demands of the Genoese is explained by their intention of exporting to Spain and to the Estates of the Duke of Savoy.[3] They were only allowed to export 5000–6000 setiers, and before the general edict arrived at the end of October, most of the Genoese had left.[4] Shortly after, the municipality of Nice asked permission to buy, but they were refused.[5] In short, a very considerable element in the potential demand on Languedoc was deflected by administrative interference.

Before the Genoese had gone (September 16), the Abondance of Lyons appeared on the scene. They proposed to buy in the eastern portions of Languedoc where shipment up the Rhône would be easy.[6] Two weeks later, the demands of Lyons had taken definite shape in a request for permission to buy 18,000 setiers along the Rhône [7] — the least fertile part of the province which raised scarcely enough for its own maintenance. Bâville refused to grant the request, and told the agents from Lyons to begin by purchasing 3,000 setiers. By October 16, prices had begun to rise, despite the prohibitions of foreign export and the careful limitation of export to Lyons and Provence. Bâville tried to deflect the Lyonese agents to Narbonne.[8] Throughout December, the merchants of Lyons, Provence, and Guienne were drawing supplies from Languedoc. Towards the end of January

[1] G[7]. 1644. Montpellier, 18 Août 1708. Bâville.
[2] *Ibid.*, 26 Août 1708. Bâville.
[3] *Ibid.*, 1 Sept. 1708. Bâville.
[4] *Ibid.*, 28 Oct. 1708. Bâville.
[5] *Ibid.*, 2 Nov. 1708. Bâville.
[6] *Ibid.*, 16 Sept. 1708. Bâville.
[7] *Ibid.*, 1 Oct. 1708. Bâville.
[8] *Ibid.*, 16 Oct. 1708. Bâville.

1709, Bâville reported that prices were still rising. He was obliged to extend his prohibitions to Guienne, though exports were to continue under cover of permits. In this manner, 20,000 setiers, purchased by Bourdonnaye, the Intendant at Bordeaux, were to be shipped to Agenois. Meanwhile, Provence had become practically dependent upon Languedoc. Bâville was trying to furnish 25,000 quintals per month.[1] In March, distress appeared in Languedoc. "Grain is as dear as in Guienne or Provence. In many places there have been popular tumults, especially in the Vivarais. In this crisis it will be impossible for me to continue with my plans to aid Provence. I shall oblige the merchants, to whom I have given permits, to go there, although they would much perfer not to ship their grain from Languedoc, where they can sell as dear as in Provence without incurring any risk."[2] By the end of the month, panic had developed. "The price of grain has declined at Toulouse, and risen slightly in Lower Languedoc, but the difficulty is no longer a matter of prices. The grain itself is lacking everywhere. There has suddenly been a complete cessation of commerce, arising in part from the fear that there will be no harvest this year. All who have a little grain have resolved to hoard it and keep it for their sustenance. All the markets have ceased in the larger towns. The towns, beginning with Montpellier, are oppressed by anxieties, rendered doubly keen by the mercurial temper of the people. Narbonne, Béziers, and Agde, which are the granaries of the province, have sent deputies to beg me to allow them to hold what they have, as it is no more than sufficient for their needs. Although it is contrary to my principles, I have issued several ordinances requiring the opening of granaries and the bringing of grain to market. I have also instigated inquiries to discover how much grain we could count on."[3]

In April, serious consequences appeared in Lower Languedoc. "The trade with Upper Languedoc had ceased." Bâville

[1] G[7]. 1644. Montpellier, 25 Jan. 1709.
[2] *Ibid.*, 15 Mars 1709.
[3] *Ibid.*, 26 Mars 1709. Bâville. See also, Montpellier, 18 Mars 1709. Bâville.

proposed "to open the granaries in the dioceses of Toulouse, Lavaur, and Alby, to take what was absolutely necessary."[1] Montpellier and Nîmes had only enough grain to last two weeks. Bâville accordingly proposed that Joubert, the Sindic of Languedoc, should go to Castelnaudary, to confer with Royer from Toulouse and with the merchants who had been buying in Guienne and Montauban. It was hoped that some division of supplies could be arranged for both Toulouse and Lower Languedoc.[2] This was finally done after much negotiation, and both Toulouse and Lower Languedoc were supplied.

The scarcity prevailing and the slight hopes of an average harvest in 1709 rendered some importation indispensable. In May, Bâville began to arrange for shipments from the Levant. The towns of Montpellier, Nîmes, Carcassonne, and Agde gave pledges to secure the residents against loss. The province as a whole furnished some funds.[3] This grain began to arrive in September and arrivals continued throughout the winter months of 1709–10.

IV

These three incidents in the history of the trade in the Rhône Valley indicate at once the possibility of actual depletion of the producing regions and the importance of the element of panic. The quantities of grain available seem to have been much less inadequate than the confusion and distress would give us reason to believe. Administrative interference did much to relieve pressure upon the supply in the granaries, and formed reserves uncertain in extent, but of great importance in time of distress, thus tending to counteract the unfortunate circumstances which so frequently fomented panics. The presence of these corrective tendencies makes it peculiarly difficult to determine how much of the excitement in time of dearth was mere unreasoning fear, and how much was well grounded apprehension.

[1] G^7. 1644. Montpellier, 19 Avril 1709. Bâville.

[2] *Ibid.*, 22 Avril 1709. Bâville à Riquet 2e. Prés. du Parlement de Toulouse.

[3] *Ibid.*, 21 Mai 1709. Bâville. See also Letters of 7 Juin 1709, 23 Juin 1709.

The most cursory reading of the official correspondence in time of dearth suggests that much of the complaint of dearth was wholly due to a failure to understand new developments in trade. The cry of *disette* appears as soon as some busybody asserts that there is not enough grain in town to last until the next harvest. No attention whatever is given to the possibility of securing grain from other points to replace grain exported. The possibility of such compensating movements is relatively foreign to the ordinary thought of the time. Each worthy burgher was possessed with the idea that famine stared him in the face, if the granaries of the town did not actually contain all the grain that would be needed till the next harvest. The largest towns had, of course, outgrown these notions, but elsewhere there was no conception of a steady flow of trade supplying the wants of the town from month to month without ever accumulating any very considerable reserve. A steady distributive trade of this type was in truth a relatively new feature in commercial life. Trade had been highly seasonal, and, except for the trade of the locality centering on the town market, the connection of the town with the larger centers of commerce was limited to the various fairs. The grain trade had never had quite the same customs as the other branches of trade, but the principle appears in this feeling that the producing region should never permit the exportation of grain unless the maintenance of the area till the next harvest was assured. When these limits were reached, the parties seeking grain should be excluded and sent elsewhere. Each town was to secure supplies for itself without regard to the needs of other towns. Combination among towns to secure a supply to be used for common needs was foreign to the ideas of the ordinary people, even in the seventeenth century, though it appears clearly in some phases of administrative policy.

In 1693, Arles and Tarascon wished to close their gates to the merchants of Lyons. The harvest in the immediate vicinity had been light, and the Lyonese merchants were active. Prices had begun to rise early in September, and even the Subdélégué suggested some limitation of shipments to Lyons.[1] In October, Lebret writes: "The inhabitants of Arles, Tarascon, and the vicinity have already sold to the Lyonese, or the merchants from Dauphiné, two-thirds of their *surplus* grain." [2] Apprehensions were repeated frequently in the letters. In November, Lebret ordered a domiciliary visitation to determine the quantity of grain in Arles, Tarascon, and other places. The investigation revealed that Arles had not enough to last till the harvest.[3] A week later, the magistrates of Arles were surprised to find that Lebret was authorizing a shipment of 600 setiers to Lyons. "We take the liberty to represent that this grain is included in the declaration which we submitted. If what remains for our own provision is deflected elsewhere, we shall no longer be able to find sustenance for our inhabitants. We have not the resources which we once possessed." [4] Lebret yielded to these instances,[5] but he had had quite a different plan for the conduct of the grain trade.

The policy that he had intended to follow is sketched in his letter of September 25: "The orders I have given to Chaiz, to discontinue his purchases, have produced the effect I had in mind. The price of grain along the Rhône has risen to a figure that will attract foreign grain, without giving the people cause to grumble. I hope to be able to continue after this fashion. When the price falls rather low, I shall give currency to the talk of dearth at Lyons; then, if the price rises to 19^{ll}–20^{ll} per charge, I shall have all purchases discontinued. In this way, I shall be able to allow Lyons to draw from Provence for more than six months. The success of this project will depend on what comes in from foreign ports, so that I shall have to maintain the strictest secrecy. None must be informed of my intentions but the little birds that I use to spread my rumors. Our principal object should be to attract foreign grain. To

[1] G^7. 1632. Aix, 6 Dec. 1693. Lebret. *Ibid.*, Arles, 22 Août 1693. Le Roy, Subdélégué. *Ibid.*, Aix, 10 Sept. 1693. Lebret.

[2] G^7. 1632. Aix, 14 Oct. 1693. Lebret.

[3] G^7. 1631. Lambesc, 13 Nov. 1693. Lebret à Bérulle.

[4] G^7. 1631. Arles, 24 Nov. 1693. Maire et Échevins d'Arles à Lebret.

[5] G^7. 1631. Lambesc, 26 Nov. 1693. Lebret à Canaples.

do that, prices must be maintained at a relatively high level, so that it will be inexpedient to publish any statement to the effect that Lyons will have no more need of the grain of Provence." [1]

The development of continuous trade was of importance in most of the towns of Languedoc and Provence and in other places, such as Rouen, Orleans, Bordeaux, and Nantes. But it would be easy to exaggerate the extent of this new feature in the grain trade. While it is true that in areas of active movement it was no longer customary to hoard the year's supply, the old self-sufficiency was still an actual fact. It is hard to stigmatize as unreasoning the apprehensions which appear in relatively infertile sections, when the season's supply is not assured.

Closely connected with the gradual transition to a continuous distributive trade were the latent defects of the old market system. These were much more potent breeders of panic than the failure to perceive the new tendencies. Uncertainty, which is the insidious cause of every panic, obscured every stage in the wholesale marketing of grain. At no step in the process was it possible to perceive clearly the extent of either supply or demand. The total amount of the crop was never accurately known, since the amount of grain hidden away in the granaries of land-owners was quite beyond any powers of calculation. Added to these uncertainties was the uncertainty as to the exact amount of grain purchased by merchants from distant towns for export.

The statistics which appear in the administrative correspondence as "États des Bleds" merely reveal the colossal extent of contemporary ignorance. In 1693, a fairly systematic endeavor was made to prepare such estimates throughout the kingdom.[2] The attempt was carried out in several provinces, but it was found that it did more harm than good. The figures for the towns were generally pretty accurate, and as the inquiry frequently revealed greater scarcity than had been realized, the

[1] G[7]. 1632. Aix, 25 Sept. 1693. Lebret.

[2] G[7]. 1630–34, *passim*.

reports merely spread panic. The inquiries were successfully prosecuted only in the regions of slight activity in the grain trade or in the consuming regions. In the producing regions, crop estimates never progressed beyond the merest guesses.[1]

This invisibility had curious results. In 1662, the Parlement of Toulouse issued prohibitions of export from its jurisdiction. Hotman was buying in the vicinity for Paris and the Lower Loire Valley. The merchants with whom he had made engagements cancelled their contracts. Hotman then proceeded to buy large quantities in the granaries of the nobility. Permits made shipments possible despite the prohibitions, and Paris and the Lower Loire were thus supplied from an area where there was sufficient scarcity apparent to give color to prohibitions.[2] This curious paradox is simply and adequately explained by the ignorance of the quantities available in the granaries. It is possible, of course, that the prohibitions were not based on any sincere conviction of their necessity, but references to riots in divers places render this supposition unlikely.

The evidence is not always quite so clear, but there are many indications that a similar explanation would frequently apply to Burgundy. In September, 1693, it was clearly the intention of the merchants to draw entirely from the granaries. "The grain merchants of Lyons, who have through their correspondents the best information about Burgundy, are quite certain of the places where the grain of preceding harvests is to be found. They assure me that the new grain and the buckwheat (blé noir), which is the ordinary food of the people, are more than sufficient for the sustenance of the inhabitants, and that Burgundy can safely dispose of its old grain."[3] The independence of the granary supplies and the local markets thus created a greater appearance of dearth than was actually warranted. The quantity existing in the granaries was never known,

[1] Excepting, of course, the estimates for single towns, such as those made by Delamare in 1709, and by other agents of Paris at various dates.

[2] Bib. Nat., Mél. Colb., 107 bis. 832. Agen, 21 Jan. 1662. Hotman. *Ibid.*, 107, 463. Agen, 11 Fev. 1662. Hotman. *Ibid.*, 107, 22. Bordeaux, 20 Mars 1662. Hotman. *Ibid.*, 108, 152v. 17 Avril 1667. Mémoire par Hotman.

[3] G[7]. 1631. Lyon, 4 Sept. 1693. Jourdain, Marchand de Lyon.

and was generally under-estimated. All these factors were more likely to create panic than to afford confidence to a people that saw its markets scantily supplied.

Finally, the informal manner in which wholesale purchases were made was sure to give rise to the wildest kind of rumors. There is a definiteness about a market which is always an element of safety. The market may be subject to great eccentricities, and there is, of course, a tendency to mild hysteria at times, but the concentration of buying on a market does render the demand an ascertainable factor. The absence of such markets in most of the producing regions made trade conditions subject to panic in the calmest moments. The administrative corresspondence is constantly revealing this curious feature, now in brief asides, now in strict injunctions to some agent, now in scornful criticism of the clumsy action of agents or merchants. Not infrequently, the first rise in prices in a period of dearth is attributed exclusively to this cause. Speaking of Burgundy in March, 1693, Bérulle writes: "there was never so much grain in that province as there has been this year. The *munitionnaire* has made all his purchases there, and there is still a vast quantity left. I am told that certain individuals in that province have purchased more than 100,000 ânées. The rise in prices is due to the slight precautions taken by the agents of the *munitionnaires*. Instead of making secret contracts for their purchases, they ride around the country in person in their *chaise roulant*. Le Noble, who was charged with the purchases, sent prices up, an écu per ânée, at one stroke, by his unskilful conduct. Still, what has contributed the most has been the formation of granaries by divers inhabitants of Burgundy, who are persuaded that grain is sure to rise. They have bought all they could and have closed their granaries; as little grain comes to market prices have risen." [1]

It is the same story in the south. "The rumor has spread here," writes Le Bartz at Marseilles in June, 1693, "that orders for large purchases are to come from Lyons. I have been told since that a man has arrived who says that he is to buy 15,000

[1] G⁷. 1631. Lyon, 2 Mars 1693. Bérulle, Intendant à Lyon.

charges. A fine beginning! His purchases should all be made before anyone knows that he is here buying; and when it is all done he must minimize the extent of his shipments. If he has really bought 15,000, he must admit only 3000–4000."[1] With all their worldly wisdom, the merchants were seldom able to restrain themselves at the critical moment following the realization that a dearth was likely. The mercantile parlance develops an idiom which expresses rather exactly the character of the wholesale trade at such periods. When the merchants hurry through the country, buying right and left in the granaries or of the peasants, seeking to secure control of the crop at any cost, they are said to "*mettre le feu sur les bleds*."[2] This idiom is of universal currency, appearing in all sections, and with all its connotation it no more than expresses that state of feverish speculation which such haphazard buying so inevitably created.

But despite all this excitement, despite all this publicity of scattered, isolated incidents in the buying of the wholesale merchants, there is never the slightest possibility of discovering how much they have bought or how much there is to buy. Every fact that tends to develop panic is paraded before the public, every detail that could allay apprehension is usually inconspicuous or secret. The merchants themselves are as much in the dark as the people. Each knows the extent of his own dealings, none can have any idea, however crude, of the extent of others' purchases. A panic is essentially unreasoning fear, but under these circumstances it is hardly surprising that reasonable men became panic stricken.

[1] G[7]. 1632. Marseille, 8 Juin 1693. Le Bartz. See also G[7]. 1632. Marseille, 1 Juin 1693. Le Bartz.

[2] Here is an example from Tournus sur Saône, from Le Noble, the *munitionnaire:* "Les lettres que je recois de Maxilly et de Saint-Jean-de-Losne me marquent, que le feu se met tout de nouveau sur les bleds qui restent en Bourgogne. . . . Le nommé Vacher d'Auxonne, et le nommé Bonnardot qui demeure du costé de Verdun et qui est frère et parent de trois ou quatre marchants du mesme nom à Lyon, ayant porté la mine de Saint-Jean-de-Losne qui ne peize que 650 lbs. à 50[ll]. C'est à dire que celle de Maxilly qui peze 750 lb. va venir à 55 ll. bien qu'elle n'etoit que 48 ll. . . . Si ces gens la qui ont desia de fort grosses parties de bleds acheptées et enarrés ont la liberté d'aller leur train dans le temps present . . . les bleds n'auront point de prix." G[7]. 1631. Tournus, 14 Juillet 1693.

CHAPTER V

Areas of Highly Localized Markets and Extremes of Misery

In regions of active trade all the difficulties can be traced to the confusion caused in the producing regions by the demands of the larger towns; in those parts where the local markets were not thus disturbed, other troubles developed out of the isolated position. No part of France escaped, whether fertile or sterile; frequented by metropolitan merchants, or so completely isolated that the local market had practically no relations with the outside world. The producing regions tributary to the great cities might be threatened with dearth, but usually relief could be procured either through prohibitions or by imports from some favored regions. In the remote sections of the back country, supplies were almost never carried off by unduly aggressive merchants, but if the crops failed in these sterile sections, it was very difficult to secure relief from elsewhere. The apathy of the few merchants of such towns was so great that little could be hoped from private initiative, so that here, too, the grain trade was in need of administrative interference. These rural sections were constantly confronted with the possibility of actual famine, and on the whole these isolated localities experienced the greatest extremes of misery.

The conditions were not characteristic of all areas where the market system was highly localized; a number of relatively isolated towns escaped the form of trouble that most threatened the independent local market. Where the locality formed an enclave in the territorial area comprised in the market system of a great city, there was little danger. Local supplies were usually adequate, and generally unmolested by the wholesale merchants. If crops failed and the province was threatened with dearth, the existence of the great trade routes offered sufficient facilities for obtaining supplies. These localities were numerous. The markets of Blois and Tours, which have been described in a previous chapter, were both of this type. So also, on the Upper Loire, were all the larger towns between Orleans and Riom. On the Rhône, such towns as Châlons-sur-Saône, Mâcon, Vienne, Montélimar, Avignon were in this position. None were regularly in trade with any large town; their supplies were obtained independently. In the Seine Basin, it is more difficult to classify the doubtful towns. The river towns for the most part were engaged in trade with Paris, except when they were beyond the usual trade limits. But there were many towns on the borders of the territory tributary to Paris which were enclaves. Rheims, Laon, Rethel, in the Marne Valley; Sens and the Yonne towns; Troyes and the upper reaches of the Seine — all these were outside the usual area of Parisian trade, and yet near enough to derive relief from the wholesale merchants in the time of dearth. In the south, many towns of this type can be found along the trade routes, both in Languedoc, on the line of the Canal du Midi, and in Guienne, on the Garonne. These places probably suffered less from the disorders of the grain trade than any other type of market area. They enjoyed all the advantages of freedom from intimate connection with the large towns, and at the same time, all the possibilities of relief assured them by the proximity of such organized trade as existed.

The special problems arising out of the highly localized market system were confined to the inhospitable cantons of central France, to the rugged sections of the north-east, and to the sandy plains of Saintonge and Angoumois. The inhabitants of these extensive regions were obliged to draw their livelihood from the sterile soil and from the forests. There was little trade, little industry, little communication of any kind with the outside world. Even in the latter part of the seventeenth century, many of these remote towns and villages seem almost literally "self-sufficing." But the dearth of records in such regions reduces us to mere conjecture, and as "self-sufficiency" should not be emphasized as a vital feature of the localized market, it is best not to insist on the probabilities. Whenever detailed descriptions come to light, some inter-market trade is revealed, a very inconsiderable trade to be sure, involving only two or three small markets, but still inter-market trade. One of the most precise reports from a region of highly localized trade is the memoir of Saint Contest on the Élection of Brive, in Angoumois.

"The élection is composed of ninety-four parishes, in half of which a considerable quantity of wine is made. Part is consumed locally, and part is sold in Upper Limousin and down Bordeaux way. The grain raised is rye, barley, patris, buckwheat, and all sorts of vegetables. These lands do not produce one-tenth of the wheat and oats needed. Those grains are imported from the vicinity of the Vicomté of Turenne, from Périgord, and from Quercy. The other sorts of grain do not suffice for the inhabitants, and the deficiency is made up by the other half of the élection, by Tulle, and by Auvergne. Pasturage is very rare. In the other half of the élection there is an abundance of rye and of chestnuts, a sufficiency of forage and pasture, and also much buckwheat and oats. There is very little commerce in the élection, and the commodities sold there are very low in price. In some cantons, there is a very delicate sort of wine, which is sold in the parishes that have no vineyards and in the vicinity of Limoges; formerly the trade was considerable . . . but since vines have been planted in Upper Limousin there has been a great diminution in the sales. The poorer wines are turned into brandy and sent down to Bordeaux . . . but that trade does not amount to much. The trade in cattle is more considerable. Wheat is so cheap that the Paris bushel sells at 5–6 sous." [1]

The interesting fact here is not so much the slightness of the general trade of the region, as the independence of central markets. Grain prices are apparently determined not by prices in Montauban, Toulouse, or Bordeaux, but by the local demand and supply. Part of the supply indeed comes from sections

[1] G[7]. 345. 16 Juillet 1687. Mémoire de St. Contest sur l'Élection de Brive.

that might at times be in touch with the Garonne Valley trade, but for the most part this little area is governed by its own local market. The medieval system, in its developed form of a market with *blatiers*, is quite adequate in *ordinary* seasons.

Auvergne, another of the relatively barren provinces, is not without trade. "This province is composed of six élections, Aurillac, Brioude, and Saint-Flour, or Upper Auvergne, Riom, Clermont, and Issoire, or Lower Auvergne. In Lower Auvergne there is the section called Limagne, which is a very fertile but not a wealthy section, as the difficulties of trade oblige the inhabitants to consume themselves what is produced.[1]

"Upper Auvergne is a mountainous country, covered with snow for six months in the year, but it possesses great advantages for grazing, which is the basis of considerable trade in cattle and cheese. The inhabitants secure their grain in Lower Auvergne." [2]

Local rural trade of this type appears also in Rouergue. Velay and the Venaissin drew supplies from the neighborhood of Millau. There was a slight trade in grain between the élections of Limoges and Bourganeuf.

In all of these cases there is some definite record, but a large portion of the territory of the kingdom does not appear in the records at all. The condition of these sections is by no means unimportant although we can do little more than speculate. Fortunately we are not entirely without evidence. The great dearth of 1693 led in some regions to the creation of crude statistics which are of especial interest by reason of the light thrown upon the distribution of population.

In Alençon, in 1693, there are detailed figures for each village, and a tabulation of four territorial divisions exhibits these results, which represent a very fair average for the region. (See table on following page.)

[1] The grain from this section was the basis of the trade of Paris, Orleans, and Lyons in Auvergne. Recourse was had to Auvergne perhaps only in years of trouble but there was always a spasmodic grain trade with this part of Auvergne.

[2] G^7. 101. 1683. Mémoire envoyée par M. de Bercy.

An inspection of the roll of parishes suggests that about one-half the population was living in villages of less than five hundred inhabitants.[1] Similar statistics for the Généralité of Pau show that the average size of villages was 200 inhabitants.[2]

Élection	No. of Parishes	No. of towns of 1000 or more inhab.	Extreme range in the size of villages	Size of towns
			persons	
Verneuil				
Chât. de la Ferté Arnault	20	. . . . .	120–450	. . . . .
Alençon				
Baillage de Moulins .	17	1	130–700	1900
Vicomté d'Effey	53	7	80–900	1000–3000
Vicomté d'Alençon . .	42	3	153–938	1100, 1180, 12,000

In 1682, in the County of Bigorre, an enumeration of the villages and towns by families gives the following results: —

Less than 10 families	10–20 families	21–50 families	51–100 families	101–200 families	201–500 families
24	85	116	15	4	9

In the whole county there were only thirteen places of more than 100 families. The characteristic size of the village was between 15 and 45 families.[3]

On the whole, there is enough evidence to suggest that the population, especially in the infertile districts, was very widely scattered in relatively small villages. There was a minimum of concentration, and for this reason these little villages must have been able to get along with very rudimentary commercial machinery. A few small villages and a central market town may well have found no development of the primitive market necessary. These out of the way regions escape notice, but it is well not to forget their existence, for the pushing of the

[1] G[7]. 1630. 5 Dec. 1693.

[2] G[7]. 1640. Sept. 1709. Déhombrement de tout le pays de Basse Navarre.

[3] G[7]. 132. Papiers des États de Béarn. Estat de Villes et Paroisses qui sont dans la Comte de Bigorre; avec la nombre des feux et des families.

metropolitan market system into these remote sections is one of the characteristic features of the late nineteenth century, a reflex movement following the perfection of central organization. So far as we have any material, it appears that the comparatively infertile sections were outside the general movement of the grain trade. The effect of a failure of crops in these regions is thus an interesting speculation. If we draw the simpler deductions that suggest themselves, we might infer that in periods of scarcity the people simply starved. This, indeed, was only too frequently the case.

An idea of the intensity of famine may best be obtained from the substitutes resorted to. In some regions there were systematic endeavors to ascertain the utility of common herbs. The most elaborate record of such attempts, with which I am acquainted, is in the papers of Dr. Gilbert Rêtif, of Pont-de-Vaux in Lower Burgundy. This was a region of great distress in 1693; it was just south of the more productive parts of the province, and unable to secure much relief, as whatever went out was sent to Lyons. The experience of that year was apparently the moving cause underlying his experiments, for when he sent his memorials to Paris in 1699, they were evidently the result of considerable labor. He used the daffodil or asphodel most frequently in his trials, but he does not seem to have considered much more than the agreeableness of his bread. The experiments most frequently took the form of giving people this asphodel bread when they supposed they were having ordinary bread; failure to perceive any difference is the principal argument in its favor. There was no consideration of the actual food value of the bread. This doctor made a trip through Angoumois and Limousin to experiment on the herbs there, — an interesting indication of the needs of that ill-favored region. The asphodel was found, and Rêtif made his suggestions. The local officials demurred; they said that the root was poisonous. He cited the doctors and herbalists of antiquity in favor of the herb. In one place the local doctors were commissioned to test the plant. They boiled it, and made "learned" notes on the properties of the mash. Then they burned it, and examined the ashes.

Next they pressed it, and subjected the liquid to such tests as could be made with the five senses of man. After this hocus pocus the herb was pronounced safe.[1]

None of the other attempts at substitution were quite as deliberate as that of the Burgundian doctor, but all sorts of expedients were tried with various degrees of success. In Rouergue, in July, 1709, the chestnuts gave out, and the people eked out the little rye and barley that remained with the asphodel.[2] The same root was used in parts of Touraine in 1709.[3] In parts of Languedoc, dog-bane (chien dent) was used mixed with rye or wheat.[4] In all these cases, the subsidiary roots were used merely to make the small supplies of grain last longer. The use was apparently not attended with any serious results. In Limousin and Périgord, turnips were used as a dilution for the grain.[5]

The Duc de Lesdiguières, writing from Dauphiné in May, 1675, says that "the inhabitants (of Dauphiné) have lived during the past winter on bread made from acorns and roots, and now they are reduced to eating grass in the fields and the bark of trees." [6]

In 1686, Bâville writes that many people in the Cevennes live on acorns and herbs.[7] In September, 1693, Bouchu, Intendant in Dauphiné, writes a most extraordinary letter. He speaks of the difficulties in the way of making investigations of the quantity of grain, and after admitting that conditions are desperate, he continues: "the hard life to which these people are accustomed is in itself a ground for hope. It is no exaggeration to say that the greater part of the provinces of Tarantais and Maurienne have lived, since 1690, on flour made from nut-

[1] G[7]. 1637. 1699. Mémoires et Documents sur le pain de Racine nouvellement inventi par M. Gilbert Rétif, Doc. en Méd. de la Ville de Pont-de-Vaux. Journal d'un Voyage en Angoulême et Limousin.

[2] G[7]. 1646. Montauban, 31 Juillet 1769. Le Gendre.

[3] Boislisle, *op. cit.*, III, 171–450. 14 Juin 1709. Turgot à Tours.

[4] G[7]. 1644. Montpellier, 30 Août 1709. Bâville.

[5] Boislisle, *op. cit.*, I, 514, 1828. 17 Jan. 1699. Bernage, Intendant à Limoges. G[7]. 138. Périgueux, 2 Jan. 1699. Évêque de Périgueux.

[6] Bib. Nat., Mél. Colb., 171, 333. Grenoble, 29 Mai 1675.

[7] Boislisle, *op. cit.*, I, 65, 265. 29 Mars 1686.

shells, in which the most well-to-do do not mix more than a tenth part of oats or barley meal. M. de Chamlay is a witness to the truth of this, and he has carried samples of this sort of bread to the King."[1]

At times some villages in the distressed regions were reduced to downright starvation, and in these crises, anything, everything was used. The accounts seem at times to indulge in an excess of statement, but the official character of the correspondence and the position of the writers make it hard to believe that the letters fail in any respect but understatement. In March, 1662, M. Bellay, a doctor at Blois, writes to the Marquis de Sourdéac, "In the thirty-two years that I have been a doctor in this province, I have never seen anything that approaches the desolation now existing at Blois, where there are 4000 (poor) who have flowed in from neighboring parishes. In the country the dearth is greater. The peasants have no bread. They pick up all kinds of meat scraps, and the moment that a horse dies, they fall upon it and eat it.

"Malign fevers are beginning at Salinier (?). The poverty is so great that there is a little barley that has not been bought, as no one had any money. The artisans are dying of hunger, the bourgeois is so grievously afflicted (that he cannot aid the poor). I have just learned that a child was found at Cheverny that had eaten its own hands. These are horrors which fairly make your hair stand on end."[2] In order to arouse the sympathy of the Parisians, and to secure relief funds, a letter from the Superior of the Carmelite Convent at Blois was printed and distributed at Paris as a hand-bill. "There are 3000 poor in the town and faubourgs of Blois. Grain is worth 200 écus per muid, measure of Paris, and prices are still rising. The poor people in the country look like disinterred corpses. . . . Whenever they find dead horses or mules or other beasts they fill themselves with the rotten meat, which destroys rather than maintains life. The poor people of the town live like pigs on bran mash, and consider themselves lucky when they get a

[1] Boislisle, *op. cit.*, I, 338, 1235. 22 Sept. 1693.

[2] Bib. Nat., Mél. Colb., 107, 344. Bellay, Médecin à Blois, 2 Mars 1662.

belly full of that stuff. They pick up decayed cabbage stalks in the gutters, and then they cook these with bran. They beg for the water in which salt codfish has been cooked. . . . In the fields and along the roads, women and children have been found dead, their mouths still full of grass." [1]

In the spring of 1694, there were reports of serious famine in various places. Near Villefranche in Beaujolais, some of the peasants had been reduced to such poverty by the failures of the crops that they no longer had any money to buy grain, and were reduced to eating raw herbs.[2] In another part of Beaujolais, the distress was due to actual physical lack of supplies. "There is not in any parish of Charollais half the grain that is needed for its sustenance till the harvest. At present the poor people live on bread made from the roots of ferns, which causes terrible outbreaks of disease. The decent people cannot stay in the churches during mass. At Charolles and Paray the poor die of hunger in the streets, without anyone being able to assist them. They are far too numerous, and grain is not to be had for money."[3] In Lower Armagnac, the Archbishop of Auch says the population is only a quarter of what it was three years before. Sickness and migration are responsible for the diminution. In many places the people live on grape pips (Pepins de raisins), roots, and ferns which they grind up to make flour." [4]

In 1709, similar extremes of misery are reported. At Valence, "les plus mauvaises herbes font à présent presque toute leur nourriture." [5] In the less fertile sections of the generality of Orleans the distress was intense. "The people in the country near Bourges, having no money to buy grain are reduced to eating herbs and roots, which they boil without any salt or other seasoning, so that grave epidemics are feared." [6] The officers

[1] Arch. Nat., A. D. XI, 37. 1662. Imprimé dans la Bibliothèque Rondonneau. "Avis Important."

[2] G^7. 1635. 1694. Deux Placets de Noyel, Receveur Général de la Taille en Villefranche.

[3] Boislisle, *op. cit.*, I, 357, 1298.

[4] *Ibid.*, I, 360. 6 Sept. 1694. Archévêque d'Auch.

[5] G^7. 1643. Valence, 14 Mai 1709. Évêque de Valence.

[6] G^7. 1640. Bourges, 3 Mai 1709. Foullé, Intendant à Bourges.

of Douzy write: "We have no grain for our maintenance. More than three-quarters of the inhabitants and the peasants for four leagues around are reduced to eating unseasoned herbs and the cattle that they kill in the fields." [1]

It is idle to deny the sporadic existence of the utmost extremes of misery, but a moment's reflection will bring these relatively isolated cases within proper bounds. In many instances the extremes were suffered only by the indigent, swelled undoubtedly in number by the heavy losses entailed by accident to the crops, but, after all, only a part of the population. Furthermore, actual lack of bread was confined to rural districts. At times the towns were possessed of very small reserves; occasionally, they were obliged to put their inhabitants on rations, as at Lyons in 1693 and 1709. But the towns did not starve. Then, too, only certain parts of the country districts suffered. I have seen only one instance of such suffering in a fertile region,[2] and in that case the lack of means was perhaps a more considerable factor than lack of grain. Despite all the highly colored statements that have been made up about the dearths in France, I cannot believe that the extremes of distress pictured were anything more than infrequent and highly localized phenomena. All the cases of the sort that I have seen have been cited here or in other places,[3] and the presumption is very strong when such striking conditions are not reported more frequently in a mass of correspondence, such as that of the Contrôle Général.[4] Conditions were bad enough, but they certainly were not as desperate as has often been represented.

[1] G[7]. 1646. Douzy, 13 Juin 1709. Les Officiers de la Pairies de Douzy.

[2] Boislisle, *op. cit.*, I, 363, 1320. 6 Mai 1694. Larcher in Champagne says, "La calamité est encore plus affreuse dans les villages, où la plupart des manouvriers ne trouvant presque plus de travail, ou du moins si peu qu'il ne suffit pas à leur gagner du pain pour eux et pour leurs familles, sont des jours entiers sans en manger un morceau, réduits à vivre de son ou de racines, qu'ils font cuire avec un peu de sel, et les plus à leur aise sont ceux qui peuvent avoir du pain d'avoyne ou de sarrazin." It is the artisans that suffer, and from lack of money rather than lack of grain.

[3] See Chap. IV. A case in Lower Burgundy.

[4] I have carefully examined the whole of the correspondence on the great dearths.

The most serious depletion of the population was due to the fevers and epidemics. These, in many cases, owed their origin to a local dearth, but the question was intimately connected with the question of poor relief. At all times, whether of abundance or of dearth, the pauper or semi-pauper class was the element in the population that suffered the miseries so graphically described by the critics of the Old Régime. There was little organized charity, and most of the attempts at relief originated with the Church. The Intendants, however, took the matter in hand in the periods of greatest distress, but at such times it was difficult to create an efficient organization. Workhouses and public works were established, but they frequently spread the epidemics and increased rather than decreased the death rate. This was Bouville's complaint of the Aumones Générales in Limousin in 1691. "This great assembling of the poor of all ages and sexes gives rise to horrible abominations, and leads to an incredible spread of disease, which is favored by the inadequate nutrition. When the grain begins to turn color, these almshouses encourage idleness, by affording a certainty of having bread and soup, and by making possible a life of licentious freedom. This general assembly of the poor should be prevented by obliging each town to feed its own poor. The paupers should be ordered to do the work assigned to them by the directors, so that none should be induced by idleness to enter the workhouse." [1]

In Béarn in 1693, the poor who had flocked into Pau were shut up in barns and houses, and given rations, but this merely made matters worse. The fevers which had already appeared increased at an alarming rate, especially among the poor, and out of 800–900 shut up in the relief houses, two hundred died within a fortnight. In the country districts thousands were suffering from extreme destitution.[2] From Montauban in 1694, the Archbishop writes: "The price of grain has already risen so high that the poor can no longer buy. Seven or eight dead persons are found at the gates of the town each day, and in my

[1] Boislisle, *op. cit.*, I, 228, 1018.

[2] *Ibid.*, I, 321, 1191. 12 Mai 1693. Sanson.

diocese of 150 parishes, 400 people die daily from improper nourishment. I myself feed 300 poor each day, in town or on my estates." [1] In 1695 the Intendant at Montauban says that the district is in a pitiable state. "The people are in misery transcending all powers of the imagination, so exhausted that they are incapable of any exertion. The sterility of previous years carried off one-half or two-thirds the population of parishes, so that in many places there are not enough people left to cultivate the soil. The distress is not equally spread, however. It is worst in Armagnac, and it may be necessary to colonize from neighboring provinces to repopulate that canton.'" [2]

The problem of poor relief was increased in difficulty by the migratory habits of the population. In June, 1693, "whole communities of the élections of Rouergue and Quercy abandoned their villages and sought food elsewhere. Near Figeac, Cahors, Villefranche, and Rodez some of these unfortunates have been found dead in the fields, with their mouths full of grass." [3]

The appearance of dearth in a canton was generally sufficient to set numbers of the poor in motion. When there was a large town near, they flocked into town; if no such hope of finding relief presented itself, they wandered from province to province, so that the infertile sections of the Massif Central were the scenes of many curious migrations of paupers. In 1692, Périgord was suffering. The poor had collected in great masses, and Bouville feared that they would set out for Limoges.[4] In 1698, a private correspondent writes from Bordeaux: "The dearth in Périgord has already caused large numbers of persons to leave their homes," "en trouppe et en famille," seeking places where grain has been stored.[5] In Roussillon, the distress is equally great. "If the king does not send grain for the sustenance of this town (Prais de Mollo) more than fifty families (220 persons) must needs leave, exclusive of six families that have already left. . . .

[1] Boislisle, *op. cit.*, I, 360, 1308. 16 Avril 1694. Évêque de Montauban.

[2] *Ibid.*, I, 391, 1432. 28 Mai 1695. Sanson.

[3] G[7]. 1632. Montauban, 19 Juin 1693. Brunot, Rec. Gén. des Finances.

[4] Boislisle, *op. cit.*, I, 297, 1122. 2 Oct. 1692.

[5] G[7]. 138. Bordeaux, 21 Nov. 1698.

All are going to foreign parts." [1] In 1705, the Curates of the élection of Cahors write: "our parishes are reduced to the sad necessity of dying of starvation or of abandoning the country unless they receive sufficient aid to enable them to subsist till the harvest. . . . Some have already abandoned their homes, and all are inclined to follow their example. Only a very extraordinary charity can stop them." [2]

These infertile districts were thus in need of a double relief; in the first place, the break-down of the local market system rendered administrative intervention necessary to secure grain from the principal grain producing regions, then when this grain had arrived, a large share had to be distributed as a charity.

In 1694 and 1698–99, Limoges and Limousin were quite dependent on the importations of grain made by the Intendant from Brittany and Bordeaux. In the fall of 1693, a letter of the Bishop of Limoges suggests that something was done to procure grain from Berry by public subscription. The local crops, however, were not consumed until the spring of 1694. Bernage perceived the necessity of extraordinary measures as early as February. "The nearer I approached Limoges, the more striking were the misery and the dearth. I was fairly frightened by the prodigious crowd of paupers, but the Bishop assured me that it was quite ordinary." Nevertheless, he straightway obtained a grant of 30,000^{ll} to procure grain in Bordeaux, Poitou, or Brittany. In March, he writes: "I urged the merchants to form a company to import grain from the neighboring provinces, but the merchants of this section do not wish to undertake anything of the sort at their own risk. Their unfamiliarity with that trade, and the many risks frighten them. I promised them armed escorts, but it does not reassure them. They would like to act as Royal agents, but they refuse to make any advances or to take any risks." Bernage proposes a scheme for royal action. The grain will have to be sold at less than the market price, but the King need not lose more than 15,000^{ll}

[1] G^7. 506. Prais de Mollo, 7 Nov. 1698. Chevalier de Landort à d'Albaret.

[2] Boislisle, *op. cit.*, II, 283, 911. 13 Nov. 1705. See also *Ibid.*, II, 255, 821. 2 Juin 1705.

on a sum of 120,000^{ll}.[1] The grain was purchased for the most part in Brittany and Poitou and was shipped to Rochefort and Bordeaux.[2] The grain arrived in May, June, and July,[3] and was distributed throughout an extensive territory. One granary was established at Angoulême, others at Limoges, Souillac, Terrasson, Pressac, and Saint-Jean-d'Angely. From these entrepôts the relief was distributed to all parts of the distressed region.[4]

In 1698, it was a repetition of the same story. The necessities of the province were early perceived. Bernage urged the merchants to engage in the trade but they refused. He borrowed from the royal tax collectors and bought grain in Brittany.[5] Périgord was equally dependent upon administrative relief. Writing from Bergerac in April, 1699, Bezons says: "the price of grain has not risen here, as I have had large quantities put on the market and have given orders to continue. I am obliged to secure wagons to transport the grain from Périgueux. The Bishop has bought grain to sell below the market price."[6] A couple of weeks later the Bishop says: "with the aid of the Intendant I have purchased grain and lentils at Bordeaux, Libourne, Saint-Foix, Bergerac, and Montleduc, whence I have them brought here (Périgueux). They are no sooner arrived than they are sold. But this trade cannot long continue, as we have not the money necessary. The province will be without grain. I ask only for 10,000 francs which I will use for lentils."[7]

Dauphiné is difficult to classify; in some respects it is an infertile, non-commercial region, but regarded in other lights it appears as a supply area. In truth, there were small sections that were fertile, which were frequently engaged in a border trade with Savoy or Lyons. The rest of the province seems to have

[1] G[7]. 1634. Limoges, 19–22 Mars 1694. Bernage.
[2] *Ibid.* Limoges, 17 Avril 1694. Bernage.
[3] *Ibid.* Limoges, 8 Juin 1694, 6 Juillet, 27 Juillet 1694.
[4] *Ibid.* 1694. Mémoire sur les Bleds acheptés pour le Limousin.
[5] Boislisle, *op. cit.*, I, 491, 1756. Summaries of several letters.
[6] G[7]. 138. Bergerac, 12 Avril 1699. Bezons.
[7] *Ibid.* Périgueux, 1 Mai 1699. Évêque de Périgueux.

hardly sufficed for its own needs. The army was also introducing complications in the trade from time to time. The border trade tended to deplete the local markets. Details are not very plentiful, but references appear in both 1698 and 1709. "The price of grain is rising steadily," writes Bérulle from Grenoble in October, 1698, "partly on account of the light harvest, partly on account of the shipments to Savoy by the Pont-de-Beauvoisin. I have felt assured that you (*i. e.* the Contrôleur Général) would approve of the prohibitions that I have issued, as there were many persons forming granaries in Savoy. The inhabitants of Bourgoin and neighboring places complained that certain rich usurers of Bourgoin bought the greater part of the grain of the region, converted it into flour and shipped it to Lyons, as the grain from Dauphiné was selling 4^{ll} per quartal higher than the inferior Burgundian grain. This movement was very considerable and caused so great a dearth that flour had risen to three sous per pound. The prohibitions have produced a decline in price."[1]

In 1709, the border trade was a more serious problem. "The Parlement of Grenoble issued an edict dispensing inhabitants of Gapençois, Embrunois, and Briançonnais, from the obligation to sell on the public markets. If the arrêt is not revoked, . . . the whole country will be reduced to famine, and we shall not know to whom to appeal for grain. I have been obliged to interrupt this letter, to go to the market place to pacify the crowd. Everyone is grumbling and complaining as they find no grain of any kind."[2]

This trade, however, was hardly more than local, merely a distribution of the provincial crop. There were no regular trading connections which could assist when the crops of the province failed. At those periods of distress, Dauphiné was quite dependent on the supplies procured by administrative activity. This phase of action appears most distinctly in a letter of Bouchu written 26 September, 1693:

[1] G^7. 244. Grenoble, 7 Oct. 1698. Bérulle. G^7. 244. Fenestrelle, 18 Sept. 1699. Bérulle. See also G^7. 243. Grenoble, 10 Sept. 1695. Bérulle.

[2] G^7. 1631. Gap, 1 Juin 1709. Évêque de Gap.

"For more than a month, I have vainly exhorted the principal towns to raise funds to buy grain in Languedoc, or in the seaports of Provence. What would have cost eighteen francs then costs 23 francs now. . . . I have assembled here in Grenoble deputies from all the towns in the province. I have spoken to each separately and then to all assembled. Even if the most moderate conclusions possible are drawn from their testimony, the province has not enough grain to maintain its inhabitants after February. The towns of Dauphiné have no revenues, so that it is not easy to devise remedies. All that I have been able to do after thorough discussion is to make a contract with one man, who agrees to advance money to the town of Vienne for the purchase of 12,000 quintals. That will relieve the most pressing needs in that canton, and some aid can be sent to neighboring places.

"At Grenoble, the price of grain is rising at each market, so that it is now selling at 4 livres, or 4 livres 5 sous per quartal. Everything was ripe for a fourth increase, when the pains that have been taken and the manifestations of popular feeling induced several individuals to sell the grain that they had in boats on the river. But there is not a large enough quantity to reduce the market price, and as the dealers made less than they had hoped for, they are not likely to continue in the enterprise. As the town has no revenue at all, I have deemed it expedient to provide for the needs of the town. So I have made a contract with an individual who agrees to deliver 18,000 setiers at Grenoble for 3 francs 10 sous per quartal, under the following conditions: He is to sell only one-half of the whole, in proportionate lots during November, December, January, and February. This first half assures me that the price of grain will not rise above 3 francs 10 sous per quartal. The other half, which he is to sell only in accordance with my orders, gives me some assurance for May and June. I have also stipulated in the contract that I can have him sell at less than 3 francs 10 sous, if I reimburse him. . . . I am working out a little scheme on this basis. By manipulating the prices of this grain, I hope to derange all the calculations of those who are hoarding grain in anticipation of a rise in price.

"As for Lower Dauphiné, the towns of Romans, Valence, Crest, and Montélimar, the trouble there is more serious than at any of the other places. The town of Montélimar proves by its registers of the flour coming in from the neighboring mills, that the annual consumption of grain is 23,000 setiers. By the register of the tithes, the year's harvest is estimated at 12,000 setiers, 3,000 setiers are needed for seed, so that there is only 9,000 setiers to supply the town. Notwithstanding all this, the price of grain is much lower there than at Grenoble where the harvest was even lighter. This is apparently due to the fact that there are few strangers in these small towns. *Each inhabitant consumes what he has, and is on the verge of a severe dearth without realizing it.* Under these circumstances, it is hard to know how to secure grain for these towns in other provinces. The cost of transportation amounts to more than the price of the small quantities of grain sold on their markets, so that any efforts to relieve them would seem to impose an unnecessary burden." [1]

This explanation of conditions in Montélimar is a complete exposition of the defects of the market system in these non-commercial regions. The improvidence and the inability to meet extraordinary conditions are both worthy of note. For the distribution of the local supply these merchants were all the machinery needed, but in those exceptional crises which occurred once in a decade or once in a generation, the local market was absolutely inadequate. Here again, we have the characteristic feature of all medieval institutions. They were carefully adapted to the ordinary conditions, and so long as nothing new appeared to change the situation, the cumbersome machinery worked satisfactorily. The least strain, the least element of novelty, anything extraordinary reduced the system to inefficient chaos. In the producing regions, the market system was unable to preserve an equilibrium between the demands of the metropolis and the country. In the non-commercial regions, the markets afforded no assistance when the usual local sources of supply failed.

[1] G[7]. 1630. Grenoble, 26 Sept. 1693. Bouchu à Pussort, Copie envoyée au Contrôleur Général.

These constant break-downs in times of crisis are the most fertile cause of our misunderstandings of the medieval régime. We forget that the system did work ordinarily, and we also forget that the effort to devise some means to meet the recurring crises is what transforms medieval into modern society. The afflictions of a crisis were borne with that resignation which we still find in the Orient. The man sat down calmly to meet his fate. If it pleased God to smite him with famine, so be it. The idea that these troubles can or should be avoided is a strictly modern idea.

PART II

CHAPTER I

Royal Regulation of the Grain Trade 1500–1660

The early history of grain trade regulation was treated by the Physiocrats from the standpoint of the protective controversy. They drew comparisons between Sully and Colbert, much to the disadvantage of the latter. They sought to identify Colbert with the protective policy that they criticised. "Colbert, despite his sincere regard for the welfare of the state, followed the wrong course and was in the end seriously embarrassed. Sully with less art had based his action on the natural principle. He regarded land as the source of all wealth, both of necessities and of luxuries. The increase of this wealth is the true interest of the state. The encouragement of commerce and industry is thus dependent upon freedom of export, for without freedom there will be no trade." [1] Sully was therefore a representative of Physiocratic ideas. Without full knowledge of their truths, he acted in accordance with their conceptions. They were thus able to describe their policy as a return to an older tradition unwisely abandoned by Colbert.

The origin of the free trade policy is doubtless one of the most interesting problems of the period, but the question cannot be answered as easily as one might be led to suppose by the insinuations of the Physiocrats. Free trade and protection mean different things at different times. The sense we attach to these terms is somewhat different from their meaning to the Physiocrats, and in the sixteenth and early seventeenth centuries they had still another meaning. There is a steady growth in the freedom of commercial intercourse, and a degree of restriction that would today be designated as protection was formerly called free trade. The distinction between tariff for revenue

[1] Forbonnais, *Recherches sur les Finances de France*, Paris, 1760, I, 292.

only and tariff to protect home industry is relatively new. In the sixteenth century, the distinction was drawn between absolute prohibition of export and permission of export subject to all duties. Such a permission of export is all that can be found in the sixteenth century, but, while there is an element of liberalism in such a policy, it is hardly what we would call free trade. The prohibitive edicts, too, must be scrutinized carefully. Prohibitions were frequently issued with the express intention of permitting export under the cover of special licenses. The sale of these licenses was a source of revenue sufficiently attractive to lead to some prohibitive legislation that was more directly related to the needs of the Crown than to the exigencies of the grain trade. Considerations of revenue, however, were seldom predominant. The trade was regulated primarily with reference to the interests of the consumers. The King intended to encourage export when harvests were good, and to prohibit exportation when there was danger of dearth.

The general terms in which royal edicts were issued might easily lead to a misunderstanding of a different type. The solidarity of the modern state and the enforcement of laws throughout the national area is likely to close our eyes to the discrepancy between the form and the reality of royal mandates in the days of the old monarchy. Edicts, general in form, were frequently local measures in reality. Some measures could not be enforced in all parts of the kingdom because of the weakness of the royal officials. More frequently, a general edict was restricted in its influence through the legitimate exercise of discretion by the local authorities. Such action was expected, and there was a real elasticity in the application of general edicts because they did not become law until published in the locality.[1] The edict did not become a dead letter merely through the indifference of the local officials; it was deliberately withheld and for cause; it never acquired legal force in that part of the kingdom. Publication did not follow as a matter of course

[1] *Ordonnance Civil.* 1667. Art. V. The commentary on this article by the eighteenth century jurists is particularly significant, *e. g.* Serpillon, Paris, 1776. See also *infra*, pp. 253, 276, 279, 280–281, 284, 288, 289, 293.

in every part of the realm, and this was particularly true in the case of detailed administrative measures like the grain trade edicts.

The tendency of the royal chancery to generalize makes it highly probable that many of the royal measures of this period were significant primarily in the Seine Basin. The weakness of the monarchy in the south during the Wars of Religion makes it unlikely that any great degree of control was exercised over that part of the kingdom, and there is sufficient evidence to suggest that the interests of the Seine Basin would sufficiently explain much that was done.

The foreign export trade from the Seine Basin has already been described.[1] In the fifteenth century most of the grain from the Oise Valley went down to Rouen, whence considerable quantities were sent abroad. The gradual exclusion of the Rouenese merchants from the Oise and the Upper Seine Basin still left the surplus of this fertile region available, though the trade was in the hands of Parisian merchants. In all probability, the volume of exports decreased on account of the increased demand of Paris, but there were years when the abundance of the harvests made foreign export possible. At such times the grain either followed the old route, down stream to Rouen, or it passed overland from Noyon to the Somme, and reached the sea at Saint-Valery. The extent of this movement cannot be ascertained, but of its existence there can be little doubt. In February, 1501, the Échevins of Paris found it necessary to adopt measures "to prevent the exhaustion of Santois, the Beauvoisis, and neighboring provinces by exports down the Somme to foreign destinations."[2] In 1508, the Échevins were informed "that peasants and others of Corbeil, Melun, Étampes, and other towns are carrying quantities of grain from Paris each day by wagons or otherwise. They go even to Champagne to buy, selling and delivering the grain to merchants who export it. . . . Furthermore, the merchants take up all that they can buy in Santois, and ship it to Rouen by way of the Seine."[3]

[1] Part I, Ch. II, §2.

[2] *Reg. du Bureau*, I, 53-54. 20 Fev. 1501.

[3] *Ibid.*, I, 148. 23 Fev. 1508.

A month later, the Provost of Merchants says that he has been besieged on all sides by merchants "desiring permission to ship grain from Paris." The destination is not given, but much probably went abroad.[1] The Parisian authorities were constantly worried by the question. It was necessary to permit the passage of grain destined for neighboring towns, but at the same time they were anxious to prevent foreign export. These fears were especially evident in 1528, and in 1536 the Provost of Merchants declared that heavy exports were being made to Rouen and that the merchants of Rouen were shipping to foreign ports.[2] In 1565, a bourgeois of Paris declared that "there were exports of grain once in four or five years, when it pleases God to grant abundant crops, and when there is dearth in Spain and Portugal." [3]

The anxiety with which these exports were regarded was the basis of much royal interference with the grain trade in the sixteenth century. The fear was quite independent of the actual volume of trade. It made no difference whether exports were large or whether they were small and infrequent. It was currently believed that a dangerous export existed and it was the uncertainty as to the extent of the trade that kept alive the fears of all officials. The remedy that suggested itself to the sixteenth century official was prohibition of trade in time of dearth and careful regulation of trade in years of plenty. Probably, too, the royal councillors were inclined to stop the export trade completely, in order to insure Paris an adequate supply. The importance of this purely Parisian influence is somewhat obscured by the general character of many of the edicts.

The general period, 1500–1660, falls into three clearly marked divisions, which indicate a moderate development in policy. From the beginning of the century until 1559, very little systematic policy can be discerned. At one moment the desire to check exports from the Seine Basin is paramount. Then, financial motives appear. There are suggestions in

[1] *Reg. du Bureau*, I, 150. 23 Mars 1508.

[2] *Ibid.*, II, 218. 27 Avril 1536. II, 225. 30 Juin 1536.

[3] *Ibid.*, V, 491. 1565.

1539 that some systematic regulation was contemplated, but nothing definite appears till twenty years later. Throughout these years, grain trade edicts were dictated by momentary expediency, without regard to large views. It was a period of empirical opportunism. Between 1559 and 1571, there were several efforts to establish an administrative department to regulate the grain trade throughout France in accordance with definite principles. These schemes failed, as the bureaucracy was not then sufficiently developed to undertake such a task. The break-down of the system of 1559 and 1571 tended to disorganize subsequent efforts to regulate the trade. Not even Colbert sketched any project quite as ambitious as these. But the traditions remained, and until the rise of Colbert the traditions were applied without material modification.

After 1571 the regulation of the grain trade presents little that is new. Between 1571 and 1660 there is merely an alternation of prohibitions and permissions of export. There is an attempt to adjust this policy to the state of the harvests, but there is no evidence that the efforts of the Crown met with any great degrée of success. The period is significant merely for the maintenance of the traditions. It is interesting to note the relative unimportance of the edicts of Henry IV upon which the Physiocrats laid so much emphasis.

I

1500–1559

The scattered edicts of this period cannot be brought within any general scheme, since each arises naturally from special circumstances. They are without logical sequence or relation. Sometimes the trade of the Seine Basin is the principal motive, more frequently the lean treasury influences the measure. The first edict of the sixteenth century is little more than a declaration that the King proposes to regulate the grain trade exclusively, without any interference from governors, barons, dukes, municipal or other officials. The preface says that it has been customary for these persons to urge the King to prohibit export in order that they might derive profit from issuing permits to the merchants desiring to engage in trade.[1] The need of such a declaration is an eloquent commentary on the confusion of jurisdictions and the weakness of the monarchy as an administrative power. Furthermore, we might infer that royal attempts to regulate the trade were more frequent than the extant edicts would suggest. This is by no means impossible. Many edicts and Letters Patent may have been lost or at least escaped the collectors of ordinances. March 12, 1515, an edict was issued, addressed to the Provost of Paris and the Baillis of Chartres, Senlis, and Vermandois: "Your jurisdictions, having abundant supplies of grain, are being daily drained, under the pretext of trade with our subjects and foreigners, to the damage and loss of our subjects, so that if the necessity arose of provisioning our towns and fortresses, it would be difficult to find sufficient supplies. Hence you are ordered to proclaim by public crier in all the towns and villages of your jurisdictions, that no grain shall be carried from the country in any manner or under any pretext whatsoever."[2] Obviously, an edict restricted to the Seine Basin, and suggested by supposed exports from the interior.

In 1535, we have a general permission of export. The harvests have been abundant so that "all merchants and other persons generally are permitted to buy grain, in such parts of the kingdom as they shall see fit, for export to such provinces or countries as they shall choose."[3] Then in 1539, there was a prohibition which was clearly a fiscal expedient. All previous edicts were annulled, and all export from the kingdom forbidden, "except when expressly permitted, under royal letters patent, and then only upon condition of paying one 'écu soleil'[4] per tonneau." This project, however, was not executed without difficulty. Many evaded the edict and exported under cover of old Letters Patent. Estimation of the amount of the extra duty was difficult, on account of the difference in measures. A special commissioner, De Neufville, was sent through the

[1] *Ordonnances des Rois de France*, XXI, 363. 12 Fev. 1507.

[2] Delamare, *op. cit.*, II, 918.

[3] *Ibid.*, *eod. loc.*, 20 Fev. 1534–35.

[4] *I. e.* the larger écu equivalent to five francs.

Seine Basin to learn what sums were due from the merchants, and to enforce the edict upon the basis of six setiers of Paris (1300 lbs.) per tonneau.[1] But the whole scheme had to be given up, because there was no administrative machinery to enforce it, and because the abundant crop made it necessary that the merchants should be freed from the uncertainties of subterfuges and evasions. Consequently, May 27, 1540, all persons were given permission to export grain to all and any countries save Geneva, without payment of the "écu soleil" per tonneau.[2]

Again in August, 1558, we find Letters Patent granting permission for six months to export freely from all baillages within the jurisdiction of the Parlement of Paris. But all customs duties must be paid.[3]

Besides these edicts and Letters Patent concerning the foreign export trade there are two other measures of significance. June 20, 1539, an edict declares the inter-provincial trade free. "We have wished and declared," it runs, "that all persons should be permitted to transport their grain, wine, etc., freely within the confines of the Kingdom, without interference from governors, their lieutenants, baillis, sénéchaux, 'gardes des ponts, ports, ou passages' or others. But understanding that our wishes have not been carefully observed in some places, and desiring to have this right guarded by a perpetual edict, so that the provinces shall be mutually aided in their necessities by this movement and trade in foodstuffs, with that intercourse and friendship which our subjects should have with each other, we have ordered that all our subjects shall be permitted to transport their grain and wine freely within the limits of the kingdom, upon paying the duties customarily paid."[4] The opening words might lead us to suppose that there had been previous edicts,

[1] All documents given by Delamare, *op. cit.*, II, 920. Edict of 20 Nov. 1539.

[2] Isambert, *Recueil des Lois, Arrêts, et Ord.*, XII, 674–676.

[3] Delamare, *op. cit.*, II, 923–924.

[4] *Ibid.*, II, 922. It is interesting also to note a reference in undated Letters Patent of Charles VIII (Lyon, Arch. Mun., Chappe IV, 381, 13). It runs: "Bien que nous avons voulu et ordonné par edit perpetuel que le trafic et négoce des bleds soient libres entre nos sujets de province en provence . . . à nostre tres grand regret sommes adverty se pratique au contraire en nostre pays de Dauphiné . . ." etc.

but the reference is doubtless to the special Letters Patent issued to various governors, in that decade. The intention was evidently to make it possible to dispense with the necessity of obtaining special royal orders to quash such local prohibitions. This object was not fulfilled, and the local authorities continued to issue prohibitions as before, recognizing nothing but special Letters Patent as competent to annul their acts.[1] The second measure is the general ordinance of August, 1539, which contains an interesting provision on the grain trade. The justices were ordered to obtain reports upon the value of the various kinds of grain and upon the current ideas of the abundance of the harvests. Information was to be derived from the merchants, who were compelled to furnish the required data gratuitously, under the penalty of fines, imprisonment, prohibition of right to continue their trade, or such other penalties as the courts might choose to impose.[2] This gives evidence of a desire to obtain information which is the most notable suggestion during the period of serious intent to regulate the grain trade. It is clearly a step in the direction of that systematic control so sincerely attempted in 1559 and 1571.

II

The edict of December 20, 1559 is the logical result of the rather aimless projects of Francis I. "We have proposed and decided to grant permission to export grain each year in accordance with the quantity which it shall be found can be shipped from our Provinces without inconveniencing our people, and in order that there shall be none of the abuses which have been in the past prejudicial to our rights and to the interest of the people, who have often been reduced to necessity before the new harvest by reason of excessive exports, while at other times unduly strict prohibitions have left their grain on their hands without profit. We have resolved to establish in Paris a Bureau composed of eight Resident Councillors or Commissioners,

[1] Evidence on this subject is too abundant to render citations necessary here. The details will appear in the following chapter.

[2] Isambert, *Recueil des Lois, Arrêts, et Ord.*, XII, pt. 2, 621, art. 102.

and a Secretary of Finance, who shall sign any decisions and orders issued by the Bureau's Treasurer, who shall receive and account for the money received from our customs, and two Sergeants. This Bureau shall be authorized to make regulations for the trade in grain and wine, in accordance with the following provisions: —

"1. This commission shall be given full authority to grant passports for the export of grain or wine from our kingdom, to alien or to native merchants, understanding always that the total of permits so issued shall be limited to the quantity which shall be declared at the beginning of each year.

"2. This commission shall regulate all details of the exportation of grain.

"3. All previous Letters Patent shall be annulled.

"4. Governors, lieutenant governors, and others in authority are forbidden to issue any orders concerning the trade.

"5. All export by land or by sea is prohibited, except so far as authorized by the Commission.[1]

"Finally, inasmuch as the preceding year has been abundant, proclamation shall be made of a general export of 50,000 tonneaux of grain, and of 100,000 tonneaux of wine, subject to increase, if more accurate information makes it seem expedient." [2]

Although it is hardly possible that this Commission or Bureau should have discharged the duties assigned to it, there are references in the archives at Lyons which show that some permits were issued by the Bureau, and that a serious attempt was made to establish the elaborate administrative machinery outlined.

February 28, 1559–60, two months after the establishment of the Bureau, Jehan Maréchal, bourgeois of Pont-de-Vaulx in Bresse, is negotiating with the Échevins of Lyons for the passage of grain which he has agreed to furnish the Duke of Savoy. He is allowed to carry his grain past the city, on condition of exhibiting within a month Letters Patent of the King *or* of the Bureau et Chambre d'Abondance recently established at Paris.[3] The Bureau was not only concerned with the subject of foreign export; all matters of royal customs on grain and

[1] The wording is condensed.

[2] Delamare, *op. cit.*, II, 924–925. 20 Dec. 1559.

[3] Lyon, Arch. Mun., BB. 81, 253. 28 Fev. 1559–60.

wine came within its jurisdiction. In March, 1561, the Échevins of Lyons had made a contract with a merchant for the delivery of 2000 ânées of grain from Burgundy. By special Letters from "the Chambre d'Abondance recently established by the King," he was allowed to ship his grain from Burgundy without paying any duties.[1] Later, in the same year, the Échevins of Lyons complained of the action of the master of the port at Mâcon. He justified himself by sending "an extract of the royal edict, with an extract of the letter sent him by the Commissioners lately established by the King at Paris. Also, a letter from the King to him in regard to the movements of trade. . . . and if you desire to understand His Majesty's wishes more completely," he writes, "you can address yourselves to the Commissioners of the Abondance in Lyons, who will communicate the Letters Patent sent them, in accordance with which I am required to send to the said Bureau (at Paris) an extract of the register that I have made of the grain and wine which have been shipped from the province."[2]

Although there may be some reason to doubt the exact purport of these rather obscure references, I am inclined to apply them to the Bureau created by the edict of December, 1559. Evidently, something had been done towards a real execution of the edict. Commissioners had been established in some of the large towns, and the local authorities had been instructed to prepare statistical reports of movements of grain and wine.

The registers of the municipality of Paris supply us with the substance of Letters Patent which do not appear in Delamare. This measure, dated at Avignon, September 25, 1564,[3] was primarily fiscal, but it is interesting because it contemplated the establishment of controllers at all ports. The rest of the edict was devoted to an elaborate statement of dues to be paid

[1] Lyon, Arch. Mun., BB. 82, 18. 4 Mars 1560–61.

[2] *Ibid.*, Chappe IV, 60 bis. 3 (13) Août 1561. Le Maître des Ports à Mascon aux Échevins de Lyon. These few facts came to light in an endeavor to trace the growth of the Chambre d'Abondance at Lyons; a search in the Departmental Archives might furnish more material upon this interesting attempt at administrative control, but the difficulties of the search would be very considerable.

[3] *Reg. du Bureau*, V, 490. 12 Fev. 1564–65.

in different provinces, but only a small part of the text appears in the registers. It is clear that the monarchy was at this time making a great attempt to extend its administrative authority.

In 1565, an edict of June 8 carries us back to the isolated edicts of Francis I. There seems to be a complete abandonment of the Bureau of 1559. This act of June 8 prohibited exports, because " the severe cold, the snows, fogs, and frosts of the present year, indicate clearly that there will be little grain at the harvest, and that we shall be obliged to depend upon the old grain which is already dear." [1]

In 1567, the aims of 1559 appear in somewhat less ambitious form. There is no commission established, but the King prohibits all exports, and announces that he intends to grant special permits when the information received from local officials shows that such favors may safely be accorded.[2] In June, 1571, this scheme is elaborated. Provision is made for systematic reports from the local officials, and the results were to be examined by the Council and used as a basis for the granting of permits. The statement of motive is like that in most of the previous edicts. The King desires " to limit the excessive export by which grain is daily sent out of the Kingdom to the detriment of our subjects, turning our abundance into dearth, and making imports necessary." " Accordingly we declare that the power of granting permissions for export is a right inherent in our Crown, which we intend to delegate to no one, infringement of which shall be deemed ' lèse majesté.' "

" None shall ask for a grant of permission to export, or for exemptions from any dues arising from exportation. All judges are hereby forbidden under pain of an equivalent fine, to make any account of such moneys, as we intend to devote these sums to the support of our army, without having them enter our Treasury.

" No grain shall be exported without express royal permission under pain of confiscation of grain, ship, wagons, horses, and fines."

[1] Delamare, *op. cit.*, II, 959. 8 Juin 1565.

[2] *Ibid.*, II, 926. 4 Fev. 1567.

These clauses were merely designed to deprive all previous acts of legal force, and to allow royal authority full sway in the creation of the new means of control, described in the following clauses: —

"All baillis, sénéchaux, or their lieutenants, shall send commissions each August to the judges of their district, seigniorial as well as royal judges, in virtue of which the said judges shall order the officers of towns, boroughs, and villages to inform themselves as to the crops. Reports shall be sent by them to the Bailli, who shall immediately inform us." Various pains and penalties are provided to enable the judges to enforce these provisions, and the treasurers of the généralités, who exercise the functions of the intendants of the seventeenth century, are instructed to gather such information as they can upon the circuits undertaken to assess the direct taxes.

The crop statistics derived from these two sources were then to be examined, and the exportable surplus determined. That quantity would then be divided among the généralités, and Letters Patent issued stating the amount that had been assigned to each. The bailli, or some other official acting in his stead, should then fix a date for the public sale of licenses for the export of grain. Any person might bid for the right to export any quantity from one tonneau or one charge to the whole quantity assigned to the district. The license was not to include exemption from duty, but the price should be sufficiently moderate to permit profit. In all cases the permits should be accorded to the highest bidder.

Minimum prices were fixed by the edict at 3 livres 10 sous tournois per tonneau or 10 sous per charge. The differences of weight and measure were provided for. The forms to be used at the auction were prescribed. Terms of payment were left to be established later in accordance with the suggestions of the baillis. In order to facilitate execution, export was restricted to specified ports, and domestic shippers were required to give security to insure the landing of their cargo at the ports specified in their sailing papers.[1]

[1] Delamare, *op. cit.*, II, 926–930.

The scheme was chimerical and its fiscal object is evident, but it indicates the nature of the policy of the time. The narrow limitations of effective royal control appear when we examine the character of these two edicts, which really attempt only to systematize the policy that was pursued spasmodically throughout the sixteenth and seventeenth centuries. The naïveté of the idea of so close an adjustment of royal regulation to crop conditions reveals the lack of comprehension of the practical difficulties of executing such a measure. For the highly organized bureaucracies of the present day it would be a serious undertaking; for the administrative system of Henry III it was an impossibility. It is hardly more than an expression of royal intentions. The desire to regulate the economic interests of the state was present; the means, the knowledge of conditions, the ideas of what might be done did not correspond in the least respect with the magnitude of the design. The ignorance of the conditions of the kingdom is perhaps the most striking feature of these curious attempts. The monarchy was working in the dark, drafting plans based upon naïve *a priori* reasoning, sketching policies which would require the exact coöperation of officials over whom the monarchy had little direct control.

The most complete illustration of the delusions cherished by the King is furnished by the frequently repeated assertions that the inter-provincial trade was free. This idea reappears at regular intervals in practically the same form. Traces can be found in the fifteenth century. Francis I states the principle very carefully in 1539 and endeavors to give the liberal policy all the weight of his authority. The edicts of 1567 and 1571 contain clauses to the same effect. In 1577, the same provision is reënacted. "Trade from province to province shall be free, and none shall be compelled to secure permits from any local officers. . . . Such persons shall stop shipments of grain only when so authorized by special Letters Patent." [1] Nothing could be more explicit, and yet the local archives of the period are full of ordinances of governors, baillis, sénéchaux, lieutenants of all sorts, mayors, provosts of merchants, syndics, or provincial

[1] Delamare, *op. cit.*, II, 705. 27 Nov. 1577.

Parlements, all prohibiting, or otherwise interfering with the domestic grain trade. In this aspect of trade regulation, the Crown claimed an authority that it never exerted. It did possess some power, but not of the type suggested by its persistent declarations that local officials should have nothing to do with the grain trade. There is an element of unreality in all this apparent activity. There is much pretence and benevolent intention.

III

After 1571, grain trade policy is merely an expression of the idea that it is good to allow exportation when crops are abundant, and necessary to prohibit export when the harvest fails. Dearth or fear of dearth led to prohibitions in October, 1573, September, 1574, and September, 1587.[1] The general edict of November 27, 1577 contains a prohibition that is essentially the outcome of fiscal necessities. It amounted to the imposition of a new duty designed to secure the funds needed to pay the Swiss debt, but the fiscal element is supplemented by a complete prohibition of export from Picardy and Champagne.

The much-discussed reign of Henry IV is but slightly concerned with grain trade regulation. In March, 1595, there was a prohibition; in February, 1601, a temporary permission of export was granted. In 1604, there was a momentary suspension of the border trade with Spain, growing out of diplomatic difficulties. To build upon this foundation the great principles of Sully's free trade doctrine requires no little imagination. Both general edicts are provided with prefaces which are filled with the spirit of the sixteenth century. The preface of the edict of March, 1595 is largely copied from the notable preface of 1557.[2] There is nothing new either in preface or provision

[1] Delamare, *op. cit.*, II, 960–962.

[2] *Ibid.*, II, 962. "*Combien que l'experience nous enseigne que la liberté du traffic que les Peuples et Sujets des Royaumes font avec leurs Voisins et Etrangers, est un des principaux moyens de les rendre aisez, riches et opulens . . . neanmoins aprés avoir reconnu que Dieu . . . nous a mis en main un Royaume composé de diverses contrées et Provinces, chacune desquelles en son endroit est autant que nulle autre de la Chrétienté, fertile et abondante . . . et que ce qui défaut en l'une se trouve facilement en l'autre; tellement que les habitans d'icelui n'ont besoin . . . d'aller emprunter le secours du voisin,*

of the act of 1595. Similarly the act of 1601, the only "liberal" edict issued, displays that combination of fiscal and commercial motives which we found in the edicts of 1540, 1577, and in less striking fashion in the edicts of 1559 and 1571. The lengthy preface confesses previous manipulation of the trade with fiscal intent. Prohibitions have been issued and exports permitted from certain provinces upon payment of extra duties. This edict grants general freedom of export for one year without payment of the extra duties. The limitation of the effect of the edict to one year is literally the only new feature. The ideas of the time appear much less clearly than in the edicts of 1557, 1559, and 1571, and the policy differs in no respect from that of Francis I in 1540, or of Henry III in 1577.[1]

The first half of the seventeenth century witnesses no real innovation in grain trade policy, though at times there is a recurrence of explicit limitation of edicts. But as this limitation was tacitly assumed in the sixteenth century, it is hardly proper to attach much importance to the formal appearance of a time clause in the edict of 1601, and those of Louis XIII.

The history of these years is little more than a catalogue of edicts. The general Ordinance of January, 1629, restates the whole policy: "Henceforth the export of grain and wine shall not be permitted, unless we are duly informed by our local and municipal officials that our provinces are sufficiently supplied. With this in view the farms of the export duties shall be let out with the reservation of the right to permit or prohibit export as is deemed expedient."[2]

lequel de son costé est tous les jours contraint d'en venir chercher en nos terres; considerans aussi que si sous prétexte de la liberté du trafic nous permettions les continuations des Traittes et transports de bleds et autres grains et légumes aux Pays Etrangers, comme nous avons fait par le passé, il seroit à craindre que pensant ayder à autrui, nostre Royaume n'en demeurast tellement dégarni, que nos Sujets aprés avoir langui sous le faix de tant de miseres . . . ne vinssent à tomber en une extrême disette . . . Nous . . . avons fait et faisons . . . inhibitions. . . ." See below, pp. 347 f., for preface of 1557.

The section italicized repeats as to substance, and in part verbally, portions of the edict of 1557.

[1] Delamare, *op. cit.*, II, 932.

[2] Isambert, *Recueil des Lois, Arrêts, et Ord.*, XVI, 328, art. 419.

Other edicts were issued as follows: —

24 Nov. 1625, a prohibition of export on account of deficient harvests.[1]
30 May 1629, permission of export, upon paying customs.[2]
30 Sept. 1631, prohibition of foreign export, with an express reservation of the inter-provincial trade. Deficient harvest alleged.[3]
19 Nov. 1639, permission of foreign export, upon payment of the customary duties.[4]
5 Oct. 1642, prohibition of foreign export on account of dearth.[5]
9 April 1643, prohibition designed to enforce the preceding act.[6]
2 Oct. 1643, prohibition of foreign export.[7]
31 Aug. and 3 Oct. 1648, prohibition of export, largely due to military policy.[8]
4 Sept. 1649, prohibition of foreign export, on account of dearth.[9]
19 March 1655, permission of foreign export for the remainder of the year.[10]

This barren review of Letters Patent and edicts can hardly have failed to weary the reader. The royal attempts have so little connection with the real problems of the sixteenth century trade that the study of the royal policy is without interest except for the antiquarian. The Crown dismissed the inter-provincial trade with the reiterated assertion of its freedom; foreign trade was to be regulated with care. But even if the intentions of the Crown had been carried out, it would have failed to touch the real issue in the grain trade, which was not the limitation of foreign export, but the regulation of domestic trade. France was not characteristically a grain-exporting country. Brittany, Languedoc, Aunis, Picardy, and Normandy sent grain to foreign countries, but only in the case of Brittany, Languedoc, and Aunis was the grain a staple export. Exportation was a relatively incidental problem in France; the serious issues involved in the grain trade were all questions of the regulation of domestic trade.

[1] Isambert, *Ibid.*, XVI, 153.
[2] H. 1803. Reg. du Bureau, vi^xx^x.
[3] Delamare, *op. cit.*, II, 963.
[4] Isambert, *op. cit.*, XVI, 514.
[5] Bib. Nat., Fr. 16740. 266, copy.
[6] Delamare, *op. cit.*, II, 963.
[7] *Ibid.*, II, 964. H. 1806. Reg. du Bureau, vi^c^iiii.
[8] Bib. Nat., Fr. 16740. 265.
[9] Delamare, *op. cit.*, II, 964. H. 1809. Reg. du Bureau, iii^c^lxiii.
[10] Bib. Nat., Fr. 16740. 264.

It is for this reason that the emphasis upon the protectionist controversy has been so unfortunate. All attention has been concentrated on royal policy, when royal policy is almost negligible, not only because the foreign trade is in itself unimportant, but because the Crown accomplishes so little. Despite the loud protestations of offended dignity, the efficient control throughout the sixteenth century was in the hands of the local officials. The Crown accomplished nothing more than the establishment of a tradition to which Colbert gave vitality.

CHAPTER II

Local Regulation of the Grain Trade. 1500–1660

The local measures are very similar in form to the royal edicts which we have been studying. They are, for the most part, prohibitions or permissions of export, combined with the system of special permits allowing exportation despite the general prohibitions. But while there is little difference in the outward appearance, there is a great difference in their purpose and in their effect upon trade. The domestic trade introduces complications that do not appear at all in foreign trade; in one, the interest of a producing region is the principal cause of solicitude; in the other, both producing and consuming regions are involved. The absence of any national boundary, too, makes it impossible to sacrifice either region, and the administrative officials are thus charged with the task of discovering some means of moderating the intensity of this conflict of interests between different parts of the same Kingdom.

The measures of local officials, whether prohibitions or permissions, were always a relatively spontaneous reflection of the public opinion in the province. In the seventeenth century, the intendants endeavored to maintain a considerable degree of detachment from local interests, but in the sixteenth century most acts were the outcome of strong local feeling. Each region sought its own welfare without much regard to the needs of neighboring sections. The consuming centers like Paris and Lyons were in constant dread of dearth, because they were dependent on distant sources of supply which might be cut off more or less completely at any time by provincial prohibitions. The producing regions also had their fears. They were not exposed to any serious danger of lack of grain, due to inadequate harvests, but the intensity of metropolitan demand constantly exposed them to the danger of excessive exports, which would seriously deplete the supplies of the province. Years of scarcity were certainly a menace to both regions. Frequently, there was enough grain physically in existence to prevent suffering in either the producing or consuming centers, but there was no means of distributing this grain equably between the two regions. The defects of the market system gave the advantage in bargaining to the consuming centers, so that there was a distinct likelihood that the producing regions would experience greater difficulty in time of dearth than the centers they supplied. This possibility was clearly realized in the grain-growing sections, and it was contemplated with panic-stricken fear. The producing provinces thus regarded the grain merchants with ill-disguised hostility. To them, the merchant meant distress and suffering in times of dearth. In the cities there was a similar feeling against the provinces. The officials were regarded as hard-hearted, unchristian beings, bent upon stopping the supplies of the large towns in order to swell their private fortunes by the sale of licenses. The peasants of the producing regions and the inhabitants of small towns along the rivers were regarded as thieves and robbers ready to attack the merchants at any moment, to steal the grain outright, or take it at less than cost.

When considered in detail, the history of grain trade regulation in the sixteenth century enables us to form some conception of the relative importance of the factors that ultimately produced the close organization of the metropolitan market. In every aspect of the problem, the sixteenth century reveals real growth. In the early years, the conflict of interests, which is never very apparent except in the areas supplying Lyons and Paris, is hardly perceptible even in the Lyons area. The increasing frequency of resort to Burgundy finally brought out expressions of local feeling, and, in 1557, the issue was joined between Burgundy and Lyons. This apparent deadlock was solved by an appeal to the King. All through this phase of the history of the grain trade, the King appears in this essentially medieval capacity. He is not an administrator, but an arbiter, not seeking to govern in the modern sense by actual administrative regulations for the welfare of the people, but serving merely to moderate the discord in the body politic. This aspect of royal activity, however, appears clearly only when the opposition of local interests has become sharp and well defined. But once this element of arbitration enters into the situation, it remains a permanent factor. In the sixteenth century, the King acted directly through edicts and patents; in the seventeenth century, the intendants assumed this function. Severally and collectively, they exerted all their influence in favor of the general welfare when local interests would naturally result in a narrow provincial policy. Social harmony was thus secured only by the active interference of the King or his personal representatives, the intendants. They endeavored to remedy the evils caused by the defective market system, and this forced them, in many instances, to assume complete control of the distribution of grain. This tendency was not very strong in the sixteenth century, as the Crown was not sufficiently informed of the details of the trade, but in the seventeenth century the policy reached its full manifestation. Intendants like Bâville would, at times, direct all details of the distribution of grain throughout their provinces during the whole period of distress.

Interests of two types were effectively represented by the local officials: the intensely circumscribed interests of individual towns, and the wider interests of those real geographical regions which formed the provinces. The relation between political boundaries and the natural divisions of the country is of significance in the history of the grain trade, as a province or government was almost certain to include the whole of a fertile area; and, as they frequently included several of those sharply defined regions, they represented a local interest of a very pronounced kind. The products of the various sections differed, and frequently the whole province was ultimately dependent upon one part for its grain supply. This natural basis of provincial boundaries made the province the best unit for regulation of the grain trade during the sixteenth century. A prohibition of export from the province permitted the ordinary local trade, but guarded the region against any disturbing influence of extra-provincial demand. The towns which were used as shipping points could give additional force to restrictive measures by prohibitions of export of grain stored within the town. The governors and the provincial parlements were usually the authorities who issued provincial prohibitions, and not infrequently both combined in their efforts to protect local interests. The Estates seldom, if ever, did anything. The welfare of the large commercial towns seeking grain was, of course, defended by the municipal officials. At Paris, the Parlement of Paris and the Châtelet assisted. The characteristic feature of administrative regulation in the sixteenth century was the persistent effort of provincial governors or parlements to limit the export trade of the province. On the part of the agents of Paris or Lyons, there was an energetic attempt to maintain freedom of trade. The former relied upon their local privileges; the latter secured royal Letters Patent annulling in whole or in part the arrêts and ordinances of the provincial authorities. The local officials joined the issue, the question was settled by appeal to the King.

The baillis and the sénéchaux were the only officials with whom we are concerned who were closely in touch with the royal government. They were charged with the general task of administration of the royal domain, and had cognizance of all matters, judicial, administrative, and financial. They enjoyed a large measure of individual initiative and possessed some ordinance making power. But they played a relatively small part in the history of the grain trade. The nature of the area under their authority made effective regulation difficult, if not impossible. As they had charge only of the royal domain, all lands belonging to the Church or to nobles were exempt from their control, forming enclaves within their jurisdiction. The baillage or sénéchausée never included a solid block of territory, and, quite apart from the confusion caused by the enclaves of extra-domain land, the limits of the baillages were never well ascertained as regards each other. In matters of judicial and financial administration this aspect of the form of the baillage was not of great importance, but such a jurisdiction was obviously unfitted to deal with questions of trade. Furthermore, the power of the bailli had been, so to speak, "put into commission" in 1498. The diversity of his authority was so great that a considerable number of assistants were required, and they gradually developed a deal of independence in the exercise of their functions. Unity of action was preserved to some degree by the formation of a council of the baillage composed of these officers. But such a body acted slowly, and, even in the sixteenth century, had begun to limit itself more and more to the judicial duties which later became its sole function.[1]

Burgundy and Lyons

The Lyonese merchants began to seek supplies in Burgundy at the close of the fifteenth century. These purchases, however, attracted little attention and caused no anxiety in Burgundy. A few years later, when the first prohibitions were issued, the Lyonese secured countervailing Letters Patent from the King. But there was no marked hostility to the Lyonese. In May, 1520, the Governor of Burgundy permitted the Lyonese merchants to export 2500 mines of grain purchased by them in Burgundy and Bassigny. Prohibitions had been issued, and the Lyonese had sent to the King for Letters Patent, giving them the right to export grain. The Governor of Burgundy yielded to the royal Letters Patent, apparently without debate, although the limitation of exports to 2500 mines may have been his own idea.[2]

In 1528, we have more details of the negotiations between Lyons and Burgundy. The Consuls of Lyons complained in August of light harvests and of attempts of Italians and others to make shipments to Savoy and Piedmont. They proposed to secure Letters Patent from the King prohibiting export from Lyonnais.[3] December 7, the Consuls assembled the notables of the town to

[1] G. Dupont-Ferrier, *Les Officiers Royaux des Baillages et des Sénéchaussées et les Institutions Monarchiques en France à la Fin du Moyen Age*, Paris, 1902, p. 119.

[2] Lyon, Arch. Mun., Chappe IV, 381, 16. 26 Mai 1520. Notarial copy of Letters Patent.

[3] *Ibid.*, BB. 47, 35. 20 Août 1528.

inform them that they had sent envoys to the King and to the Governor of Burgundy in order to secure the right to export grain from Burgundy. The Consuls asked for money with which to purchase grain on the account of the municipality.[1] A month later, one Henry Guimbre was commissioned to go to Burgundy to buy one thousand mines of grain on the account of the municipality. January 30, Letters Patent, dated January 15, arrived from the Court, authorizing these Lyonese exports from Burgundy. These Letters were at once forwarded to Guimbre.[2] Letters and reports indicate that the purchases in Burgundy aroused no opposition, either official or popular.[3] In the letter of May 6, it is remarked, however, that the Lyonese "merchants hesitate to ship to Lyons, on account of the rioting that occurs there, and because *prices are higher at Villefranche and Belleville and other places which are passed on the way down.*"[4] There was only grain enough at Lyons to supply the city for two days,[5] and the anticipation of difficulties in Burgundy or on the way had already suggested resort to other provinces. On April 23, the Consuls had resolved to send agents to the Parlement of Grenoble to secure the right to export from Dauphiné. May 11, Letters Patent were received from the court, authorizing Lyons to export three thousand ânées of grain from Dauphiné, Viennois, Forez, and Velay. Letters were also received from the Governor of Auvergne and Bourbonnois, permitting the export of one thousand setiers of grain.[6] At the end of the month, more royal Letters Patent arrived, covering exports from Dauphiné.[7] On September 13, royal Letters Patent were issued, covering further exports from all these provinces.[8]

[1] Lyon, Arch. Mun., BB. 47, 164. 7 Dec. 1528.

[2] *Ibid.*, BB. 47, 183, 191. 7 Jan. 1528–29, 20 Jan. 1528–29.

[3] *Ibid.*, BB. 47, 200, 233, 248. 10 Fev., 20 Avril, 6 Mai 1528–29.

[4] This is a singularly direct illustration of an important consequence of the independence of the divers municipal markets.

[5] Letter of 6 May.

[6] Lyon, Arch. Mun., Chappe IV, 381. 18, 11, 25 Mai 1529. Copies des Lettres Patents de François I et des Lettres du Gouveneur d'Auvergne et de Bourbonnois.

[7] *Ibid.*, Chappe IV, 381, 19. Original. 30 Mai 1529. Autres Lettres Patentes 13 Sept. 1529. Chappe IV, 38, 124.

[8] *Ibid.*, Chappe IV, 381, 20. 13 Sept. 1529.

These frequent royal Letters Patent seem to be directed against a customary provincial prohibition. Their object was to anticipate possible objection, rather than to annul prohibitions that had actually been issued by the provincial authorities. It was an attempt to secure that freedom of the provincial trade so vainly enunciated in the general edicts. At this period, there was almost no obstacle in the producing regions, save inertia.[1]

In September, 1539, there is a suggestion of a more positive desire for protective prohibitions in the producing sections. Royal Letters Patent were issued prohibiting export from Burgundy. These were doubtless obtained by direct intercession at Court.[2] The King was equally accessible to other influences, however, and in October, Letters Patent were given the Consuls at Lyons authorizing citizens of Lyons to export grain from Burgundy, Bresse, Bourbonnois, Auvergne, and Dombes.[3]

This use of royal Letters Patent continued for the next twenty or twenty-five years. There were occasional Patents prohibiting export from Burgundy, as, in September, 1540 and October, 1544; more frequently there were grants of privilege to Lyons.[4] On one occasion the Lyonese addressed themselves directly to the Governor of Burgundy, who permitted the export of one hundred mines of grain.[5]

In 1556–57, the attitude of the Burgundian officials changed. They no longer assented readily to the export of grain to Lyons but discussed seriously the expediency of permitting any export. Royal Letters Patent received little more attention than other forms of request.

The harvest of 1556 was not abundant, and considerable exports to Lucca and to Malta tended to exhaust Burgundy

[1] See also Lyon, Arch. Mun., Chappe IV, 381, 25. 2 Fev. 1530. Lettres Patentes of François I.

[2] Dijon, Arch. Mun., G. 256. 13 Sept. 1539. Ord. du Bailli de Dijon, portant mandement aux Maire et Échevins de Dijon de publier les lettres Patentes de François I du 4 Sept. 1539.

[3] Lyon, Arch. Mun., Chappe IV, 393, 32. 28 Oct. 1539.

[4] Dijon, Arch. Mun., G. 256. 28 Sept. 1540. 28 Oct. 1544.

[5] Lyon, Arch. Mun., BB. 61, 102–119. 18 Juillet, 21 Sept. 1543. *Ibid.*, Chappe IV, 393, 34 bis. 26 Oct. 1543. *Ibid.*, Chappe IV, 393, 37. 26 Oct. 1545. *Ibid.*, Chappe IV, 393, 38. 11 Dec. 1545.

and to excite the apprehensions of the Lyonese. Joined to these unusual demands upon Burgundy and Lyons was the quartering of the army of the Duc de Guise, then at Lyons. This naturally stimulated the Lyonese merchants to greater activity in Burgundy. The officials there became apprehensive and prohibited export. "At Auxonne, Seurre, Châlons, Mâcon, they prevent the shipment (February, 1557) of the grain that the merchants customarily buy for the provision of Lyonnais. . . . They even prevent the passage through Burgundy of the grain purchased in Franche Comté and lands under the jurisdiction of the Empire." [1]

The prohibitions were thus more positive and more deliberate than formerly, and they were the direct outgrowth of fear of dearth.

The Consuls of Lyons resorted to the old expedient. Royal Letters Patent were secured February 24, 1557, granting Lyons the privilege of exporting 30,000 charges of grain from Burgundy, Bresse, and Dombes.[2] But this policy no longer had an immediate effect as before. On March 13, new Letters Patent were granted with the same end in view.[3] But this did not clear away the obstacles. The local officials proceeded to negotiate and bargain. The twentieth of the month, the Governor of Burgundy made an agreement with the Commissioners of the Consuls at Lyons. The whole negotiation is an illuminating instance of the nature of royal authority. The Letters Patent of the King were absolute grants of the privilege of exporting grain from Burgundy, but the document embodying the result of the negotiations states "that in consideration of the Letters Patent of the King of Feburary last, the said Barthelemy Alexandrin, bourgeois of Lyons, and Jacques Guimbre, Commissionaire of the King at the fortifications of Lyons, both in their private capacities, and as Commissioners of the Échevins of Lyons,

[1] Lyon, Arch. Mun., Chappe IV, 393, 34. 26 Mars 1542. Chappe IV, 393, 40. 10 Fev. 1556–57. Procès Verbal faite par M. Jehan de Fournel. Con. du Roy: Lieu. Gén. en la Sénéchaussée et Siège Présidial de Lion. The whole of the above is an account drawn from this document.

[2] *Ibid.*, Chappe IV, 393, 41. 24 Fev. 1556–57.

[3] *Ibid.*, Chappe IV, 393, 42. 13 Mars 1556–57.

have signed the treaties and conventions which follow: viz: — the said Sieur de Saulx, Governor of Burgundy, grants them the right and privilege of exporting 500 mines of the grain that they have assembled at Maxilly and vicinity, with the understanding that said grain shall be carried down the Saône to Lyons . . . and in return, said Alexandrin and Guimbre have agreed to carry to Dijon 250 mines of grain, which they shall be required to purchase in Bassigny and Langres, or other places outside the government of Burgundy, in those granaries in which they have been buying. This they shall do within a month. . . . And when the said quantity of 250 mines of grain shall have been delivered at Dijon, the said de Saulx promises to grant them the privilege of exporting 500 mines of grain from Maxilly on like conditions of delivering 250 mines at Dijon."[1] The Governor of Burgundy thus imposed such limitations as he deemed necessary upon the royal order.

The Échevins of Lyons were not very well satisfied with this rather hard bargain, and proceeded to obtain fresh Letters Patent from the Court.[2] These recite the whole story. "Inasmuch as by our Letter Patent of February 24, we have permitted the Consuls and Échevins of Lyons to export 30,000 charges of grain from Burgundy and other provinces . . . and notwithstanding this, the Lieutenant of the Governor of Burgundy has not only persisted in his refusal, but even seized and arrested all the grain that the said petitioners had purchased and transported from Lorraine, Franche Comté, Champagne, and Bassigny, together with the boats on which the grain was loaded at Maxilly and other parts of the Saône, . . . Accordingly, we order the release of all the grain belonging to the petitioners or to merchants supplying Lyons, whether the grain is of the growth of Burgundy, Franche Comté, Lorraine, or other lands."

Meanwhile, Grolier and Guimbre, the agents of Lyons in Burgundy, were doing their best to overcome the insistence of the Lieutenant, Villefrancon, upon the dearth and the necessities of Burgundy itself. Guimbre writes from Dijon, March 31, —

[1] Lyon, Arch. Mun., Chappe IV, 401, 46. 20 Mars 1556–57.

[2] *Ibid.*, Chappe IV, 401, 46. 31 Mars 1556–57.

"Today, I have presented M. de Villefrancon with the Letters of the King, which he has treated as he has the previous Letters. Then, in accordance with your last instructions I presented him with the petition of which I enclose a copy.[1] He would give me no reply. I asked for an acknowledgement of having seen the Letters of the King, but he refused that request also. . . . The said Seigneur was persuaded to grant permits for the export of your grain only with great difficulty, and to secure the permits for the rest of the grain covered by the first contract, he has forced me to sign another, agreeing to leave at Maxilly 250 mines of grain instead of those that I was to deliver at Dijon a month hence. His reason for doing this is that Dijon is not adequately supplied, and the 250 mines are to remain at Maxilly for six weeks, where the people of Dijon can go to get them if they have need. . . . As for the grain that Nicholas Molle has sold you, you cannot expect to receive it for a long while. Still less, the grain at Saint-Jean-de-Losne, on account of the strict prohibitions and the order given the Lieutenant of that town by Villefrancon, and despite all these fears, there are 4000 ânées at Saint-Jean-de-Losne, more than the town could consume in two years."[2]

Towards the end of April we begin to get reports of the results of the Lyonese attempts to execute the royal Letters Patent of March 31. They began at Mâcon[3] and gradually worked up the river, exhibiting the royal Patents and bidding the municipal authorities to publish their contents by the public crier. "We have found the local officials very respectful and obedient to royal commands and by that authority we have secured the release of much grain. It is true that last Saturday, upon arriving at Auxonne, we found that Villefrancon, advised of our action on the lower river, had sent a commission prohibiting exports. This was executed an hour before our arrival, so

[1] This petition is apparently the document, Chappe IV, 411, 60 bis. Placet de MM. les Échevins de Lyon à M. de Villefrancon, Lieu. au Gouvernement de Bourgogne.

[2] Lyon, Arch. Mun., AA. 32. Dijon, 31 Mars 1556–57. Guimbre.

[3] *Ibid.*, AA. 32. Mascon, Mardy de Pasques, 1557. Grolier. Rapport d'un Procès Verbal fait à Mascon.

that we left immediately for Dijon to speak with Villefrancon. After making the necessary remonstrances, . . . he finally granted us the right to export all the grain that had been purchased by the city or by merchants for the provision of the city. . . . Since the publication of the right of export several persons have manifested much energy in shipping grain to Lyons. . . . We have sent copies of the Patents to Langres, and have left Dijon for Maxilly to publish them there." [1] But Villefrancon's concessions were not as complete as this letter would seem to indicate. The commissioners write on May 1st: "Villefrancon permits the export of 1700 mines of grain. Since that promise, too, he has agreed to allow the shipment of all the grain we have at Maxilly. We expect that there will be forty boats ready to leave by the sixth day of May, carrying more than 5000 ânées, belonging in part to the city, in part to merchants." Then, just as their mission has succeeded, they admit the reality of the apprehensions which have actuated Villefrancon and the local officials. "The Maire and Échevins of Dijon," they say, "have agreed not to interfere with our shipments in the future, unless there is urgent need as in this present year, during which they say that they have suffered as much from dearth as we have. *For this reason*, we have not published our letters by crier, as we have in other places." [2]

The Échevins of Lyons, however, were anxious to bring suit against Villefrancon for his interference with the trade, and the commissioners were instructed to collect evidence. Grolier replied to these directions of the Échevins in a long letter defending Villefrancon's conduct:

"I have received your letters of April 27," he writes, "ordering me to neglect no opportunity of gathering information in all the places where Villefrancon had the grain boats stopped. In reply, I may say that in all the towns of Burgundy where our Patents have been published we have had notarial copies made of the orders and prohibitions of Villefrancon in virtue

[1] Lyon, Arch. Mun., AA. 32. Auxonne, 27 Avril 1557. Grolier et Guimbre.

[2] *Ibid.*, AA. 32. Auxonne, 1 Mai 1557. Guimbre et Grolier. Also AA. 32. Auxonne, 2 Mai 1557. Grolier.

of which the merchants were stopped. This is incontrovertible evidence of the wrongs done the city of Lyons, and of his disobedience of royal commands. Furthermore, we have taken depositions of witnesses at Saint-Jean-de-Losne of the arrest and seizure of the grain boats, and of the exaction of illegal dues by the measurers and other officers established by Villefrancon. . . . But I have not wished to initiate any proceedings, for reasons which it will please the Councillors of Lyons to consider. In the first place, the principal object of our voyage was the prompt shipment of the grain purchased by the town and by merchants. This we could not have compassed, if Villefrancon had supposed that we were inclined to proceed against him; and it would have been absolutely impossible, if he had learned of such inquiries before the grain had left Auxonne. We should then have been in a much worse position than before, as he has the complete confidence of Sieur d'Aumale, of the Duchess of Valentinois, and generally of the brothers of the House of Guise. They would have supported him, *as Burgundy is certainly suffering from dearth, and would have profited from the enforcement of his prohibitions.* All this we were able to infer from the fact that mere publication of the general permission of export, without our having first informed him, had so irritated him that he had issued prohibitions in all the places we had passed through. I was thus constrained in much perplexity to follow the maxim of the great dramatist, 'Ne quid nimis,' which proved to be good policy, for by means of the diplomatic language that I used with him, . . . we are sending down to Lyons nine to ten thousand ânées, . . . and since my return to Auxonne Villefrancon has sent me several missives directed to the officers of all the river towns, instructing them to allow the Lyonese boats free passage.

"Secondly, I felt that the Échevins should be satisfied with meeting the present necessity without indulging in any formalities against a Governor of Burgundy who has the support of most of the members of the 'Conseil Privé,' and who could easily justify himself by proving the dearth that existed in his provinces. Furthermore, after hearing the reasons which had influenced Villefrancon, I recognized that he is a virtuous man, and that any of the Échevins of Lyons would have done as much had they been in his place."[1]

The local prohibitions in Burgundy in 1557 are the earliest manifestation of a consciousness of real danger from the exports of the wholesale merchants. From this time, the local policy in Burgundy is the outcome of a persistent dread of exports in years of scarcity. The exact extent of the sufferings of Burgundy cannot be known, for no information was ever gathered that could decide such a question. None the less, we are frequently confronted by such admissions as those just cited from the letters of the Commissioners of Lyons. Grolier and Guimbre evidently believed that the dearth in Burgundy was an actuality. It was not, of course, a wide-spread famine; that, as we have seen, was rare and confined primarily to the infertile sections of France, but dearth could bring many serious consequences in its train, even without becoming actual famine. The recurrence of dearths, more or less acute in both consuming and producing regions, is the basis of all the local regulations and negotiations concerning the grain trade in this region.

In 1559–60 there was some little difficulty, and light crops induced the Governor of Burgundy to issue prohibitions. The Échevins of Lyons procured Patents from the King and secured permits from the Governor.[2]

In 1570, the old problem recurred. In September, the Parlement of Dijon prohibited export from the province, and enjoined the officers of Auxonne, Saint-Jean-de-Losne, Seurre, and Châlons to prevent shipments. The sergeant of the Parlement made a trip to Maxilly and Pontaillier to enforce the execution of the ordinance. He had the local officials collect information about the merchants who were amassing stores or securing grain for shipment by giving earnest money. He made a tour of the

[1] Lyon, Arch. Mun., AA. 32, 89. Auxonne, 6 Mai 1557. Original. AA. 32, 83. Copy of above.

[2] *Ibid.*, BB. 81, 212, 242, 257. 28 Nov. 1559, 4 Fev. 1559–60, 12 Mars 1559–60. Délib. Consulaires.

Saône towns and stopped several boats.[1] The Échevins of Lyons endeavored to secure from divers local authorities permission to export, but without much success. The Syndic of Dijon writes in January: "I have communicated your letters to the Estates. They have begged me to grant no permits, and, in very truth, grain is so dear in these parts that any accident to the coming crops would reduce us to famine. Furthermore, the Estates have obtained Letters Patent from the King prohibiting export from the Province." [2] Lyons then proceeded to get Patents from the Court, securing, in February, the right to draw 10,000 ânées of grain from Burgundy.[3] These were followed in April by a similar permit for Bassigny.[4] But these were not executed without difficulty. The Parlement of Dijon refused (June 20) to register either Patent, "until inquiry had been made into the necessities of the province." [5] A letter of April 8 also suggests that many difficulties were encountered by the merchants and agents of Lyons. The municipal officers did not attach much credit to the royal Patents.[6] In September, after the harvest, the Patents were executed by order of the Governor of Burgundy.[7]

In 1572–73, the necessities of Burgundy were pressing, but the authorities seem to have become more accustomed to the situation and permitted limited exports to Lyons without quite so much negotiation. The Échevins of Lyons continued to keep their agent at Court busy securing royal Patents to overrule the action of the Estates or of the Governor, and a couple of letters from this agent show the devious method employed. But these Patents granted by the King, "à la barbe des États de Bourgogne," [8] do not seem to have had any great effect. The Governor apparently felt free to decide the case according to

[1] Dijon, Arch. Mun., G. 256. 23 Sept. 1570. Ord. du Parlement.

[2] Lyon, Arch. Mun., Chappe IV, 411, 60 bis. Dijon, 13 Jan. 1571.

[3] *Ibid.*, Chappe IV, 401, 48. 8 Fev. 1571. Lettres Patentes de Chas. IX.

[4] *Ibid.*, Chappe IV, 401, 49. 6 Avril 1571.

[5] Arrêt joined to above piece.

[6] Lyon, Arch. Mun., AA. 29. Dijon, 8 Avril 1571. Châtillon.

[7] *Ibid.*, Chappe IV, 401, 50. 6 Sept. 1571, and letters of the Governor annexed.

[8] *Ibid.*, AA. 98, 4, 5. Amboise, 3 Fev. 1572, 5 Avril 1572.

his own judgment. "You are such near neighbors of this province," he writes to the Échevins of Lyons (May 20), "that you must know how great the dearth is, and yet I have endeavored to close my eyes to all this indigence, and have granted you a second permit for the export of 500 mines of wheat to succor you in your present need. But at the same time, I feel it necessary to make this final, and shall not grant any more permits, as I must prevent further exports from this province, or I shall soon be in the midst of severe famine. You are out of the danger which threatened you, as we have left the trade relatively free, and have not made any very searching inquiry into the quantity of grain shipped to Lyons."[1] Evidently, the Governor is acquiring the habit of a close regulation of the grain trade, seeking to adjust the permission of export as exactly as possible to the needs of his own province, and of Lyons. He endeavors to keep himself informed of local conditions as far as it was possible in his time, and while he recognizes the necessity of some limitation of export to protect Burgundy, he does not make his prohibition absolute to the detriment of Lyons. He seeks to reconcile the conflicting interests of his province and the distant city.

In 1573, there were suggestions of trouble, both in the spring and in November, after the harvest.[2] A letter of De Rubys, an agent of Lyons, speaks in strong terms of the actuality of the dearth in Lower Burgundy,[3] and the letter of Charny in November discloses an equally serious condition and a careful endeavor to adjust his policy to all the necessities of the case.

There is somewhat more information for 1579, although the situation seems to have been hardly more serious. Prohibitions had been issued by the Estates. The Échevins of Lyons had obtained Letters Close from the Queen Mother and from Mandelot, Governor of Lyonnais, urging the Burgundians to grant the export of 10,000 mines of grain. The Parlement of Dijon

[1] Lyon, Arch. Mun., AA. 29, 150. Paigny, 20 Mai 1572. Charny, Lieu. du Gouverneur.

[2] *Ibid.*, Chappe IV, 401, 51. 14 Mai 1573. Lyon, Arch. Mun., AA. 29, 28.

[3] *Ibid.*, AA. 36. Châlons-sur-Saône, 25 Mai 1573.

refused to acceed to the petitions of the Lyonese, and supported the Estates in their policy of prohibition.[1] Charny refused to do anything definite. "I will do what I can," he writes, "and I will add this word. The necessity which you fear should make you henceforth husband your supplies better than you have in the past. Your town has drawn from Burgundy in the last twelvemonth quite enough to leave you adequately supplied."[2]

After the harvest of 1585, there was a similar stringency and the same negotiations and conflict of authorities, with the difference that the Parlement of Dijon played a larger part in the affair than previously.[3]

From this time, there is little evidence of acute trouble until 1628. Difficulties continued for three or four years, but the material is not abundant enough to make it possible to give a definite account of the period, even if it were worth while. There are almost no new features, and with the scattered information at hand, it is difficult to arrive at any conclusion as to the severity of the crisis.[4] Prohibitions, Royal Patents, and Letters indicate spasmodic trouble during the decades of the forties and fifties, but here again we have not adequate basis for a continuous narrative, although it is evident that the problem which was so acute in the latter sixteenth century had reappeared in its old form. From this time, indeed, the conflict of interest between Burgundy and Lyons became steadily more serious. The consideration of this development, however, must be postponed for a later chapter. We have only to observe that the defence of local interests in Burgundy was undertaken primarily by the Governor and by the Parlement of Dijon, the municipalities acting in subordination to the provincial authorities.

[1] All this appears in the act of Parlement of Dijon, 8 Oct. 1579. Lyon, Arch. Mun., AA. 29. Copy.

[2] *Ibid.*, AA. 29. Paigny, 10 Oct. 1579. Charny.

[3] *Ibid.*, Chappe IV, 401, 54, 55, 56, 57. 27 Sept. 1585, 12 Fev. 1586, 13 Fev. 1586, 27 Fev. 1586. *Ibid.*, 427, 1. 14 Juillet 1586. Lyon, Arch. Mun., AA. 71. Langres, 2 Dec. 1586. Maire et Échevins. Dijon, Arch. Mun., G. 265. 14 Dec. 1585, 31 Mai 1586, 10 Juin 1586, 24 Oct. 1586.

[4] *Ibid.*, Chappe IV, 61–68; AA. 72, 82. 26 Fev. 1628. AA. 78, 8. 20 Nov. 1629. AA. 103, 14. 29 Dec. 1629.

The Seine Basin

In the Seine Basin the different economic and constitutional conditions exerted a great influence upon the form and character of local regulation. The fertility of the region and the tendency to foreign export transformed completely the economic aspect of the grain trade problem. The weakness of the provincial organization and the greater opportunity for direct royal control had a marked effect upon the power of the governors of Champagne and Picardy. There were no provincial Estates and no local parlement, so that the governor was the only local official possessing jurisdiction over a wide area. The most cursory consideration of conditions in this region suggests a greater degree of political solidarity than existed between Burgundy and Lyons, while the conflict of interest in economic matters was not likely to be so acute. Furthermore, the obvious political preponderance of Paris deprived the play of political forces of that relative equality which gives such an interest to the negotiations between Lyons and Burgundy. Then, too, the Court was hardly an impartial arbiter in the affairs of the Seine Basin.

The most striking feature of local regulation here in the early sixteenth century is the effort of the Parisian authorities to regulate shipments from Paris to other towns or to foreign parts.[1] The foreign exports in 1501 from the sources of Parisian supply have already been mentioned. These were met by despatching letters from the Parlement of Paris to the Bailli of Amiens and the Sénéchal of Ponthieu.[2] But at the same time, there was complaint that "the inhabitants of Melun, Corbeil, Étampes, and other places in the vicinity purchase considerable quantities of grain at Paris daily, and also buy in Champagne and at

[1] It is proper to observe that there are traces of such regulations at Lyons, especially in 1580, when Lyons permitted exports to Crest, Montélimar, Valence, and other towns on the river and in Dauphiné. Lyon, Arch. Mun., BB. 104, 30, 32, 33. BB. 105, 35, 65, 89. Chappe IV, 401, 53 bis. There are frequent instances of the arrest of all boats endeavoring to pass Lyons. Chains were stretched across the Saône near the Archévêché, and a keeper appointed who would allow specified classes of trade to pass. But these movements of grain from Burgundy to points below Lyons were rare, so that these cases must not be understood to imply conditions such as existed around Paris.

[2] *Reg. du Bureau*, I, 53, 4.

Meaux, so that there is ground to apprehend dearth at Paris." [1] These complaints were repeated at a meeting held a few days later.[2] In 1504, the central and eastern provinces appealed to Paris for grain to relieve their distress.[3] In 1508, Paris was also treated as an entrepôt whence grain could be secured for export to points outside the Seine Basin. "The peasants and others of Corbeil, Melun, and Étampes are carrying large quantities of grain each day from Paris, by wagons and other means of transportation. They also go to Champagne to buy, selling and delivering the grain to merchants who export it. Similar exports are made from the Lower Loire, so that grain has become dear at Paris. Other merchants take up all they can buy in Santois and ship down the Seine to Rouen." [4] Prohibitions were issued. Then, a month later, the Provost of Merchants said that he had been importuned by divers merchants for permits to export grain. The merchants asserted that exports had been restricted sufficiently to remove all possibility of danger, so that the Provost proposed to allow merchants to export limited quantities of grain up or down the river, on the condition that they should expose equal quantities for sale at Paris.[5]

In 1521, there was more trouble from exports. Considerable quantities of grain were being shipped from Paris under cover of darkness. Consequently, orders were issued against any movements of grain boats after dark, and chains were stretched across the river.[6] Strict control of exports was still maintained in the following spring, when one unlucky merchant was caught after getting his grain away from the city. He was brought back and fined.[7]

In 1529, "great crowds of people daily carried considerable quantities of grain away from Paris, and by reason of these

[1] *Reg. du Bureau*, I, 53. 20 Fev. 1501.
[2] *Ibid.*, I, 54. 27 Fev. 1501.
[3] *Ibid.*, I, 92, 99–100. 9 Août 1504, 15 Jan. 1505.
[4] *Ibid.*, I, 148. 23 Fev. 1508. (Parts of this have been cited previously.)
[5] *Ibid.*, I, 150. 23 Mars 1508.
[6] Delamare, *op cit.*, II, 354. Arrêt du Parlement, 7 Avril 1521.
[7] *Reg. du Bureau*, I, 272. 27 Mai 1522.

exports dearth was feared. It was decided that the inhabitants of neighboring towns should be allowed to draw limited quantities of grain from this town for their provision, but that the gates should be guarded to prevent the passage of any grain without the permission of the Provost of Merchants."[1] This control was at times exercised with too much rigor. In 1532, for instance, the municipal authorities had received royal orders to permit no exports from the town, which they enforced so strictly that they refused to allow a religious house at Poissy to carry through Paris the grain that came from its farms at Brie. The Parlement interfered and the grain passed on.[2]

These regulations of passing grain were directed primarily against shipments to Rouen, which were all too frequently designed for export. In 1528, there was much dispute as to the jurisdiction over this trade. The Provost of Paris asserted that it belonged properly to him, the Provost of Merchants declared that this jurisdiction had always been exercised by the municipality and not by the Châtelet. The King settled the dispute temporarily by instructing the Parlement to defend the municipality in the exercise of this control of the grain trade. "Henceforth they shall grant permits for the export of grain, but they shall require security to guarantee that the grain is not exported from the Kingdom." It was this fear of foreign export that led to the complete prohibition of all movements of grain down the Seine in the spring of 1536. The Provost of Merchants declared that "heavy shipments of grain had been made to Rouen and to other parts of Normandy, and that the Norman merchants exported the grain amassed at Rouen and other places. Grain was lower in Normandy than at Paris. Permission to export grain from Paris was withdrawn. Letters were to be sent to the King to inform him of the trouble occasioned by these exports. All permits should henceforth be signed by the Provost of Merchants."[3] Persistence in this resolution is indicated by the deliberation of June 30, when it was

[1] *Reg. du Bureau*, II, 54. 8 Avril 1529.
[2] *Ibid.*, II, 140. 16 Jan. 1632.
[3] *Ibid.*, II, 218. 27 Avril 1536.

decided that no general permissions to export grain should be granted.[1]

This aspect of the trade in the Seine Basin becomes less and less important. During the latter part of the century, indeed, there is a change in the relation of the Parisian demand to the available supply, which renders export from the region less frequent and more obviously inexpedient. Prohibitions of export from Paris become practically permanent,[2] and only in 1596 does the permission of limited export to neighboring towns reappear.[3]

Although the conflict of interest between the producing sections and Paris was less intense than that between Lyons and Burgundy, there are instances of prohibitions in Champagne and Picardy. Such action by the governors appears in 1529, 1530, 1531, 1556, and 1587, so that it is no exaggeration to describe this type of regulation as extremely irregular.[4]

The comparative weakness of the provincial organization and the fertility of Champagne and Picardy rendered it unlikely that the action should be provincial, for quite apart from the governor, there was little probability that the supplies of a whole province would be sufficiently jeopardized to warrant general action. The distress, so far as it existed at all, was intensely localized, so that the opposition came more naturally from municipalities than from provinces. This opposition is in no wise different from the municipal action in Burgundy, except

[1] *Reg. du Bureau*, II, 225. 30 Juin 1536.

[2] *Ibid.*, V, 93. 21 Mai 1561. *Ibid.*, V, 234. 25 Juin 1563. *Ibid.*, VIII, 579. 8 Mai 1586. *Ibid.*, VII, 332. 4 Jan. 1576. In June, 1563, an exception was made in favor of Meaux.

[3] *Ibid.*, XI, 261. 12 Juin 1596. Circular letter to the towns of the vicinity offering them limited quantities of grain.

[4] *Ibid.*, II, 59. Août 1529. Prohibition by Governor of Picardy. *Ibid.*, II, 59. 2 Sept. 1529. Prohibition by Governor of Champagne. *Ibid.*, II, 75. 31 Août 1530. Prohibition by Governor of Picardy. *Ibid.*, II, 133–134. 24 Nov. 1531. Reference to Prohibitions by the Governors of Champagne and Picardy.

Ibid., IV, 45. Dec. 1556. Vague reference to prohibitions in Picardy, not necessarily by the Governor.

Delamare, *op. cit.*, II, 1011. 3 Juillet 1587. Decision to get letters from the King ordering the Governor of Champagne to permit export, hence suggesting prohibition by the Governor himself.

in its independence of general provincial action. It is not a phenomenon confined to the Seine Basin, though the absence of other forms of opposition naturally throws the municipal opposition there into stronger relief. It is perhaps just to distinguish two forms of this interference with the grain trade, the official and the unofficial: the former, prohibitions issued by municipal authorities; the latter, the manifestations of popular fear in riots directed against the grain merchants. Properly speaking, this popular interference was illegal, and generally so largely due to mere panic, that it would be quite unworthy of formal treatment, it if were not at times the only indication of the unsatisfactory working of the grain markets in this region. Unfortunately, this type of opposition does not attract much attention in the scanty records that we possess for the sixteenth century, and it is only in the early seventeenth century that it becomes noticeable.[1]

Action by the town becomes pronounced in 1626. The Provost of Merchants was told on April 25 by divers merchants "that their trade in grain had been interrupted, and that all the towns whence they were accustomed to ship grain had issued prohibitions against export, especially Rouen, Chartres, Soissons, Noyon, Chaulny, La Fere, Roye, Peronne, Montdidier, Saint-Quentin, Vitry-le-François, Châlons, and Melun. The governors and officers of these aforesaid towns were so strict that they could ship no more grain, so that Paris would be reduced to famine."[2] The Provost of Merchants repaired straightway to Fontainebleau to secure Patents from the King ordering the towns to release the grain held by Parisian merchants. The King acceded readily enough, reiterating the prohibitions to export from the Kingdom and ordering the local officials to interfere in no wise with the grain trade.

These municipal prohibitions are somewhat incomprehensible, as the merchants declared that exports to foreign ports were continuing from many of the towns in Picardy which had cut

[1] *Reg. du Bureau*, I, 54. 27 Fev. 1501. Delamare, *op. cit.*, II, 1002. 7 Avril 1521. *Ibid.*, II, 1009. 1 Juillet 1573. *Ibid.*, II, 1011–1012. 7 Juillet 1587.

[2] H. 1802. Reg. du Bureau, vii^{xx}ii.

off the trade with Paris. Thus, one Sieur de Saint-Genis deposed before the officers of the Châtelet: "that the merchants have made purchases in Champagne and Picardy, that they are prevented from shipping by the governors and judges of the towns . . . that there are large quantities of grain at Saint-Quentin, Peronne, Montdidier, and other towns of Picardy which do not cease to leave the Kingdom, despite the prohibitions." Sieur du Poix said that the couriers from Cambray had informed him that a considerable quantity of grain had been sent from Peronne to Cambray. Sieur Ferrand declared that Vitry, Châlons, Chartres, Noyon, Soissons, and other places had closed their gates. Another witness said that there were 800 muids of grain in Vitry, and that the officers had forbidden the sale of more than two bushels to any bourgeois."[1] Doubtless the towns of Picardy regarded export as the regular trade, and, finding it necessary to sacrifice either the Parisian or the Flemish market, preferred to give up the relatively infrequent Parisian trade.[2]

In March, 1643, the merchants summoned before the Échevins of Paris mention prohibitions in some of the towns of the Seine Basin. Chartres, Provins, Elboeuf, Pont-de-l'Arche, and Oudan are explicitly mentioned.[3] Another document enumerates Meaux, Provins, Saint-Jean-des-Jumeaux, Lizy, Rèbes, Coulommiers, Château-Thierry, and refers to reports mentioning other towns.[4] Doubtless, there is some confusion here between popular violence and official action, but much of the opposition was the work of local officials. In 1649 the merchants say that they have made extensive purchases, but that they are unable to bring their grain down to Paris on account of prohibitions and open violence. "It will not suffice to send parchments,"

[1] Bib. Nat., Fr. 21634. 177. Du Landy, 27 Avril 1626. Procès Verbal faite en l'Assemblée de la Police Générale au Châtelet.

[2] It is fairly certain that Paris did not draw supplies regularly from the towns mentioned as exporting.

[3] H. 1806. Reg. du Bureau, iiii^{c}xl. 28 Mars 1643. Enquête pourquoi les bleds sont si rares à Paris. Prohibitions on the Oise are mentioned in 1630. Bib. Nat., Fr. 21641. 136. 16 Dec. 1630. Déposition de Denis de St. Genis.

[4] *Ibid.*, vi^{c}vi. 2 Oct. 1643.

they say, "and, unless the Grand Provost and a Company of Archers are sent to chastise the rebels, there is no hope of a successful prosecution of the affair."[1] Further deliberations at Paris resulted, September 12, in the sending of a circular letter to the municipal officers of Châlons, Vitry, Château-Thierry, Meaux, Nogent-sur-Seine, Provins, Montereau, Melun, Soissons, Noyon, and Beaumont-sur-Oise. The replies to these letters appear, but they are hardly more than purely formal acknowledgments of the receipt of the circular.[2] Châlons and Vitry, however, sent a more creditable excuse for their action: "We have too much sympathy for your needs to deny you our aid, . . . but the present exigencies are so obvious and so pressing, that we have been obliged to seek means of obviating the difficulty. We interfere with our trade only with regret, and in order to preserve our supplies we are forced to deny aid even to our farmers, our vinegrowers, and our neighbors. The eagerness displayed in conveying grain to Paris after the opening of the river has so exhausted our town of wheat and rye that we have not enough to last until the coming harvest. We have no hope of receiving anything from the country districts, partly because of the general sterility of the season, and partly because the merchants from the frontier are going the rounds of our villages and carrying off the small reserves that remain. . . . In order to show you our condition without any reserve, we enclose an enumeration of the grain in the town of Châlons. According to this investigation there are 13,888 setiers belonging to bourgeois, 2,740 setiers in reserve, and 9,828 setiers belonging to outsiders (Forains). Of this we have had to contribute 2,000 setiers of rye to the support of his Majesty's armies, so that we have none too much for the support of 16,000 persons."[3]

The officials at Vitry write: "The sterility of the year has been so extraordinary, and our town has been so exhausted that we have not enough to last the sixth part of the year, and

[1] H. 1809. Reg du Bureau, iii^{c}lix. 10 Sept. 1649. See also *ibid.*, ii^{c}iiii^{xx}vi. 20 Août 1649. Cites prohibitions at Châlons and Montereau.

[2] *Ibid.*, iii^{c}lvi. 12 Sept. 1649.

[3] *Ibid.*, iiii^{c}xxxi. 1 Oct. 1649. Maire et Échevins de Châlons. Three or four setiers were needed per person each year.

most of this supply is in the hands of the merchants. We have thus been obliged to seize what we could. We are suffering from extreme dearth. Even if we wished, we could not permit the transport of grain to Paris, as the prohibitions have been issued by our Bailli or his Lieutenant, and in the event of shipments the people might well execute the threats that have been made to rob the merchants." [1]

The Parisian encroachment upon the sources of the supply of Rouen in the seventeenth century led to attempts to limit the movement by means of prohibitions. The first of these appear in 1630 and 1643,[2] but this phase of the grain trade does not become very striking until after 1660.

Normandy and Languedoc

In Normandy and Languedoc we find the local authorities playing still another rôle. Both of these provinces were relatively independent, politically as well as economically. Their commercial ties with foreign countries, too, were, in some respects, closer than their relations with the rest of France. Local regulation thus assumed the form of limiting the freedom of export to foreign parts, so that local policy was connected with the question of foreign rather than of domestic trade. This independent local regulation of the trade of the maritime provinces is a valuable illustration of the great qualifications that must be made in regard to the application of the ostensibly general royal edicts. In these provinces, as in central France, royal authority was exercised in large measure through Patents, directed to the local officials, and, as in the other provinces, many of these Patents were a direct response to local demands and suggestions, so that this type of royal action is hardly more than local policy indirectly expressed through the medium of royal orders.

In Normandy, the political situation was complicated, the provincial organization still retained much vigor, and although

[1] H. 1809. Reg. du Bureau, iiii^cxxxiii. Vitry. 11 Oct. 1649.

[2] Delamare, *op. cit.*, II, 1014. *Ibid.*, II, 1015. 1630. H. 1806. Reg. du Bureau, iiii^cxl. 28 Mars 1643.

the authority of the Estates declined in the course of the sixteenth century, the Parlement continued to exert much influence. The governor was not a conspicuous figure. The Bailli of Rouen and the municipal officers played a relatively subordinate part. Ordinarily, the Estates confined themselves to suggestions as to grain trade policy in preference to undertaking positive regulation, so that the appearance of royal control and supremacy was maintained in form, if not in reality. The submissiveness of these local bodies is striking. In February, 1500, we hear that prohibitions had been issued at the time of the last meeting of the Estates, "at the request of the Estates."[1] On April 1, 1505, there was a deliberation under the presidency of Louis Dare, Lieutenant of the Bailli. The officers of the baillage were present, and the meeting decided to represent to the Lords of the Exchequer of Normandy the danger of continued export of grain. The following day, letters were sent to the King urging prohibition of export.[2] In June, 1506, an assembly of the Estates of the baillage was held, at which delegates were present from the Estates of the Vicomté of Pont-Audemer and of the Vicomté of Auge. All were of the opinion that letters should be sent to the King to secure prohibition of export.[3] There was a constant dread of export and these requests to the King or protests against the action of some officials in granting special permits continued at frequent intervals. The full details of the internal politics, however, could be obtained only by careful study in the Archives at Rouen.

In Languedoc, there was less submissiveness to royal authority. The Estates issued positive prohibitions in January, 1496–97, January, 1508–09, November, 1513, October, 1524, December, 1529, November, 1529, December, 1530, November, 1531, October, 1532, November, 1534, October, 1535, and October, 1538.[4] Later in the century, the political relations of the various authorities became more complicated, and the Estates acted

[1] *Invent. Som. des Arch. Mun., Rouen,* 91. 11 Fev. 1500.

[2] *Ibid.,* 92. 1–2 Avril 1505.

[3] *Ibid.,* 94–95. 15 Juin 1506.

[4] *Invent. Som. des Arch. Dept., Haute Garonne,* C. II, 1, 6, 10, 19, 22, 23, 24, 25, 26, 27, 28, 32.

less vigorously. In this early period, the Estates at times flatly refused to obey royal orders. Thus, in December, 1504, they would not authorize the execution of the missives of the King permitting the export of two hundred charges of grain for His Holiness the Pope. Likewise, they refused to permit the shipment of two or three thousand charges by Florentines provided with similar passports.[1] The Estates, however, issued special permits on their own authority.[2]

But the Estates were not the only power acting in Languedoc. In December, 1523, we find a prohibition of export issued by the Sénéchal of Carcassonne, limited, of course, to his jurisdiction, but as this included Narbonne, the most considerable grain port in Languedoc, the act was important.[3] A few scattered letters from Clermont-Lodève, the Lieutenant Governor, indicate that he also took an active interest in the grain trade, issuing permits and at times prohibitions.[4] One of these letters discloses the persistent effort to discover the precise extent of the available supply, and to regulate prohibition and permission in such manner as to dispose of the surplus. " Despite a light harvest," he says, " divers merchants and others have amassed large quantities of grain, and are now endeavoring by various subtle means to secure the right to export, although it would exhaust the country and be highly prejudicial to the interests of the inhabitants. . . . Accordingly, all royal officers in each town of the diocese of Maguelone are ordered to assemble the consuls, sindics, and procureurs, bidding them to make diligent search of the quantity of grain available and careful estimates of the amount needed. Reports shall be made within a week, and from these a general report for the diocese shall be drawn up before the Procureur of the Sénéchaussée of Beaucaire, in order to acquaint the King with the facts, so that he may issue such declarations as may seem proper." [5]

[1] *Invent. Som. des Arch. Dept., Haute Garonne*, C. II, 4.

[2] *Ibid.*, C. II, 6, 15. Jan. 1508–09, Nov. 1520.

[3] Vaisette, *Hist. Gén. de Languedoc* (2e Édition), XII, 389.

[4] *Ibid.* (2e Édition), XII, 405. 4 Oct. 1526. XII, 418. 11 Mai 1527. XII, 439. 22 Nov. 1527. XII, 440. 24 Dec. 1527. XII, 451.

[5] *Ibid.*, XII, 439. 22 Nov. 1527.

In the latter part of the sixteenth century, the governor became more important, representing the increased influence of the royal power. But this is a phase of constitutional history that has little to do with the grain trade in particular.[1] In any event, the policy is simply that of limiting export by means of prohibitions and special permits. When the acts are royal, they are suggested by various local officials or bodies, and are the outcome of immediate needs, rather than of visionary ideas, such as influenced so many of the general edicts.[2]

Judgment upon particular incidents of trade regulation in the sixteenth century is now impossible. Material is too scanty and the survival of what we have has been too much influenced by special circumstances to make it a safe basis for an expression of opinion. Mistakes there must have been; in some years prohibitions were doubtless unnecessary and inexpedient. Direct corruption, too, played its part in the history of the negotiations between merchants and officials, and between the officials of various sections and the Court. But there is no necessity of reaching any conclusions upon these matters, all of which can safely and wisely be allowed to rest in oblivion.

The larger aspects of the situation, however, are not veiled in this impenetrable obscurity. Our information is sufficient to reveal the general conditions of the period, and the results are an interesting chapter in the history of the growth of administrative control. Official action deserves commendation for its perception of the necessity of emphasizing the fundamental community of interest between different provinces. The hostility between town and country was restrained by the officials who steadily became more convinced of the necessity of close interdependence. In the absence of definite market machinery

[1] *Invent. Som. des Arch. Dept.*, *Haute Garonne*, C. II, 38, 44, 50, 53, 129, 133, 135, 255, 272, 287.

[2] The inquiry could be pushed into some other regions, notably the Lower Garonne and Lower Loire valleys. Material for these regions, however, is not available in print, and work in local archives of these sections was abandoned for want of time. The results would merely add to the variety suggested as characteristic of local regulation.

for the adjustment of the interests of the provinces and the capital, the officials did their best to secure the equable distribution of grain that would have been assured by the existence of centralized price-making. The sixteenth century leads to little; but a sound body of tradition was developed, which exerted a powerful influence upon Colbert and upon the intendants of the late seventeenth century. This early period is thus the foundation of all that follows, and it is difficult not to feel respect for the individuals who labored sincerely in obscurity to make possible the accomplishment of a later generation.

CHAPTER III

Colbert's Place in the History of the Grain Trade

When Colbert obtained the King's favor in 1660, he began a reorganization of the administrative system which soon gave new meaning to the traditions of the monarchy. The grain trade did not secure much of the great minister's attention, and may well be considered one of the least important departments of his activity. But the general administrative development was not without effect. The centralization of control included the grain trade within its scope, and, while the policy of preceding generations was not radically modified, the change in general political conditions made the actual effect of the old policy somewhat different. In the sixteenth century, we found an evident desire to regulate the foreign export trade in accordance with the state of the harvests. At one time, the judges were required to send reports, later a Bureau was established to undertake both the task of collecting information and of regulating the trade. Then the King proposed to discharge these duties directly through his council. But at no time was much accomplished. Information was scanty, the central officials had little besides vague rumors to direct their policy, and the exigencies of the case practically limited their action to the Seine Basin. The efficient control of the trade was largely the work of local authorities, acting indeed through royal Patents, but none the less directing the policy in accordance with the local needs, of which they alone possessed anything like accurate knowledge. Lack of information was thus the principal cause for the failure of royal efforts to control the grain trade in the sixteenth and early seventeenth centuries. There was no dispute as to what should be done, but an efficient execution of the policy was possible only if the central officials were furnished with an intimate knowledge of local conditions.

It is in this respect that the significance of the general administrative changes becomes most apparent. The intendant, who had existed in divers forms since the days of Henry III, finally became the efficient administrative officer that was so prominent in the last century and a half of the history of the monarchy. Given charge of the financial areas, called the intendancies, which were ordinarily of considerable territorial extent, obliged to make circuits of his district annually in order to apportion the direct taxes, and in close contact with all the various local officials, royal, seigniorial, and municipal, no one was better able to obtain accurate and systematic information of the condition of the country. Furthermore, unlike any previous royal officials, the intendant under Colbert gradually became charged with the duty of regular correspondence with the Contrôleur Général. The early intendants had been special commissioners, ordinarily sent out for a specific object, so that their task consisted either in acting in accordance with instructions given at the beginning, or in reporting at the conclusion of their mission, after the manner of the maîtres des requêtes, from whose numbers these early intendants were largely drawn. The intendants of the early seventeenth century were legally under the obligation to correspond with any secretary of state demanding information.[1] But this obligation was never enforced to any appreciable extent. Scattered letters from intendants previous to 1660 may be found, but there is no evidence of any regular correspondence in either national or departmental archives. The history of the office, too, would suggest that it does not present the characteristic blending of judicial and financial functions until after 1651. The administrative correspondence between Colbert, his brother Colbert de Terron, and a few of the intendants in western France was thus a far-reaching innovation. This rather personal correspondence begun by Colbert, just previous to his rise into prominence, developed with his gradually increasing influence. During the early years of his activity, when his official position was ill-

[1] Boyer de Sainte Suzanne, C. V. E., Baron de, *Les Intendants de la Généralité d'Amiens*, Paris, 1865, p. 21.

defined and his power was dependent upon personal influence, this correspondence remained personal.[1] Later, when his personal power had become more definitely connected with the "Contrôle Général," he systematized the correspondence, and began the formation of the public administrative archives.[2] The development of the informing function of the intendants was thus one of the most direct results of the personal influence of Colbert. Nor was any function of the new administrative official more important or more literally unique. It was a phase of that effort to create a true administrative government which was from this time on the primary object of the monarchy.

The novelty of the idea is interestingly revealed by the correspondence itself. At first, it is relatively barren the moment the intendant takes leave of matters of pure administrative routine. The much desired information about agricultural and industrial conditions is merely a collection of current rumors. At times such letters passed without comment, but occasionally Colbert turned impatiently upon the intendant and proceeded to give him a lesson in letter writing. Thus, in 1670, Daguesseau had written from Bordeaux that frosts had injured the vines. Colbert replies: "I am already informed that there will surely be less wine in some of the vineyards, notably in Grave and Langon, but I am told that this diminution will be offset in other localities where there is abundance. It is very important for the royal service that you should rise above vulgar rumor to penetrate the real truth of the situation. When I ask for information, at the King's instance, you must not be satisfied by the reports made by interested persons, or by those mediocre minds that draw conclusions from the odds and ends of information they happen to possess. In this particular case, the King is not particularly concerned with the product of the vineyards of Grave and Langon; the interest of His Majesty is in the welfare of his people, he asks only if Frenchmen and foreigners will export more wine in one year than in another, for that is the only means of bringing more or less money into

[1] Preserved as the Mélanges Colbert, at the Bib. Nat.

[2] The Series G[7]. at the Arch. Nat. See Boislisle, *op. cit.*, I, Introduction.

the Kingdom."[1] Ordinarily, no statistical information was expected. The intendants wrote their general impressions of the state of the harvest, based either upon their journeys in their généralité or upon reports of merchants and officials. Tables of prices, however, appear from time to time in the earlier correspondence, and quite frequently in the letters of the Contrôle Général (*i. e.* after 1677). In 1693, there was an attempt made to collect systematic statistics of quantities of grain, population, and prices. Commercial statistics, which are almost non-existent before this time, were sent occasionally in strict tabular form. In 1682–83, we have elaborate figures, month by month, of all trade passing up or down the Canal de Languedoc. We have compilations from the registers of the customs bureaux of grain passing the limits of the *Cinq Grosses Fermes*. Some statistics of other trade movements appear, but on the whole, it is clear that systematic statistical compilations were impractical on account of the irregularity of trade. In September, 1677, for instance Colbert had asked for details concerning the export of grain to foreign ports from Normandy. Le Blanc replied that "the certificates of the clerks at the customs houses of the department of Rouen showed that, during the months of July and August, there had been no exports from Dieppe, Havre, Honfleur, or Rouen."[2]

The persistent efforts of Colbert, his ceaseless criticism of inadequate reports, his constant emphasis upon the importance of full information created precedents which gathered headway gradually, and finally bore fruit in the fulness of the reports and letters of the period 1683–1715.[3] The correspondence of the intendants remained centralized in the Contrôle Général, and affords an insight into conditions of the time rivalled only by the elaborate governmental publications which begin in the prin-

[1] Clément, *Lett. Inst. et Mém.*, II, 567.

[2] Bib. Nat., Fr. 8751. 203 ff. Colbert à Le Blanc, 13 Sept. 1677.

[3] The correspondence continued throughout the century, but became scattered between 1715 and 1730. Most of the later correspondence is in the Departmental Archives, which are doubly important as the intendants correspond with their subdélégués. The correspondence of an intendant in Dauphiné (1720–40) is preserved at the Bib. Nat. as one of the annexes au fonds Français. The papers were preserved by the intendant as private property!

cipal European countries in the latter half of the nineteenth century.

The development of this new source of information was not without a far-reaching influence upon the question of grain trade policy. With fuller knowledge of local conditions, it became possible to exert more effectually the influence that the monarchy had aimed at since the days of Henry III. The main lines of policy persisted; the change was primarily in the degree of execution. But there was one element of novelty. The reduction of custom duties both domestic and foreign was one of Colbert's most cherished projects for general commercial reform, and it appears in his regulation of the grain trade. From May, 1669 to April, 1674, exportation of grain was permitted for the most part without the payment of any duties at all, and qualification is made necessary only by the requisition of one-half the ordinary dues between January, 1672 and April, 1673. Thus, for nearly five years, the grain trade enjoyed a freedom that was at that time absolutely unique. So far as I am aware, the idea of according this degree of commercial liberty was original with Colbert. In the grain trade, there had never before been any conception of permission of export that did not require the payment of all customs, royal and seignorial. The first systematic campaign against the local duties was that initiated by Colbert, culminating in his so-called "protective" tariff of 1664. While there is no denying the "protective" elements in that edict, it is none the less true that it contains much besides. It was directed quite as much against local duties as it was against foreign imports, and it is hard to say whether we should emphasize most the firm conception of complete freedom of domestic trade that appears in this treatment of local duties, or the "protective" duties levied on foreign imports.[1]

The contradiction involved in this question of policy is fundamental. Some aspects of Colbert's policy are unquestionably

[1] A letter of 23 Juin 1673, Colbert à de Ribeyre, Intendant at Tours, would seem to connect this policy of exemption from duties with "mercantilist" reasons. "La grâce que le Roy a faite à ses peuples de leur permettre l'enlèvement de leurs bleds, sans payer aucuns droits, a eu pour fin d'attirer l'argent des pays estrangers dans le royaume." Clément, *Lett. Inst. et Mém.*, IV, 262.

the antecedent of much latter-day "protectionism," but there are other elements in his work which held quite as high a place in his mind, and which exerted a more direct influence upon his time. In these aspects, he appears as the keen economist, fully cognizant of elementary principles, one of the first to perceive many of these principles, and, as a result, an ardent advocate of a policy which was designed to liberate trade from all obstacles hindering automatic adjustment. Colbert is at once the precursor of the modern protectionist and of the modern free trader, both in policies and in fundamental ideas. The conceptions of each school appear in embryo in Colbert's letters, and both schools influence his policies. Protectionism Colbert received as the heritage of Barthélemy Laffémas and Montchrétien. The free trade tendency in his thought seems to be a consequence of his perception of the possibility of equable physical distribution of commodities through differences in price. Both his free trade policy and his protectionism are results of his firm belief in national solidarity; the former affects his attitude toward domestic or inter-provincial trade, the latter affects foreign trade. Colbert's foreign grain trade policy, however, in so far as it was not purely traditional, was distinctly a free trade policy, and the insistence upon the idea of a trade that should be free even from customs duties was a long step toward free trade. The contribution of that idea is, in fact, the one element of originality in Colbert's treatment of the grain trade.

Except for this period when all duties were removed, Colbert followed the old policy of permitting exports when crops were abundant, of prohibiting exports in times of dearth, of granting freedom to the inter-provincial trade at all times. His attention was primarily directed toward securing information about crop conditions, in order to make the necessary adjustments. The variations of the harvests, however, fall into two fairly defined periods: 1669–75, good harvests with continuous permission of export; 1675–83, alternations of good and indifferent harvests, leading to a corresponding alternation in policy.

The years preceding 1669 leave little trace, except for an edict of December 2, 1661, which is the only instance of royal regulation of the grain trade in this time. This prohibits export to foreign countries, but makes very express declaration of the freedom of the inter-provincial trade.[1] No special limitation of time is mentioned in the edict, and as harvests were unfavorable in 1662, and for several years following, this prohibition was doubtless applied for a considerable period, if not to the whole interval up to 1669.[2]

May 20, 1669, we have the first of the edicts permitting export. The edict mentions the abundance of the harvest and declares that "all subjects shall be permitted to export, to sell, and to transport their wheat and other grain to such kingdoms, states, and provinces, as they please, up to the first of October next, without paying any export dues."[3] The explicit limitation in time is new, and continues to be one of the means by which Colbert maintains a close supervision of the trade.

September 27, 1669, the edict of May 20 was renewed for a period of six months, but further limited to the provinces of Poitou, Touraine, Anjou, Normandy, Picardy, Soissonnais, Champagne, Burgundy, Bourbonnais, and Berry.[4] Further continuations were issued in March and August, 1670. In connection with this last renewal, it is interesting to note the circular letter of Colbert of August 22: "As the term of the edict of March 18 will soon expire, and as His Majesty could perhaps grant a continuation of those privileges, do not fail to let me know whether or not the harvest has been good in

[1] H. 1816. Reg. du Bureau, iii^e^xiii. 2 Dec. 1661. Ext. des Reg. du Conseil.

[2] See especially a circular letter of Colbert to the intendants, 15 Juillet 1663: "La saison qui a esté jusqu'à présent assez déréglée, et les pluies fréquentes qui sont arrivées dans le milieu de l'esté, diminuant en quelque façon l'espérance qu'on avoit conçue de la fertilité de l'année, . . . je vous écris ces lignes pour vous prier de m'informer en détail de l'estat auquel sont à présent les biens de la terre dans vostre généralité, et si, suivant les apparences, la récolte sera bonne; me marquant . . . les endroits du pays qui auront esté affligés de la gresle ou d'autre accidens, et ceux qui n'en auront rien souffert." Clément, *Lett. Inst. et Mém.*, IV, 216.

[3] Delamare, *op. cit.*, II, 933.

[4] *Ibid.*, II, 933.

your généralité this year. Send me also the price of grain, so that His Majesty can decide what is most advantageous for his subjects."[1] It is difficult to be sure that reports were actually received from the intendants, but I should be inclined to think that such was the case, and that this, as well as other renewals, was granted only after Colbert had definite assurance of the condition of the harvests.[2] Further continuations were issued February 28 and May 30, 1671, with the same exemptions from duties. The exemptions were limited to half the ordinary duties in the edicts of December 31, 1671, and October 26, 1672. The complete exemption was restored in April, 1673, only to be withdrawn the following year, in order to obtain money for the war.[3]

After 1675, the condition of the harvests resulted in an alternation of prohibition and permission of export. There are prohibitions issued July 6, 1675, September 11, and October 6, 1677, May 16, 1679, and June 24, 1681. Export was permitted generally December 31, 1675, June 4, 1678, June 1, 1680, August 7, 1683.[4] How closely these royal edicts were adapted

[1] Clément, *Lett. Inst. et Mém.*, IV, 233. 22 Août 1670.

[2] The bulk of material made it impractical to note all letters, especially the ordinary crop reports, and there is every reason to believe that many letters are missing in the collection preserved.

[3] Delamare, *op. cit.*, II, 934–937.

[4] *Ibid.*, II, 938, 965. Clément, *Lett. Inst. et Mém.*, IV, 285, note (26 Juin 1681). A. D. XI, 37. Edicts of 11 Sept. and 6 Oct. 1677, 1 Juin 1680, 7 Août 1683. (There was a prohibition in August, 1682, but the edict is lost. References appear in the letters.) The Collection Rondonneau, at the Archives Nationales, is a comprehensive collection of edicts and Letters Patent, arranged chronologically and by subjects. It was made by a private person connected with the Parlement, and even at the time it had a semi-official character and was used by the advocates and judges. At the death of the collector, Rondonneau, it was purchased by the Government. It is now one of the most important and trustworthy sources for the study of royal ordinances from 1660 to the Revolution. After 1683, Delamare is less complete, and the series A. D. XI, 37, adds many edicts to his list. The policy, however, is a simple continuation of that of Colbert in all respects, including the exemptions from duties and the control of the trade, by means of annual or semi-annual edicts that are renewed if circumstances permit. There is a very complete series of edicts from 1683 to 1715. From 1686 to 1689, export is permitted and exemption is granted from duties. After 1692, prohibitions alternate, and the serious crop failures make the prohibition most frequent till after 1700, when there was another period of free export.

to local conditions is necessarily somewhat uncertain, but the special exemptions of some provinces from general provisions, and the careful inquiries made by some intendants before publishing the edicts would suggest that these measures were much more real regulations of trade than were the royal edicts of the sixteenth century.

Breteuil, the Intendant at Amiens, writes from Aire, June 19: "I received the edict (of June 1) concerning the permission of the export of grain to foreign countries. The news gives much pleasure on all sides, but before publishing it formally, I have thought it wise to write to all the officers of the baillages, élections, and towns, to inform me precisely of the conditions of the crops in their districts. While waiting for their reply, the possibility of injury to the harvests from hail or other accidents will be past. *I will not publish the edict until there is that certainty concerning the harvest that your letter enjoins.*"[1] Colbert replies, June 27: "You have done well to postpone the publication of the edict for the export of grain until you are sure of the conditions of the harvest. But as I learn from all parts that the harvest will be fine, I do not doubt that you have published it by this time."[2] A few days later, Colbert writes again: "As you have published the edict, and as you feel assured of an abundant harvest, let me know if there is really likelihood of considerable exports from your généralité."[3] There are other cases in which the general edicts were suspended in particular localities, so that it is not unfair to conclude that these edicts of Colbert were really executed in those districts where special reasons did not lead to local exemptions arranged between Colbert and the intendants.

Allusion has already been made to the repeated assertion of the freedom of the inter-provincial trade. The declaration appears formally in subsidiary clauses of some edicts, as in December, 1661, more frequently it is assumed, as indicated by divers letters, which are called forth by local limitations

[1] G^7. 84. Aire, 19 Juin 1680. Breteuil à Colbert.

[2] Bib. Nat., Mél. Clair., 463, 453. Colbert à Breteuil.

[3] *Ibid.*, 463, 478. Colbert à Breteuil, 4 Juillet 1680.

upon freedom of circulation. "The grain trade between the provinces of the kingdom has never been restricted," says Colbert in many letters to intendants.[1] Colbert must have realized that this statement was by no means justified by the facts, but he persistently refused to recognize the existence of any problem in the domestic distribution of grain. Such blindness to obvious facts is hardly comprehensible, as he is singularly practical in most political questions, and rarely misled by preconceived notions. But here he seems to be hopelessly involved in confusion by his strong feeling of nationality. At all events, he never gave any attention to the domestic grain trade, dismissing it with the declaration that it ought to be perfectly free and upbraiding any officials who endeavored to restrict the freedom of movement within the Kingdom.[2]

Colbert, however, did not confine his regulation of the foreign trade in grain to purely general measures. His desire to adjust policy to local conditions and his perception of the essential differences in the interests of some provinces led him to adopt a means of control more cognizant of local needs than the general edicts of his predecessors. His general edicts were issued with the express injunction to intendants to publish them only if the conditions in their généralité warranted such action. Consequently, an adequate conception of the regulation of the trade requires study of Colbert's dealings with special provinces.

Burgundy

In the history of the trade in the Saône Basin, there are two incidents of special interest. The first was an outgrowth of Colbert's desire to reduce the obstacles to trade created by local customs, the second case is an illustration of the working of the administrative system at times when the slowness of communication might have had serious results.

[1] Clément, *Lett. Inst. et Mém.*, IV, 277, 282. 26 Oct. 1679; 18 Dec. 1680. *Ibid.*, IV, 286. 16 Juillet 1681. References of this type can be multiplied without difficulty.

[2] Read in this connection the letters cited in ch. I, of this part, apropos of prices and grain movements.

Colbert was aware of the importance of Burgundy as a source of grain supply, and was anxious to secure adequate outlet for the large crops of 1671. There had been complaint that trade was slow, that prices had fallen to such a point that returns were slight even when it was possible to sell. News of large shipments from Provence and Languedoc to Italian ports suggested the possibility of an outlet for Burgundy, either in Languedoc and Provence, or in export to Italy.[1] The intendant replied that the trade proposed could not be profitably undertaken because of the heavy tolls and local customs. Colbert then writes: "If it is true that the tolls on the Saône and Rhône prevent the export of grain, some remedy can be found. You must look into the matter with the farmers of the customs of the Saône. Find out how much grain has actually been shipped down the river during the last six months, and if the quantity is not considerable, persuade the farmers to remit half the customs, explaining to them that by that means they will gain much more than by levying duties on the present basis. As soon as they have consented to the diminution, the King will issue an order reducing all the tolls on the Rhône by one-half." [2] Without waiting for any reply, an ordinance was issued on April 2, covering both the town octrois and the other tolls levied along the rivers Saône and Rhône.[3] This was followed, at the end of the month, by another order removing the remaining half of the old dues.[4] The attempt to stimulate this export trade was a failure, and the chief effect of the acts was to relieve the Lyonese trade of the burden of duties. This was not contemplated in the orders, however, and when it was learned that the merchants were availing themselves of this opportunity, interpretative orders were issued May 31 and June 3, expressly forbidding the application of the exemption from duties to the grain going to Lyons.[5]

[1] Clément, *Lett. Inst. et Mém.*, II[2], 651–652. 22 Mars 1672.

[2] *Ibid.*, II[2], 652, note 1. 1 Avril 1672.

[3] Delamare, *op. cit.*, II, 934.

[4] Clément, *Lett. Inst. et Mém.*, II[2], 652, note 1. 20 Avril 1672.

[5] Delamare, *op. cit.*, II, 935.

In 1678, the crops had been fine and a general permission of export had been issued June 4. The following harvest was less abundant, and the inconvenience and danger of foreign export became evident in the spring of 1679. This feeling ultimately resulted in the prohibition of May 16, 1679, but the difficulty in Burgundy arising from export over the Alsatian border had already reached an acute stage by May 11. The only royal edict governing the case was that of June 4, 1678. A letter of the Sindic of Burgundy throws much light upon the legal standing of the edict in Burgundy: "I was extraordinarily surprised," he writes, "when I was shown the edict of June 4, 1678 by which the King permits the export of grain. The edict was in the hands of the clerks of the customs office at Bellay. They told me that the farmers of the Cinq Grosses Fermes had secured the edict and that the director at Lyons had sent it to them. This edict, like the prohibitory edict, is addressed to the intendants, but it is not signed by any of them. It has never been published in Burgundy,[1] and was issued upon the supposition that there was a large quantity of grain in the various provinces. But grain is scarce everywhere. These reflections, in connection with the dearth and the high prices current, have obliged me to oppose the execution of that edict, partly to prevent the famine which would be inevitable if exports were permitted, partly to prevent rioting and popular outbreaks."[2] An accompanying "procés verbal" indicates that the sindics and officers of the baillage of Bugey confiscated large quantities of grain that had been prepared for export. The vigor of the local officials is thus beyond doubt. Bouchu, the Intendant, was less certain of the proper course to follow. He submitted the whole case to Colbert without, however, taking any action against the local officials. By May 31, Bouchu had received

[1] Publication had perhaps been purposely withheld in Burgundy, if we may judge from similar cases elsewhere. At such times copies sent in unofficially, as here, always made some difficulty, though it seems to have been a principle of administrative law that no general edict applied to any particular jurisdiction until published by the officials to whom it was addressed.

[2] G[7]. 156. St. Rambert, 11 Mai 1679. Balme, Sindic en Bourgogne.

the prohibition of the 16th, which of course settled the whole dispute.[1]

The discretion possessed by the local authorities and the diversity of the official staff were important sources of elasticity in the administrative system of the seventeenth century. The officials were not expected to be servile media of central activity. General edicts were to be applied only if adapted to local conditions.

Picardy, Champagne, and Normandy

The northern provinces furnish instances of both types of special action, both special royal orders and exemptions from general edicts upon the initiative of the intendants.

In November, 1672, a royal order was issued discharging exports from Picardy and Champagne from the payment of half the ordinary dues. There is an implication that full dues are paid from other provinces, though the general edict of October 26, 1672 seems to have been still in force.[2] The order of April 11, 1676 was more explicit. Export from Picardy and Champagne is expressly permitted, but strict prohibitions are levied against export from other provinces.[3] In 1678, permission of export was granted in general by the edict of June 4, but in Picardy and Champagne this right was withdrawn by an edict of July 23, prohibiting export.[4] Then, after the harvest, exports from Picardy and Champagne were permitted,[5] by edicts of October 22, 1678 and January 7, 1679. A letter to Miroménil, Intendant in Champagne, suggests that Picardy and Champagne were exempted from the general prohibition issued May 16, 1679.[6]

The intendants also used their discretion. In June, 1681, Faultrier, in Hainault, issued a prohibition of export from his

[1] G[7]. 156. Dijon, 15 Mai 1679. Bouchu encloses the letter of Balme and the "procès verbal." Dijon, 31 Mai 1679. See also Colbert's letter of 24 Mai 1679, sending the edict of 16 Mai. Bib. Nat., Mél. Clair., 461, 569.

[2] Delamare, *op. cit.*, II, 936.

[3] *Ibid.*, II, 937–938.

[4] *Ibid.*, II, 939, cited in edict of 7 Jan. 1679.

[5] *Ibid.*, II, 965, cited in edict of 16 Mai 1679. References in a letter of Breteuil to Colbert. G[7]. 84, Arrêt. 31 Oct. 1678. Breteuil says that the permission will have a good effect. Edict of 7 Jan. 1679. Delamare, *op. cit.*, II, 939. A. D. XI, 37.

[6] Bib. Nat., Mél. Clair., 462–471. Colbert à M., 19 Juillet 1679.

department before the general edict appeared.[1] Scarcely a month later, Colbert writes to Bazin at Metz: "As you find it inexpedient to publish the prohibition of export, there is no reason why you should not suspend it."[2]

In regard to Normandy, there is little that is worthy of note. Méliand, at Caen, prefers not to publish the edict of June 1, 1680, permitting export. "I have received the edict for the permission of the export of grain from the Kingdom, and I should have published it as you order. But the continual rains in these parts for the last six weeks render the harvest so uncertain that I have felt obliged to defer the publication of the edict. I may say that the grass in the meadows is covered with water, and that the grain is lodged in many places. There are no apples anywhere."[3]

The following year conditions were reversed. A general prohibition was issued June 24, but crops in Normandy were good. Colbert writes to Le Blanc at Rouen: "I am glad to hear that there will be an abundant harvest in the généralité of Rouen, and that prices have been falling each market day. Consequently, you can suspend the publication of the edict to prohibit export."[4]

Bordeaux

In the south, the necessity of special attention was even more marked; local authorities were more independent and conditions differed widely from those of the northern provinces. At Bordeaux, in 1663, the municipality endeavored to regulate the grain trade in its own interest by preventing the passage of shipments from the Upper Garonne. This action, which was hardly warranted by conditions, evoked an immediate protest. In April, Colbert received an anonymous letter from Bordeaux, stating the case of the exporting merchants: "This letter

[1] Bib. Nat., Mél. Clair., 464, 323. C. à Faultrier, 18 Juin 1681.

[2] *Ibid.*, 465, 25 v. Colbert à Bazin, 11 Juillet 1681. See also Letters between Colbert and Breteuil. *Ibid.*, 467, 110. Colbert à Breteuil, 6 Août 1682. G^7. 84. Amiens, 16 Août 1682. Breteuil à Colbert.

[3] G^7. 213. Caen, 17 Juin 1683. Méliand. A very characteristic report of conditions.

[4] Bib. Nat., Mél. Clair., 465–49 v. Colbert à Le Blanc, 24 Juillet 1681.

is designed to show you how you can render a great service to the provinces of Languedoc and Guienne. They are burdened with direct taxes; they have an abundance of grain but no hope of selling. The Garonne is covered with loaded grain boats. The granaries of the province are full, but the municipal officers of Bordeaux prevent the passage of grain. Numbers of English, Dutch, and Flemish merchants have made extensive purchases of grain that is spoiling in granaries on the Tarn and Garonne. They are not likely to come again after this experience. All because of the obstinacy of the Jurats of Bordeaux, which M. de Saint-Luc is unable to overcome. The King would be sure of the tax receipts, if the passage of this grain were permitted. It is to the interest of His Majesty that money should come into the kingdom from foreign countries." [1] Colbert took immediate action. The question was brought before the Council and the Jurats of Bordeaux were ordered to exhibit the titles, in virtue of which they had taken to themselves this authority over the grain trade. The intendant was instructed to examine the documents produced and to terminate the affair, establishing freedom of trade on the Garonne.[2] Le Jay, however, was much less prompt than Colbert desired him to be, and as no news was forthcoming, another letter was despatched on the seventh of June.[3] In the course of the following month, the case was brought to a conclusion. The town had practically no authority. There was a charter of Henry II, which Colbert considered quite irrelevant, and a royal Patent of June, 1662, giving the city the right to take one-third of the grain passing the town, upon condition of paying the market price.[4] After the harvest,

[1] Bib. Nat., Mél. Colb., 115, 454. Avril, 1663. Bordeaux. This is a very characteristic form of the so-called "Mercantilism" of the period, but it would seem necessary to distinguish this from the more systematic form. The immediate effects of specie movements are alone in view in these statements of the necessity of obtaining specie, and it would be difficult to prove that a dearth of specie was not sufficiently common to give great importance to the current movements of coin and bullion. Such a mercantilism is quite distinct from the money-hoarding system that is too frequently represented as the universal economic doctrine of the seventeenth century.

[2] Depping, *Correspondence Administrative*, III, 26–27. 5 Mai 1663.

[3] Clément, *Lett. Inst. et Mém.*, IV, 207–208. 7 Juin 1663.

[4] *Ibid.*, IV, 215. 13 Juillet 1663.

Bordeaux complained of excessive exports and rising prices, and petitioned for authority to interfere with the trade on the river. Colbert did not attach much weight to their complaints, but he did urge the intendant and the premier président of the Parlement to look into the matter to see if there was any ground for the fear of dearth.[1] He desired above all things to afford Montauban and Languedoc an adequate market for their grain, so far as it could be done without really imperilling Bordeaux. Le Jay writes very reassuringly a month later. He is in correspondence with Pellot at Montauban, and they are both agreed upon the necessity of keeping the river free for the exportation of grain from the upper waters. "If there should be any considerable change in conditions," he says, "or if an excessive export should cause prices to rise unduly, Pellot and I could come to some understanding about the proper means of producing such limitations of shipments as should be necessary."[2]

From this time, the intendant at Bordeaux was in unquestioned control of the grain trade; for the most part he followed the general edicts but there are exceptions. One of the most interesting cases arose in July, 1675. A general prohibition had been issued on the sixth, but the weather was fine in the south and the prospect of an abundant harvest was assured. On the nineteenth, Colbert wrote to de Sève, recommending him to suspend the publication of the prohibition. De Sève replied that he had already done so, and that he had written to Paris on the eighteenth to inform Colbert of his action.[3] Similar exceptions to the general edicts appear in 1681 and 1682. In 1681, a prohibition had been issued, but crop reports from Guienne were favorable, so that Colbert wrote: "I am glad that the harvest promises to be abundant in Guienne; there is no reason why you should not suspend the order prohibiting export.

[1] Clément, *Lett. Inst. et Mém.*, IV, 220. 25 Sept. 1663. Colbert à Pellot, Int. à Montauban. Depping, *Corr. Admin.*, III, 341.

[2] Bib. Nat., Mél. Colb., 117 bis, 817. 22 Oct. 1663, Bordeaux. *Ibid.*, 117 bis, 818. Pellot à Le Jay.

[3] *Ibid.*, 172, 179. Bordeaux, 25 Juillet 1675. de Sève. Bib. Nat., Mél. Clair., 796, 323. Colbert à de Sève, 25 et 29 Juillet 1675. Some of the letters are lost, but a full account appears in the letter of de Sève of 25 Juillet.

But I doubt if that will lead to trade with Spain, as the harvests are good there."[1] A similar prohibition was issued in 1682, and Colbert was so uncertain as to conditions in Guienne, that he practically left the intendant free to publish it or not. "I send you the edict," he says. "You will let me know whether you decide to publish it or not."[2] Some of his uncertainty was shared by de Ris and by Foucault, who was located at Montauban, but made a trip to Bordeaux at this time. Foucault writes, on the twenty-fourth: "I arrived here this morning, and my first care was to confer with de Ris on the condition of the harvest. . . . He tells me that the crops have been poor throughout his department. Nevertheless, the price of grain has fallen, and this confirms my opinion that it is not expedient to prohibit export, particularly as I have just received letters from Montauban, which represent conditions there as unchanged."[3] The hesitation seems to have continued for some time, for on the first of October, we still find Colbert writing to de Ris: "although grain has gone up a little, I do not think it necessary to prohibit export."[4]

Languedoc

Languedoc necessitated more special treatment than any other province in the Kingdom. The normal trade of the province was with Spain and Italy. There was little community of interest with the interior; the principal, if not the only, question was the relation between Upper and Lower Languedoc. Ordinarily Lower Languedoc was relatively self-supporting, and as Upper Languedoc had a surplus, it was obliged to export. In times of dearth, however, as we have seen in a preceding chapter, Lower Languedoc might suffer if export were permitted. The frequent necessities of Provence and the difficulty of diverting the grain of Languedoc thither are the most interesting features of the efforts to control the trade of Languedoc. It

[1] Bib. Nat., Mél. Clair., 465, 28. Colbert à de Ris, 16 Juillet 1681.

[2] *Ibid.*, 467, 138. Colbert à de Ris, 17 Août 1682. *Ibid.*, 136. Colbert à Foucault, 17 Août 1682.

[3] G[7]. 390. Bordeaux, 24 Août 1682. Foucault.

[4] Bib. Nat., Mél. Clair., 467, 248. Colbert à de Ris, 1 Oct. 1682.

is a clear indication of the fact that Provence was a group of distinct markets which were less favorable, on the whole, than the equally distinct markets in Italy and Spain.

In Languedoc, too, the intendant enjoyed much more independence than elsewhere. Bâville was dubbed the "King of Languedoc," and the phrase does not connote too much. But it is quite as important to realize that the powers of the intendant in Languedoc were exceptional as it is to remember that the relative impotence of the intendant at Lyons is equally exceptional, on account of the prestige of the governor and the power of the municipality.

The earliest information from Languedoc consists of a few letters written in the spring of 1662, but apparently they give us only the latter part of the episode. Bezons had been discussing the expediency of prohibiting export, and finally issued a prohibition on his own authority, March 20. There was trouble in Upper Languedoc in regard to shipments to be sent down the Garonne, and, to remedy this, guards had to be despatched to protect the grain boats.[1] Prices continued to rise at Narbonne, so that Bezons felt quite satisfied with his conduct. The harvest promised well, and there was reason to hope for a speedy termination of the stringency.[2] The weather continued fine, and by the end of July, Bezons writes that it will be quite necessary to permit export, unless it should be proposed to divert the grain of Languedoc towards the interior, by shipping up the Rhône or down the Garonne. The Rhône presents many difficulties and he would hardly care to advise such a course.[3]

In 1668, there were no prohibitions, but there was no demand for the grain of Languedoc, as Italy was supplied, either by her own grain or from other sources.[4] After 1670, trade improved and for three years was carried on without any official interference.[5] In fact there is little evidence of any special regulation till 1678.

1 Bib. Nat., Mél. Colb., 107, 20. Béziers, 20 Mars. 1662. Bezons à Colbert.

2 *Ibid.*, 107, 92 v. 28 Mars 1662. Bezons à Colbert. Pézenas.

3 *Ibid.*, 109 bis, 936. 23 Juillet 1662. Bezons à Colbert.

4 Depping, *Corres. Adminis.*, I, 378. 10 Nov. 1668, D'Oppède à Colbert.

5 G^7. 295. Statistics of exports, 1670, Languedoc.

The harvests in 1677 had been deficient and general prohibitions had been issued. Provence, however, declared that the coasting trade with Languedoc was necessary. Marseilles asked for permits to import 25,000 charges from Languedoc. But these demands were treated very suspiciously. December 17, Colbert writes to Rouillé, Intendant in Provence: "As for the grain that you say is needed by Marseilles, I will say that the King has not intended to interrupt the trade between the provinces of the kingdom. Express prohibitions have been made against export from frontier provinces without licenses, and it is quite certain that Languedoc will not permit the shipment by sea of the 25,000 charges that you demand. The profit that could be made by carrying the grain to Genoa or Spain, instead of Marseilles, is too great, and it is so easy to change the route. You ought not to be surprised by the strictness of the prohibition. It is hard to believe that Marseilles alone can have need of 25,000 charges of grain. . . . Furthermore, as Marseilles is a free port, there would be nothing to prevent shipment to foreign parts, once the grain was landed."[1] Rouillé replies that he has not written of the distress in Marseilles without having made investigations. The town has only enough to last through January. Nor did he intend to give the impression that the 25,000 charges were for Marseilles alone.[2] As a matter of fact, exports of considerable quantities of grain were passing from Languedoc to Messina, and perhaps to other parts of Italy.[3]

In January, 1678, Rouillé renews his demands, but this time is very humble: "If you will do me the favor to procure a few licenses for the export from Languedoc of a moderate quantity of grain for the province, especially for Marseilles and Toulon, I will use them only in case of real necessity and with all the proper precautions. Prices are everywhere one-third higher than is usual."[4]

[1] G[7]. 1. (copie), 17 Dec. 1677. Colbert à Rouillé.

[2] G[7]. 458. 28 Dec. 1677. Rouillé à Colbert.

[3] G[7]. 295. Pézenas, 14 Jan. 1678. à Colbert. G[7]. 295. Estats des achepts de bleds fait par la Cie. de Commerce de Cette, pour estre porté à Messine. Mars, 1678.

[4] G[7]. 458. Aix, 25 Jan. 1678. Rouillé.

The shipments to Italy from Languedoc continued, and Daguesseau discovered that the army contractors had been shipping down the Rhône and thence to foreign ports, on the strength of licenses issued before the recent prohibitions.[1] But it is hard to believe that there was really any great dearth in either Provence or Languedoc, as general permissions of export for those provinces were issued May 14 and 27.[2] Bad weather in Provence, however, diminished the prospect of good harvests, and these permits were no sooner issued than Rouillé began to doubt their expediency. This was before he had received the edict of May 27 for Provence.[3] A week later, he was even more firmly convinced that the permit should not be published. Prices were already above the maxima of previous years, and were still rising.[4] There is little information from Languedoc, but apparently export was permitted only under cover of special licenses. In November, the Company at Cette asked for licenses for export to Italy. Daguesseau did not like to grant them, so that there was doubtless some apprehension in Languedoc. In January, we find Daguesseau and Rouillé entering into correspondence, in order to arrange exports to relieve distress in Provence. Colbert practically ordered Daguesseau to devote his attention to assisting his neighbor,[5] and thus promptly quieted the fears of Provence.[6]

Daguesseau, meanwhile, had been investigating conditions in his province. In the producing regions, "I find everywhere considerable quantities," he says, "more than will be consumed before the harvest. Were it not for Lower Languedoc, where prices are always high, and for Provence, it would be advisable to permit general export. But as it is necessary to harmonize

[1] G[7]. 295. Toulouse, 9 Mars 1678. Daguesseau encloses a list of these exports. Toulouse, 16 Mars 1678. Daguesseau à Colbert.

[2] Delamare, *op. cit.*, II, 938. Clément, *Lett. Inst. et Mém.*, II, 853. A. D. XI, 37. 27 Mai 1678.

[3] G[7]. 458. Aix, 7 Juin 1678. Rouillé.

[4] G[7]. 458. Aix, 14–15 Juin 1678. Rouillé. See also letter of Aix, 6 Août 1678.

[5] G[7]. 295. Montpellier, 19 Nov. 1678. Daguesseau au C. G. and other letters.

[6] Bib. Nat., Mél. Clair., 461, 37. 13 Jan. 1679. Colbert à Rouillé. *Ibid.*, 461–479. Clément, *Lett. Inst. et Mém.*, IV, 271. Colbert à Rouillé, 27 Jan. 1679.

these conflicting interests, I think it wise not to open the door completely by granting absolute freedom of export, and yet on the other hand, I would not close the ports. In short, I should advise a qualified permission, allowing shipment only from Narbonne, which is the export point for Upper Languedoc. As the quantity of 50,000 setiers which you allowed for Provence has all been shipped, I think that His Majesty could now permit the export of 100,000 setiers to foreign parts, on condition of paying the customary duties. If you will please divide this quantity into two licenses of 50,000 setiers each, I will use them only to facilitate the passage of grain from Upper to Lower Languedoc and will not publish the second until I see that there is plenty of grain in Lower Languedoc to suffice for some time. I do not think that I can do more to prevent abuses than by following the course adopted last year. No preference or personal discrimination is shown, those who are first ready to put to sea receive the permits." [1] Colbert assented to these propositions and forwarded the licenses. "It is almost impossible to prevent influential people from getting permits which they use as a source of revenue. Accordingly, avoid using these licenses, if you can, and grant general freedom of trade." [2] A few days later, Colbert decided to issue an edict permitting export generally from Languedoc.[3] But Daguesseau did not publish the royal edict, issuing instead an order of his own, permitting export from Narbonne but from no other ports.[4]

Then come complaints from Provence: "I had hoped that I would not be obliged to write you again about the dearth in this province," writes Rouillé, April 8, "but everything has been against us this year. The severity and length of the winter, which still continues, has held back the crops which never in the memory of man gave less promise. The little grain that remains has been hoarded, and prices have risen. The people

[1] G[7]. 295. Lavaur, 4 Fev. 1679. Daguesseau à Colbert.

[2] G[7]. 1. 17 Fev. 1679. Colbert à Daguesseau. Bib. Nat., Mél. Clair., 461, 158. 17 Fev. 1679. *Passports.*

[3] *Ibid.*, 461, 182–183. 24 Fev. 1679. Colbert à Daguesseau.

[4] *Ibid.*, 461, 291. Clément, *op. cit.*, IV, 272, note. 24 Mars 1679. Colbert à Daguesseau.

of Marseilles sent to Languedoc, last month, but as there has been a general permission of foreign export there, prices have risen so high that the merchants do not engage in the trade sufficiently to supply Marseilles. . . . The Échevins of Marseilles have already been obliged to seize several small boats that were going to Italy."[1] There was a threat of a general grain riot at Marseilles, but the crisis passed without actual outbreak.[2]

These accounts from Provence mystified Colbert completely. "I am particularly surprised," he writes, "by your statement that the merchants have had difficulty in buying grain in Languedoc, except at excessive prices. Languedoc does not complain, and is continually demanding freedom of export. You will admit that it is difficult to reconcile such conflicting reports. However, the King bids me write in strong terms to M. Daguesseau to have him correspond with you and consider if it is necessary to prohibit export from Languedoc."[3] Colbert again took matters into his own hands without waiting for a reply; a prohibition of export from Languedoc was issued April 18. This evoked a long letter from Daguesseau who insisted upon continuing his previous policy. "The edict will do no good to Provence and will do much harm to Languedoc."[4] Colbert disliked to insist and finally gave Daguesseau instructions to act as he thought best.[5] Daguesseau finally published the prohibition of foreign export, but the coasting trade with Provence was continued under bond.[6] The correspondence is rather voluminous even after this, but there is nothing of importance until the harvest introduced new elements.

The news that crops were good in Languedoc induced Colbert to issue a special ordinance, permitting export from the province

[1] G^7. 458. Aix, 8 Avril 1679. Rouillé au C. G.

[2] G^7. 458. Aix, 11 Avril 1679. Rouillé à Daguesseau and enclosure of a letter from Marseilles, 8 Avril 1679.

[3] Clément, *op. cit.*, IV, 272, note. 20 Avril 1679. Colbert à Rouillé. Bib. Nat., Mél. Clair., 461, 394. 20 Avril 1679. Colbert à Daguesseau. *Ibid.*, 461, 418. 27 Avril 1679. Colbert à Rouillé.

[4] G^7. 295. Montpellier, 29 Avril 1679.

[5] Bib. Nat., Mél. Clair., 461, 488. 11 Mai 1679. Colbert à Daguesseau.

[6] *Ibid.*, 461, 521. 18 Mai 1679. Colbert à Daguesseau.

but not to foreign ports.[1] This tended to stimulate the movement of grain from Languedoc to Provence, much to the relief of all concerned. General permission of foreign export from Languedoc was withheld solely on account of the needs of Provence,[2] and letters from Rouillé indicated that this difficulty was likely to continue, as crops were light in Provence.[3]

Complete freedom of trade from Languedoc was considered seriously, but Colbert warned Daguesseau that even if such permission was granted, it must not be published until he had assured himself that the needs of Provence and Dauphiné were adequately supplied.[4] Shortly after this, Daguesseau sent in a report of conditions in his province: "There have been divers accidents which have rendered the harvest in Upper Languedoc less abundant than was expected. There are no oats anywhere, and prices are high. There is very little wheat in the mountains, more in the plains, but less than last year, so that wheat is high considering the season. Prices have risen even since the harvest in Lower Languedoc, on account of the hoards made by merchants in hopes of complete freedom of export. On the whole, there will be no extraordinary abundance of grain, but there will probably be enough, not only for Languedoc but also for the neighboring provinces. Prices will doubtless run high throughout the year. At the same time, it is certain that the people of Upper Languedoc cannot live or pay their taxes, except through the sale of their grain, and I have noticed that even when there were complaints of dearth, Upper Languedoc always has some old grain left. Furthermore, there is an unusual crop of millet in Upper Languedoc and in the mountains, and, as millet is the ordinary food of the peasants, this will compensate in some measure for the light wheat crop. I feel that it would be advantageous to permit export until October or November, quite as much to complete the sale of the old grain, as to give the people some means of procuring money. But this permission should be limited to Narbonne

[1] Clément, *op. cit.*, IV, 275, note. 2 Août 1679.

[2] *Ibid.*, 9–10. Août, 1679.

[3] G[7]. 458. Aix, 15–16. Août, 1679. Rouillé à Colbert.

[4] Bib. Nat., Mél. Clair., 462, 151. 17 Août 1679. Colbert à Daguesseau.

as an outlet for Upper Languedoc." [1] Colbert assented to this proposition and sent an edict permitting export from Narbonne until November 30.[2]

The dearth in Provence continued,[3] and there was some difficulty in other provinces. This revived Colbert's old project of turning the grain of Languedoc inward. He writes to Daguesseau, November 23: "I doubt if the King will continue the permission of export from Narbonne. There is ground to apprehend a serious dearth in the kingdom, so that if Languedoc has too much it can easily ship to the neighboring provinces by land or by sea." [4]

Daguesseau, of course, finds some basis for disagreement. He will see that no grain leaves Narbonne except for other ports of Lower Languedoc or for Provence. But he does not think it wise to allow exports from Lower Languedoc even for Provence. There is very little grain in Lower Languedoc.[5] A couple of weeks later, he takes a new point of view. The Estates have asked for permission to export from Narbonne, Vendres, Sérignan, Agde. He feels "that His Majesty can safely grant this permission, for it would take some time for foreigners to learn of it, even after the permission were published locally. Then they will have to enter into correspondence with their agents, so that they could not very well begin actual shipments before the end of March or the first of April. They would not then have a very long time before the harvest. But as regards Lower Languedoc, from Béziers and Agde to the Rhône, it is important not to remove the prohibitions." [6] This is the special permission from Narbonne dressed up in different words with new excuses. But it is as incomprehensible as ever to Colbert, who evidently cannot conceive of the extreme specialization of trade routes, to which Daguesseau's policy was adapted. Colbert accordingly

[1] G^7. Toulouse, 23 Août 1679. Daguesseau à Colbert.

[2] Bib. Nat., Mél. Clair., 462, 220. 7 Sept. 1679. Colbert à Daguesseau. G^7. 295. Montpellier, 23 Sept. 1679. Daguesseau à Colbert.

[3] G^7. 458. Marseille, 26 Sept. 1679. Aix, 17 Oct. 1679. Bib. Nat., Mél. Clair., 462, 316. 6 Oct. 1679. Colbert à Rouillé.

[4] *Ibid.*, 462, p. 462. 23 Nov. 1679. Colbert à Daguesseau.

[5] G^7. 295. Pézenas, 4 Dec. 1679. Daguesseau à Colbert.

[6] G^7. 295. Pézenas, 19 Jan. 1680. Daguesseau à Colbert.

returns to the charge: "I must confess that the demands of the Estates for export from Narbonne have seemed quite extraordinary to His Majesty. He receives daily complaints of dearth from Provence, Dauphiné, and Burgundy, and it seems to him that, if there is too much in Upper Languedoc, there is nothing to prevent shipping to Provence, or up the Rhône to those provinces which lack.[1] As prices are high there it would be very advantageous to Languedoc, and would not be so prejudicial to national interests, as export to foreign countries."[2]

Daguesseau replies: "As regards export of grain from Upper Languedoc, I shall have the honor to inform you that there are shipments daily from Narbonne to Provence, but the consumption of that province is not sufficient to discharge Upper Languedoc, which ordinarily has a great abundance of grain and has no other means of obtaining money and paying taxes. This is what obliges the Estates to demand freedom of export from Narbonne, even to foreign countries. To send grain up the Rhône to Dauphiné and Burgundy is not practicable, on account of the great expenses of transportation. The Rhône is so swift that a great number of horses is required to get boats up the river. Then, too, there are frequent delays arising from the contrary winds which are very strong in the Rhône Valley. Furthermore, there are heavy dues, on account of the tolls, which are levied quite close to each other. The difference in the price of grain among these provinces is not great enough to cover all these expenses. This is a route that has not been tried except for salt; as that trade *is regular and annual*, a company has been formed which has undertaken that work for a fixed price. But that is a great establishment and the same method could not be applied to the grain trade.

"Accordingly, Languedoc has only two routes for the disposal of its grain: the sea which is the usual outlet both for Provence and foreign countries, and the Tarn and Garonne, for shipment through Bordeaux. But this latter route is available

[1] Note through here the insistence on the idea of equable national distribution as a result of differences of price.

[2] Clément, *op. cit.*, IV, 278. 1 Fev. 1680. Colbert à Daguesseau.

only when there is dearth in Guienne, when that demand is supplied before there is any resort to Languedoc. Thus, it is necessary to facilitate export by sea. The uncertainty of the coming harvest can alone cause hesitation. As you have asked for my opinion, I may say that there are only two courses open. You may permit export from Narbonne, even to foreign ports, with the understanding that prohibitions are to be issued towards the close of April, if the news from Languedoc or Provence gives reason to fear for the harvest. Or on the other hand, you may leave the present prohibitions in force until the latter part of April, deciding then to continue or to remove them, in accordance with the news you receive at that time." [1]

The letter had the effect desired; Colbert agreed to a permission of export from Narbonne, even to foreign ports, but to take effect only on March 15. A drought in Lower Languedoc made Daguesseau hestitate to publish the edict but, as prices did not rise, he finally issued it.[2] This drought, however, practically destroyed the crops of Lower Languedoc, and that fact exerted a great influence on Daguesseau's policy in regard to the latter part of 1680. Writing June 5, he says: "The crops in the dioceses of Narbonne, Béziers, and Agde are entirely ruined. . . . In some places, they have ploughed their wheat fields and sown millet in order to get some crop. I have never seen desolation equal to that in some localities, and it is certain that most of the farms in these three dioceses will not yield enough to serve as seed." [3] Conditions became more serious in the course of the month and other dioceses were affected so that, while the crops were good in Upper Languedoc, there was practically nothing in the rest of the province. This made Daguesseau unwilling to publish the general edict for permission of export issued June 4.[4] Colbert assented. "The King," he says, "leaves you full discretion to publish the edict or not, according

[1] G^7. 295. Montpellier, 17 Fev. 1680. Daguesseau à Colbert.

[2] Bib. Nat., Mél. Clair., 463, 137. 22 Fev. 1680. Colbert à Rouillé. *Ibid.*, 463, 159. 29 Fev. 1680. Colbert à Daguesseau. G^7. 295. Montpellier, 29 Mars 1680. Daguesseau à Colbert.

[3] G^7. 295. Toulouse, 5 Juin 1680. Daguesseau.

[4] G^7. 295. Toulouse, 2 Juin 1680. Daguesseau.

to the information you secure in your province. I should say, however, that reports from all the other provinces indicate a considerable abundance."[1] The difficulties experienced in Lower Languedoc, in August, September, and October, fully justified Daguesseau's policy, but the details of these relief works are hardly relevant here.[2]

The last three years present little that is new or interesting. The correspondence in regard to crops, dearth, and abundance continues, although it is less voluminous. It is a ceaseless repetition of the same theme. Prohibitions, in time of dearth; permission, if there is plenty. The whole attention of the administrative staff is given to finding out the facts, disentangling the complicated commercial conditions which are of influence, and seeking to achieve some crude adjustment of supply to demand. The apparent complexity of the grain trade policy is wholly due to its intimate connection with current conditions. The simple idea, foreshadowed vaguely in the time of Francis I and more clearly sketched in the edicts of 1559 and 1571, persists with little change in form to the close of our period. But the rather intricate mass of detail presented in connection with Colbert's efforts will have failed of its purpose if it does not suggest that Colbert realized, to a considerable extent, the dreams and intentions of his predecessors.

[1] Bib. Nat., Mél. Clair., 463, 494. 18 Juillet 1680. Colbert à Daguesseau.

[2] G^7. 295. Toulouse, 21 Août; Cette, 2 Sept. 1680; Montpellier, 7 Sept. 1680; Montpellier, 29 Sept. 1680; Montpellier, 15 Oct. 1680. Bib. Nat., Mél. Clair., 463, 642. 28 Août 1680.

CHAPTER IV

Regulation of the Domestic Grain Trade, 1683–1709

After the death of Colbert, there was a much greater change in the efficient regulation of the grain trade than appears upon the surface. Royal edicts for the control of foreign trade appear with increasing frequency and form an almost unbroken chain throughout the remaining years of the reign. In these edicts there is no sign of a new policy, and if it is too much to assert that they were without influence on the trade, it is none the less true that the relative importance of royal activity was very greatly reduced by the energetic and efficient control exerted by the intendants. Their policy must be regarded as the continuation of the efforts of the sixteenth century officials to regulate the domestic trade. The influence of Colbert is manifest, and, in this sense, there is at least an apparent connection with the traditions of royal policy. But the influence of the central administration is not that of an authority controlling export trade; it is rather a new representative of the crown acting as arbiter between conflicting local authorities. The intendant was a personal representative of the Crown, and, although resident in the district, in the late seventeenth century he was charged with the care of general rather than local interests. The intendants trained by Colbert were the product of many influences; they brought together administrative traditions that were formerly entirely distinct. They inherited the policy of the old local officials, many of whom no longer possessed the power whose trappings they still retained, but they also received the impress of the powerful personality of Colbert, and were filled with a solicitude for the commonweal that was entirely new in a French administrative official.

It is fortunate that this transformation of the administrative system should have been completed just before the critical years of the late seventeenth century. For many years the domestic grain trade had presented no great problem, nothing but dreary persistence of old traditions. Some of the seeming quietness of the early seventeenth century is probably due to the accidental loss of important records. But when every qualification is made, there seems to have been no development of importance in the early years of the century, and even after the rise of Colbert, the regulations of the domestic trade are of the traditional type.

The relative fertility of the years of Colbert's ministry removed the domestic trade from the sphere of active administrative supervision. There was a recrudescence of old prohibitive regulations in some places; the Parlement of Toulouse, for instance, issued prohibitions in 1660, and the Jurats of Bordeaux interfered with the trade, as we have already seen. There is some indication of active regulation in the Seine Basin in 1660, but these efforts of the Châtelet and Échevinage did not assume a sufficiently positive character to make them of immediate importance. Those years were, indeed, of interest as regards the extension of the jurisdiction of the Châtelet, but they do not disclose any change in administrative policy. The activity of the officials in the Seine Basin in 1660 was largely based on the old traditions, presenting no novelty, but better informed than previous similar efforts. The difficulties arising from the location of Orleans appear very distinctly in 1662–63, and the letters of the Intendant and of the Maire afford considerable insight into conditions.[1] With these exceptions, the administration of Colbert has little significance from the standpoint of domestic policy. He himself was but slightly interested, partly because he felt that the reiteration of the declarations that the inter-provincial trade should be free was all that was necessary, partly because the grain trade as a whole was of subordinate interest to him.

Ten years after the death of Colbert, the first of the great dearths created a crisis in the regulation of the domestic trade such as had never before existed. There had been failures of the crops that were almost as serious, although the area affected

[1] Bib. Nat., Mél. Colb., 108, 188, *passim*.

in 1693 was probably more extensive. But never before had such a dearth occurred at a time of rapid growth towards metropolitanism. The danger from metropolitan demand that had ever been present was rendered doubly intense by the great change in commercial practice. The change was apparent even before 1660, but there had been no dearth sufficiently severe to reveal all the consequences of the new developments around Lyons and Paris.

This crisis came upon France just as the changes in the administrative system had created new officials admirably suited to grapple with the new problem. The intendants were, for the most part, in control of the trade, but there were other officials, too, who had acquired new powers. The struggle between the Châtelet and the Échevinage at Paris had smouldered for generations, without notable results of any kind. There are signs of change as early as 1630. The Châtelet was gaining in prestige, and by 1660 was definitely in the possession of new powers which made it one of the most important influences in the Seine Basin. The Échevinage made a futile attempt to regain its old authority, but the general control of the grain trade passed to the Châtelet. The time demanded new policies and new officials, or old officials with new powers, prepared for the crisis.

The character of the official body precluded the possibility of any definite scheme for the regulation of the trade. The need was not for men with preconceived ideas, whether favoring restriction or complete freedom of trade; it was a time that called for men conversant with all the details, provided with the authority and the will to do whatever a concrete case demanded. Openness of mind, the administrative rather than the theoretical temperament was needed. It is this spirit that was most conspicuous in the intendants, and in this they exhibited most strongly the finer qualities of Colbert. But there was great diversity of opinion and policy. Intendants in different districts pursued distinct policies. The one believed in prohibitions under certain conditions; the other asserted the advisability, nay, even the necessity, of complete liberty.

Advocacy of freedom of inter-provincial trade was not uncommon. We find de la Bourdonnaye writing from Bordeaux, that grain is a "commodity that cannot be given too much freedom of circulation." . . . "Only complete freedom of trade can produce abundance." "The least constraint will spoil everything."[1] D'Argenson at Paris says: "Freedom of trade in grain is a public benefit, restraint alarms and ordinarily produces nothing but unfortunate results." He makes some concession to the old views, but persists in his belief that freedom is essential. "If it be necessary to prohibit at times the transport of grain from province to province, it would seem best to exempt the large towns like Paris and Lyons from the effect of such restriction."[2] Bouchu says that prohibitions are unwise in any case, since "they are always the cause of the increase in prices, and even of the scarcity of grain in the markets, because they render the people more inclined to hoard. The object of the prohibition, too, is rarely attained, for the officials charged with the execution of the orders are easily corrupted."[3] In 1709, the Contrôleur Général writes: "The first thing that the King deemed necessary when the lightness of the harvest of 1708 became known was to establish an entire and absolute freedom of trade in grain from province to province, so that those having too much might succor those that lacked. His majesty has never approved of having his intendants shut themselves up in their departments, preventing the export of grain."[4] This was apparently a very bold assertion of the old policy of freedom for the inter-provincial trade, but it is nevertheless an indication of the persistence of the old idea, with perhaps an increased vitality. Notwithstanding these wide-spread and forceful assertions of the liberal ideal, the effective policy retains, as before, a very considerable element of restraint. Sanson, writing from Soissons, states the policy that is most successfully applied to the grain trade. "I think," he says, "that the trade cannot be stimulated too much in times of abundance nor watched

[1] Boislisle, *op. cit.*, II, 103, 358. 19 Jan 1702.

[2] *Ibid.*, I, 509, 1811. 24, 27 Dec. 1698.

[3] *Ibid.*, II, 2, 4. 18 Sept. 1699.

[4] *Ibid.*, III, 204, 532. 8 Sept. 1709. C. G. à Le Gendre.

too closely in time of dearth. It is necessary to go from one extreme to the other, according to the different circumstances."[1]

This course advocated by Sanson was not new. It is fundamentally the idea of the local officials of the sixteenth century, but its adaptation to circumstances led to progressive modification. There had long been a feeling that the trade must be regulated, the great question was, How? In the sixteenth century, the prohibition and an assertion of the old market regulations were the only modes of regulation proposed. At the close of the seventeenth century, the prohibition became a more flexible instrument, by reason of a systematic development of special licenses. The purely reactionary endeavor to maintain the old markets, too, gave way to attempts to regulate the markets on an entirely new principle. The old system had sought to preserve the independence of the local market from metropolitan influence. The new attempts were in the direction of subordinating the local markets to the metropolitan market. Prices, instead of being made on the local market, were to be determined by the metropolitan market. This idea appears most clearly in a letter of Daguesseau where the preponderant influence of Paris is treated as an established fact: "Paris, so to speak, determines the prices of grain for a great part of the Kingdom. When Paris is sufficiently supplied and grain is reasonable there, less is drawn from the provinces, and local prices follow approximately the prices at Paris."[2]

The prohibition and the license system were designed to perform the work that would be done by a well-organized metropolitan market; they were to assure an equable distribution of available supply. The new regulations for the markets were steps towards the metropolitan market itself. One was a temporizing policy, the other was a constructive policy; in the one case, the intendant acted constantly as *Deus ex machina*, in the other case, he sought to render trade independent of external interference. The license system was much less novel than the new market regulations. Licenses had been issued

[1] Boislisle, *op. cit.*, II, 125, 444. 19 Oct. 1702.

[2] *Ibid.*, III, 102, 313. 24 Fev. 1709.

quite generally throughout the sixteenth century, and the abortive projects for the regulation of foreign trade present in full the idea of regulation by prohibition and license as it was realized in the domestic trade in the late seventeenth century. The license system, then, is new chiefly in respect to the high degree of systematization, and in the actual application of the policy to the concrete facts.

But while, in a general sense, these two modes of regulation appear during this period, they do not appear in the same regions, nor have they an equal degree of historical significance. The effort at constructive market regulation was practically confined to the area described in previous chapters as the upper Seine Basin. This was the primary supply area of Paris. Here the trade was relatively regular. Supplies were seldom actually inadequate, and it was fairly well realized that the chief problem was to distribute the grain equably. Downright prohibitions were infrequently resorted to, and a careful control of markets was ordinarily adequate. In Burgundy, the possibility of exhaustion was greater; the fertile area of the province was not extensive, local needs were considerable, the Lyonese demand insistent and heavy. A short crop was really a just cause for apprehension. Prohibitions and licenses consequently play a great part in the Rhône Valley trade. Conditions were not very different in Brittany and Languedoc, where there was an additional complication by reason of the frequency of export to foreign countries.

The other parts of France present somewhat different problems. There is nothing that is worthy of the name of grain trade policy except at Orleans, where conditions are very curious. Situated on the southern edge of the Beauce, with a possibility of securing additional supplies from Saumur, Brittany, or even from Auvergne, it might seem as if Orleans enjoyed a singular security in respect to its food supply. But Paris exerted so great an influence on all these sources that Orleans was often seriously affected. The city was not possessed of the legal right to interfere with the movements of trade on the river, where the shipments were designed for Paris. In the producing regions, there was, of course, the possibility of buying, but only in competition with Paris. This, too, was less easy, as the city could usually be supplied from the Beauce, so that the merchants of Orleans were not accustomed to buy regularly in the lower Touraine. In times of dearth, too, the grain of the Beauce tended to flow toward Paris rather than to Orleans. The city was thus occasionally placed in the curious situation of being in want, when an abundance was floating by on its way to Paris.

Our consideration of policy will fall naturally into three divisions: the attempt at constructive market regulation in the Seine Basin; the development of licenses in Burgundy, Languedoc and Brittany; the policy of the officials at Orleans, the most typical enclave.

The Seine Basin

In the Seine Basin, some peculiarities are presented by the presence of the Châtelet and the Échevinage. The municipality of Paris retained much of the power enjoyed in the sixteenth century, and the Provost of Paris continued to occupy a unique place. He and his lieutenants increased their authority, despite the appearance of the intendants. The Intendance of Paris, indeed, was created later than most of the others, and the intendant there never possessed the wide field of activity that characterizes the office in the more distant sections of France. The proximity of the Court and the extensive jurisdiction of the municipality and of the Châtelet, all conspired to render the intendant of Paris inconspicuous.

Besides this complicating fact that the trade of the region was, in part, controlled by the Châtelet and the Échevinage of Paris, the history of the latter part of the seventeenth century is somewhat confused by the keen rivalry of the two Parisian authorities. The Châtelet was reaching out for more power, the Échevinage was striving to retain at least its old prestige and influence.

This question of jurisdiction is not without significance as it throws light on the character of the authority of the Châtelet, which was quite different from that of the intendant, and there can be little doubt but what the nature of its power had an important influence upon the policy of the Châtelet and upon the development of new means of controlling the grain trade. The Châtelet had the supervision of the trade on land; the Échevinage had the regulation of the river trade. The jurisdiction of the Châtelet covered infringements of the market regulations in the immediate vicinity of Paris and any illegal conduct occurring during the transportation of the grain to Paris. The old market regulations were primarily ordinances fixing market hours for bourgeois and merchants, excluding merchants from markets within ten leagues of Paris, reserving specified markets to bakers, prohibiting the buying of grain off the markets, along the roadside or in the streets of the town, and also prohibiting partnerships among the merchants. Violence on the part of the inhabitants toward the grain merchants fell naturally within the criminal jurisdiction of the Châtelet. This authority was not unlike that exercised by the baillis and sénéchaux of the fifteenth and sixteenth centuries, when these functions were acquired by the Châtelet.[1]

The Échevinage of Paris, represented primarily by the Provost of Merchants, had gradually acquired jurisdiction over all water-borne traffic. With the grain trade, this involved the right to prevent the passage of grain through Paris, and even the right to control all the movement on the river down to the bridges at Mantes, which were the boundary between the Rouenese and the Parisian spheres of influence. The most characteristic features of the jurisdiction of the Provost of Merchants were his right to require the shipment of grain purchased with the intention of bringing it to Paris, to prevent the stopping of the grain at intermediate points by the mer-

[1] Bib. Nat., Fr. 21624. 53. Le sommaire des moyens allégués par M. le Prévôt des Marchands et Échevins en l'assemblée qui se faisoit 19 Dec. 1660. H. 1805. Reg. du Bureau, vii^{xx}vii. sans date; H. 1825. *Ibid.*, cxxx. 31 Jan. 1675; H. 1826. *Ibid.*, v^{c}xxxi. 21 Jan. 1678; H. 1835. *Ibid.*, 161. 28 Juin 1695; *passim.* G^{7}. 1632. Paris, 20 Sept. 1693. Dubois. Mémoire pour les Prévôt des Marchands et Échevins, de Paris. G^{7}. 1635. Dec. 1694. Petition au Parlement de Paris. Many other references can be given for details of this interesting episode in constitutional history. The story runs along through the Registres du Bureau.

chants themselves or by the officials or inhabitants of river towns, and to regulate the sale of grain from the boats at the ports of Paris. These powers involved incidental acts which were less precisely determined. Thus, the Provost of Merchants had some oversight of the quality of grain sold, of the measures used, and of the various circumstances which might prevent shipment from the point of origin. The merchants were not supposed to store their grain after it was bought, longer than was necessary to accumulate a boat-load. The execution of this provision of course involved some interference with the trade on land in the river towns. Similarly, when market dues were exacted in these shipping points, the merchants could appeal to the Échevinage of Paris, representing that such dues were not properly levied on grain that was purchased in the country and merely brought into the river town for shipment. This, of course, raised the question of the right to buy outside the market.

This confusion as to the nature of the incidental powers of the Échevinage was the basis of the whole conflict of jurisdiction with the Châtelet. The officials of the latter body asserted that they had authority over the grain trade as long as it was on land, whether it was to be shipped to Paris by land or by water. The Échevinage declared that its authority covered the trade entering Paris by water, from the time and place of purchase to the sale on the ports at Paris.

The merits of the case presented a rather nice point of law. Appeal to precedent was useless, as there had been in the past little effort to regulate the up river trade before it reached the river town. Furthermore, there was scarcely any means of settling the question legally, so that in practice the jurisdiction over the up river trade, while on land, ultimately fell to the body most capable of exercising this new branch of trade regulation.

In the respect of possessing means of executing its policy the Châtelet had an overwhelming advantage. The type of regulation was practically the same as that applied to the land trade near Paris, so that the accustomed measures could be easily extended to this wider field which lay equally within the general jurisdiction of the Châtelet. The special commissaries and the *Huissiers à cheval* were efficient agents for the execution of the policy and orders of the Lieutenant Civil, who was the principal official representing this aspect of the jurisdiction of the Châtelet. The Provost of Merchants, on the other hand, found himself confronted by a relatively new problem, and without any means of executing his policy, save commissioners whose effectiveness depended largely upon the good will of the local officials invited to execute their orders. Besides these advantages, the Châtelet obtained additional hold upon this jurisdiction through the union in one person of the offices of Lieutenant Civil and Provost of Merchants. This happened several times in the middle of the century, and, as the office of Lieutenant Civil was the more important of the two, the functions of the Provost of Merchants were confused with those of the Lieutenant Civil, establishing precedents which were later extremely awkward for the Échevinage. In this rather devious manner, then, the Châtelet extended its authority and its traditional regulation of markets to the whole area of Parisian supply.

This novel extension of an old power was not without significant effects. The Châtelet proposed to control the Parisian grain trade, and to exercise this control, not through the system of prohibitions and licenses devised by the provincial authorities and inherited by the intendants, but by a systematic regulation of the local markets and the grain merchants. This policy was not undertaken as result of any scheme conceived at one time by any individual, but, by a process of evolution, it came to be the policy of the Châtelet. It was a projection of the oldest ideas of grain trade regulation into an entirely new sphere, in which these old ideas were transformed under stress of circumstance. The Châtelet ultimately gave definite form to commercial customs which became the basis of a new type of market organization.

The control of the trade in the Seine Basin was thus in the hands of three distinct types of authority: the Châtelet; the municipality of Paris, and, to some extent, other municipal officers; and lastly, the intendants. At times, they worked harmoniously, more frequently there was considerable friction, so that the ultimate result was quite different from that contemplated by any official or group of officials. The history of this complicated tangle of policies and authorities will be clearer if we include in our study the years 1660–63. The situation at that time is a sort of interlude between the older local regulation and that of the three great dearths that mark the closing years of the century. There were no general provincial prohibitions, but many of the towns interfered with shipments of grain. There was also much trouble arising from the disorganization of the local markets.

In 1660, there was no serious difficulty until early summer. Then the towns on the Marne, Oise, and Seine began to interfere with the movement of grain. At Meaux, Crécy, and a few other places, the townspeople pillaged the boats of the merchants.[1] The interruption of traffic soon became so serious that the Châtelet, in October, sent commissioners to many river towns to discover the cause of the cessation of traffic. They went up the Oise to Noyon, up the Marne to Châlons, up the Seine to Port-Moutain, in the vicinity of Bray and Provins. In each town the granaries were inspected, formal reports drawn up, and the officials and townspeople were questioned.[2] Considerable quantities of grain were found, and the inquiry suggested that the trouble arose primarily from the improper conduct of merchants and municipal officials. In the minds of the commissioners, both merchants and officials were equally guilty. At Châlons, they were told by the Lieutenant General of the town, "that there were 400,000 setiers which could be exported without inconveniencing the town. The cause of disorder in sale of grain was that the Parisian merchants, after buying, would not remove their grain from the granaries in the time agreed upon. They obliged the sellers to bring suits

[1] H. 1815. Reg. du Bureau. cciiiix^{xx}iv, 24 Juillet 1660.

[2] Bib. Nat., Fr. 21641. 190 ff. Delamare's papers. Original Procès Verbaux, copies, and extracts.

The commissions are of 16 Oct. 1660, and appear in Delamare's *Traité de la Police*, 2d ed., II, 376. The commissioners were divided into three groups, one for each river valley.

against them to force them to clear the granaries." [1] At Soissons, the commissioners learned of serious abuses in regard to the marketing of the grain. The Parisian merchants bought in the streets of the town, or on the highways outside the gates.[2] In both places there was evidence of partnerships among the merchants, and at Soissons there were many assertions that the town officials were engaged in the trade and used their official position to further private ends.[3] A more elaborate description of these associations and the accompanying practices appears in an order of July, 1660. It declares in the preamble that information has been given "that certain merchants have recently formed granaries at Paris and disseminated divers false rumors, although the grain is in good condition in the principal provinces. And to contribute to the success of their pernicious design, they have made agreements to buy all the grain of the provincial merchant immediately upon arrival, for fear that the latter would be satisfied with the ordinary honest gain of a merchant. Once possessed of the grain, they could sell at whatever price they pleased. Not content with all these illegal practices, they have ridden post through the provincial towns to spread the false rumors, and to make them more credible they have purchased small quantities of grain at high prices to keep prices up. In consequence of these actions, the inhabitants of some towns have risen and endeavored to prevent shipment to Paris. Then, to profit by their malice, the merchants bring their grain to market a little at a time." [4] All these acts were prohibited again and again, both by the Châtelet and by the Échevinage. The ordinance of the Provost of Paris was followed, August 7, by an ordinance of the Provost of Merchants. The merchants were enjoined to ship their grain to Paris without any delays in transit, and to sell the whole

[1] Bib. Nat., Fr. 21641. 190. Oct. 1660. Châlons-sur-Marne.

[2] *Ibid.*, 250, 254. 6 Nov. 1660. Le Proc. du Roy au Sr. Martinet, fermier du droit d'estallage.

[3] *Ibid.*, Soissons.

[4] Bib. Nat., Fr. 16743. 108. 29 Juillet 1660. Delamare, *op. cit.*, 2d ed., II, 374.

boat-load at one price.[1] October 26, the Échevinage again took this matter in hand: "All partnerships and associations in the grain trade are hereby annulled and cancelled. Merchants are forbidden to enter into any contracts of this nature in the future. They are enjoined to make their purchases separately, each on his own account, and to divide within a month all grain which they now hold in common." [2] In November, the Châtelet issued an ordinance on the same subject.[3]

This dread of associations dominates all the evidence taken by the commissioners of the Châtelet in 1660. They were searching eagerly for just such abuses, and it is hardly surprising that they found what they were looking for.

The chief result of these inquests was the shipment of large quantities of grain to Paris and the accumulation of information that showed the Parisian officials the necessity of regulating the trade. The conflict of jurisdiction between Châtelet and Échevinage became more intense. The Échevinage resented the action of the Châtelet and the whole case was presented to the Council.[4] The immediate decision favored the Échevinage, and when difficulties arose in the following year, commissioners were sent out by that body to regulate all aspects of the river trade. These commissions are the first indication of trouble; two were sent up the Seine and Oise to Soissons, and two up to Châlons. Their commissions were very similar to those of the Châtelet of the preceding year.[5] Shortly after these commissions were issued, the Provost at Châlons proceeded to limit the export from the town to such quantities as he should permit. All the merchants were inscribed on a roll, and permits were issued in order, as the Provost deemed expedient.[6] In the following month there were similar restrictions

[1] H. 1815. Reg. du Bureau, ccclvi. 7 Août 1660.

[2] H. 1815. *Ibid.*, v^c^iiii^xx^vii. 22 Oct. 1660.

[3] Delamare, *op. cit.*, 2d ed., II, 377–378. 26 Nov. 1660.

[4] H. 1815. Reg. du Bureau, vii^xx^vii. Long account of both sides of the case from the point of view of the Échevinage.

Bib. Nat., Fr. 21642. 53. Similar statement of the case by the Châtelet.

[5] H. 1816. Reg. du Bureau, clxi. 18 Juin 1661; *Ibid.*, clxiii. 18 Juin 1661.

[6] H. 1816. *Ibid.*, ix^xx^xix.

at Vitry.[1] Other towns followed their example, and the trade suffered from this species of interference for the rest of the season. Ordinances were issued both by the Châtelet and by the Council, cancelling the prohibitions of the local officials and ordering immediate shipment to Paris. But these measures were not entirely successful.[2] In September, more commissioners were sent out by the Échevinage to go up the rivers to send down grain.[3] Difficulties at Châlons continued, and finally, in January, 1662, one of the Échevins was commissioned to travel through "the provinces of Brie and Champagne, accompanied by four horsemen, to execute the ordinance of December 2, and in consequence, to cause to be shipped to Paris such grain as merchants of Paris or others shall have in store, destined for the provision of this town. He shall also see to it that the merchants are not prevented or hindered in any way in the purchase and transport of grain. He shall cause the granaries to be opened and have the grain placed on sale, and to that end, if need be, have it carried to the neighboring markets. He shall also inquire into the acts of violence which are committed to prevent shipments of grain. Similarly, he shall investigate the associations, monopolies, or other evil practices, and the transport of grain from the kingdom." [4] He was given plenary power to act in the name of the town and to call upon any judicial officers for assistance. The commission is interesting because of the inclusion of the power to regulate the markets, and the recommendation of an investigation of the practices of the merchants. But it was an undertaking which was not really carried out. The principal prohibition of export was at Châlons; and there, despite all that had been done in the fall of 1661, despite the plenary powers of Mouthers, the Échevin of Paris, the restrictions were maintained at least as late as May 6. The merchants were still compelled to dispose of a large proportion of their grain to the Échevins of Châlons, as a condition

[1] H. 1816. Reg. du Bureau, clxxii. 5 Juillet 1661.

[2] H. 1816. *Ibid.*, ii^c^liiii, cites arrêt of 2 Sept. 1661. Delamare, *op. cit.*, II, 382, 2d ed.

[3] H. 1816. *Ibid.*, ii^c^liiii. 20 Sept. 1661.

[4] H. 1816. *Ibid.*, iii^c^xxxvii. 14 Jan. 1662.

of being allowed to export the rest.[1] The conclusion of the episode does not appear, but the mission of Mouthers was apparently a failure.

These years are instructive because they made the Parisian authorities realize that the delayed shipments and prohibitions might be due even more largely to defective market organization than to the actual lack of grain so frequently alleged by the officials in the producing regions. The minute investigations of the Châtelet in 1660 were entirely new, and revealed a situation that was quite unlike the utopian dreams of Colbert and his predecessors. The necessities of Paris made them feel the vital importance of uninterrupted trade, and their careful investigation of the causes of the municipal prohibitions was destined to inaugurate great changes. The main lines of the policy of the future appear in the Procès Verbaux of the Châtelet, and more definitely in the commission of Mouthers. It is to be a policy of regulation of merchants and markets, which are to be made to work without the constant interference of administrative officials. But these years do no more than suggest the break with the old traditions. The details of the policy are not clear; the active agents in its execution are uncertain.

After 1662, there is a long interval during which there are few incidents worthy of note. The Échevinage had petty cases brought before it from time to time, but the regulation of the grain trade does not again become important until 1693. Then, all the issues of 1662 reappeared. The officials in Champagne declared that dearth was such an immediate menace that prohibitions were necessary. The Parisian officials were more inclined to believe that the real source of all the trouble lay in the disorganization of the markets and in the associations of merchants designed to create corners and to control prices. As a matter of fact, there was probably some truth on both sides.

The general history of the years 1693–94 differs slightly from that of other years of dearth. Apprehensions arose in part from

[1] H. 1816. Reg. du Bureau, iiii^{c}iiii^{xx}. 14 Fev. 1662. H. 1816. *Ibid.*, iiii^{c}xix. 12 Avril 1662. H. 1816. *Ibid.*, iiii^{c}xxii. 13 Avril 1662. H. 1816. *Ibid.*, iiii^{c}lxvii. 6 Mai 1662.

the light crop of 1693, and the poor prospects for the succeeding harvest filled the summer and fall with violence and unrest. In January, 1693, the first complaints began to come in from the outer edge of the Beauce. The Lieutenant of the Prévôté at Montargis writes: "There is a man here acting for M. Berthelot of Plaineuf, who is shipping all the wheat in our province. He says that it is for the Invalides. Every one complains of the granaries he is forming, for it is certain that we shall be without grain in a month. If I had not taken pains to stop six grain boats last year, we should have suffered from famine, and the situation is much more serious this year as there is no old grain from the preceding harvest."[1] The Procureur du Roy writes about the same time: "We are all persuaded that this grain of M. Berthelot cannot be shipped without causing a dearth in this little province which scarcely raises enough for its own maintenance."[2] In May, the Provost of Merchants issued an ordinance which refers to interference with the grain trade in "many places of Brie, Burgundy, and Gâtinais." "The inhabitants have even maltreated the merchants and cut the ropes of the boats."[3] The violence is especially notable at Montargis and vicinity. "At Rogin, three or four peasants, or rather their wives, took twenty to thirty bushels of grain from the *blatiers* who had come to buy in that parish."[4] In August, the local authorities at Châlons were roused to the point of taking measures to secure grain on the account of the municipality. Much of this was for the indigent, but the pressure of dearth was beginning to be felt generally. Larcher, the Intendant, also complained of high prices and danger of scarcity.[5] Shipments were prevented at Nogent-sur-Seine.[6] In January, 1694, there was real suffering at Rheims: "Out of

[1] G^7. 1632. Montargis (Jan.–Fev.) 1693. Gaillard à Creil, Intendant à Orléans.

[2] G^7. 1632. *Ibid.* M. Le Proc. du Roy à Creil.

[3] H. 1834. Reg. du Bureau, 204. 15 Mai 1693.

[4] G^7. 1632. Montargis, 30 Mai 1693. Monard, Prévôt des Maréchaux,—*i. e.* chief police officer.

[5] G^7. 1630. Châlons, 26 Août 1693. Échevins de Châlons. Châlons, 27 Août 1693. Henri, Évêque de Châlons. Châlons, 8 Sept. 1693. Larcher.

[6] H. 1834. Reg. du Bureau, 340. 9 Sept. 1693.

the 25,000 or 26,000 persons, of which the town is composed, 11,000 or 12,000 are reduced to begging, and have to be supported by alms. But all the pains that have been taken have not prevented the death of 4,000 within the last six months." [1] About the same time, Châlons and Vitry were hard pressed. There was no prohibition at Vitry, but the port of Châlons was closed by the Échevins.[2] The other details may be easily inferred, but as the bulk of the information is not large, it is hardly safe to imagine a very extensive dearth. There were no general prohibitions and the municipal interference came more largely from the inhabitants than from the officials. On July 10, the Châtelet sent out commissioners. The commission declared "that several ill disposed people had made divers monopolies to evade the royal ordinances, and had diverted from its proper course much of the grain that should have been brought to Paris or to neighboring markets." [3] MM. Poiret and Chevalier went through Hurepoix, the Beauce, and Vexin, MM. le Maistre and du Mesnil, through France, Valois, and Picardy, Delamare and le Page, through Brie, Burgundy, and Champagne. "The results of these investigations confirmed the conjecture that the malice of men had been much more truly the cause of the dearth than actual scarcity of grain. The commissioners found the grain of the preceding harvests on all sides, in the farms, in the houses of the wealthy bourgeois, and in the granaries of the merchants. They enjoined each individual to carry a certain quantity of grain to the nearest market and to bring back a certificate from the judge. They attended the markets themselves, as far as their itinerary would permit, and they had the satisfaction of seeing abundance reëstablished by the grain they had sent to market."

The commissioners Delamare and le Page reached Sens, Thursday, July 22. Saturday they were told that there was a riot in the central square where the market was held. "They

[1] Boislisle, *op. cit.*, I, 349, 1272. 13 Jan. 1694. Lieu[t]. Gén[x]. du Conseil, et Échevins de Reims.

[2] G[7]. 1634. Châlons, 17 Jan. 1694. Larcher. G[7]. 227. Placet des Maire et Échevins de Châlons.

[3] Delamare, *op. cit.*, 2d ed., II, 1053. 10 Juillet 1694.

went thither . . . and finally discovered that a rich cultivator of a village near Sens, who worked his farm himself, had his barns filled with old grain, but nevertheless came each market day to buy more. He always paid more than the current price and forced prices up. . . . That day, at the opening of the market, the man's wife had come and forced prices up three sous per bichet, which had caused the people to attack her and to besiege the house to which she had fled. . . . The woman was sent to prison. . . . The Provost of Sens went to the village where she lived, and found the grain as indicated. A part was confiscated and the farmer fined.

"All these pains that the commissioners took in the provinces had indeed for their object the relief of all, but their principal intention and care was always to reëstablish abundance on the markets of Paris. The movement which they gave to trade, getting the grain out of the places in which it was hoarded and having it brought to market, gave the merchants and *blatiers* an opportunity to buy, and made the grain work its way down towards the capital. The discovery and the opening of the granaries on or near the rivers, the great numbers of boats which they had loaded and sent down to Paris, were a great aid. Furthermore, they spread a terror among the merchants by their investigations of the practices of those who had caused high prices by their usuries [1] and monopolies, by the imprisonment of some of the principal offenders and the suits against others. . . . The merchants were thus obliged to confine themselves within the limits of legitimate trade.

"By these means the price of grain diminished at Paris, ten days after the departure of the commissioners, from 54^{ll} per setier to 36^{ll}. Two days later prices fell to 32^{ll} and in the same week to 28, 27, 26; at the end of the month wheat was at 20. This fall in prices continued to Martinmas when the best wheat was selling at 15 to 16^{ll}. Thus ended that apparent dearth and that period of high prices which lasted nearly two

[1] Doubtless purchases on earnest money, which enabled a man to control a large supply by means of a small sum of ready money. The right to the crop was frequently secured by loans to the farmers.

years."[1] The fall in prices was, of course, due in part to the harvest, which naturally relieved much of the pressure. However, it is probable that Delamare's interpretation of this particular year in this region is just. The element of panic was always great, even in regions where there was little serious trouble, and this unreasoning fear which disorganized trade was doubtless the whole basis of such difficulties in 1693–94 as were not directly due to the illegal conduct of the grain merchants.

The Échevinage had also made an attempt to enforce the market regulations and to restrain the grain merchants. In December, 1693, fines of 500ll apiece were imposed upon Philipon, the widow Cressy, Channes, Mercier, the widow Chaillot and de la Noue, all of Bray, "for having purchased grain in the country districts of the peasants and farmers, both threshed and unthreshed, and for having gone out of town to meet the peasants bringing grain to the markets, and for having bid up prices one against another, both outside and on the markets, and for having set prices higher than that of the opening of the market."[2] There are also orders against the delaying of shipments on their way to Paris, and against associations of merchants.[3] The principal denunciation of these practices is that of October 19, 1694. "The excessive dearness of grain having forced us to investigate its causes, we have recognized that several provincial merchants, expecting that their contraventions would not come to our notice, have formed associations to increase prices. Furthermore, they did not ship to Paris the grain that they had purchased in Champagne, Brie, and other provinces, intending to buy and sell amongst themselves, for great profits were made in that way. They accordingly

[1] Delamare, *op. cit.*, II, 1054–55, 2d ed.

Some of the Procès Verbaux of these commissions are now in Delamare's papers at the Bib. Nat., and some of this evidence has been used previously. But I do not feel sure that all the Procès Verbaux are now in Delamare's collection. Some may have been lost, the rest might perhaps be found in the Série Y at the Arch. Nat.

[2] H. 1834. Reg. du Bureau, 382. 1 Dec. 1693.

[3] H. 1834. *Ibid.*, 482. 18 Mars 1694. H. 1834. *Ibid.*, 494. 2 Avril 1694.

neglected to bring their grain to Paris, so that it reached Paris only after having passed through divers hands and after the price had been very considerably increased. Furthermore divers persons, induced by reprehensible avarice, preferred the grain trade to more honorable professions in which they were engaged, and made extensive purchases in the said provinces both in the towns and in the country; this they do by means of agents who compete with the ordinary merchants." The intentions of the Échevinage were thus quite as far-reaching as those of the Châtelet, but its lack of executive power was a serious obstacle. In order to enforce the ordinances which the merchants had infringed in the manner described, the Lieutenant General of the Baillage of Vitry was ordered to enforce the regulations in Champagne.[1] An ordinance was actually issued November 15, 1694, by the Châtelet. The activities of the Châtelet appear, in part, in Delamare's description of his tour, but even more distinctly in the account of the prosecution of Jean Roger.

Roger had been engaged in the grain trade since 1656, when he established himself at Paris. He had long been one of the principal merchants of Paris, and it is beyond question that he changed the character of his business considerably in 1693. Up to that time, he had bought principally in the vicinity of Soissons. In that year, he transferred his operations to the upper Seine Valley.[2] As early as January, 1693, Roger is accused of being the most unprincipled and most avaricious of the grain merchants. "He is absolute master in all the markets where grain is exposed for sale, and of the farmers, cultivators, and the minor merchants, to whom he gives the law personally or through his factors. . . . It is known that the said Roger, since the months of May and June (1692) has taken up grain in the markets of Provins, Mary-sur-Seine,

[1] H. 1835. Reg. du Bureau, 63. 19 Oct. 1694. See G[7]. 1635. Letter of De la Reynie, 4 Dec. 1694, apropos of Le Blanc's Ordonnance of 15 Nov.

[2] Bib. Nat., Fr. 21642. 368. Factum pour Jean Roger (imprimé). This is a defence of Roger. There is a reference to him in H. 1816. Reg. du Bureau, lxxxvii. 5 Avril 1661.

Bray, Nogent, Sergines, Pont, Montereau, Sens, Melun, and other places, in farms, in tithe barns, and in the houses of private individuals. It is a prodigious quantity in all, which would have sufficed to supply Paris for a year. It would be impossible to imagine what has become of it all, were it not for the immense granaries which he has in divers places. . . .

"Viard, whom every one knows, is also under agreement with Roger and Crécy, to subject France to famine. They engage in (commercial) war with the provincial merchants both in the provinces and at the Port de la Grève, trying to render themselves masters of their grain.. Viard, Roger, La Bague, and Tournois write to their factors to ship no grain by land or water, except by their express orders." [1]

These were the general accusations against Roger, and the presence of these memoirs in Delamare's papers doubtless indicates that they furnished the initial impulse in the suit against Roger. At all events, proceedings were well under way in the middle of July, 1694, shortly after the departure of Delamare on his commission of July 10. De la Reynie, Lieutenant de la Police at Paris, writes on the fifteenth: "I have seen by what we are doing in the Roger affair that Colmet, farmer of the 'minage' at Bray, has done much to cause the disorders there. It is important that you should amass as much evidence as possible against him, not only as regards his doings at Bray, but in other places. . . . He has come to Paris since the imprisonment of Roger to confer and receive instructions. He will return to Bray Saturday, and you can have him arrested on the writ that I have issued against him." [2]

Delamare reached Bray at eight o'clock in the evening, on the eighteenth. The next morning, Colmet was arrested and his papers confiscated. Besides ten letters of Roger to Colmet, accounts of all their dealings were found. These indicate that the size of the business of Roger was hardly exaggerated:

[1] Bib. Nat., Fr. 21642. 290 et 293. 15 Jan. 1693. Mémoire des auteurs de la Cause de la Cherté des Bleds, par Leger de la Verbissonne.

[2] *Ibid.* 309. Paris, 15 Juillet 1694. De la Reynie à Delamare.

	Remittances of money	Shipments of grain	Grain in Bray and vicinity
27 Aug. 1692—15 Jan. 1693.........	73,595 ll	45,298 ll	28,298 ll
15 Jan. 1693—30 April	55,497	49,783	5,719
30 Apr. 1693— 6 Nov.	98,013	96,988	1,526
6 Nov. 1693—15 Mar. 1694........	60,480	56,655	3,825
15 Mar. 1694—13 June	65,128	62,626	2,502[1]

The next day witnesses were summoned to testify in regard to the case. Much of this testimony has been used in another connection and a repetition here is needless; suffice it to say that there was abundant evidence that Colmet had disorganized the trade at Bray and in the surrounding towns, buying in the country, forming granaries at Bray and buying much that was offered at the market. The trade of the region was, to a great degree, in his control. The general accusations were thus justified in large measure.

The principal point legally, however, was the question of partnerships and agreements with other merchants. On this subject the accusations are admitted even by the "Factum pour Roger." "Asked if it was not true that the partnership with Huge had been kept secret in order to raise the price of grain, the defendant replies that, if this was kept secret, it was only because the 'Commissionaires Facteurs' might have claimed 30 sous per muid as fee, although the merchants of Paris have always been exempt from this due.[2] Furthermore, these partnerships between merchants have always been practised, and it would be difficult to furnish the ports without clerks or partners in the provinces, and inasmuch as the grain has always been sold at the price current when the boat arrived, the public has suffered no injury. . . . If the partnership had been formed by several merchants of the same province to buy all the grain and thereby render themselves masters of the price, . . . that would be a case contemplated as illegal by the law. . . . Furthermore, if the defendant has entered into partnerships, they are with provincial merchants more than ten leagues from Paris. The utility of this type of establishment is so well recognized

[1] Bib. Nat., Fr. 21642. 300. Notes faites par Delamare des "Papiers trouvées Chez Colmet." 19 Juillet 1694.

[2] This form of question and answer seems to be adopted merely for convenience.

at the Hôtel de Ville, that when disputes arise between the merchants of Paris and their partners in the country, the Provost of Merchants decides the case in accordance with the clauses of the partnership agreement."

The question of delaying shipments with reference to the condition of the market was more difficult. A specific case was alleged, and no effort was made to deny the fact, but a defence of a rather slippery character was forthcoming.

"By a letter written by the defendant to Huge, to delay for a few days the shipment of 100 muids of grain which they had put into partnership, the defendant shows that this was done not with the intention of making a great gain, but merely because he had other grain on the ports. . . . As for the gain on that 100 muids, it is true that it came to 1800^{ll} apiece, but that profit ought not to be considered unjust if all the risks of the trade are considered." [1]

The defense set forth in this little pamphlet is extremely clever and very well calculated to calm the popular feeling against the defendant. But the evasiveness of the answers is significant. The one point that was really sound was the assertion that partnerships had become legal through the tacit recognition by the Provost of Merchants. That was the crucial question. The law of the case ultimately depended upon the legality or illegality of the trading partnerships and associations of merchants; the merchants could produce decisive evidence to prove that such partnerships had long existed; the authorities could produce a long series of prohibitions. The case is important for bringing a definite issue between the traditional prohibition of partnerships and the actual development of partnerships among the merchants. Both the Châtelet and Échevinage had cried out against these associations of merchants in 1660–63, and again in the years 1693–94, to say nothing of spasmodic outbursts in the interim.[2] Both official bodies were inclined

[1] All these citations are from the Factum pour Jean Roger. Bib. Nat., Fr. 21642. 368. ch. 7 of the Factum.

[2] It is possible that the edict of Sept. 1690 for the creation of 60 grain brokers at Paris should be cited in this connection. The measure, however, seems to be

to attribute much of the trouble to the dealings of these associated merchants. On the whole, they were probably right in their judgment of the situation, but they did not have any means of distinguishing between legal and proper partnerships and the partnerships formed with a distinct intention to manipulate the Parisian market. Roger had doubtless been engaged in wholesale manipulation of the local and the Parisian markets, but the most that could be done was to impose a fine. In short, officials had put their hands on the real difficulty, but they had not found the true remedy. The practices of Roger and his associates were made possible by the inadequacy of market organization. The creation of wholesale markets was the most effective means of keeping the merchants within proper bounds. Visibility of supply and a proper correlation of local and metropolitan interests were the true solution of the problem.

After 1693, the effort to suppress partnerships ceased to play an important part in the regulation of the trade. The old laws remained on the registers, but there was no such serious attempt to enforce them as in 1693, though the popular dread of monopolies always kept the subject in view.

The years 1698 and 1699 served to emphasize an element that the Parisian officials were disposed to overlook, the possibility of a serious depletion of local supplies in the producing regions. There had been prohibitions in Soissons in 1693–94, but Soissons was not one of the most important sources of supply, and the Parisian officials were more impressed by the quantity of grain on the Seine and Marne than they were by the scarcity in Santerre and Soissonnais.

Our information for these years is singularly incomplete; the Châtelet and Échevinage do little in the Upper Marne, so that we have nothing but scattered letters from Larcher, the Intendant in Champagne. He had been strongly impressed by conditions in 1697, when the markets had been very notably disturbed in November by activity of the merchants and *blatiers*.

more or less of a financial expedient, and I do not like to take it too seriously. See Delamare, *op. cit.*, II, 967, 970. H. 1834. Reg. du Bureau, 75, 147, 272–282. G[7]. 1630. Châlons, 1693.

The high prices lasted only three or four markets at Châlons and Vitry, however, and although he resorted to prohibitions at Sedan and Mézières, he did not interfere with the Parisian trade. But he was disposed towards a prohibitive policy. Otherwise he would hardly have been so ready with his general prohibition in September, 1698: "I have been through the cantons of Rheims, Rethel, and Sainte-Menehould where I have found that there is very little grain and that prices are rising daily. . . . Here in Vitry, which has the largest grain trade of any town in the province, and the only town where the merchants have granaries, I discovered by means of an inquiry that there is about 30,000 setiers, Parisian measure. This is hardly sufficient for the subsistence of Vitry, and the succor of Rheims, Châlons, Saint-Dizier, and Joinville. I have given orders that none should leave Vitry except for those towns, and I have sent word to the Provost of Merchants, so that he may not be surprised if the merchants of Vitry send no grain to Paris, where I hear there is abundance and lower prices than here in Champagne." [1]

The Contrôleur Général thought that Larcher was somewhat over-anxious,[2] but the difficulties in Champagne increased. Prices rose steadily. There were constant complaints, and many of the larger towns had sent deputations, representing that there had been no wheat at the markets for several weeks. Larcher did his best to meet the trouble, but he could not do much, as the wheat crop had been a failure and there was little old wheat. The best farms had scarcely yielded enough to serve as seed. Fortunately, barley, oats, rye, and buckwheat were plentiful and three-quarters of the rural population was living on those grains. But even these were excessively high, and it was to be feared that supplies would be exhausted before the end of the year. The common people were becoming anxious, and distributions of public grain were necessary to allay the fear. At his suggestion, indeed, Troyes, Rheims, Sedan and other towns had held several markets with grain brought in from

[1] G^7. 228. Vitry, 21 Sept. 1698. Larcher.

[2] Apostille sur la lettre.

outside. Other towns would have liked to adopt the same policy, but lacked the necessary funds, and could find none to undertake the enterprise. Besides, they did not know where to procure grain and they feared violence.

At the end of the month, Larcher issued an ordinance prohibiting export from the province, cancelling all contracts "for the delivery of grain, and urging the peasants to thresh and bring their grain to market." A copy was sent to the Contrôleur Général, who replied: "There is no desire to condemn the ordinance, but it cannot be approved. The essential thing is that the prices of grain diminish." [1] Despite the ordinance, difficulty was experienced at Troyes; [2] in February, Châlons was obliged to purchase grain on public security.[3]

There was little positive regulation on the part of the Châtelet that is of great importance. Delamare, however, was not inactive, and a trip to Bray, made in January, 1699, seems to have been influential. The object of the trip was doubtless the same as in 1694, but although the grain merchants were found to be guilty of various illegal practices, nothing seems to have been done. The ordinary market at Bray was completely disorganized,[4] but an informal market had grown up and the significant fact is Delamare's acquiescence in this illegal commercial custom. He says, in his *Traité de la Police:* "The market is held Friday, but the peasants and *blatiers* have become accustomed to bring their grain to town on all days of the week, exposing it for sale at the Halle, so that there is a sort of continuous market. This *extension* of the market is not authorized by any regulation. Custom alone has established it, but according to the testimony of the officers and inhabitants experience has shown that it is useful to the trade." [5]

[1] All the above in Boislisle, *op. cit.*, II, 500, 1787. Nov. 16.

[2] G[7]. 228. Troyes, 7 Dec. 1698. Maire et Échevins, 23 Dec. 1698.

[3] Boislisle, *op. cit.*, I, 518, 1838. 8, 16 Nov. 1699.

[4] Bib. Nat., Fr. 21643. 317. Procès Verbal à Bray-sur-Seine, 3 Jan. 1699. I infer that this is the basis of the notice on the market at Bray in the *Traité de la Police.*

[5] Delamare, *op. cit.*, II, 977, 2d ed. Bray-sur-Seine.

The perception of the practical value of a continuous wholesale market was of importance, because it exerted a controlling influence upon the policy pursued by Delamare at Vitry in 1709, where conditions were gradually tending in the same direction. The suppression of partnerships was abandoned as a policy, and there was an obvious unwillingness to interfere very much with the trade. Even the prohibitive policy of the Intendant was very mildly criticized, and Delamare, the principal agent of the Châtelet in this phase of its action, was more than ever inclined to adopt a purely empirical policy, founded on commercial usages.

By 1708, de Harouys had become Intendant in Champagne, a man much less inclined to use prohibitions than Larcher had been. Harouys could not escape entirely from the idea of a control of trade by licenses, but his intentions were liberal. This is indeed the striking feature of the policy pursued in the grain trade in the latter part of 1708 and the first six months of 1709, when the Intendant and the Contrôleur Général had control.

Some little pressure had appeared soon after the harvest of 1708, but Harouys was determined not to issue prohibitions. In November, 1708, he told the merchants of Vitry and Perthois that they would be allowed to continue their trade with Paris, on the basis of licenses.[1] This policy was continued throughout December, January, and February. Harouys considered it eminently successful and wrote, February 13: "After having prevented the merchants from scouring the country and selling to each other, I have established a complete freedom for the circulation of grain by means of licenses. I have had the satisfaction of seeing prices fall, at a season when every one expected them to rise. The markets are adequately furnished. . . . I have been opposed in this policy only by the officers of police, most particularly by a regulation issued by the Lieutenant of Police at Sézanne. . . ." The grain of one Robert was seized, a part confiscated, and a general order issued, prohibit-

[1] G[7]. 1642. Châlons, 9 Dec. 1708. De Harouys. G[7]. 1642. Châlons, 21 Jan. 1709. De Harouys. G[7]. 1642. Châlons, 11 Fev. 1709. De Harouys.

ing trade in grain in the Baillage of Sézanne. Harouys annulled the order of the Lieutenant of Police.[1] The Parisian officials, however, did not approve of this act, and their criticism induced Harouys to abandon the policy of giving licenses.[2] The trade was left to itself for a while, but the license system was ultimately restored.

At Vitry, the local officials found it necessary to make some provision for the needs of the town itself, and in March all merchants were ordered to sell to the town at the market price 5 setiers of every 100 exported. This was sold to the indigent by the Subdélégué at Vitry.[3]

These were the measures proposed by the general administrative staff to avert distress. It is merely the result of the distrust of the traditional prohibitive policy. The merchants were left almost entirely to their own devices, with a slight restraint designed to safeguard the local interests. The only constructive element in the policy was this endeavor to enforce upon the wholesale trade its responsibility for local wants.

This policy was shown to be inadequate by the course of events in April, May, and June. The first sign of trouble came from Bassigny. "The subdélégués of Langres and Chaumont write me," says de Harouys April 1, "that since you have deemed it expedient to suspend the use of licenses, the merchants of Burgundy and other provinces have entered Bassigny and are carrying off all the grain, without regard to the prices they have to pay. That little district which is usually one of the surest resources of Champagne will soon be exhausted."[4]

Two weeks later, disasters affecting the crop increased the apprehension throughout the province. "All the municipal corporations come to me to demand grain for public granaries. From Perthois to the Meuse on one side and to Troyes on the other, Vitry is the only town that can furnish them with supplies.

[1] G7. 1642. Châlons, 13 Fev. 1709. De Harouys.

[2] G7. 1642. Paris, 26 Fev. 1709. Daguesseau au C. G. G7. 1642. Châlons, 28 Fev. 1709. De Harouys.

[3] G7. 1642. Paris, 14 Mars 1709. Lallement. G7. 1642. Vitry, 26 Mars 1709. M. le Subdélégué à Vitry.

[4] G7. 1642. Châlons, 1 Avril 1709. De Harouys.

But quite apart from the fact that there are only 30,000 setiers in Vitry, the merchants of Paris and several factors . . . have purchased so large a quantity that the granaries of Vitry will be exhausted if some measures are not taken at once. I am quite well aware that the provinces should succor Paris, but in order to prevent the exhaustion of Champagne, the matter must be conducted with some system."[1] An additional complication appeared in the necessity of securing provisions for the armies in the Low Countries. These purchases were made almost entirely through the intendants, and generally quota were levied on the various towns.[2]

The town of Châlons considered itself seriously threatened. An exact enumeration of all the grain in the town was made, and it was found that there was only enough for six or seven months. No grain was then coming in from the country, and the neighboring villages were quite dependent upon Châlons.[3] A committee of nineteen had been formed to take charge of the grain trade. They were to fix the price of grain and of bread, to decide what villages should be allowed to buy bread and grain in the town, and to determine the quantity of grain which should be assigned each week to the inhabitants.[4]

All these provisions indicate the fallacy underlying the whole policy of prohibitions, the notion that the true basis of calculation is the condition at any one moment, supposing that all trade were stopped. The town that could not see within its walls enough grain to last till the harvest was sure to raise the cry of dearth, or, even as at Châlons, when there was just about enough to last till after the harvest (six months from April). The conception of a continuous flow of trade was entirely foreign to the thought of the ordinary bourgeois of the time, and it is only fair to say that trade was hardly regular enough to warrant much general confidence. Still, the maintenance of trade with proper market regulations was the only

[1] G[7]. 1642. Châlons, 14 Avril 1709. De Harouys.

[2] G[7]. 1642. Châlons, 16 Avril 1709. De Harouys.

[3] G[7]. 1642. Châlons, 27 Avril 1709. De Harouys.

[4] Bib. Nat., Fr. 21648. 234. Imprimé. Chambre Particulière pour la police des bleds dans la Ville de Châlons.

remedy. The mere shutting of the gates of each town was quite inadequate.

In a sense, it is unfair to insinuate that a continuous circulation of trade was not desired. The more accurate statement would be that the trade was forever stopping in times of dearth, and, as no one seemed to be able to keep it moving, every one proceeded to hold what he had. This all appears in a letter of de Harouys of April 30: "As regards the 15,000–20,000 sacks of wheat and rye that you ordered me to buy to be sent to Charleville, I must tell you that the agents I sent to the élections of Vitry and Sainte-Menehould have just come back without having been able to buy a single sack. At first, when every one feared an extreme dearth, which is now only too certain, those who had grain in store, whether from their farms or from purchases, made no difficulty about selling. The only obstacle was the violence shown by the people. But now matters have come to such a pass that those who have grain are afraid to sell, for fear of the violence with which they are threatened." [1] Rheims was threatened seriously by this general cessation of trade. "Here, we are all in the throes of dearth," write the Lieutenant General and the Échevins. "Not one grain of wheat comes to the market. The little that we have is being consumed, and even the grain grown in our élection is stopped everywhere. Yesterday we sent some carters to Pouilly and Héry, with an escort of fifteen men to get 120 setiers of wheat, that we had bought. All in vain. The peasants assembled with arms and prevented the passage of the grain. . . . Sieur de Vige, whose grain has already been a great aid, told us that he had a large quantity at Verdun and in that vicinity, but that it would be impossible to get it here without an escort of regular troops." [2] It is the same story at Troyes. "Yesterday we sent a convoy of twenty wagons with a company of archers to Chavange, to bring in the grain that we have bought for the

[1] G^7. 1642. Châlons, 30 Avril 1709. De Harouys.

[2] G^7. 1642. Reims, 29–30 Avril 1709. Lieu. Gén. du Conseil et Échevins de R., à Harouys.

G^7. 1642. Reims, 30 Avril 1709. M. le Lieu. Gén.; Savary, Ancien Maire; et d'Origny, Avocat du Roy au C. G.

provision of our town. We had reason to believe, too, that the licenses and orders of the intendant would be respected and would facilitate the passage of the grain. But things were carried to such a point that not only were the sacks of grain stolen, but the archers and carters were quite unable to resist the force of three villages combined in a body of three thousand strong, so that our men were obliged to seek safety in flight after being exceedingly misused." [1]

Meanwhile, exports to Paris continued from Vitry and to some extent from Châlons.[2] This trade was carried on under cover of licenses, and violence did not manifest itself there as soon as in the country districts. It is this factor that rendered the situation really serious, — a continuance of exports from the shipping ports, despite a cessation of the movement from the country districts. But riots soon began in Vitry and Châlons. The first trouble at Vitry was on May 10, when the people endeavored to prevent shipments to Rheims and to Paris.[3] De Harouys immediately began to assemble troops; in the course of a fortnight regiments were sent up from the Beauce to maintain order. There was a tumult at Châlons, but no one was killed.[4]

This seems to have been the crisis. The month of June passed more quietly, and although the promise of the harvest was not great, it inevitably tended to relieve pressure. It was at this time that Delamare made his first trip to Champagne, after the worst period of congestion, but while trade was still completely disorganized. Up to that time, there had been no successful attempt to restore the normal conditions of circulation, and this was the problem to which Delamare addressed himself.

Among the papers now at the National Library, there is a memoir of 1709, which seems to contain an outline of the policy Delamare proposed to adopt. If it was not drawn up before

[1] G^7. 1642. Troyes, 8 Mai 1709. Maire et Échevins. See also letter of the Notables of Troyes, 11 Mai 1709. G^7. 1642.

[2] G^7. 1642. Châlons, 9 Mai 1709. De Harouys.

[3] G^7. 1642. Châlons, 12 Mai 1709. De Harouys.

[4] G^7. 1642. Châlons, 18 Mai 1709. De Harouys.

he actually reached Vitry, it must have been written soon after his arrival:

"In order to maintain the continuity of trade between Lorraine, Bar, Alsace, and Vitry, and between Vitry and Paris, three things must be done:

1* The foreign (*i. e.* to Vitry) merchants must be given facilities for selling their grain on the day of its arrival.

2* The grain purchased by merchants of Vitry, which they now retain in granaries or storehouses in concert with merchants of Paris, must be set in motion towards Paris.

3* The Bourgeois must be prevented from making stores, and must be compelled to carry their grain to market.

"To succeed in this:

"It will be necessary to have at Vitry a fund of 60,000ll in charge of a trustworthy and solvent man, who shall act as if he were a private merchant.

"Freedom of trade must be guaranteed the merchants.

"The commission agent shall buy only such grain as shall be left at the end of the market, at the market-place, the Halle, or the central square.

"As soon as a merchant of Vitry shall have a boat-lod of grain, he shall be obliged to load it at once and ship to Paris, or sell to the commissioner, who shall appear as a merchant willing to buy.

. . . .

"The commissioner may go to Lorraine and Bar or elsewhere if the Royal agent shall consider it expedient.

. . . .

"The commissioner shall have granaries at Vitry to store his grain, until he shall have enough for a boat." [1]

The document thus has all the aspects of being a detailed project of the policy to be followed, and in general it was followed. The buyer was never established, but the significant feature of the project is its emphasis upon market organization, and the obvious intention to solve the difficult problem by direct commercial machinery, rather than by external administrative regulation. It was a project, first and last, to keep the trade moving, and to make the markets work.

The execution of the task involved many unforeseen difficulties, but most of these were surmounted. "The merchants of Paris were then at Vitry. They had already sent five to six hundred muids to our ports, at my instance. I secured a continuance of this assistance by visiting again the granaries and storehouses of the merchants. I drew up a Procès Verbal of the quantity

[1] Bib. Nat., Fr. 21646. 94.

of grain still held by them, and they agreed to sell it for the sustenance of Paris.

"This increased demand revived trade. I saw several foreign merchants come to Vitry bringing grain in carts or pack saddles. I spoke to them, and assured them of protection whenever they should have need of it. I permitted them to sell daily in the central square, which had not been done before.[1] They then brought so great a quantity of grain that they did not find a ready sale for all of it. This forced me to hire granaries for them in order not to have them become disgusted with the trade."[2]

But Delamare did not propose to confine his attention to Vitry, and hearing of difficulties at Troyes and at Sézanne he went thither, — first to Troyes, and not without misgivings:

"When I left Vitry, I was afraid that the trade there would languish. It can be kept in movement only by force. Every one has an idea that wheat will be worth 100^{ll} at Easter. Here (Troyes) the people are ready to rise at the slightest provocation. The houses of the magistrates and of several of the richest inhabitants have already been invested twice with threats of incendiarism. . . . It must be confessed that the disorder of the market contributed much to maintain these movements. There was scarcely any attempt at control. I restored order and enforced the regulations, especially that requiring all persons to bring grain to market. Eagerness to secure grain and the desire on the part of some to form hoards impelled them to go out to meet the grain on the highways. All was stopped in the suburbs so that little reached the market place. I now send squads of archers out on the highways on market days. All comes in to the market. I give the 'menu peuple' preference for two hours, and the minor grains have gone down by a half."[3] Similar reforms were made at Sézanne. A trip was made down the Aube, and another to Bray and Provins.[4]

[1] Note the influence of the investigation at Bray in 1699.

[2] Delamare, *op. cit.*, 2d ed., III, Supp. 39.

[3] Bib. Nat., Fr. 21647. 86. Troyes, 4 Sept. 1709. Copie avec apostilles.

[4] *Ibid.* Sézanne, 16 Sept. 1709. Copie.

"But while I was at Sézanne, I learned that the inhabitants of Vitry kept the grain in their granaries and wished to sell at the excessive price of 60^{ll} some even for seventy and eighty. This obliged me to return to Vitry. I found three to four hundred muids of wheat and had a part delivered to our merchants of Paris and to their agents. I fixed the price of this wheat at 50^{ll} per setier, founding my action on that clause in the ordinances which forbids selling at higher prices in granaries than in the market, for 50^{ll} was then the market price.

"The grain, which I was thus drawing from the granaries of Vitry, was replaced literally every day by the Lorraine merchants. They bring in grain continually, and scarcely a week passes without the arrival of eight or ten muids. They are beginning to bring barley also, of which there is an abundance in their country. This grain from Lorraine is purchased by the merchants of Vitry for the provision of Paris." [1]

Delamare seems to have then returned to Sézanne and continued the investigations interrupted by the bad news from Vitry. But no letters were preserved. October 20, he is back in Vitry. "I have learned," he writes, "that the measures I had taken to prevent the bourgeois, the merchants, and the people from going out to meet the grain were successful, and have caused a considerable diminution in price. . . . The people are much pleased . . . but the wealthy bourgeois and merchants are not. I have learned since my return from Sézanne, that divers persons have been harrassing the Lorraine merchants and other foreigners, even to the point of refusing to buy their grain. The foreigners, having learned of my return, came to me. I reassured them and helped them to sell their grain for a price with which they are well satisfied. . . . Others continue to arrive daily. There are continual convoys from Lorraine, Bar, the bishoprics of Toul and Verdun, some from Alsace and I am even told that some are en route from Franche Comté.

[1] G^7. 1643. Vitry, 29 Sept. 1709. Delamare, original. Bib. Nat., Fr. 21647. 3. Same letter. Copy. This duplication indicates that Delamare kept copies regularly, but that some of the originals sent were lost, and so do not appear in the Series G^7. It is possible that some of these Delamare letters may be in the cartons of the Série G^7. called "Lettres Communs."

All the foreigners, with whom I have spoken, have told me that there was no town more convenient for them." [1]

The ordinance of October 21, which we have already discussed in a previous chapter, concluded the practical work of the first visit to Champagne. The influence of the energetic commissioner can hardly be denied. His untiring persistence, his great knowledge, both of the old regulations and of the conditions of trade, his desire to do nothing unpractical, to keep the trade moving at any cost, all combined to render his work singularly important at this critical moment in the history of the grain trade.

But after Delamare had left Vitry, the old jealousies and the avarice of the merchants of Vitry interrupted the steady flow of trade that he had started. This necessitated a second visit, and Christmas Eve, 1709, found Delamare again at Vitry. The Lorraine merchants had left Vitry almost entirely, bringing their grain to Saint-Dizier. Delamare purchased grain in Lorraine by his agents and had it shipped to Vitry. This started the stream again, and by means of coaxing and negotiation the trade was completely revived. Various ordinances were issued both at Vitry and other places to regulate the markets, but there was little in his policy that did not appear in his work on the first visit. He also made a hurried trip to Lorraine, and that trade continued to be the basis of the relief afforded, not only to Paris, but to the larger towns of Champagne, especially Rheims and Châlons. The work of the commissioner was thus of immediate value, as well as being the most significant step historically in the organization of the wholesale market in grain.[2]

The regulation of trade in the Seine Basin was thus largely controlled by the Châtelet. The difficulties were primarily difficulties of marketing, and as early as 1660 there was a manifest desire to abandon mere prohibitions for measures regulating the conduct of merchants, without actually stopping trade. The first attempt of the Châtelet was directed against the

[1] Bib. Nat., Fr. 21647. 129 v. Vitry, 20 Oct. 1709. Delamare.

[2] Delamare, *op. cit.*, 2d ed., II, Supp. 41 ff. Also letters. Bib. Nat., Fr. 21648. 1, 3, 9, 34, 282. G⁷. 1643. 1 Jan. 1710, 23 Mars 1710.

associations of merchants. The old prohibitions were renewed, and commissioners were sent out to collect evidence for prosecutions. The investigations of 1660–63 produced no immediate effect, but prosecutions were undertaken on a larger scale in 1693. The troubles of that year were certainly due in no small measure to the operations of Jean Roger and his associates. He was selected as the most conspicuous offender and a determined effort was made to secure a conviction that would serve as an example to other merchants. The legal intricacies of the case were too considerable, however, and no decisive action resulted. The failure of this policy left the Châtelet with no precise scheme for the regulation of the trade, but at this point, the personality of Delamare became important. In his work at Bray in 1693 and later in 1699, he became acquainted with modifications of the market system which had developed there under the stimulus of a growing volume of trade. The old market regulations were no longer strictly observed, and instead of trade being confined to two days of the week, buying and selling of grain became a daily event. This informal market, too, was a wholesale, rather than a retail, market. In these new practices, Delamare saw the solution of the problem. The cessation of trade in time of dearth could be overcome by sound market regulations, above all, by increased facilities for daily buying and selling. The great desideratum was movement rather than regulation. Both the provinces and Paris would be secure against dearth so long as the grain could be kept in motion. This was a natural outgrowth of the earliest policy of the Châtelet. It is the fundamental feature of all the regulations from that source throughout the century. But the means of securing the much desired continuity of movement were not perceived until Delamare furnished the excellent example of his visits to Vitry, in 1709 and 1710. His measures not only relieved distress in the Seine Basin, but led to a great advance in market organization. All the fundamental conceptions of wholesale marketing appear in his letters and orders of 1709, and it is the first time such ideas had been applied to the marketing of a bulky commodity of relatively uniform character.

Burgundy and Lyons

In Burgundy, the traditional policy of the sixteenth century underwent little change. Although intendants assumed many of the functions previously discharged by provincial and municipal officials, the new officers did not bring new policies as in the Seine Basin. Every factor in the Parisian supply area led administrative activity into new channels, in Burgundy everything tended toward the persistence of the old traditions.

In Champagne, greater quantities of grain were available, and the possibility of securing additional supplies from Lorraine gave the trade of Vitry and Châlons a very broad basis. Delamare's policy was founded on these features of the trade, and it is by no means certain that his liberal policy would have been equally successful in the absence of such resources for the large markets.

In Burgundy, there was little concentration of trade, no possibility of securing supplementary resources, such as those of Lorraine, and a smaller general surplus in the producing region itself. None of the Saône Valley towns controlled as large a volume of trade as Vitry, or Bray, though there is a perceptible tendency towards concentration at Gray. The Saône Valley was able to draw grain only from Burgundy proper and Bassigny; the Vosges and the Jura cut off communication with other grain-raising sections, and the foot-hills were more suitable for vines than for wheat. Wheat culture was thus confined to the favored regions of the province that contributed regularly to the supplies of Lyons. Then too, Lyons was more dependent upon Burgundy than Paris upon the Upper Marne. Paris could and did draw grain from several other regions. Lyons could procure supplies elsewhere only with difficulty, so that the demand of Lyons pressed upon Burgundy with even greater severity in years of dearth than in years of plenty. This difference in the intensity of metropolitan demand inevitably produced a degree of apprehension in Burgundy that seldom, if ever, existed in Champagne. The province was barely capable of supplying the Lyonese in times of average fertility, in times of dearth all were skeptical. Under such conditions a policy of market regulations designed to keep the grain in motion was not sure of success. There was less grain to move and it was never possible to be sure that enough remained to support trade till the next harvest.

A sweeping condemnation of the prohibitive policy in Burgundy is unwarranted. The province possessed only a relatively small surplus, and the Lyonese demand was great enough seriously to deplete the Burgundian supply. The only remedy was the prohibition. The expediency of the measures is largely a question of the particular circumstances. The intendants are to be judged only by the accuracy of their perception of the extent of the available supply. A crude, haphazard application of prohibitions, merely on account of popular rumor, is hardly defensible. But if the extent of the depletion is carefully investigated, and the prohibitive measures are issued only after thoughtful consideration, it is fairly evident that the intendant was doing all that was humanly possible to meet a trying situation.

In the spring of 1693, prohibitions were issued in Burgundy, much to the disappointment of the Lyonese. Bérulle, the Intendant at Lyons, was very much put out. He declared that the prohibitions were not justified by conditions, and that it was a device to enable the Burgundian officials to make illicit gains in the grain trade. The prohibitions were ostensibly the outcome of an investigation made by the intendant, which showed only 32,000 charges beyond local needs.[1]

"If it were true," says Bérulle, "that there were only 32,000 charges left in Burgundy, I could but approve of what they have done. But this memoir is not accurate. There are still more than 300,000 charges in Burgundy as will appear by the enclosed memoir. The commissioners sent to investigate the quantity of grain in most of the towns were satisfied with taking the declarations of the owners of the granaries, without having the grain measured. They did not visit the villages near the Saône, and were content to accept the common reports of the quan-

[1] G^7. 1631. Estat contenant la quantité de bleds qui se sont trouvés dans la province de Bourgogne au mois de Mars.

tities there. The subdélégués, who are all engaged in the grain trade, have concealed the truth from M. d'Argouges, in order to oblige the merchants who had large stores to sell to them at low figures." [1] Bérulle enclosed an estimate prepared by "a rich merchant of Burgundy." [2] The accusations against Burgundian officials are even more sweeping in a letter, written in June. He then tells the Contrôleur Général that the Sindics of Burgundy have imposed upon him by their false reports that there were only 32,000 charges of grain in the province. "They are all engaged in the grain trade, as well as most of the Councillors of the Parlement of Dijon. They have even bought standing grain by giving earnest money. I have just been told that the Sindic of Bugey, Sr. de Blame, a man of whom many complain, was the real author of the tumult at Louhans. It was stirred up by him to prevent the Lyonese merchants from shipping their grain, so that he could buy it cheap. That is the way it is done in Burgundy." [3]

On the whole, there would seem to be some foundation in Bérulle's contention that the Burgundians under-estimated the available supply, but the course of events indicated that he had over-estimated the supply considerably. He acted on the assumption that there was plenty of grain in Burgundy, and issued many certificates to merchants. Cherishing the hope that the Contrôleur Général would be brought round to his point of view, he neglected to make any great efforts to obtain supplies from the south.

These certificates did not give the Lyonese merchants the right to export from Burgundy, but they were an assurance that those merchants would be given the benefit of any permits that should be issued. Feeling confident that they would get the grain out in some way, these merchants bought extensively in Burgundy. They proceeded to accumulate large hoards, "and rendered themselves the masters of all that remained in the country." "These monopolists," says Le Noble, "together

[1] G^7. 1631. Lyon, 14 Mai 1693. Bérulle.

[2] *Ibid.* See besides the mémoire, the letter of 30 Mai 1693.

[3] Boislisle, *op. cit.*, I, 325, 1199.

with the Lyonese bakers are the cause of all the disorders which have occurred. Having a common understanding, the grain which is permitted to be exported is sent down only when the need is most pressing, so that the highest prices are realized."[1]

The high prices and the panic, which were the outcome of these practices, made it very difficult to ship grain from Burgundy. As the "munitionnaires" enjoyed special privileges, contracts were made with them. But they were hindered both by the officials and the people. In June, a shipment was seized by the subdélégués.[2] In July, the boats were stopped at Châlons.[3] In August, grain boats were stopped at Mâcon and at Tournus.[4] This, too, is but a slight indication of the violence.

At the end of the month, the officials at Seurre write to Dijon "to find out what it is best to do in their extremity."[5] An agent of the municipality of Dijon writes: "I come from Bassigny where the dearness of grain frightened me. At Langres, where I am at present, I do not dare to make offers to buy grain. There are more buyers than there is grain, and I assure you that if it were worth twenty écus per mine, and people dared to ship, I scarcely know where I could go to buy. . . . In these parts every one trembles for the future, and resolutions are formed to let no grain leave the province until every one is supplied."[6]

Lyons was also in distress. In the middle of August, the last 100 sacks in the granaries of the Abondance were distributed, and 1500 charges were taken from the royal quartermaster at Lyons, despite his protests.[7]

Inasmuch as every one was suffering to a considerable extent, each endeavored to shift all the blame to the other's shoulders.

[1] G[7]. 1631. Auxonne, 3 Mai 1693. Le Noble au C. G.

[2] G[7]. 1631. Lyon, 18 Juin 1693. Bérulle, notes letter of 15 Juin.

[3] G[7]. 1631. Châlons-sur-Saône, 14 Juillet 1693. Le Noble.

[4] G[7]. 1631. Lyon, 5 Août 1693. Bérulle. 17 Août 1693. Bérulle. (Other cases *passim.*)

[5] Dijon, Arch. Mun., G. 256. Seurre, 28 Août 1693. Maire et Échevins de Seurre.

[6] *Ibid.*, G. 266. Langres, 30 Août 1693. Mosseur.

[7] Boislisle, *op. cit.*, I, 330, 1216. 18 Août 1693.

The Contrôleur Général, however, was not inclined to conceal his opinion that the main trouble lay in the conduct of Bérulle, the Intendant at Lyons, and in the activity of the municipality.

"The whole trouble," he writes, "comes from the obstinate perseverance with which Bérulle and the Consulate have endeavored to draw grain from Burgundy, neglecting to procure supplies in Provence, despite the orders that I gave them from the King. Both are worthy of blame, with this difference, that the former is at fault by reason of his rash confidence in the promises of Le Noble, and in his hope of an abundant harvest in Burgundy. In addition to this, some of the Consuls have shown an extraordinary desire to make themselves masters of the purchases of grain needed for the sustenance of the town. They continue to manifest the desire in regard to the purchases in Provence.

"Throughout the late spring I received complaints from Burgundy almost daily, mostly from d'Argouges, who declared again and again that Burgundy was being exhausted by the Lyonese merchants. This obliged me to write to Lyons, ordering them to cease to buy in Burgundy and to go to Provence. By my express orders, M. Le Noble (the munitionnaire) was charged with furnishing Lyons with the small quantities of Burgundian grain that would be needed until the grain arrived from Provence. If sufficient pains had been taken at that time to secure grain in Provence, only eight or ten thousand ânées would have been needed from Burgundy, and these Le Noble was to furnish. But the officials at Lyons neglected to make purchases in Provence, and subjected themselves to the necessity of continuing to depend on Burgundy; to cover this second mistake, a third was made, in contracting with Le Noble to procure in Burgundy such grain as they might need." [1]

The crisis was so severe at Lyons and delays in the south were so considerable that the grain already purchased in Burgundy had to be shipped to assist the town. The boats stopped at

[1] G^7. 1631. Lyon, 30 Août 1693. Canaples à Barbezieux, Copie avec apostilles faits par le C. G. The authorship of the marginal notes is placed beyond doubt by a letter of Canaples, Lyon, 22 Sept. 1693.

Châlons, Mâcon, and Tournus were released, and some small lots allowed to pass on new permits.[1]

But there is almost no note of any shipments from Burgundy after November, 1693. Until the following harvest, Lyons was obliged to seek sustenance elsewhere. The qualified prohibitions in March, 1693, thus seem to have been justified whether the inquiry of d'Argouges was accurate or not. Bérulle's insistence upon the possibility of considerable exports from Burgundy did nothing but increase the distress and violence.

After the harvest of 1694, trade began again, though the intendants kept it under close supervision. Ferrand had issued a prohibition in August.[2] The authorities at Lyons protested, and, at the command of the Contrôleur Général, negotiations between the intendants began.[3] Ferrand agreed to allow the shipment of a limited quantity, but did not feel sure of the exact amount. He was certain, however, that it would be unwise to allow the merchants liberty to buy as they chose. "To avoid the export of a larger quantity than is permitted, d'Herbigny should choose those whom he desires to charge with the undertaking. A list should be sent to Ferrand, and each week these persons should submit a statement of their purchases."[4]

This was the more ordinary state of affairs, for the lack of concert between the intendants in 1693 was unusual. This is the outcome of the conflict of interests. The intendant in Burgundy is in favor of a relatively complete prohibition. The officials at Lyons insist upon having the right to make some shipments from Burgundy. The intendant in Burgundy recognizes the necessity of some concessions and proceeds to negotiate in regard to the amount. Licenses are then issued through the Lyonese officials to the merchants.

[1] G^7. 1631. Lyon, 1 Sept. 1693. Bérulle, Lyon, 4–5 Sept. 1693. Canaples, *passim*. G^7. 1631. 6 Sept. 1693. G^7. 1630. Buxy, 7 Sept. 1693, d'Argouges, etc.

[2] Boislisle, *op. cit.*, I, 374, 1360. 16 Août 1694.

[3] G^7. 1633. Lyon, 8 Sept. 1694. Bérulle, enclosed letter of Ferrand to him.

[4] G^7. 1634. Dijon, 27 Nov. 1694. Ferrand.

G^7. 1633. Mémoire sur les Bleds necessaires pour la ville de Lyon. (Envoyé avec la lettre de M. d'Herbigny. 23 Nov. 1694.)

This system is somewhat less crude than the sixteenth century system. The latter was more or less haphazard. There was little feeling of community of interest between the divers groups of local officials. The intendants were less attached to their locality, and were always controlled to some extent by the Contrôleur Général at Paris. Everything rendered negotiation easier in the seventeenth century, and there was a conscious effort to discover the real extent of the exportable surplus.

Soon after the harvest of 1698, Ferrand, the Intendant in Burgundy, found it advisable to prohibit the export of grain. The Contrôleur Général took the special precaution of writing to the Consuls of Lyons, instructing them to place little reliance upon Burgundy. Ferrand sent word that he could permit the export of only 9,500 ânées, a quantity that was considered to be sufficient to enable Lyons to wait for aid from Languedoc, Provence, and foreign countries. The licenses for this grain were divided between the Abondance and the merchants.[1] These shipments were all to be discharged at Lyons before Christmas.

In January, d'Herbigny was begging Ferrand to restore complete freedom of trade between Lyons and Beaujolais, Mâconnais, and Brionnais. Ferrand was not at all disposed to accede to the request. "Grain is cheaper in every part of the department of M. d'Herbigny than it is in Burgundy," he writes to the Contrôleur Général. "If we have any grain, it is much better for us to keep it to assist you in case of need (*i. e.* for the army), than to send it to a province where it is desired merely to create greater abundance and to decrease the price of grain, but where prices are continually lower than in Burgundy."[2] Later in the month, prices fell notably at Lyons, and the Abondance discontinued its purchases in Burgundy.[3] From this time, we hear little of Burgundy till July.

[1] G⁷. 358. Lyon, 25 Juillet 1699. Relation très sincère à M. le Maréchal de Villeroy de la conduite des Prévôt des Marchands et Échevins de Lyon et des Directeurs de l'Abondance.

[2] G⁷. 159. Dijon, 5 Jan. 1699. Ferrand. The statement about comparative prices is questionable, though it is quite possible that prices in parts of Burgundy should be higher than at Lyons.

[3] G⁷. 358. Lyon, 18 Jan. 1699. d'Herbigny.

Then, there were many demands for freedom of trade between Burgundy and Lyons. This was readily explained by Ferrand. "It is because I have been very careful to give no permits except in concert with d'Herbigny. The merchants of Burgundy see themselves on the eve of the harvest and apprehend a considerable loss from the decline in price that will follow the harvest. Some have shipped to Lyons without licenses, through the connivance of the farmers of the octrois. I stopped this abuse by new orders. It will, of course, be necessary to remove the prohibition after the harvest, but storms may injure the crops, and, as Lyons is in no need, it is well not to take any steps until the harvest is assured." [1]

The presence of this supply available for exportation just before the harvest may well be cited as an indication that exports to Lyons might have been more freely permitted. It is indeed a case that illustrates the crudity of the device, but we must remember that there was literally no means of knowing how much these merchants had secreted, just as there was never any evidence to show that they really possessed a considerable quantity. Relatively small amounts might easily give rise to a rather marked demand for licenses. This ignorance of the available supply was the most dangerous feature of conditions in Burgundy, and that alone would justify prohibitions at such a time.

The years 1708–09 present no new phases of grain trade policy, so that a detailed treatment may be omitted.

The history of the dearths in Burgundy, then, points rather strongly to the conclusion that prohibitions were necessary to assure the satisfaction of the needs of the province. In 1693, when the evidences of dearth were not taken seriously at Lyons, the substantial accuracy of the judgment of local officials in Burgundy was abundantly confirmed by subsequent events. Despite all the confidence of Bérulle, Lyons was not able to secure any great quantity of grain in Burgundy during the late season. Supplies had to be procured hurriedly in the south,

[1] Boislisle, *op. cit.*, I, 535, 1894. 20 Juillet 1699. On the 23d, freedom of export was granted.

and the inevitable delays reduced Lyons to sore straits. In 1698, and in 1709, the intendants limited exports from Burgundy. Lyons sought provisions in the south, and little difficulty was experienced in the north. The expediency of the prohibitions in Burgundy can hardly be doubted. They were the only means of forcing the Lyonese to enlarge the area of their supply market.

Languedoc

Most of the features of the policy characteristic of Languedoc have appeared, either in the discussion of Colbert's relations with Daguesseau, or in connection with the study of the exhaustion produced by uncontrolled trade. The policy in regard to the exports of grain to maritime ports is not notably different under Bâville. In 1709, however, the severity of the dearth obliged Bâville to undertake the general direction of the internal trade of the province. In August and September, 1708, he found it necessary to send away the Italians who had come to buy at Narbonne, and other coast ports. Then the demands of Lyons and Provence must needs be satisfied. After much effort, the Lyonese were driven out of the districts along the Rhône, and forced to go to Narbonne. The supplies of the province were next attacked in the Upper Garonne, by a movement down towards Bordeaux. This was limited like the trade with Lyons and Provence to a trade with licenses. By March and April, 1709, the distress in Lower Languedoc was extreme. All the markets were disorganized and the regular circulation of trade completely suspended. Bâville was obliged to take measures to assist the larger towns, opening granaries in the dioceses of Toulouse, Lavaur, and Alby, to supply the most pressing wants in Lower Languedoc. Besides this, he issued divers market ordinances, though he did not adopt anything like Delamare's policy. His treatment of conditions in Languedoc was indeed the exact antithesis of Delamare's. The latter endeavored to restore the normal conditions of a trade passing properly through the markets. Bâville went to the other extreme, practically running the trade himself. His personal control went to the length of procuring grain from the Levant, partly on the security of the province, partly on the security of divers towns.[1]

Lebret, in 1693, plays a different part in the trade. The Lyonese merchants were buying freely around Arles and Tarascon, and the needs of Lyons were so pressing that he perceived the necessity of permitting these purchases. But at the same time, he proposed to stimulate imports of Barbary grain, and with that in view he secured control of a quantity of grain which he proposed to place on the markets in such way that both ends should be gained.[2] Thus, in one way or another, the intendants supplied the defects of the imperfect market organization. Here, helping to determine the quantity that was really available for export, there distributing grain when the markets had broken down, in a third place, trying vainly to make the towns realize the meaning and significance of a steady flow of trade.

Brittany

In Brittany, licenses were used extensively to authorize domestic trade at times when foreign export was prohibited. The regularity of trade had reduced the granting of licenses to a system. The merchants of Quimper, Concarneau, and other towns sent the intendant a statement of their projected shipments immediately after the harvest. He then secured royal licenses for carrying these amounts to the domestic ports indicated by the merchants.[3] Even Nantes could draw supplies from Lower Brittany only upon royal licenses, and the correspondence of the years of dearth is filled with the details of the administration of this license system. When other towns were dependent upon coastwise grain trade, they, too, were obliged to secure licenses to permit shipment.[4]

[1] This whole episode will be found in part I, ch. IV.

[2] See part I, ch. IV.

[3] G^7. 181. Hennebont, 22 Sept. 1699. Dutel, Commis. du Roy.

[4] G^7. 181. Rennes, 4 Oct. 1699. De Nointel. Letter enclosing a list of licenses needed by Nantes and Saint-Malo.

G^7. 181. Saint-Malo, 7 Nov. 1699. Sainte-Marie.

G^7. 181. Nantes (28 Nov. 1699, date of receipt). De Mianne.

G^7. 181. 11 Dec. 1699. De Nointel. Says he has delivered the licenses;

In 1709, to expedite matters, it was arranged that "Ferrand should issue permits upon the presentation of certificates from the Provost of Merchants of Paris. When supplies for the army were needed, Ferrand should be given notice of the quantity necessary."[1] In the course of a year or so, the care taken at first was no longer used. Ferrand began, after a while, "to charge his subdélégués with the issue of the necessary permits." Then these subdélégués began to commission their inferiors for the same duty, "so that there was a great opportunity for abuses in the granting of licenses."[2]

Furthermore, general permissions that were issued at Paris were not always promptly received and enforced. Not infrequently the merchants learned of the ordinance through their correspondents, so that we have the curious situation described in a letter of May 5, 1702: "I take the liberty to address Your Excellency apropos of the loading of certain barques and other vessels with barley and wheat. The masters demand sailing papers to carry this grain to Spain and Portugal, on the strength of an Order in Council of March 28 which permits export. In this jurisdiction (admiralty of Nantes) we have heard nothing of such an Order, and as there are several orders prohibiting export, I have thought it wise to write to you."[3] The order of March 28 had been sent to Brittany, but for some inexplicable reason, it had not been sent around. It was finally published in the middle of May, too late to be of any value to the merchants.[4]

similar details for the year 1701 will be found in the letters G7. 182. Rennes, 27 Avril 1701, and many other letters.

[1] G7. 1641. 3 Oct. 1709. Deliberation d'une assemblée tenue chez M. Daguesseau. See also G7. 1642. Saint-Malo, 17 Oct. 1710. Ferrand, with enclosed memoir of licenses granted.

[2] G7. 1642. 17 Nov. 1710. Clairambault. See also G7. 1642. 6 Nov. 1710. Laurencin, Marchand à Nantes à M. Ferrand. Speaks of clandestine export to Spain. G7. 1642. Rennes, 3 Dec. 1710. Ferrand acknowledges receipt of letter apropos of the abuses mentioned by Clairambault. Says that he has reprimanded the two subdélégués.

[3] G7. 182. Nantes, 5 May 1702. Dangy, Lieu. de la Marine à Nantes.

[4] G7. 182. Paris, 11 Mai 1702. de Messureaume. G7. 182. Nantes, 16 Mai 1702. Dangy.

Orleans

It is extremely difficult to give any definite conception of the policy followed at Orleans, because there is so little positive action and so much discussion and negotiation. But the position of the town brings out strongly one feature of the seventeenth century trade, and the conduct of the officials illustrates the gradual break-down of the old ideas and the development of new commercial usages.

The custom among the Marne Valley merchants of bringing their grain down to a point near Paris and then storing the grain to wait for a good market had produced among the Parisian officials a strong determination to enforce the old regulation requiring the immediate and continuous shipment of all grain from the point of purchase to the ultimate destination. A regulation of this sort was, of course, calculated to preserve the independence of trades supplying different towns from the same source of supply. In the Marne Valley, this was of little consequence, as there was no large town between the shipping points and Paris. In the Loire Valley, it was quite another matter. The slight surplus of Auvergne, coming down the river, might either stop at Orleans or continue to Paris. Grain coming up from Saumur or Nantes could likewise be applied to supply the demand of either Orleans or Paris. The rigorous enforcement of the provision requiring continuous shipment made it necessary to decide upon the final destination before the grain was shipped. This, of course, prevented any very exact adjustment to the conditions at Orleans or Paris, especially as there was an additional factor in the more energetic punishment of violence done to shipments destined for Paris.[1] If strict law were followed, the trade supplying Orleans must have been entirely distinct from the trade supplying Paris. The Parisian grain passed through Orleans, but only physically, without influencing the market, and was technically incapable of being applied to the satisfaction of the demand of Orleans. This limitation of the movements of grain was favorable to Paris, but prejudicial

[1] G[7]. 1632. Orleans, 20 Dec. 1693. De Creil.

to intermediate points, and in this respect, the Parisian officials stood in the way of that fusion of the entire wholesale trade which would be the final result of the completed wholesale market system. The persistent protest of Orleans against this rigid specialization of lines of trade is thus one of the forces tending to break down the old medieval system and to substitute for it the more highly organized market system, which seeks to meet the needs not only of a tyrannical metropolitan demand but also the local demands of all parts of the area. In the upper Seine Basin, no town was large enough to protest with effect, and ordinarily there was no need. Orleans, however, was naturally an entrepôt of the Loire Valley trade, and its own needs were such that it was quite essential that the whole trade of Loire should pass through the market at Orleans. The separation of Parisian trade from that of Orleans could not be maintained.

Some of these aspects of the relation between Orleans and Paris appear in 1662, in the letters of Brachet, the Maire of Orleans.[1] But the significance of the case can be perceived only by reading between the lines. In 1694, the situation is more completely revealed by the letters of Bouville, the Intendant. "The whole country between La Charité and Châteauneuf will suffer severely, because no grain leaves Berry or Bourbonnais, and of that coming up the river none passes Orleans except for Paris. There is also great dearth towards Montargis and around Blois and Beaugency, as I do my best to prevent them from stopping boats. However, sir, as most of the merchants of Orleans have marked Paris as the destination of their grain, it is certain that Orleans will be without grain in a short time, if we are obliged to allow all grain to pass that is billed for Paris in the *Lettres de Voiture.* All the rural districts will suffer, as they draw their provisions from the large towns." [2] Later he writes: "I beg you not to compel the merchants to carry their grain to Paris; I am persuaded that this liberty

[1] Bib. Nat., Mél. Colb., 108, 246, 380, 382, 464, 475, 543, 557, 653, 745.

[2] G[7]. 1635. Orléans, 17 Avril 1694. Bouville; La Charité, 27 Avril 1694. Bouville.

will procure aid for us here, and that more will even be shipped to Paris than the quantity promised by the merchants. Once the Loire towns are supplied the people will not be inclined to interfere with the passage of boats. I am acting in concert with the merchants here, and if Miroménil does as much at Tours, I hope that all the Loire towns will be supplied and that the rural districts will feel the benefit. Paris will also find much assistance, for, besides the grain that passes daily on the Canal, all the grain that comes into the country towns in the Beauce will go to Montlhéry, and then to Paris. Everything depends upon freedom of trade." [1]

In 1699 and 1709, there was little real trouble at Orleans. The harvests had been fairly abundant and the town served as an entrepôt. So far as there was any apprehension, it was more like what we find in any producing region. In this case, the fear was of excessive shipments from the Beauce, where much of the town's supply was procured.

In general, two distinct types of policy appear in these closing years of the seventeenth century. The new constructive market regulations of the Châtelet in the Seine Basin, on the one hand, and the development of the old sixteenth century policy in the hands of the intendants in the other parts of France. The policy of the Châtelet was not without its traditional basis, but novel results were obtained. A well-organized wholesale market was created at Bray and at Vitry; the trade was kept moving; and this idea of continuous circulation through the markets was definitely adopted as the basis of future regulation of the Parisian trade.

The trade in other sections of France was less highly organized. The local markets still played so large a part in the distribution of grain that the policy adopted by the Châtelet would have been impossible. In Burgundy, in Languedoc, and in Provence the local markets were still the basis of trade, and in every crisis this market machinery proved inadequate. The

[1] Boislisle, *op. cit.*, I, 360, 1309. 18 et 23 Avril 1694. Bouville. See also G[7]. 1635. Orléans, 27 et 28 Avril 1694. Bouville.

old relief measures of the sixteenth century were applied, but with more care, a better knowledge of conditions, and a more accurate perception of the character of the problem. In 1698 and 1709 the regulations of the intendants in Burgundy and Languedoc were on the whole distinctly successful. These regulations may have been a poor substitute for improved market organization, but in the absence of the metropolitan market, these inferior substitutes were necessary.

CHAPTER V

Conclusion

Political Theory and the Administrators

Throughout our period, grain trade policies fall into two distinct types. On the one hand, the Crown insists on the essential harmony of interest between different parts of the kingdom; on the other, the local officials are ever harrassed by the imperfect adjustment of inter-provincial interests. The Crown declares, in edict after edict, that " France is more fertile than any other kingdom in Christendom, that a dispensation of kind providence has granted to one province what its neighbor lacks, so that by mutual succor the wants of all are supplied." The correspondence of local authorities, however, instead of depicting this harmonious exchange of the blessings of Heaven, reveals a bitter strife, accompanied by mutual recrimination, abuse, and violence. The Crown endeavors to bring home to its recalcitrant subjects the ideal of interdependence.

All royal measures were designed to bring about the ideal social state that hovered before the eyes of sixteenth century statesmen as the goal of human endeavor. No province should be utilized for the relief of some other kingdom until the needs of France had been supplied. No province should be allowed to impose any obstacles to complete freedom of trade between different parts of the kingdom. No unpatriotic merchants should be allowed to increase their private fortune at the expense of the commonweal, by selling grain to foreigners when dearth was possible.

The local officials were not concerned with ideals, with the growth of nationalism, or with any large conceptions of social interdependence. They saw only a discordant conflict of man with man, of town with town, of province with province. The one motive apparent to them was self-interest, a determined, rapacious effort on the part of each man, or each group, to secure the complete satisfaction of its wants without reference to the needs of others. The large towns sought grain in the provinces, and carried off great quantities, usually regardless of the needs of the locality. The peasantry plundered grain boats destined for the large towns, assaulted and abused local merchants. The merchants sought their own ends without consideration for town or country. The country people suffered at times from depletion of local supply, but as long as there was no actual violence the merchant gave their situation no thought. Paris or Lyons might be reduced to intense distress, but the merchant would delay his grain boats another day or another week, if he could secure an additional sou per bichet.

But the theoretical and practical points of view were not in antagonism. While the Crown and such writers as Laffémas and Montchrétien were developing the idea of the state as a social organism, the administrators were actually organizing the ill-coördinated feudal monarchy into the firmly-knit national state.

The earliest expression of the idea of this new nationalism is the preface of an edict of Henry II. It possesses more distinction of style than most of the effusions of the chancellries of the sixteenth century, but the constructions are still labored and awkward. This edict of February 14, 1557 granted complete freedom of trade in all commodities except grain, — a change of policy that was considered to be so great a departure from ordinary custom that some explanation was deemed necessary. The preface, accordingly, proceeds to an elaborate defence of free trade.[1]

" It has always been known by common experience that the principal means of making the people of a kingdom, country, or

[1] There are occasional expressions of similar sentiments in the provinces, notably a passage from the papers of the Estates of Languedoc. A resolution of 14–25 Sept. 1501 reads: "Que pour prévenir la famine, requête soit fait aux Commissaires du Roy, afin qu'ils empeschent plusieurs seigneurs, nobles, et marchands d'amasser les bleds, et de les vendre hors du pays, *attendu que les trois sénéchaussées sont tout un corps mystique*, que l'une pourra bailler ses bleds à l'autre pourveu que les bleds soient portés par terre." *Invent. Som. des Arch. Dept., Haute Garonne*, Série C., vol. II, p. 2.

province, well-to-do, rich, and opulent, is freedom in the trade and commerce in which they are engaged with their neighbors. They sell, barter, and exchange the goods, merchandise, and commodities which they bring from their country, to bring back others which they lack, together with gold, silver, and other things useful and necessary. If it were not for trade, the commodities and fruits of each kingdom, country, province, all their specialties and manufactures must needs be consumed by the subjects and inhabitants, so that the greater part of their commodities and fruits would be relatively useless, so that the landlord would be disappointed in his hopes of profit, and the laborers and artisans would receive no return for their industry. Consequently, upon the petition of the Third Estate at the last general assembly of the principal Estates of our kingdom, that they should be allowed to enjoy the freedom of trade needed during this time of war, and the exemption from the export duties recently levied, we have remembered that God, by his blessed grace, has given us a kingdom composed of divers countries and provinces, each of which is in itself as fertile as any lands in Christendom, abounding in a variety of commodities, so that what is lacking in one is found in another. The inhabitants of this kingdom, indeed, are constrained by no necessity of food or other useful articles, to ask assistance of their neighbors, or of foreigners. But, on the other hand, it is more reasonable that each should (freely) seek his gain from his land, his labor, his industry, or his commerce, and that in doing this he should serve himself, his country, and others, by the benefits flowing from trade. . . ." [1]

Here is a fairly clear conception of a country within which there is a certain territorial division of labor, potentially a self-sufficing economic entity, and yet engaging freely in trade with other nations because there is a greater advantage in complete freedom of trade than in restriction, even within national boundaries. There is no tinge of the narrow-minded hatred and distrust of foreigners, no trace of the delusion that the gain of one party necessarily involved loss on the other side, no hint

[1] Fontanon, *Ordonnances des Rois* (1610), I, pp. 958 f.

of the short-sighted confusion between money and the real wealth of a country. The short, highly abstract passage suggests the conception of the metropolitan area and that freedom of trade which is most expedient between such areas.

The same type of "free trade" doctrine appears in Bodin and in an anonymous tract ordinarily ascribed to du Haillan. Their statements are interesting as they reveal more completely the ideas underlying their views. In the *Discours sur le rehaussement et la diminution des Monnoies* (1578), Bodin says that trade with foreign nations is indispensable, and then proceeds: "Even if we could do without their goods, we should nevertheless trade, buy, sell, exchange, lend; nay we should give some of our goods to foreigners, if it were only to maintain intercourse and friendship between them and us. . . . We owe them that charity by a natural obligation. We must share with them the goods with which God has blessed us."[1] The treatise of du Haillan, which appeared in 1586, expresses similar views: "Every one knows that trade consists in the interchange of commodities, and although certain people of rank have endeavored to restrict the freedom of trade, supposing that we can dispense with foreign commodities, it is really impossible, . . . and even if it were possible, we should none the less share what we have with our neighbors, as much from the duty of charity, which commands us to succor others, as to maintain friendship with them."[2] In this sixteenth century "free trade," the economic question is judged entirely in the light of religious and philosophical cosmopolitanism.

This conception of a community of interest appears in various kinds of local material. In such cases, Christian duty is supplemented by the sentiment of nationality. Thus, in 1504, Lyons and certain towns of Burgundy and Auxois desired to purchase grain at Paris to relieve their distress. A meeting of the municipal authorities of Paris, held November 29, 1504, resolved that something should be done to aid their neighbors. A more

[1] Cited in Baudrillart, *Bodin et son temps*, p. 176. I have been unable to obtain the use of a full text of the *Discours*.

[2] Fournier, *Variétés, Historiques, et Littéraires*, VII, 185. Discours de l'Extresme Cherté. 1586.

general meeting was called to consider the matter further. On January 15, it was finally decided that it was proper to assist their fellow-countrymen in time of trouble, but that it would not be wise to allow strangers to go to Santerre and other places where the Parisian merchants buy, so that it was arranged that the purchases should be made by Parisian merchants and turned over to the Lyonese at Paris.[1]

The last decade of the sixteenth century reveals a change in contemporary ideas. In 1596, Barthélemy Laffémas published his first treatise, and began his energetic struggle to secure the adoption of his policies. His proposals were fundamentally different from anything suggested by previous sixteenth century politicians; the active measures suggested were new, the predominance of purely economic over political, religious and cosmopolitan motives was notable, the conception of the economic unity of the State was more aggressively and clearly asserted.[2] The influence of Sully in the ministry of Henry IV long made the efforts of Laffémas unavailing, but the persistence and energy of the man finally resulted in the appointment of a commission to consider his projects for the encouragement of industry and commerce and to take such action as was necessary. The work of Laffémas falls into two general divisions: the treatises, stating his doctrines, and the papers of the Council of Commerce, which embody his views.

He advocated the exclusion of foreign goods and of foreign influence as far as possible, the stimulation of domestic industries, the improvement of means of communication, the encouragement of more careful stock breeding, the protection of inventors

[1] *Reg. du Bureau*, I, 98–100. See also letters between Rouen and Paris, 1528. *Ibid.*, II, 16. References can easily be multiplied in the local material.

[2] The inaccessibility of the treatises of Laffémas makes this account of his work general in character, but the complete publication of his political acts in connection with the Conseil de Commerce reveals the larger elements of his policy. See Champollion-Figeac, *Documents Historiques Inédits, tirés des Collections Manuscrites de la Bib. Nat. et des Archives, ou des Bibliothèques des Départements*, IV tom. Paris, 1848. Coll. des Docs. Inédits pour servir à l'Hist. de France. The papers of Laffémas are published in Vol. IV. For a complete catalogue of the works of Laffémas, see Boyer de Sainte Suzanne, *Les Intendants de la Généralité d'Amiens*, p. 552.

of mechanical labor-saving appliances. Except for the financial reforms of Colbert, there is almost no phase of his activity which does not find its counterpart in the "Procès Verbaux" of the Conseil de Commerce of 1601. In fact, most of the industries encouraged by Colbert were marked out by Laffémas for attention, and, in many cases, much was done. Underlying this policy was a strong consciousness of nationality; in a word he advocated "Colbertism" before Colbert.

The views of Laffémas were like those of his contemporary, Montchrétien. Litterateur, bon-vivant, and duellist, Montchrétien became interested in the economic problems of his time after a residence in England rendered necessary by his skill with the rapier. He returned to France determined to urge the government to adopt measures to promote the industrial and commercial prosperity of France, and thus impose a much-needed check upon the growing preponderance of English and Dutch industry and commerce. Poet by nature, familiar with the political works of the Greek philosophers, he writes with an elegance and breadth of view that gives his penetrating analysis a rare distinction.[1]

Montchrétien has a real perception of the reciprocal economic interests of the community. In one passage, he likens the interdependent arts and industries to "a marvellous chain of interlacing rings of gold, vitalizing and attracting within its scope all affairs of this world, as did the chain which the poet Homer puts in the hands of Zeus."[2] In another passage, he suggests the analogy that inspired much of Spencer's sociological work, and that still haunts the literature of the subject. "There is a great similarity between the well-organized state and the bodies of animals. Animals are controlled by three faculties, which are different manifestations of one force, rather than distinct forces. The doctors call these faculties, spirits. The first is the vegetative, possessed in common with trees and plants; this force has its seat in the liver and the blood. It

[1] Antoyne de Montchrétien, *Traité de l'Économie Politique*, dédié au Roy et la Reyne, en 1615. Réimprimé par Funck-Bretano. Paris, 1889.

[2] Montchrétien, *op. cit.*, p. 17.

nourishes the body, and is dispersed through the members by the veins. The laborers and farm hands correspond to this element in the body politic. The second faculty, that of feeling ('sensitive'), has its seat in the heart. It is the source of the natural heat of the body and is diffused by the arteries. In the state, the artisans and journeymen represent this faculty. The third is the animal, and has its seat in the brain, where it directs the instincts and actions, and by means of the nerves imparts movement to the whole body. To this faculty may be compared the merchants.

"By these three types of men, — laborers, artisans, merchants, — the whole state is nourished and sustained. Through them, all profit comes and is made, and in the various digestions, as in the natural body, it is always transformed with advantage." [1]

Dropping the metaphor, in another passage, he emphasizes the national character of this economic entity. "France is the most complete 'corps du Royaume' that the sun can behold from his rising in the East to his setting in the West. The members are more diverse and yet more perfectly arranged in the symmetry demanded of a finely organized state." Then after enumerating various natural sources of wealth, he continues, "the greatest of these is the inexhaustible abundance of men, if they can only be properly directed. . . . Indeed, the spectacle of France, teeming with men, might lead one to believe that she was burdened and in distress, but it is only a lack of order. Its greatest blessing may become, through ignorance or neglect, its greatest curse. But who does not know that organization is the prime requisite for the efficient functioning of a state? The exquisite harmony of their constituent elements is the primal manifestation of the power of great organic bodies." [2]

While conceiving economic, as well as political interdependence, it is clear that Montchrétien's political ideas led him to suppose that the areas coincided. He failed to perceive that complete economic interdependence exists only within the limits of the market.

[1] Montchrétien, *op. cit.*, 32–33. [2] *Ibid.*, 23–24.

The immediate influence of Montchrétien was very slight. The Court of the Regency had other interests. But Colbert's connection with Laffémas is involved in little doubt. The papers of the Council of Commerce form a part of the collection of manuscripts at the Bibliothèque Nationale coming from the library of Colbert. The only uncertainty attaches to the date of acquisition, and this may well be supposed to be relatively early in Colbert's ministry, when he was most busily assembling documents of previous administrations. On the whole, it is highly probable that Colbert was acquainted with the ideas of both Montchrétien and Laffémas. The influence of this early seventeenth century writing upon Colbert was probably considerable, and may be regarded very properly as the beginning of the policies and ideas grouped under the term, "Colbertism."

Although the fundamental conceptions that seem to underlie seventeenth century policies are outlined by Montchrétien, there is nevertheless a marked development in the precision of the ideas, and many subsidiary points are brought to light. Our own studies of the market system have revealed the importance of the machinery for the distribution of commodities over the market area. This diffusion of material things is the most direct manifestation of economic organization. The laws of price, value, and price-making are the basis of the economic structure of society. Some perception of the nature of these problems accordingly might well be expected of these early theorists. Bodin had disposed of one of the mysteries in regard to money and prices, but he contributed little to an understanding of the importance of the subject of value and price. Montchrétien proceeded a step further, drawing distinctions between real wealth and money, and between value and price. "It is not the abundance of gold and silver, or the quantity of diamonds and pearls that makes a state wealthy — it is the ease of producing the necessities of life and articles of clothing. The more of these commodities possessed, the greater the wealth."[1] Elsewhere we find: "The real value of commodities is immovable, but not the momentary price, which

[1] Montchrétien, *op. cit.*, 241.

depends upon many factors. Nothing is dear which has not been cheap and nothing is cheap that may not become dear. Nor do prices always follow the changes in the value of money." [1] But he does not get beyond these elementary distinctions. The importance of differences of price in stimulating movements of commodities is clearly perceived by Colbert, though seldom well stated. The idea appears frequently in his letters, and he is often mystified by the absence of the movements he expects. March 22, 1672, he writes to Bouchu, Intendant at Dijon: "I am informed that there have been heavy shipments of grain from Provence and Languedoc to relieve the dearth in Italy and Naples. These exports have rendered grain very dear in those provinces, which should result in the movement of a great quantity of grain from Burgundy and Champagne. As I do not hear from you of any shipments down the Saône, and as there is nothing more important for all of these provinces than the relief of the dearth in Provence and Languedoc and a movement of specie to Burgundy and Champagne, I beg you to go to one of the river towns, and establish yourself there as permanently as your affairs permit. Procure information of everything that is going on, urge the merchants to ship, enter into correspondence with Provence and Languedoc with that in view, remove all obstacles that the merchants may encounter, and if necessary, let me know and I will send any orders of which you have need." [2]

This little incident reveals the conceptions of Colbert. The nation is an economic unit, and within it there is complete mobility of commodities in response to differences in prices. Prices should differ in the various provinces only by the amount

[1] Montchrétien, *op. cit.*, 257.

[2] Clément, *Lett. Inst. et Mém.*, II, 651–652. See also *ibid.*, IV, 298. Letter of 15 Avril 1683. "Lorsque les bleds sont chers dans une ville, l'industrie de tous les hommes, françois et estrangers, consiste à porter des marchandises dans les lieux où elles sont chères." See also G[7]. 1. 8 Nov. 1679. Colbert à M. d'Herbigny, Int. en Dauphiné. "La grande application, que les particuliers ont à tirer les bleds de la province de Dauphiné, est une preuve constante qu'il est plus cher dans les lieux ou on le veut porter que dans cette province, ainsy vous voyez que cela prouve une chose contraire à celle que l'on veut vous prouver. . . ." Also Bib. Nat., Mél. Clair., 462, 423. Colbert à M. Bouchu. 8 Nov. 1679.

of the cost of transportation. In short, he has in mind the fully organized metropolitan area. He assumes its existence, although the evidence of facts might well have disillusioned him.

These ideas were rapidly diffused and at the close of the century were very generally known. The best indication appears in the interesting discussion of the fixation of the price of grain in 1709. The inadequacy of some impracticable proposals was clearly explained in the course of the controversy. One anonymous writer points out that the chief difficulties lie in the impossibility of an absolutely uniform price, and in the diversity of measures. "The merchants are stimulated to buy and sell only through the hope of gaining through the transport of their grain. If the price is uniform they will find no profit in moving grain.

"Unless a uniform measure is introduced, the merchants will evade the established prices by means of the diversity of measures. But if it be supposed that these difficulties were surmounted by fixing the price of grain with reference to the distance of the sources of supply from the consuming area, and by a reduction of measures to weight, it would still be necessary to overcome the disposition to form granaries." [1]

The other most important aspect of metropolitan organization is suggested by the mercantilistic idea of the balance of payments. This is, of course, an anticipation of the results of the perfected use of negotiable paper. The system was rapidly taking shape during the closing years of the century, although it had hardly attained the completeness that is connoted by the mercantilistic idea of a definite balance of payments between countries, to liquidate their commercial dealings. This element of mercantilism is significant as it emphasizes the unity of the metropolitan or national area as against other areas.[2]

[1] G^7. 1635. Mémoire contre la fixation des bleds.

[2] I have not been able to trace the history of this idea of a balance of payments. The mercantilist doctrine is generally said to begin in the late sixteenth century. I have seen little real evidence of it in French sources, and no definite conception of a balance of payments, prior to Colbert. It appears in his "Mémoire sur le Commerce," *Lett. Inst. et Mém.*, II, cclxix, but he does not lay so much stress upon the idea as do later writers.

The larger aspects of the metropolitan distributive organization were thus conceived by the last generation of the seventeenth century. This anticipates by nearly one hundred years the full realization of the idea. But it does not necessarily follow that this anticipation enabled the politicians materially to accelerate the growth towards the new form of organization. Questions of policy are decided upon the supposition that certain organic relations already exist, and the policy is necessarily vitiated to a great degree by the failure to adjust policy to fact. Under such conditions the energies of the statesman may be misdirected. The encouragement of domestic industry by Colbert, for instance, could exert relatively little influence upon the growth of the economic area, though the industrial side of his policy was, to him, one of his most important spheres of activity. So far as he exerted any influence by those efforts, the results differed considerably from his expectations.

The economic policy of the Crown was thus based upon unfounded assumptions, since it failed to appreciate the strength of the centrifugal forces in the community. The Crown was ever prone to assume that the state was a closely organized national unit, when in reality the degree of territorial interdependence was far less considerable than was supposed.

The edicts of 1559 and 1567 illustrate the general tendency in its extreme degree. The Crown assumed that it possessed an administrative system that could carry out a general ordinance involving a vast amount of executive detail. That was a less comprehensible mistake than the assumption, in the royal edicts, that the problem of grain trade regulation was primarily a question of excessive exports to foreign ports, and that an assertion of complete freedom of inter-provincial trade was all the regulation that was needed in the domestic trade. This false view of the situation was due to a belief in a national economic unity that did not exist. The policy was, therefore, necessarily ineffective.

The policy of Colbert conveys the same moral. But Colbert is two different men: he was at once a theorist and a man of action; he had a capacity for setting aside all general ideas when it was necessary to act. His general ideas led him astray only in regard to the regulation of domestic trade. He always assumed complete freedom of inter-provincial trade and probably never understood the seriousness of the problems presented by the domestic trade.

The growth of a national policy of regulation in the hands of the "practical men," the local administrators, is difficult to trace. But despite the confusion caused by conflicts of interests and opinions, several periods may be distinguished. In the first, two groups appear in conflict, the producing regions and the large consuming center. At Paris, an additional complication is introduced by the energy and wealth of the wholesale merchants. They perceived opportunities for profit that frequently subjected both town and country districts to severe strain. In this first period, opinions are influenced almost exclusively by the interests of the group with which the official is most intimately concerned. In this manner, an issue is joined, and the clash of interest becomes evident to all. Once the difficulty is clearly seen, there is a distinct change in the character of official regulation. The more conscientious officials seek means of harmonizing the discordant interests and no longer insist stubbornly upon the complete satisfaction of the desires of the group they represent. This leads to much groping and tentative experimentation, most of it fruitless, but ultimately a solution is discovered. Then, the new idea is applied systematically and all the consequences and details are worked out. The clearest instance of the first stage of this process is the history of the relations between Lyons and Burgundy in the sixteenth century. For twenty or thirty years the presence of the Lyonese excited little comment in Burgundy, but after 1529 the conflict of interests gradually appeared. The Burgundian officials were prone to seek refuge in prohibitions. The Lyonese secured from the King full permission to buy grain in Burgundy. Soon the right to seek supplies along the Upper Saône was regarded as one of the privileges of the town. In the producing region, meanwhile, the prohibition became more frequent. Finally, an unusually severe failure of crops produced an acute crisis in 1557. The Lyonese proposed to buy extensively, but the people of Burgundy were bitterly opposed to the action of the Consuls of Lyons. On the one hand there was refusal to permit further exports, on the other, defiant assertion of intention to carry off the grain under cover of royal privileges. The divergence of interest is hard for us to understand, but the bitter recrimination, the threats of the Lyonese to prosecute Villefrancon, the violence all along the river, all testify to the intense reality of the discord.

The acute crisis of 1557 was, in itself, the beginning of a new departure in policy. The necessities of Lyons led to the sending of Grolier and Guimbre to Burgundy. They started with a firm conviction of the justice of the complaints of Lyons; they returned with a realization that there was much to be said on the other side. Their long association with Villefrancon brought both sides to an appreciation of the difficulties of the situation. A compromise was made; Villefrancon abandoned his policy of absolute prohibition, and the agents of Lyons contented themselves with securing carefully restricted permissions of export.

The difficulties of the situation of Burgundy were not sufficiently great to lead to a complete solution of the grain trade problem. The intermittent character of the problem and the tolerable success of official regulation established this temporary expedient as the fixed policy of the region. The discord between the groups called for no delicate remedy, and after 1557 and 1573 there is no further progress in the regulation of the grain trade in the Rhône Basin.

If the records of the Parisian Échevinage were still extant, we should probably be able to trace a similar clash of interest between Rouen and Paris in the fifteenth century. Paris was habitually buying grain in the vicinity of Rouen. Merchants from Rouen were buying in the Valley of the Oise for foreign export. This cross movement of trade was inconsistent with the spheres of influence that had been created by the "Compagnie Française" of the Parisian merchants, and by the

"Compagnie Normande" of the Rouenese. After a period of recrimination and rivalry, both parties became reconciled to the inevitable, compromised, and applied the idea of distinct spheres of influence to the grain trade.

In neither of these instances is the increase in social harmony and the promotion of closer economic interdependence the result of vague general ideas deduced from theological precept or national sentiment. In each case, the increasing economic unity of the community is brought about by an empirical solution, more or less complete, of a concrete difficulty. The conflict of interest reveals the necessity of coöperation and interdependence, and the concentration of attention upon the question ultimately results in the discovery of some means of reconciling the hostile groups, and bringing them together as parts of a larger group.[1]

The later history of the trade in the Seine Basin is more interesting. There, the conflict of interest was more complicated. The old territorial antagonism persisted. Champagne felt in some measure the hostility towards Paris that Burgundy felt towards Lyons. But the feeling in Champagne was so weak that it serves merely to emphasize the lack of close relations between the province and the capital. In this region, the development of close economic interdependence was the result not of the conflict of territorial groups, but of Parisian groups: the merchants and the general public.

The problem was peculiarly fitted to bring about a general reconciliation of conflicting interests. The merchants forced the Parisian authorities to regulate the trade with reference to Paris, but the ubiquity of the wholesale merchants made it impossible to found any adequate regulations upon Parisian

[1] Ratzenhofer lays down as a social law that small, relatively independent groups are constantly being merged into larger groups. Undoubtedly a true observation, but historically the interest centers upon the manner in which the fusion of small groups is brought about. It is not a process that accomplishes itself. It is the result of persistent efforts of individuals to reduce social discord and to promote harmony. The absence of human volition in the operation of Ratzenhofer's laws is purely fictitious. It is the result of an exclusion of the concrete details, which is justifiable only if the exclusion is constantly borne in mind. Ratzenhofer, *Zweck und Wesen der Politik.*

interests alone. The merchants exerted quite as much influence upon conditions in the producing regions as they did upon the Parisian markets. Any regulations would have to cover the activity of the merchants from the time grain was bought in the farms or on the local markets to the final sale at the Halle or Ports of Paris. If the regulations were to be successful, they must obviously command the sympathy of the provinces. Thus, the solution of difficulties which were primarily Parisian involved the working out of a general reconciliation of all the groups affected by the grain trade throughout the Seine Basin.

Within the period covered by this study, we find the first two phases of the solution of the problem. The years 1630–60 reveal the sharp conflict of interest between the great wholesale merchants and the Parisian public. The latter part of the century is marked by the persistent efforts of the Châtelet to find the proper means of controlling the grain merchants, and of confining them within proper limits.

The uncertainty of the officials in 1660, the adoption of the policy of prohibiting associations and partnerships, the failure of the policy, — all this administrative muddle has been related at length. From 1660 to 1693, little was accomplished beyond the collection of information. The officials gained a deeper insight into the details of the situation, but the grain trade problem was no less acute than it had been in 1660. Then, this aimless groping was suddenly brought to an end by Delamare's perception of the importance of the development of the general wholesale market at Bray. The solution of the problem by the establishment of wholesale markets had occurred to no one; it was too great a departure from old precedents; but therein lay the possibility of ending the discord and unrest in the trade of the Seine Basin. Once a steady flow of trade was established, all the panic and distrust in the producing regions disappeared; the merchants shipped more regularly to Paris, because of the certainty that no exorbitant profits could be realized by delaying the boats. The visits of Delamare to Vitry in 1709 and 1710 sealed the victory of administrative regulation. Thenceforth, it was only necessary to carry out the brilliant idea which would make possible the national unity that had so long been the dream of theorists and politicians.

The development of social institutions seems to be the result of conscious individual effort to diminish the intensity of social conflict, and this effort is much more than an automatic reaction upon the environment. There is not any inherent reason for assuming the presence of this desire to improve the physical and social conditions of life. In fact, the fatalistic attitude is the more natural, and actually the more wide-spread. Plague, disease, and famine are regarded in primitive society as a divine judgment, an act of God from which man should not seek to escape. If there be any truly spontaneous reaction between men and their physical surroundings, this fatalism must be regarded as the true social law.[1] The individual feels helpless in the presence of the great forces of nature.

The fatalistic attitude discloses its value as a social power in the oriental countries. The famines recur periodically, sweeping off vast numbers of individuals who accept their doom with resignation. The difficulties in those countries may have been more or less acute than the similar troubles in France during the sixteenth and seventeenth centuries. The actual extent of physical distress is not the significant feature. The recurring famines in the Orient lead to no change. The market system that is adequate for the ordinary years breaks down regularly under the stress of dearth, but nothing is done to create a market system that shall work even in time of dearth. It is the will of God that misfortunes come, the efforts of men cannot avail, wherefore struggle against the powers of nature?

If this attitude had prevailed in Europe none of the modern structure of western civilization would have come into being. There was no social law necessarily bringing about an alleviation of the intensity of conflicting interests. Progress is not inherent in the environment; it is the result of conscious human effort to deal with concrete problems. The true background of the history of the grain trade is the firm conviction that the troubles of the famine years could and ought to be remedied.

[1] Townsend, M., *Asia and Europe*, 1901.

In this respect, this chapter in history is merely typical of the history of Western Europe. It is the record of an extraordinary mastery of the physical and social environment by the resolution and acumen of many relatively obscure individuals, lawyers, administrators, and statesmen.

It is a gradual process, a series of victories over the environment that begins in those regions where the difficulties are least serious. Thus, in the grain trade, the most fruitful development occurs in the Seine Basin, where the actual physical distress of famine was least intense. In Burgundy, where distress was greater, nothing of permanent importance was done. In the infertile regions, the history of years of dearth is merely a harrowing record of disease and death. But the solution of the problem discovered in the Seine Basin was subsequently applied to the relief of distress throughout France. The perfection of distributive machinery both as regards market technique and physical transportation made dearth a tradition handed down from "the good old times."

APPENDICES

APPENDIX I

FRENCH DRY MEASURES OF THE OLD RÉGIME

WEIGHTS and measures of the old régime present a problem of great difficulty, partly on account of their diversity, partly on account of the difficulty of securing information. Some of the official standards still exist, and these together with documentary evidence constitute the basis of our information. The principal documentary evidence is the royal examination of measures in Northern France made in 1673. This had special reference to the grain trade, and, as it is summarized by Delamare in his *Traité de la Police*, it is easily accessible. Commercial dictionaries of the period also give considerable information. The relation of the old measures to the metric system has been worked out by the Vicomte d'Avenel in his *Histoire Économique de la Propriété, des Salaires, des Denrées, et de tous les Prix en Général, depuis l'an 1200 jusqu'en 1800.* (Paris, 4 tom., 1894–98.) He nowhere gives a detailed account of the method followed in conversions, and the omission is unfortunate, to say the least. In the conversions given here, all equivalents are based on his figure of 1.56 hectoliters per setier of Paris.

The complexity of measures before the Revolution was of two kinds: differences in content of measures having the same name, differences in the names of the measures used. Differences in the names of measures were not unrelated to sectionalism based on cultural, political, and commercial bonds. In most cases, each district used the same names for measures. Barring minor exceptions, there was a distinct system of measures in the Seine Basin; three systems, in the basin of the Rhône and Saône; a distinct system in Brittany, in Guienne, and in Gascony. Sometimes, the system was distinct throughout, sometimes, the smaller measures had the same name while the larger measures of account were different in name and content.

Dry Measures of Paris and the Seine Basin[1]

1 boisseau of wheat weighed 20 livres.

3 boisseaux	=	1 minot	=	60 livres.
4 minots	=	1 setier	=	240 livres.
12 setiers	=	1 muid	=	2280 livres.

The setier and the muid were measures of account, the boisseau and the minot were actual measures. These names prevailed throughout the Seine Basin and nearly always bore the same relation to each other, though the content of the measures differed widely in different towns. In a few towns different primary units were used, the bichet and the mine. The bichet contained 40 livres when filled with wheat, and the mine, 50 livres. But even in these places, quantities of wheat are usually given in setiers or muids.

Taking d'Avenel's figure of 1.56 hectoliters for the Paris setier, we have the following table of English equivalents: —

1 boisseau	=	20 livres	=	.3575 bushels.
1 minot	=	60 livres	=	1.0725 bushels.
1 setier	=	240 livres	=	4.29 bushels.
1 muid	=	2880 livres	=	51.48 bushels, 3120 pounds.

The measures of Paris were somewhat larger than the measures of the same name used in the provinces. Delamare gives a list of rough equivalents for most of the towns of the Seine Basin. The most important differences for the purposes of this study are: —

Soissons,

1 setier	=	80 livres
3 setiers de Soissons	=	1 setier de Paris.

Châlons-sur-Marne,

1 setier	=	12 boisseaux du pays.
1 setier de Paris	=	13½ boisseaux du pays.

Vitry-le-François,

1 setier	=	12 boisseaux du pays.
1 setier de Paris	=	14½ boisseaux du pays.

Bray,

1 setier	=	8 boisseaux du pays.
1 setier de Paris	=	9 boisseaux du pays.

[1] Delamare, *op. cit.*, II, 744–745. These are presumably the wheat measures. For the other grains the measures were somewhat different. See H. 1823. Reg. du Bureau, ii^{c}xxix. 24 Mars 1671. Resolution that oats should be sold by wheat measure of 24 boisseaux per setier, instead of the former oats measure: H. 1822. Reg. du Bureau, 29 Août 1669. Assembly to consider the reform of measures: H. 1822. Reg. du Bureau, ii^{c}lvii. Text of Royal Ordinance of October 1669.

At Orleans the names were similar, but the system was different: —

1 mine	=	50 livres of wheat.		
12 mines	=	1 muid	=	600 livres.

The muid at Orleans was thus equivalent to 2½ setiers of Paris.

In Brittany, grain was usually sold by the tonneau. This measure varied in different ports. According to Posthelwayt's *Universal Dictionary of Commerce*,

The tonneau at Auray contained	2200 livres.
The tonneau at Hennebont	2950 livres.

At other towns the measure lay between these extremes.

In the Rhône Basin, there were three sets of measures; those of Burgundy, represented by Dijon, those of Lyons, and those of Languedoc and Provence. The Lyonese were so active that the Lyonese measures were used frequently both in Burgundy and in Languedoc.

The measures of Dijon were: —[1]

1 quatranche	=	42 livres of wheat.		
4 quatranches	=	1 quartau	=	168 livres.
2 quartaux	=	1 bichot	=	336 livres.
2 bichots	=	1 emine	=	672 livres.

Assuming these weights to be given according to Paris standards, the equivalents would be: —

1 quatranche	=	2 livres more than 2 boisseaux de Paris.		
1 quartau	=	8 boisseaux de Paris (Approx.)	=	2.86 bushels.
1 bichot	=	16 boisseaux de Paris (Approx.)	=	5.72 bushels.
1 emine	=	¼ muid, mesure de Paris (Approx.)	=	11.44 bushels.

At Lyons, the unit was the boisseau. Six boisseaux made one ânée, and this was the ordinary grain measure.

1 ânée = 8 setiers de Paris or ⅔ muid = 34.32 bushels.

In Languedoc and Provence, quantities were usually given in "charges." The system of measures, according to Posthelwayt, was: —

1 setier	=	90 livres.		
4 setiers	=	360 livres	=	1 charge.

[1] Delamare, *op. cit.*, II, 745.

The equivalents cannot be figured with certainty as it is not clear what kind of weights Posthelwayt has in mind. He uses "pounds," but I doubt if he means English pounds. I presume the unit intended is the local unit, as the figures are in round numbers. The livre in the Rhône Valley was somewhat less than the livre of Paris. At all events the setier of Languedoc was a much smaller measure than the setier of Paris.

APPENDIX II

GLOSSARY OF ADMINISTRATIVE TERMS

ADMINISTRATIVE terms have not been translated in the text, as there are no English equivalents that would not be more misleading than helpful. In the second part, a brief treatment of certain phases of administrative history has been deemed essential, but it has not been possible to discuss these topics comprehensively in the text, and some recognition of the constitutional problem is necessary. The constitutional history of the period is singularly involved, and, in the light of new material, much of it is being rewritten. The dictionaries of Dareste de Chavannes and of Chéruel are already obsolete in many respects. The recent monographs are not always at hand.[1] Some terms frequently used in this study do not receive much attention from the general historian. Consequently, a few concise descriptions of the functions of officials may assist the reader, though it is impossible to do more than call attention to the historical problems involved.

Avocat du Roi. — A member of the staff of the baillage supposed to give advice on legal matters. His functions seem to have been essentially advisory.

Bailli. — The bailli was the administrator or steward of some part of the royal domain or of a seigniorial domain. In the south, the official of this type was called sénéchal, but the functions were substantially the same. In the twelfth and thirteenth centuries, the

[1] Dupont-Ferrier, G., *Les Officiers royaux des baillages et sénéchaussées.* Paris, 1902.

Jacqueton, G., *Documents relatifs à l'administration financière en France de Charles VII à François I.* 1443–1523. Paris, 1891.

Hanotaux, Gabriel, *Les Origines de l'institution des Intendants des Provinces.* Paris, 1884.

Arbois de Jubainville, Henri d', *L'Administration des Intendants d'après les Archives de l'Aube.* Paris, 1880.

Jouvencel, Henri de, *Le Contrôleur Général des Finances sous l'ancien régime.* Paris, 1901.

Delamare, *Traité de la Police,* gives many details not easily found elsewhere, and many references are given in Viollet, P. *Histoire des Institutions Politiques et Administratives de la France.* 3 vols. Paris, 1890–1903.

bailli or sénéchal was a general administrative officer not unlike the steward of the English manors. The growth of the royal domain, and the increase in royal power made the bailli more of an administrative official. He possessed both financial and judicial functions. In all respects he was accountable to the Parlement. He managed the revenue of the royal domain, and, as a judicial officer, he exercised the rights of the Crown. Within the confines of the domain, he had final jurisdiction over petty cases, and, subject to appeal to the Parlement, jurisdiction in first instance over nearly all other matters. As representative of the Crown, he possessed an ill-defined jurisdiction over the seigniorial courts. The "cas royaux" were in the jurisdiction of the bailli, and as they received the fees they were anxious to extend the royal authority. In 1498, the bailli were forbidden to exercise judicial functions in person. The authority still remained vested in the office, but the actual exercise devolved upon the lieutenants of the bailli. In the fifteenth and sixteenth centuries, the financial functions of the bailli were overshadowed by the development of new taxes and a financial system in which the domain was no longer the administrative unit.

Baillage. — The area under the jurisdiction of a bailli. The complications in regard to the baillages arose from the fact that the administrative boundaries had little relation to local geography. The baillage included, in most cases, all portions of the royal domain in a given region. Frequently, as the result of historic accident, a village would be attached to one baillage when every fact of geography or convenience would place it more naturally in another. Then, too, there were frequent disputes over jurisdiction. Even in 1789, the Crown did not possess precise knowledge of the confines of the baillages.

Châtelet. — The castle used as official residence by the Provost of Paris. The term is used in a general sense to refer to the jurisdiction of the Provost. It is particularly appropriate after 1498, when the office of Provost was put into commission.

Consul. — The title given the members of the municipal corporation in the south of France. In a general way, they may be compared to the Échevins of the north, and the aldermen of the English boroughs.

Contrôleur Général des Finances. — It is scarcely too much to say that no two Contrôleurs Généraux had the same authority or power. The title was old even in Colbert's day. In the sixteenth century, the Contrôleur was merely an auditor. The title was given to Colbert to conceal the fact that he was to exercise the functions of Surintendant des Finances. The Surintendant was the principal minister of finance, and Sully had exercised a predominant influence while he held that office. Colbert's authority was the result of a combination of several offices in his hands. Some of these functions became definitely associated with the Contrôle Général and were included in later commissions. Some of the offices were regularly conferred upon the Contrôleur Général. After the death of Louis XIV the Contrôle Général became the center of the constitutional struggle.

Échevin. — The title of a member of the municipal corporation in the north of France.

Élection. — A division created in the fourteenth century to facilitate the assessment and collection of the direct taxes. The assessors were originally elected by the land-owners of the district, hence the name, but the election soon ceased to have any real meaning. In the later period, the élection is an administrative division of the généralité.

Généralité. — An area formed originally with reference to the collection of the direct taxes. By a very complicated process of growth, the division came to be the general administrative area under the supervision of the intendant. The number of généralités was constantly changing. The boundaries were at times the old provincial boundaries, but more frequently their limits bore no relation to any of the older administrative divisions.

Intendant. — The title intendant is used in several distinct meanings during the sixteenth and seventeenth centuries. The Intendants de Justice of the sixteenth century were royal officers sent from Paris to attend to fairly specific judicial matters. During the Wars of Religion, Intendants d'Armée were frequently attached to the armies. In the early seventeenth century, the intendant developed new functions in connection with the taxes. This change was really a fusion of offices that had formerly been distinct. The Intendant de Justice was given the functions of the Receveurs Généraux. The change is difficult to trace in detail, but it was this new development that brought the intendant into close contact with the généralités, and made him a local administrative officer. Colbert emphasized these administrative functions and made the intendant an efficient agent of the central administration. Under Louis XV, the authority of the central administration diminished and the intendants became more independent. Apart from the differences in the powers of the intendants at different periods, there are important differences in their authority in different places. In Languedoc, the intendant enjoyed a large measure of discretion. Bâville was called the "King of Languedoc." At Paris, the intendant was not very important. At Lyons, local influences were strong and the intendant complained at times that he scarcely knew what was being done.

Lieutenant Civil. — In 1498, the judicial authority was taken from the Provost of Paris and given to the Lieutenants at the Châtelet. Both the lieutenant civil and the lieutenant criminel claimed precedence. The dispute remained undecided until 1630, when the lieutenant civil was given precedence. He thus exercised general supervision over all the work of the tribunal.

In some of the baillages, there was an official with this title.

Lieutenant Criminel. — After 1630, the lieutenant criminel exercised the criminal jurisdiction of the Châtelet, subject to the general control of the lieutenant civil. In the absence of the lieutenant civil the lieutenant criminel presided.

This title also appears in some of the baillages.

Lieutenant Général. — The lieutenant général was a resident of prominence empowered to discharge all the functions of the bailli throughout the baillage, when the bailli was absent. As the duties of the bailli increased, more and more of his power passed to the lieutenant. In the larger baillages, there were lieutenants généraux in all of the important towns. Technically, they had jurisdiction throughout the baillage; in practice, they did little outside of their immediate vicinity. They discharged the functions of the bailli, not only when he was absent from the baillage, but also when he was merely occupied in some other part of his baillage. After 1498, the lieutenants généraux were the real administrators of the baillages.

Lieutenant Particulier. — This lieutenant was a subordinate of the lieutenant général, and had jurisdiction only within the portion of the baillage most immediately subject to the lieutenant général. The lieutenant particulier was not supposed to act if the lieutenant général could be found, and the lieutenant général was supposed to be accessible at all times. If all went well, there would be nothing for the lieutenant particulier to do.

Parlement. — The Parlements of French history were judicial and administrative bodies, in which the judicial functions steadily gained the upper hand. Legislative power, in the true sense of the term, they never possessed. The Parlement of Paris was somewhat different in attributions and organization from the provincial Parlements of Toulouse, Grenoble, Bordeaux, and Dijon. For the purposes of this study, the most important feature of the activities of the provincial Parlements is their resistance to the increase of the power of the Crown in the provinces. Although these Parlements technically possessed no legislative authority, refusal to publish unpopular royal edicts, and the enforcement of edicts more in accord with local interests, gave them the means of exerting much real influence. The Parlement of Paris did not come into conflict with the Crown in any matters pertaining to the grain trade. It seldom did anything more than confirm the measures of others.

Procureur du Roi. — A royal attorney attached to the staff of the baillages to defend and supervise the judicial interests of the Crown.

Provost of Merchants (*Prévôt des Marchands*). — At Paris, Lyons, and some other cities the chief municipal officer was called Provost of Merchants. This was a souvenir of the origin of the municipal charter in a grant of privilege to the merchants of the town. The jurisdiction varied in accordance with the charter, and the actual importance of the office was largely dependent upon the political situation in the locality.

Provost of Paris (*Prévôt de Paris*). — The Provost of Paris was an administrative officer of the royal domain possessing roughly the same attributions as a bailli. The resemblance, however, does not extend far. The influence of the Crown in the Isle de France was so strong that the character of the official and of the office were exceptional in many ways. The edict of 1498 withdrew all direct judicial administration from the hands of the Provost and assigned it to the lieutenants civil and criminel. There was no specific division of powers, and the struggle for precedence that ensued was not settled until 1630.

Sénéchal. — See *Bailli.*

Sénéchaussée. — See *Baillage.*

Subdélégué. — The subdélégué was an agent of the intendant, appointed by him and directly subject to his authority in all respects. There were subdélégués in some of the généralités early in the seventeenth century, but it was not until 1709 that they became universal. From that time on they become increasingly important. The powers of the subdélégué cannot be described very definitely, variations in different localities were considerable, and, even in the same généralité, their powers changed in many important respects.

BIBLIOGRAPHY

MANUSCRIPT MATERIAL

This statement of manuscript material should not be treated as a comprehensive manuscript bibliography. A complete list of the sources that might be used in a study of the grain trade would be too voluminous in extent and too general in character to be of any assistance. The sources for such work are almost entirely official documents, and the variety of jurisdictions coming in contact with trade was so considerable that research can be continued indefinitely. In some "dépôts d'archives" there are cartons of material entirely devoted to the subject of grain trade regulation; such collections of material are of value as indicating the jurisdiction that is most active in the locality, and as affording some general ideas of conditions. But these selections of material are seldom to be trusted, and it is generally necessary to examine all the general documents of the authorities acting.

The quantity of material that was available forced me to limit my work to what may be called the Parisian and the Lyonese manuscripts. The Parisian material included the correspondence of the central authorities at Paris from 1657–1710; the extant records of the Échevinage of Paris, and the records of the Châtelet in so far as they were collected by Delamare.

Of these three sources of information, the general correspondence of the Contrôleur Général with the intendants is least satisfactory. The letters contain an extraordinary variety of information, but most of it is irrelevant and letters are most infrequent in the regions of the most active development.

This correspondence has an involved and curious history which still appears in the manner in which it is preserved. It is divided into three large masses, and small volumes of letters may be found where they are least suspected.

1. The "Mélanges Colbert," preserved at the Bibliothèque Nationale, consist of the letters addressed to Colbert by intendants, private persons, and various officials with whom an incidental correspondence developed. This covers the years 1658–77. Many of these letters

have been published by Depping, in his *Correspondence Administrative*,[1] but the publication by no means exhausts the letters of general interest, and there is reason to believe that the selection was not made with great care. Judgment of the value of Depping's publication is doubly difficult because of a change in the classification of MSS. at the Bibliothèque. The bulk of the Colbert Correspondence figured at that time as "Volumes Vert," and if we may judge by the numbers reported by Depping in his bibliography, the present collection of correspondence has been augmented by the addition of other volumes. Exactly what has happened, the present staff at the Bibliothèque does not seem to know. For the purposes of the present study the volumes "Mélanges Colbert," 101–126, were examined carefully, but on account of the apparent barrenness of this material, the remaining volumes, 126–176 bis, were covered by the selection of the correspondence for May and June of each year. The letters addressed to Colbert in the "Mélanges" stop at 1677. The letters of the intendants to Colbert after that date are preserved at the Archives Nationales, série G^7. The correspondence in these later years is even more extensive than in the early period, as well as being more general in character. The letters in the "Mélanges" represent a correspondence with only a few of the intendants, those included in the Department of Colbert, as Secretary of the "Maison du Roi, etc."[2]

2. The most extensive mass of letters written by Colbert is now preserved at the Bibliothèque Nationale, in the "Mélanges Clairambault," vols. 461–468. These are copies in a secretarial hand of letters written between 1679 and 1681. Nearly all of these have been published by Clément in his *Lettres, Instructions, et Mémoires de J. B. Colbert.* Scarcely anything of importance has been omitted. These letters are supplemented at times by collections made by the intendant to whom letters were addressed. At the Bibliothèque Nationale, Fonds Français, 8751–52, there are the original letters addressed by Colbert to Le Blanc, Intendant at Rouen, 1681. At Amiens, in the Bibliothèque Communale, four volumes of letters

[1] Depping, G. B., *Correspondence Administrative sous le Règne de Louis XIV*, tom. IV, Paris, 1850–55.

[2] The history of the Departments of State at this period is most helpfully treated by A. de Boislisle, in the Introduction to the *Correspondence des Contrôleurs Généraux*, and in the appendices on the Council of State in his edition of the *Mémoirs of St. Simon*, vol. IV, 377–439; V, 437–482; VI, 477–512; VII, 405–443.

addressed to Breteuil are preserved. (Amiens, Bib. Comm., 508. Letters 1680–83.) Other collections could probably be found. It is wise to observe that we posses. only the letters of the closing years of Colbert's ministry, and that our judgments of his work are probably affected by this ill-balanced preservation of material.

3. The Papers of the Contrôle Général des Finances which now constitute the serie G^7. at the "Archives Nationales" are the most voluminous mass of general material connected with the period. Both sides of the correspondence appear: the letters of the Contrôleur Général and the letters of the intendants. Beginning in 1677, the correspondence gradually becomes more voluminous until 1715, and then diminishes in value until it ceases in 1733. After that date, most of the letters are to be found in the Departmental Archives. The publication of documents from this correspondence by the late A. de Boislisle,[1] is excellent in every respect. The documents are well selected and the indications of what it was necessary to omit are singularly complete. But the mass of material is so great that the printed volumes can do no more than give the reader an accurate conception of what can be done with the MSS. This *fonds* consists of general correspondence, classified by généralités: Cartons, 1–537.

In addition to this, there is much material classified by subjects, including 35 cartons on the grain trade: Nos. 1630–65. This separation of material was made, at the time, to facilitate the work of the administrative staff. The special cartons on the grain trade contain all the correspondence of the years 1693–94 and 1709–10.

In this series it was possible to utilize only: —

(1) Cartons 1630–65.
(2) General cartons containing the correspondence for the last years of Colbert's ministry: 1667–83.
(3) General cartons containing the correspondence of the years 1698–1700, a period of dearth only slightly less important than the years 1693–94, 1708–09. The letters on this dearth were originally collected with the other grain material, but were spread through the general cartons by Boislisle.

No attempt was made to cover the years 1683–93, 1695–98, 1700–08. It is certain from other evidence that there was little pressure from scarcity in those years, and so little information appears in years of plenty that it was not deemed expedient to spend time in searching the MSS. of those periods.

[1] *Correspondence des Contrôleurs Généraux des Finances avec les Intendants des Provinces*, 3 tom., Paris, 1874–97.

The General Cartons actually examined were: — 1, 15–16, 71, 79, 84, 87–89, 101, 112, 124, 131–132, 137–141, 156–157, 159–162, 171–172, 178–187, 213, 223–224, 227–232, 239, 243, 257, 276, 294–309, 337–338, 345, 355, 358–361, 374, 390, 394, 405, 417–420, 425, 429–433, 449, 451–453, 458–459, 463–471, 491, 495–496, 506, 512–513, 518–527, 551.

The most serious omission is the neglect of the letters addressed to the intendants by individuals. For the period 1683–1730 there are eighty cartons (Nos. 552–634). During the years of dearth information of importance might be contributed by individuals. Lack of time rendered the exploitation of that material impossible.

The local Parisian material is associated with the Échevinage and the Châtelet, and here the difficulties of research reach a maximum. The archives of the Échevinage were almost completely destroyed by the Commune in 1871; only the "Registres du Bureau de la Ville" remain, a very brief record of the principal activities of the Échevins after 1499.[1] These are preserved at the Archives Nationales as part of "série H." These have been printed down to 1610, though one or two volumes are still in press. The manuscript registers were used for the period 1610–1710, Nos. H. 1796 and ff. The registers are practically duplicated by a series of notes and papers on loose sheets, which were used by the secretary as the basis of the registers, but as these are more difficult to handle, the latter were used. The registers were indexed by the secretary, year by year, so that there is little trouble in using these records.

The records of the Châtelet have survived intact, but the jurisdiction was so comprehensive and the organization of work so slight that it is wellnigh impossible to find one's way around in these MSS. The trouble is increased by the extremely difficult notarial hand in which these records are written. The Châtelet was unquestionably the jurisdiction most intimately in touch with the grain trade in the seventeenth century, but the difficulty of utilizing the material at first hand made it necessary to depend largely upon Delamare. All his papers are preserved at the Bibliothèque Nationale, so that it is possible to supplement his printed volumes in many respects. My confidence in Delamare for the more important grain trade material contained in the records of the Châtelet is based upon two facts.

[1] *Histoire Générale de Paris. Registres des Délibérations du Bureau de la Ville de Paris.* 1499–1610. tom. XIV, Paris, 1883–1908.

In the first place, the general registers of the Châtelet, the "Bannières," were certainly utilized by him in preparing his *Traité de la Police*. Consequently we can trust him for the larger outlines of the activity of the Châtelet, even prior to his own day. He knew as much as anyone can, without an extraordinary acquaintance with this complicated jurisdiction. In the second place, after 1660, Delamare is indubitably the best informed man in France in regard to grain trade regulation. In addition to his historical or antiquarian knowledge, he possessed first hand knowledge of conditions throughout the Seine Basin, acquired as commissioner of the Châtelet.

Delamare's information is accessible in several forms: —

(1) The general material in the second volume of the *Traité de la Police*.

(2) The description of the two visits to Champagne in 1709–10, in the supplement to the 2d edition of the third volume. (Paris, 1722.)

(3) The papers at the Bibliothèque Nationale. These papers fall into three classes: — notes for the *Traité de la Police*, which seldom contain anything not printed; letters passing between Delamare and various people, both private individuals and public officials; lastly, "procès verbaux" which should properly be at the Archives Nationales among the papers of the Châtelet. These letters and "procès verbaux" are scattered through several volumes — Bibliothèque Nationale, Fonds Français, 21641–50. The other volumes among Delamare's papers are of little value for the study of the grain trade, though there is much on commerce and industry. But although it is safe to trust Delamare for the general results of the work of the Châtelet and for many facts, it is probable that a careful utilization of the papers at the archives would yield much. Research will be difficult, and it is possible that nothing might come, even of protracted search. All the clues to be found in Delamare were traced down without result in the papers of the commissioners, but those particular documents had been abstracted by Delamare and are among his papers. None the less, the most considerable possibility of discovering new material is presented by the archives of the Châtelet. It remains to be seen if Delamare's work is to be the only attempt to master this material.[1]

In addition to these general deposits, much scattering material was examined, both at the Bibliothèque Nationale and at the Archives. At the Bibliothèque, the MSS. on "Commerce" and "Police"

[1] The Bannières have already been worked over by M. Tuéty, but little has been added to Delamare.

in the "Fond Français" were inspected, for the most part without result. The most important MSS. were the volumes in the "Collection Moreau." 1061. Pièces sur le Commerce de Paris. 1062. Registres des Compagnies Françaises, 1449–67. There are three volumes of Compagnies Françaises, 1532–61, but the entries are so brief that they have no historical value for the purposes of this study.

The famous "Mémoires sur les Généralités," of 1698, were left untouched chiefly from a lack of time, and partly from the idea that they were not particularly important for this study. At the Archives Nationales, the most useful of the small groups of material was the "Bibliothèque Administrative" (Rondonneau). This is a collection of ordinances, edicts, and letters patent, beginning in the middle of the seventeenth century. There are two series, one arranged chronologically, the other by subjects. The grain edicts, A. D. XI, 37–40 supplement Delamare at many points.

The work in the Municipal Archives at Lyons was less difficult in one sense, because there was no doubt as to which authorities were acting, but here again it was necessary to utilize the general records, so that a large mass of material had to be searched for the requisite data.

The importance of the grain trade at Lyons resulted in the collection of many papers on this subject, and these are still catalogued independently. But these documents would not be a safe guide for a knowledge of Lyonese conditions. The one entirely trustworthy source of information is the series of municipal registers. These are much more voluminous than the Paris registers, and, as they begin almost a century earlier (1428), it was impossible to examine this material thoroughly. The difficulty of research is increased by the inadequacy of the *inventaire sommaire* of the Registers, which the archivists warned me not to trust.

The papers which relate especially to the grain trade are of three kinds: —

(1) Série HH. Chappe IV. Letters Patent of the Crown, or of Provincial Govérnors.
(2) Série GG. Chappe IV. Papers relating to the Chambre d'Abondance. Some concern its organization; some are the papers of the Chambre: accounts, records of the deliberations of the Chambre, and letters from its agents, 1667–69.
(3) Série FF. HH. Chappe VII. Various papers concerning the detailed regulation of the trade, Assizes of Bread, ordinances concerning bakers, the ports, etc.

The Letters Patent are a valuable and interesting source. The documents of the Abondance are of unequal value. The accounts are of little use historically, except as indicating the degree of regularity in the functioning of the Chambre. The Registers of Deliberations are valuable, and should have been utilized more carefully. The letters of Du Pradt to the Directors of the Abondance constitute one of the most important pieces of evidence in regard to the seventeenth century grain trade. But on the principal question, the history of the Chambre, these special papers were uncertain and vague. Still, it was evident that the critical years in the history of the trade were the years that left some trace in these scattered papers. The main body of facts could, therefore, be obtained by reference to the Consular Registers for the years indicated in Letters Patent, accounts of the Abondance, and such other incidental references as suggested notable occurrences.

The third class of material was of no value for this study.

The Consular Registers for the critical years were examined, and as there were frequent references to deputies charged with regulation of the grain trade, it was deemed expedient to seek fuller details among their letters. Some important letters thus came to light.

Citations in the municipal archives at Lyons present a few unusual features. The documents were very carefully inventoried and classified in the eighteenth century by one Chappe, and his work is still the basis of the arrangement of the parts of the archives inventoried by him. Documents are cited by the letters of the series and by the volume and page of the manuscript Inventaire. The Consular Registers of the Série BB., and the Letters in Série AA. were not included in Chappe's Inventory.

Work at Lyons covered the following material:[1] —

(1) Letters Patent, etc. Série HH. Chappe IV, 381, 393, 401, 411, 422, 427. Each liasse is cited by the reference to the first document.

(2) Papers of the Abondance: —
General, GG. Chappe IV, 443, 448, 450, 451–452, 453, 460, 461–642.
Accounts, GG. Chappe IV, 481.
Deliberations, GG. Chappe IV, 538.

(3) Registres Consulaires. BB. 19. 352, 24, 47, 61, 81, 82, 85, 91, 105, 116.

[1] Here, as elsewhere, I cite only those MSS. which proved to be of value.

These Registers exist in duplicate for the most part, there being the minutes taken during meetings and the copy prepared later. The latter are, of course, most convenient.

(4) In Série AA., of thirty-three liasses examined, only two contained letters of importance for the grain trade — Nos. 29, 32.

A few days' work was done in the Municipal Archives at Dijon to clear up the early history of the Lyonese in Burgundy and Bassigny. In the time available it was possible to examine only such material as lay on the surface: letters patent, extracts from the municipal records, vouchers turned in by commissioners stating work done, etc. These results should be controlled by study of the municipal registers, but for the purpose in view the scattered documents were probably trustworthy. The work covered Série G. 241, 256–266 inclusive.

I trust that this statement will indicate the general character of the material that can be utilized for a study of the grain trade. The subject necessitates constant reference to general municipal registers and to administrative correspondence. Furthermore, it is essential to cover a large territory, so that comprehensiveness of research is almost impossible. The necessity of abandoning any hope of comprehensive treatment made me neglect price statistics. Materials exist for the preparation of interesting figures, but the general statement of the conditions of the time seemed to be essential to a proper interpretation of such statistics, and it was evident that there would only be time for the prosecution of this first stage in the work.

PRINTED LITERATURE

The extent of the MS. sources available for the treatment of this subject made the printed literature relatively less important, as regards the completed book. The studies of Araskhaniantz, Afanassiev, and Naudé were exceedingly helpful at the beginning, but concentration on the market problems of the domestic grain trade carried the work into a different field, and the results suggested a somewhat different account of royal policy. The influence of these authors was thus of a nature that cannot easily be indicated by footnotes in the text, and for that reason I take this occasion to recognize an indebtedness that is real even if it cannot be precisely indicated.

Works Relating Specifically to the History of the Grain Trade during the Sixteenth and Seventeenth Centuries

Araskhaniantz, A. *Die Französische Getreidehandelspolitik bis zum Jahre 1789 in ihrem Zuzammenhange mit der Land-, Volks-, und Finanzwirthschaft.* Leipzig, 1883. In Schmoller: Staats und Socialwissenschaftliche Forschungen, IV. This is the most considerable attempt at monographic treatment of the history of the grain trade in the sixteenth and seventeenth centuries, but it is only proper to add that it is unfinished. The author's studies were interrupted after two years' work, and, as there was little prospect of a resumption of the task, the results obtained were published. The magnitude of the project was such that the author was scarcely more than well started when work was discontinued. He was able only to bring together the material that lay on the surface, and as the questions of policy are most conspicuous, his attention is largely absorbed by the political aspect of the trade. His treatment is not very helpful as he does not read the edicts critically and does not realize the necessity of a sharp distinction between the "foreign" and the "domestic" trade. There is no indication of a perception of the preëminent importance of the problem of distribution within the confines of the kingdom.

Bethouart, A. *Histoire du Blé dans la Beauce.* Chartres, 1888. A compilation of a few scattering notices of prices, dearths, and crop conditions. Of no serious value.

Biollay, L. *Les anciennes Halles de Paris.* Mémoires de la Soc. de l'Hist. de Paris et de l'Isle de France, III (1876).

Boislisle, A. de. *Le Grand Hyver de 1709.* Revue des Questions Historiques. Avril, 1903, p. 445. An excellent account of the external aspects of the episode which played so large a part in the crisis of the history of the grain trade. Contains references to the material available for study of the meteorological conditions, as well as the most important general descriptions in contemporary material.

Boissonade, P. *La Production et le Commerce des Céréales, des Vins, et des Eaux de Vie en Languedoc, dans le seconde moitié du XVIIe siècle.* Annales du Midi, XVII (1905). Also published separately. 32 pp. A very interesting study of the agricultural side of the subject, but so brief in the portions devoted to the commercial movement that it was of little assistance. Although local material was utilized, little information is given on the commercial aspect of the subject that does not appear in greater detail in the MSS. consulted for the present study.

Chassaigne, M. *Essai sur l'ancienne police de Paris: l'approvisionnement.* Revue des Études Historiques, 1906. (Mai, Juin, Juillet, Août.) Largely concerned with the regulation of the retail trade in food stuffs.

Gras, L. J. *Prix du Blé à St. Étienne pendant trois siècles (1640 à nos jours) d'après les mercuriales.* 1906. Soc. d'agriculture de la Loire. (This work has been inaccessible.)

Louandre, Charles. *De l'alimentation publique sous l'ancien monarchie française.* (This I have not seen.)

Marsy, Comte de. *L'approvissionnement de Paris sous Louis XII. Difficultés au sujet d'acquisitions de blé faites à Noyon, 1501–03.* Bulletin de la Soc. de l'Histoire de Paris et de l'Isle de France (1877).

Naudé, Wilhelm. *Die Getreidehandelspolitik der Europäischen Staaten vom 13ten bis zum 18ten Jahrhundert.* Berlin, 1896. A well considered statement, but necessarily brief. The explanations of the French policy are hardly supported by detailed study.

de la Porte, Guillaume. *Avis de G—— de la P—— Hotteux es Halles de Paris.* Paris, 1621, Fournier: Variétés, Historiques, et Littéraires, tom. III.

Works Relating to the History of the Grain Trade in the Eighteenth Century

These books were consulted and many of them exerted an indirect influence upon the present study.

Afanassiev, Georges. *Le Commerce des Céréales en France.* Paris, 1894. Traduit du Russe sous le direction de Paul Boyer. An interesting beginning of a study of the most difficult period in the history of the grain trade. There is evidence of much patient research, but the main problems of the period are scarcely touched.

Babeau, A. *La lettre de l'Etat contre la cherete en 1724.* Paris, 1892.

Biollay, Léon. *Les Prix de Blé en 1790.* Paris, 1885.

Biollay, Paul. *Études économiques sur le XVIIIe siècle. Le Pacte de Famine.* Paris, 1885. Disposes of the charges against Louis XV in regard to the alleged syndicate for the control of grain prices.

Boisguillebert, Pierre le Pesant de. *Ouevres diverses.*

Bond, G. *Le Pacte de Famine. Histoire du Blé en France.* Paris, 1889. A more popular statement of the case than Biollay's, but no less destructive of the old legend.

Frotière de ia Messelière, M. *Boisguillebert et la liberté des grains.* Paris, 1903.

Galiani. *Dialogues sur les Blés.* 1770.

Gazier, A. *La Guerre des Farines.* (Mai, 1775.) Mémoires de la Soc. d'Hist. de Paris et de l'Isle de France, VI, 1879.

Herbert, Claude Jacques. *La Police des Grains: Essai sur la Police Générale des grains, sur leurs prix, et sur les effets de l'agriculture.* Berlin, 1755.

Letaconnoux, J. *Le Commerce des Céréales dans la Bretagne.* The proofs of this work were kindly placed at my disposition. Its publication is announced.

Le Trosne. *La Liberté du Commerce des Grains toujours utile et jamais nuisible.* Paris, 1784.

Marion, M. *Une Famine en Guyenne, 1747–48.* Revue Historique, XLVI, pp. 241–287.

Mercier de la Rivière. *L'Intérêt Générale de l'Etat, ou la liberté du Commerce des Blés.* Amsterdam, 1770.

Morellet. *Réfutation de l'ouvrage qui a pour titre " Dialogues sur le Commerce de Blés."* 1770.
Roubaud. *Récréations économiques, ou Lettres de l'auteur des Representations aux Magistrats à M. le Chevalier Zanobi, principal interlocuteur des Dialogues sur le Commerce des Blés.* 1770.
Valran, G. *Misère et Charité en Provence au XVIIIe siècle.* Paris, 1899.
Vaudin, Bataille. *Histoire de la Charité jusqu'en 1789.* Paris, 1897.

INDEX

INDEX

Bei Fragen zur Produktsicherheit wenden Sie sich bitte an:
If you have any questions regarding product safety,
please contact:

Walter de Gruyter GmbH
Genthiner Straße 13
10785 Berlin
productsafety@degruyterbrill.com